LOVE RELATIONSHIPS IN THE JOHANNINE TRADITION

SOCIETY
OF BIBLICAL
LITERATURE

DISSERTATION SERIES

William Baird, Editor

Number 58

LOVE RELATIONSHIPS IN
THE JOHANNINE TRADITION
Agapē/Agapan in I John and the Fourth Gospel
by
Fernando F. Segovia

Fernando F. Segovia

LOVE RELATIONSHIPS IN THE JOHANNINE TRADITION
Agapē/Agapan in I John and the Fourth Gospel

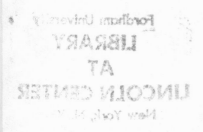
Scholars Press

Published by
Scholars Press
101 Salem Street
P. O. Box 2268
Chico, CA 95927

LOVE RELATIONSHIPS IN
THE JOHANNINE TRADITION
Agapē/Agapan in I John and the Fourth Gospel

Fernando F. Segovia

Ph.D., 1978   Advisor:
University of Notre Dame   Dr. Elisabeth Schüssler Fiorenza

BS
2545
$L6S4$

$Cop. 2$

Library of Congress Cataloging in Publication Data

Segovia, Fernando F.
    Love relationships in the Johannine tradition.

(Dissertation series / Society of Biblical Literature ;
no. 58) (ISSN 0145-2770)
        Bibliography: p.
        1. Love (Theology)—Biblical teaching. 2. Bible.
N. T. John, 1st—Criticism, interpretation, etc.
3. Bible. N. T. John—Criticism, interpretation, etc.
I. Title. II. Series: Dissertation series (Society of
Biblical Literature) ; no. 58.
BS2545.L6S43   226'.506   81-9407
ISBN 0-89130-533-5   AACR2

Manufactured in the U.S.A.

To my Parents, Fernando and María del Carmen

ACKNOWLEDGMENTS

The completion of a work such as this presupposes and entails the contributions--whether direct or indirect, academic or otherwise--of countless individuals. To all concerned I should like to express my deep and sincere feeling of gratitude. Above all, I should like to thank the following:

First and foremost, the director of the dissertation, Dr. Elisabeth Schüssler Fiorenza, for a gentle and gracious mixture of scholarly and exegetical excellence, critical and constructive advice, and friendly and continuous encouragement. To her I owe a major part of my expertise in the field of New Testament studies.

Secondly, the readers who composed the Examining Board for the dissertation: Dr. Joseph Blenkinsopp; Dr. Josephine Massyngberde Ford; Dr. Charles Primus; and Dr. Robert Wilken. It was my privilege to do extensive work under the direction of these scholars during the course of my studies at the University of Notre Dame. I should also like to mention in this regard the chairman of the Examining Board, Dr. Anton Hermann-Chroust, whose knowledge, company and conversation it was my pleasure to enjoy over the years.

Thirdly, the chairman of the Theology Department at the University of Notre Dame, Rev. David Burrell, C.S.J., for the financial assistance that made my graduate studies and this work possible.

Finally, my parents, whose continuous dedication to Christian principles and a Christian life have provided and continue to provide a source of inspiration and hope in my own life.

CONTENTS

Chapter

Chapter

Chapter

ABBREVIATIONS

AnalBib	Analecta biblica
BiLe	*Bibel und Leben*
BJRL	*Bulletin of the John Rylands Library*
BWANT	Beiträge zur Wissenschaft vom Alten und Neuen Testament
BZNW	Beihefte zur Zeitschrift für die neutestamentliche Wissenschaft
FRLANT	Forschungen zur Religion und Literatur des Alten und Neuen Testaments
HNT	Handbuch zum Neuen Testament
ICC	The International Critical Commentary
JBL	*Journal of Biblical Literature*
JTS	*Journal of Theological Studies*
MüTZ	*Münchener Theologische Zeitschrift*
NovTSup	Novum Testamentum Supplements
NTD	Das Neue Testament Deutsch
NTS	*New Testament Studies*
NTSMS	New Testament Studies Monograph Series
RB	*Revue biblique*
RNT	Regensburger Neues Testament
StANT	Studien zum Alten und Neuen Testament
TRu	*Theologische Rundschau*
TS	*Theological Studies*
ZNW	*Zeitschrift für die neutestamentliche Wissenschaft*
ZThK	*Zeitschrift für Theologie und Kirche*

CHAPTER I

STATE OF THE QUESTION--METHODOLOGY

In the last few years the question of the existence of
a Johannine "school" in early Christianity--or, as different
exegetes would have it, a Johannine "circle," "community,"
"group," or "sect"--has been the subject, directly or indirectly, of several studies dealing with the Johannine writings.[1]
This question can hardly be called "new" at all; it is as old
as the history of the interpretation of the so-called Johannine
literature. In this regard, the first chapter of the recent
monograph by R. Alan Culpepper, *The Johannine School*, is particularly valuable and informative, since Culpepper collects
and summarizes the opinions of many a Johannine scholar on the
subject of a "school," extending as far back as Dionysius of
Alexandria.[2]

The survey shows that scholars have over the years,
and indeed over the centuries, proposed an almost infinite
variety of theories and working hypotheses designed to account
for the great similarities as well as for the more subtle differences that exist between the Gospel and the three Letters
and to explain the many difficulties and unevennesses that the
text of the Gospel presents in its own right.[3] This is one of
those problems or questions that is never really fully resolved:
at the precise moment that a new theory is propounded, there
takes place the resurrection of an older, forgotten theory or
the creation of yet a new one.

If the number of solutions has proved to be innumerable,
one may expect the respective methods employed by these scholars
to arrive at such solutions to be just as diversified. Culpepper has conveniently reduced these to their common denominators, and it will prove beneficial to enumerate them at this
point:[4] (a) first of all, scholars have relied heavily on the
external evidence provided by the Church Fathers; (b) the

1

terminology and style of the Johannine writings have been
studied and analyzed in close detail; (c) scholars have also
turned their attention to the conceptual and theological
parallels and developments within these writings.[5] Culpepper
would add his own approach as a fourth--and largely ignored--
common denominator, viz., the study of the structure and life
of ancient schools.[6]

     The present study does not seek to propose yet a new
solution; rather, it seeks to test and refine an already existing theory. Its goal and dimensions are, therefore, more
modest. The working hypothesis in question is one which has
been gathering momentum in the last decade or so, viz., the
theory that the author of I John was actively concerned with
and engaged in the redaction of the Gospel of John.[7] The present study will take as its point of departure what constitutes
the most advanced variation of that theory--I say "most
advanced" because it presents a more complex view of the redactional process than had hitherto been supposed--as presented in
the work of Jürgen Becker.[8]

     From the point of view of methodology, the present
study will scrutinize Becker's theory by means of a variation
of the third common denominator described above. Those passages
within the Farewell Discourse which Becker identifies as coming
from the pen of the author of I John or of someone in the very
same life situation deal at length with the theme of ἀγάπη
(Jn 13:34-5; 15:1-17; 15:18-16:15). I propose, therefore, to
seize upon this common and important theme and to determine its
meaning in I John, in the disputed sections, and in the rest of
the Gospel. Thus, I propose to determine whether this key
theological term displays the same meaning throughout or
whether there takes place a radical reinterpretation thereof
--does there exist a group which operates in a very particular
and fixed thought-world, but which feels free nonetheless to
reinterpret this thought-world?[9]

     In this first chapter that follows, I wish to pursue
in greater detail the main points raised in the preceding paragraphs. First of all, therefore, I shall mention briefly the
most recent works dealing with the Johannine community. I
shall then proceed to discuss the question of the relationship

of I John to the Gospel, including the working hypothesis mentioned above, i.e., that the author of I John was involved to
a considerable degree in the redaction of the Gospel. Thirdly,
I shall present an overview of those works that have dealt
thematically with ἀγάπη and its meaning in the Johannine writings in order to show how my approach shall differ from these.
Finally, I shall conclude with an exposition of the development of my own work.

Recent Discussion of the Johannine Community

Since the year 1972 five separate studies have been
published all of which deal to one degree or another with the
question of an ongoing Johannine group responsible for the composition and redaction of the Johannine writings. I shall present them chronologically.

The first two studies--articles published in scholarly
journals--were authored by Wayne Meeks (1972)[10] and D. Moody
Smith (1974).[11] Meeks concentrates primarily on what one could
call a sociological approach in order to describe the community
behind the documents, while Moody Smith utilizes a review-of-
the-literature approach to provide an outline of the history
of the Johannine community from its inception.

The following three works were book-length studies of
the Johannine community. In 1975 Oscar Cullmann published a
study titled *Der johanneische Kreis* in which he sought to connect the Johannine group with the Hellenists described in
Acts 6.[12] That very same year saw the publication of a dissertation by R. Alan Culpepper--already alluded to above--that
dealt with an investigation of the structure and life of ancient
schools.[13] Finally, in 1977 another dissertation appeared,
written by John Bogart, that examined the problem of perfectionism in the Johannine community.[14]

Wayne Meeks (1972)

The main purpose of Meeks' article is, as he puts it,
to ask once again an old question, the answer to which has, in
his opinion, not done justice to the validity and importance
of the question itself. In asking the question anew, Meeks

proposes to overcome the given obstacles inherent in the question itself by approaching it from a different angle altogether,
viz., employing a different methodology.

The basic question has to do with the "special patterns of language" that the Fourth Evangelist employs to
describe the figure and role of Jesus Christ in the Gospel.
Already in 1925 R. Bultmann had singled out one of these patterns as fundamental to an understanding of the Johannine
puzzle: the myth of the descending/ascending revealer.[15] The
solution, Bultmann argued, was not to be found in a *religionsgeschichtliche* comparison with other contemporary patterns of
pre-existence, but rather in an attempt to understand the
logic of the myth itself. Bultmann proposed that the pattern
involved the idea of revelation, but that the evangelist had
deliberately modified the myth, concentrating instead on the
fact that Jesus was the revealer. In other words, the gnostic
myth had been "Christianized."

Meeks remarks that neither Bultmann nor the reaction
that followed[16] managed to extricate themselves from reducing
myths to theological categories and to consider myth as myth,
i.e., in terms of its own logic. It is this attempt, therefore, that constitutes the essence and purpose of his own study.
Given that the pattern of the descending/ascending revealer is
fundamental to an understanding of the Gospel, Meeks proposes
to examine what the pattern itself discloses within the literary structure of the Gospel and to see what this disclosure
reveals about the community that utilized it.[17] In order to
achieve this result, Meeks borrows a methodology from the
social sciences:[18] the interpreter must assemble and dissect
the various occurrences of the same myth in order to arrive
at the basic underlying pattern or structure of the myth.[19]
And this pattern will, in turn, "discover the function which
the myths have within the group in which they are at home."[20]

The application of the method to the myth of the
descending/ascending revealer in the Gospel discloses a very
close association with an anti-Jewish polemic or controversy.
In this regard, Meeks' findings confirm the main hypothesis of
J. L. Martyn's work, *History and Theology in the Fourth Gospel*,
concerning the centrality of Pharisaic Judaism in the *Sitz im*

Leben of the Gospel.[21]   Thus, Meeks finds that wherever the
motif occurs in the Gospel, the point is made that the men "of
this world," i.e., "the Jews," could neither understand nor
accept the "one from above," i.e., Jesus. Whereas Jesus knows
where he comes from and where he is going, the Jews simply do
not know anything at all.[22]   Only a few do know, and these are
the disciples.

        From this association of the myth with a virulent anti-
Jewish polemic, Meeks concludes to the "sectarian" character
of the Johannine community. Those who utilize the myth are
exposed as a "small group of believers isolated over against
'the world' that belongs intrinsically to 'the things below.'"[23]
The myth, therefore, functions as a vindication of the group's
existence: it is this group that has received revelation and
has separated itself "from the world"; those that attack them
are ignorant of the group's superior standing.[24]

        Thus, the renewed asking of the question leads Meeks
to a view of the Johannine community as a "sect"--a group that
separated itself fundamentally from "social reality" into an
exclusivistic and totalistic community. A major element of
this separation involved the development of a language peculiar
to itself, a set of symbols which reinforced and sharpened this
exclusivistic outlook.[25]

        Although Meeks concentrates on the middle phase of the
Gospel, i.e., the work of the evangelist and the anti-Jewish
polemic, he considers the Johannine community to be more than
an ephemeral phenomenon.[26]   The group exhibited a prehistory,
from which part of the narrative and the discourse materials
may be dated, as well as a posthistory, from which insertions
and the Johannine Letters may be traced--that is, taking the
stage of the evangelist as the point of reference. With the
Letters, Meeks argues, one can see the sect becoming even more
"sectarian" in belief and praxis.[27]

D. *Moody Smith (1974)*

        From the point of view of methodology, this study by
Moody Smith differs radically from the sociological approach
undertaken by Meeks. As he himself states in the prologue,
the study concerns itself primarily with secondary literature

on the Johannine writings, attempting to discern by means of
"clarification, summary, and assessment" whether significant
patterns of thought are emerging with regard to the Johannine
puzzle.[28] Yet, despite this procedural difference, the outcome, i.e., the picture of the character and development of the
Johannine group, is remarkably similar to that of Wayne Meeks.

For example, like Meeks before him, Moody Smith posits
--again taking the main body of the Gospel as the point of
reference--a prehistory and a posthistory of the Johannine community. Thus, the protracted use of similar terminology and
conceptual apparatus indicates the existence of a "traditioning" community.[29] Moreover, this "traditioning" community
betrays throughout a "sectarian consciousness," which Moody
Smith defines as "a sense of exclusiveness, a sharp delineation of the community from the world."[30] The only difference
between this characterization and that of Meeks is the importance that the latter attaches to the possession of an esoteric
system of symbols which functions as a vindication of the community's self-consciousness.

As far as the early history of the sect is concerned,
Moody Smith sees the formation and composition of both narrative and discourse material as stemming from this period.
Recent scholarship has been able to recover these stages by
means of form and redaction criticism. On the one hand, he
accepts the existence of an underlying *sēmeia* source behind
the Gospel, the *Sitz im Leben* of which may originally have been
a polemic against the followers of John the Baptist.[31] On the
other hand, he also accepts an early tradition of Jesus' sayings formulated by a Spirit-filled community.[32]

The activity of the community at the time of writing
of the Gospel is taken to be an anti-Jewish, anti-synagogue
polemic. In this regard, Moody Smith also accepts the main
lines of J. L. Martyn's theory concerning the *Sitz im Leben*
of the Gospel. It was at this time, Moody Smith continues,
that narrative and sayings were brought together, the latter
using the former as an anchor.[33] Furthermore, a redaction of
the Gospel followed--this is the posthistory aspect--which
included the additions of chapters 21 and 15-17.[34]

Besides the epithet "sect," Moody Smith describes this "traditioning" community by a variety of other terms, all of which appear to be synonymous, e.g., "a peculiarly Johannine strain of thought," "indigenous to a school," or "to certain early Christian circles or churches."[35] All of these terms reflect the existence of a group with an ongoing tradition, a sectarian consciousness, that endured for a considerable period of time. The Johannine Letters reflect a later stage of that tradition, a time when the sectarian consciousness of the community became much sharper.[36] Therefore, the author of I John was a part of that ongoing "traditioning" process.

Oscar Cullmann (1975)

The method of presentation followed by Cullmann in this study is not unlike that employed by D. Moody Smith: it is essentially a review of secondary literature. To a large extent the work incorporates exegetical opinions already adopted and set forth by Cullmann in other occasions.[37] At the same time, a critical summary, a sifting and weighing, of the various directions shown by present Johannine research is undertaken. The purpose of this constructive review is said to be the provision of a prolegomenon, an introduction, to a commentary which is to follow later. As such, this work pre-sents a very definite thesis concerning the *Sitz im Leben* of the Gospel and its process of formation, but its validation must either be sought elsewhere or await further publication.

With regard to the process of literary composition, Cullmann adopts the same threefold sequence held by both Meeks and Moody Smith: tradition--both oral and written; evangelist; and redaction (by someone other than the evangelist).[38] How-ever, Cullmann downplays completely any possible theological conflict that might exist between these three stages of the process; rather, he subordinates the first and third stages to the second. It is the evangelist that emerges as the central focus of the process, a man of strong personality who influ-ences very strongly the traditions available to him and the man (or men) who follow him.[39] Thus, Cullmann spends little time in searching out the peculiarities of either tradition or

redaction, considering the Gospel as it stands as possessing
a clear unity of thought and purpose.

Instead, Cullmann devotes much of his time to tracing
the roots of this particular theological perspective. He
would agree with both Meeks and Moody Smith that ultimately
it is sectarian Judaism that furnishes much of the conceptual
matrix that informs the theology of the Johannine group.[40]
But Cullmann is unique insofar as he proceeds to trace the
earliest Christian beginnings of this theological perspective.
In a comparison of the theology exhibited by Stephen and the
Hellenists of Acts 6-8 with Johannine theology, Cullmann finds
that the two have very important elements in common.[41] He
concludes, therefore, that this group of Hellenists, who had
emerged from the ranks of sectarian Judaism (and specifically
from the movement of John the Baptist), were not only con-
temporaries but also disciples of Jesus.[42] Furthermore, this
group of Hellenists constitutes the very beginnings of the
"Johannine" circle.

After their expulsion from Jerusalem, the Hellenists
engaged in a mission to the area of Samaria--they already
shared many theological beliefs in common with the Samaritans,
since the latter also formed part of syncretistic, sectarian
Judaism, but now the influence of Samaritan theology became
much stronger[43]--where they proved to be rather successful.
Following the fall of Jerusalem in 70 A.D., the Johannine group
settled in Transjordania (or maybe Syria), an area where other
groups from sectarian Judaism were to be found and where open
syncretism was the norm. It is at this stage that the Gospel
is written.

As Cullmann envisions it, the *Sitz im Leben* of the
Gospel encompasses two very important concerns of the community
and the evangelist. First of all, this brand of Christianity
feels that it must justify itself as a viable form of Christianity besides Synoptic Christianity. The situation is not
one of open conflict, but rather one of a search for recognition.[44] In the Gospel the evangelist carries out this project
of justification by joining together a historical event of
Jesus' life and the situation of the community at the time of
writing, so as to derive the latter from the former. Secondly,

this brand of Christianity feels that it must defend itself
against the open syncretism that surrounds it and, as a result,
engages in a series of polemics with its neighbors, e.g., it
defends itself against the claims of the followers of John the
Baptist and against a docetic movement.

The Johannine "circle" thus emerges as an ongoing and
consistent brand of Christianity--indeed, one of two major
brands--which traces its roots back to Jesus himself. Its
theological conceptions do not seem to undergo any changes in
the history of the group.[45] Furthermore, Cullmann is adamant
in denying this circle the category of a "sect." It is important, however, to realize what it is that Cullmann understands
by that term: whereas both Meeks and Moody Smith understand
"sect" to mean an exclusivistic and totalistic community,
Cullmann sees it in terms of a polemic against the church,
i.e., a sect would be a religious group that engages in a
bitter polemic with the larger church.[46] Although the Johannine group sees itself as being different from Synoptic Christianity, it does not attack the latter in the justification
of its own position.

The evangelist is also presented as a disciple of the
Lord, an eyewitness, who testifies to the roots of this brand
of Christianity in Jesus himself.[47] He, in turn, was surrounded by the Johannine circle, whose spokesman he was. It
was other members of the group that carried out the redaction
of the evangelist's work--primarily the addition of ch. 21--
and composed the Johannine Letters. Thus, the Letters belong
to a man who formed part of this monolithic group and who was
under the strong influence of the evangelist.[48]

R. Alan Culpepper (1975)

As it has already been pointed out above, Culpepper
seeks in this dissertation to understand the Johannine community or group in terms of "school" and what it means to be
a "school" in antiquity. His point of departure is the looseness with which the term has been employed by generations of
Johannine scholars.[49] The term "school" has come to mean,
Culpepper argues, different things to different exegetes. As
a result, and following a method which had already been

employed with respect to other Christian writers,[50] Culpepper
decided, first of all, to observe and describe the constituents
of schools in Graeco-Roman antiquity and, secondly, to see
whether these essential elements were to be found in the Johannine literature as well. If the answer turned out to be positive, then the Johannine community could in effect be called a
"school," and exegesis would narrow somewhat its ongoing investigation of this peculiar group.

     As primary data for his investigation Culpepper selected
nine schools of antiquity on the basis of three main criteria:
(a) all had been established prior to the composition of the
Gospel of John; (b) all trace their origin to a founder (except
for the school of Philo); (c) all have the potential of revealing the factors which influenced the Johannine community.[51]
After an extensive study of these schools, Culpepper arrives
at a series of characteristics which are to be found, more or
less, in all of these schools:[52] interest in the ideal of
friendship; a sense of tradition; a sense of discipleship; a
degree of organization; an interest in learning and studying;
a particular relation to society; a degree of control over
their teachings.[53] Although some of these elements are rather
amorphous (e.g., relation to society, where a tremendous variety of attitudes may be observed within this group of nine
schools), the most important characteristic or common denominator is that of teaching, learning, studying, and writing. This
constitutes the *sine qua non* of a school.[54]

     In the search for these characteristics in the Johan-
nine literature, Culpepper finds that they are all indeed present and that, as a result, the Johannine group could in principle and by definition be called a school.[55] Above all, the
primary and distinguishing characteristic of a school--its
learning activity--is quite prominent, he argues, in the literature. The community does engage in teaching, learning,
writing, and studying.[56]

     Furthermore, it is this activity that is systematically
carried on that accounted for the composition of the Gospel.
While the Beloved Disciple was alive, the school was subject to
his guidance and direction; when he died, the activities of the
school continued in direct imitation of the founder's role.[57]

Like Meeks and Moody Smith, Culpepper also accepts the main
lines of J. L. Martyn's thesis concerning the *Sitz im Leben* of
the Gospel and proceeds to fit his own theory into it. Thus,
he argues that the synagogal opposition gave rise to the study
of the scriptures and the interpretation of the traditions
about Jesus given to the community by the Beloved Disciple in
order to use them against the Jews.[58]

      Culpepper is much more definite than the previous three
scholars about the place of the Letters within the history of
the community. First of all, the Letters are said to come
from a time later than that of the Gospel and from a hand
other than that of the evangelist.[59] Yet their author was a
member of the school, who appealed to the traditions of the
Beloved Disciple in the face of docetic and libertine aberra-
tions on the part of some within the community.[60] The emphasis
was no longer that of abiding in the Spirit, but of abiding in
the teaching of the Spirit.

      The Johannine "school," therefore, endured from its
foundation under the guidance of the Beloved Disciple into the
second century, when it was wrecked by the docetic dissension
that arose in the community. Its main activity throughout was
one of studying and teaching, interpreting and writing, i.e.,
all the activities that form the *sine qua non* of the concept
of a "school."

      It should also be mentioned that Culpepper does not
rule out the possibility that the "school" formed part of a
"sect," but his understanding of the latter term is quite different from that of Meeks and Moody Smith. Culpepper understands a sect as being "characterized by its devotion to the
teachings of a founder or its adherence to a set of principles."[61] Yet, if one employs the exclusivistic and totalistic
picture of a sect adopted by Meeks and Moody Smith and com-
pares it with Culpepper's picture of a Johannine school, it
would indeed appear that the proposed school would have a sectarian consciousness.[62]

John Bogart (1977)

      The point of departure for Bogart's study is very sim-
ilar to that of Wayne Meeks, i.e., both address themselves to

a particular exegetical puzzle within the Johannine literature.
In the case of Meeks, this puzzle is the myth of the descending/
ascending revealer in the Gospel; Bogart begins with what
appears to be a contradictory position regarding the attitude
of perfectionism in the First Letter.[63] Whereas I Jn 1:8-10
consists of an attack on those who adopt a perfectionist stance,
I Jn 3:6-10 seems to put forward precisely such a doctrine.
In the resolution of this problem, Bogart proceeds to give an
attempted historical reconstruction of the Johannine community.[64]

      The first stage of the community considered by Bogart
is that of the Gospel itself; thus, he does not deal with the
pre-Gospel or preliterary stages at all. The Gospel, he
believes, presents a good example of that attitude he has
labelled "perfectionism": on the one hand, it presents the
believer as already possessing eternal life (spiritual perfectionism); on the other, the believer is seen as enjoying the
state of salvation and as living in ethical purity (ethical
perfectionism).[65] In a history-of-religions approach to the
attitude of perfectionism, Bogart finds that, besides the
Johannine literature, the phenomenon is also found in Jewish
apocalyptic literature.[66]

      The second stage of the community appears to take
place after the Gospel had been written. This stage centers
on the introduction from the outside of a gnostic view of creation and man, a view which apparently many from the community
accepted and developed into a docetic-libertine brand of Christianity.[67] Bogart is adamant in insisting that these ideas
were introduced from the outside, that they could not have been
developed from the Gospel in and of itself.[68] He believes,
however, that it is impossible to identify the origin of these
ideas.[69]

      It was the reaction against this development--which, in
turn, constitutes the heretical perfectionism attacked in I Jn
1:8-10--that constitutes the third stage of the community. The
author of the First Letter wrote directly against these
docetic-libertine Christians and sought to recall the community
to the "orthodox" brand of perfectionism contained in the

Gospel of John.[70] It is this perfectionism that is given in
I Jn 3:6, 10. However, in this affirmation of the traditional
attitude of the community, the author in effect supplants perfectionism with a type of "gradualism": man may become perfect,
but only over a long period of time.[71] In combatting his
opponents the author was forced to modify the traditions of the
community.

      At the end of the study, Bogart addresses himself to
the question whether the Johannine community may be called a
"sect," and in doing so he has in mind the understanding of
this term adopted by E. Käsemann[72] and W. Meeks.[73] He concludes
that the community was indeed a sect--a term which he defines
as "being both peculiar in doctrine vis-à-vis the rest of the
church, and defensive and alienated vis-à-vis the world around
it"[74]--but not on account of its gnosticizing christology nor
on account of its self-referring system of symbols; rather, it
is on account of its perfectionist stand that the community may
be called a sect. This is the *sine qua non* of sectarian consciousness.[75]

      By the time that I John was written,[76] Johannine chris-
tology and soteriology are brought completely into the orthodox
camp of mainstream Christianity. Along with this shift there
occurs a cessation of the perfectionist stance in the community in favor of gradualism, so that this unique phenomenon
within the New Testament in effect disappears. At the same
time, Bogart claims that the sectarian spirit nevertheless continued in the community, not so much vis-à-vis the church, but
vis-à-vis the world.[77]

Summary

      In conclusion, I would like to summarize the views of
these five recent studies on the Johannine community by concentrating on two themes which are important to my own study.
These two themes are: (a) the sectarian consciousness of the
community and (b) the role of I John within this community.

      With regard to the first theme, it seems fair to say
that these recent studies would support the view that the community did indeed possess a sectarian consciousness; perhaps
the only dissenter would be Oscar Cullmann, who, however,

understands "sect" from the rather narrow point of view of a
struggle against the larger (Synoptic) "church." The others
would stress different elements associated with the sociological concept of a sect: Meeks would place the primary emphasis
on the symbolic language being used; Moody Smith would limit
his description to the exclusivistic and totalistic stance
taken by the community; Bogart would stress the attitude of
perfectionism; and Culpepper--dealing with the supposedly narrower term of "school"--would follow basically Meeks and Moody
Smith.

        As far as the second theme is concerned, all the
exegetes but J. Bogart--who really does not address the issue
directly--would assign the authorship of the First Letter to
a hand other than that of the evangelist. Furthermore, all
the exegetes but J. Bogart, who would see a certain relaxation
of the sectarian attitude, and O. Cullmann would place I John
within this sectarian consciousness and indeed see the Letter
as manifesting a heightening or a sharpening of sectarianism
in the community.[78]

        Thus, the general direction of thought seems to be
that the Johannine community was basically a sectarian group--
whether "school" or not--and that I John represented a later
stage of the same community (indeed, a different author who
was probably very close to the evangelist) which manifested
an even greater sectarian consciousness. None of these authors,
however, seriously considers the possibility that this author
(i.e., the author of I John) could have had a hand in the
redaction of the Gospel. In the study of ἀγάπη that follows,
I wish to keep these two themes in mind: does the community's
understanding of ἀγάπη reveal its sectarian attitude? Does the
understanding of ἀγάπη in I John betray an even more sectarian
outlook? I now turn more specifically to the question of the
relationship of I John to the Gospel.

Relationship of I John to the Gospel

        The exegetical position that the author of I John is
to be distinguished from that of the Gospel--a position which
is espoused by W. Meeks, D. Moody Smith, O. Cullmann, and

R. Alan Culpepper--has gained much acceptance in the last two decades of Johannine research.[79] There are only a handful of dissenting voices from this emerging scholarly consensus.[80]

It was not really until the publication of C. H. Dodd's article on the similarities and differences, both stylistic and conceptual, between I John and the Gospel that this opinion began to take root.[81] The year was 1937. Prior to this time the question of common or different authorship had been a see-saw battle. Thus, for example, one finds H. J. Holtzmann (1881-2),[82] J. Martineau (1891),[83] C. von Weizsäcker (1899),[84] E. F. Scott (1906)[85] and H. Windisch (1930)[86] arguing for the latter position, while J. Drummond (1903),[87] R. Law (1909),[88] A. E. Brooke (1912),[89] V. H. Stanton (1920),[90] and B. H. Streeter (1924)[91] sought to defend the tradition of common authorship.

In his commentary on the Johannine Letters, published nine years later (1946), Dodd reiterated the position taken in the previous article.[92] Although the thesis was immediately attacked upon publication by a series of scholars (primarily on linguistic grounds),[93] it began to gain more and more adherents as time went on. In the process, the theory was also advanced and strengthened to the point that it has become scholarly consensus. In what follows I would like to trace this development in terms of its most salient points. I shall begin with C. H. Dodd, continue with an article on the under-standing of tradition in I John by Hans Conzelmann (1954)[94] and an article on the different eschatological perspectives of both documents by Günter Klein (1971),[95] and conclude with a reference to a "school" of thought which has recently begun to assign certain sections of the Gospel to the author of I John.

C. H. Dodd (1937)

Writing in England in 1937 and acknowledging the con-sensus opinion at that time concerning the relationship of I John to the Gospel--a position which was largely determined by the work of A. E. Brooke and which argued for common author-ship[96]--Dodd is very much aware of the novelty of his own theory. It is perhaps for this reason that he begins his argumentation by remarking upon the general correctness of the

existing theory: there are great similarities between both
writings in terms of theological standpoint, terminology, and
style. The question is whether such similarities warrant the
attribution of common authorship.

Dodd's theory is that they do not, because there are
also differences--differences in theological standpoint, terminology, and style--that are best accounted for by positing
two authors, one of whom, the author of the Letter was strongly
influenced by the other's work, i.e., the evangelist and/or his
Gospel. All these differences may be summarized in a very general way by a certain "aesthetic" or "emotional" impression
made upon the reader by a simple reading of both writings:
"There is surely to be felt in the Fourth Gospel a richness,
a subtlety, a penetrating quality about the style which is
missing in the Epistle."[97]

From the point of view of style, Dodd argues that a
detailed study of such stylistic elements as grammatical words
and particles, compound verbs, idiomatic expressions[98] and
rhetorical figures leads one to conclude that the style of
I John is indeed less sophisticated and more monotonous than
that of the Gospel. The differences may be more reasonably
explained in terms of an "imitator" of his master's work.[99]
Furthermore, a detailed study of the terminology of both writings leads one to the same conclusion, since quite a few of
what one could call *termini technici* of the Gospel are totally
absent from the Letter--thirty-three terms to be exact.[100]

Those stylistic and terminological differences are
further strengthened by significant theological variations
between the Gospel and the First Letter. First of all, Dodd
argues that the strong Jewish element evident in the Gospel
seems to disappear from I John completely--the Letter has no
Old Testament quotations, one direct allusion to it, and very
few indirect echoes.[101] Secondly, the Letter is said to present three theological doctrines which are much closer to
"common Christianity" than to the tradition of the Fourth
Gospel, viz., an imminent eschatological expectation; a belief
in the redemptive efficacy of the death of Christ; and a more
primitive conception of the Spirit.[102] Finally, Dodd points
out that the gnosticizing elements within the Letter are much

more salient and less restrained than their counterpart in the
Gospel.[103]

The combined effect of these differences is to place
the unity of authorship of the two writings in serious doubt.
Therefore, Dodd argues, it is much easier to reconcile both the
similarities and the differences between the two writings if
one adopts a theory of different authorship--thus accounting
for the differences--and a theory of discipleship--in effect
accounting for the similarities. This position may be essentially described as a "school" hypothesis: "The author of the
Epistle was a disciple of the evangelist and a student of his
work."[104] It should be mentioned as a final point that Dodd
does consider briefly the possibility that the author of I John
may have had a hand in the redaction of the Gospel, but rejects
it by a reference to the underlying unity of thought present
throughout the entire Gospel.[105]

Hans Conzelmann (1954)

Conzelmann's brief study reinforces Dodd's conclusions
from what the latter might call a difference in theological
standpoint.[106] No one, Conzelmann begins, can deny that there
do exist differences and similarities between the Gospel of
John and the First Letter, thus raising the problem of the
literary relationship between the two writings. The way to
solve the problem, Conzelmann continues, is by focusing methodologically on the differences in order to see how the one
writing may be interpreted by the other. His own proposal is
to examine the issue of eschatology from this particular perspective.

Dodd had already examined this difference in eschatology, arriving at the conclusion that I John had reintroduced
an imminent eschatological perspective which was not to be
found in the Gospel. Conzelmann's research, however, leads
him to a rather different conclusion. His precise point of
departure is the use and meaning of the prepositional phrase
ἀπ' ἀρχῆς in I John; this expression provides a key with which
to open and bring to light the relationship in eschatological
perspectives.

The prepositional phrase is used in the Letter in two
different ways. On the one hand, it may refer to the absolute
beginning, i.e., the beginning of the world, as in 1:1; 2:13,
14; 3:8. This meaning may be found in the Gospel as well,
viz., the Prologue.[107] On the other hand, it may signify the
beginning of the church or the historical appearance of Jesus,
as in 2:7, 24; 3:11; II Jn 5. It is this ecclesiastical meaning that is lacking altogether in the Gospel.[108]

The emergence of this technical meaning, Conzelmann
continues, may be explained by the new problems which have
arisen in the community, specifically, the emergence of false
teaching among the ranks. In this new situation the author
of the Letter looks upon the past stages of the community as
tradition and invokes this tradition in order to justify and
strengthen his own position: it is he who is in contact with
"the beginning."[109] Therein the difference between Gospel and
Letter becomes quite clear. Whereas in the Gospel the contrast had been one of belief versus unbelief, in the Letter
it is presented as correct belief versus incorrect belief.
Likewise, whereas in the Gospel a Christian could be distinguished by a knowledge of the kerygma, in the Letter it becomes
a question of reflective knowledge. In other words, for the
author of I John the Gospel has become set tradition.[110]

With this emergence of tradition and set doctrine one
also finds a difference in eschatological perspective. From
the realized eschatology of the Gospel one finds a shift
toward an eschatology that is being realized: the "true
light" (2:8) only shines insofar as correct doctrine and correct praxis are maintained.[111] Thus, Conzelmann argues, the
eschatological consciousness of the community becomes historicized, dependent upon the struggle between truth and error.

In Conzelmann's study, therefore, the author of the
Letter is regarded chiefly as an *Imitator* of his master's work,
i.e., the Gospel.[112] Thus, he stands directly in connection
with and under the influence of this work, which has at this
time become his own ecclesiastical tradition: he uses and
reshapes, invokes and reinterprets. Like Dodd's view, this
view may also be considered a variation of the "school" hypothesis; indeed, in his *Outline of the Theology of the New Testament*

(German original, 1954) Conzelmann speaks of a school of the evangelist from which the epistles are derived.[113] Further-more, in that very same work Conzelmann rejects the theory that the community may have been a "sect."[114]

Günter Klein (1971)

Klein's rather voluminous study of the question of authorship is by far the most self-consciously methodological of the three, examining critically the manifold solutions that have preceded his own work and, at the same time, pointing out the direction that any further research must follow in this area (including his own, of course).[115] At the very beginning of the article, Klein states that the question of the Johannine mystery has begun to receive some elucidation from two differ-ent directions: (a) the emergence of the history of Johannine Christianity as a preeminent problem; (b) the recent considera-tion of Johannine style from a sociological point of view.[116]

However, this new area of research has concentrated for the most part on the traditions that underlie the Gospel, i.e., the pre-Gospel stages.[117] Methodologically, Klein argues, there is another possibility open to the Johannine exegete, viz., a consideration of the development of Johannine tradition and Johannine "literature" after the composition of the Gospel. One way to examine the later stages of that tradi-tion is to presuppose that the Gospel itself has gone through a process of redaction within a Johannine group and to proceed on that basis to separate tradition (i.e., Gospel) from redac-tion.[118] This is certainly a valid approach in Klein's view, but it does present some grave risks.[119]

Klein proposes yet another way of dealing with the *Nachgeschichte* of the Gospel by comparing the Gospel and the Letters of the corpus with one another in order to see whether a shift in theological reflection has taken place.[120] If such a shift has indeed taken place, then one can argue on behalf of the different authorship of the Letters and, at the same time, elucidate further the later, i.e., post-Gospel, stage of the community. Like Conzelmann before him, Klein concentrates on the issue of eschatology. However, before proceeding to summarize Klein's findings on behalf of different authorship,

it might be well to consider briefly his evaluation of previous works employing this methodology, including those of
C. H. Dodd and H. Conzelmann.

Prior to the work of Hans Conzelmann, all comparisons
of the Gospel and the Letters had been conducted on what Klein
calls the principle of *Sondergut*, i.e., a specific emphasis of
the material present in one of the writings, but absent from
the other.[121] Such an approach, Klein argues, is very much
lacking in methodological rigorousness, since its results may
also be explained by other means. Thus, for example, one can
argue form-critically that the differences are due to the different *Gattungen* being employed by the same author.[122] In
Klein's view, the three theological differences proposed by
C. H. Dodd fall victim to similar argumentation.[123] With
Conzelmann's study the situation changes drastically, since he
chooses to concentrate not on *Sondergut*, but rather on material
common to both writings--the expression ἀπ' ἀρχῆς--in order to
see whether different interpretations are present.[124]

Similarly, Klein proposes to examine the problem of
eschatology from the starting point of common terminology
between the two writings, e.g., the contrast φῶς / σκοτία, the
expression ἐσχάτη ὥρα, and others.[125] Furthermore, he states
that this particular choice of motifs will not raise the
doubts that Conzelmann's choice does.[126] The conclusion is
that there is indeed a fundamental difference between the conceptions of eschatology of the two writings. In terms of the
contrast light/darkness, this difference may be explained as
follows: whereas the Gospel presents a chronologically undifferentiated opposition between "light" and "darkness" (they
are opposing powers on an existential level), the Letter his-
toricizes this opposition by having the epoch of "light" follow that of "darkness."[127] Thereby, the First Letter addresses
itself explicitly to the theologically relevant problems of
time and history.

This conclusion is further reinforced by an examination
of the other eschatological terms. As a result, only a theory
of different authorship can account for this divergence. Likewise, the divergence does elucidate to a degree the later stage
of the Johannine tradition. This later stage is conceived of

in terms of a variation of the "school" hypothesis: the author
of I John had the Gospel before him and reinterpreted the
eschatological terms that he found therein in terms of his own
situation. Thus, Klein argues, Conzelmann's statement to the
effect that the author of I John "das Johannesevangelium
bereits als feste Autorität vor Augen hat" is essentially correct.[128] This author engaged in a revision of his master's
work, particularly the latter's eschatological doctrine, adopting its terminology, but reinterpreting it drastically.

*I John as Redactor of the
 Gospel*

        None of the above studies seriously considers the pos-
sibility that, granted the theory of different authorship, the
author of I John--or perhaps someone in the same life situa-
tion--could have helped to redact the Gospel as well. Dodd
raises the question, but dismisses it quickly.[129] Klein specifically refers to J. Becker's findings concerning the redaction of the Gospel, but does not mention Becker's thesis that
the redaction may be connected with I John as well.[130] The
reason is partly, no doubt, the goal of these studies, i.e.,
the theory of different authorship.

        Yet, rather recently a number of opinions have been
raised proposing precisely such a hypothesis: the author of
I John or someone who shared exactly the same life situation
(both variations are found) did have a role in the redaction
of the Gospel. I do not wish to present these theories in
detail at this point, since they will be examined closely in
Chapters III and V below. I should merely like to enumerate
the proponents that constitute this "school" of thought and to
present the most salient points of their theories.

        The works of Georg Richter[131] and Hartwig Thyen[132] may
be considered together, since they both present the same point
of departure and arrive at rather similar results. The *Aus-
gangspunkt* is in both cases a study of chapter 13 of the
Gospel, i.e., the Washing of the Disciples' Feet. Not only do
both men find in this chapter two different renditions of the
same episode (one of which, made up primarily of vv. 10-17, is
attributed to a later redactor),[133] but also they both see the

redactor of this chapter as engaging in a thoroughgoing revision of the entire Gospel.[134] Furthermore, both men associate
this undertaking with the author of I John.[135] They argue that
the theological *Akzent* of the hypothetical revision matches
that of I John as well.

Again, the works of Jürgen Becker[136] and R. Schnackenburg[137] may also be considered together, since they are more
cautious in associating the Gospel with I John. First of all,
both men see the redaction of the Gospel as involving more than
one person, as consisting of different layers. Thus, for
example, Becker assigns 15:1-17 and 15:18-16:15 to one redactor,
while attributing 16:16-33 to another. Likewise, Schnackenburg
attributes 15:1-16:4a to one redactor and assigns 16:4b-33 to
another.[138] Secondly, both men prefer to speak of a "situation like that of I John" and of someone in that situation
rather than to speak of one and the same author.[139] As in the
case of Richter and Thyen, both Becker and Schnackenburg argue
that the theological *Akzent* of the revision clearly matches
that of I John.

All of these studies presuppose the different authorship of the First Letter,[140] and their results in turn serve
to confirm and further strengthen this exegetical opinion.
Their methodology is similar to that of Conzelmann and Klein
insofar as they point out the fundamental theological differences between the Gospel on the one hand and the Letter on the
other. They do seem, however, to lack that rigorousness that
characterizes Klein's work, since for the most part (above all,
Richter, Thyen, and Becker) they do not spend much time at all
on I John, being content to draw parallels between it and the
redactional insertions attributed to it within the Gospel.

Summary

The present study on ἀγάπη also partakes of the presupposition that I John was written later than the Gospel and
that it comes from a different hand than that of the Gospel.
The mounting evidence on behalf of this opinion--starting
above all with the work of C. H. Dodd--is simply too overwhelming and too persuasive to be bypassed. At the same time,
the present study will serve to confirm and strengthen a bit

further this exegetical opinion, insofar as a theologically
different notion of ἀγάπη is to be found in the First Letter
when compared to its counterpart in the Gospel.

From the point of view of methodology, the present
study takes to heart the methodological restrictions imposed
upon any further research by the work of Günter Klein. Thus,
it deals not with *Sondergut*, but rather with a term that is
common to both Gospel and First Letter, viz., the noun ἀγάπη
and its verbal form ἀγαπᾶν. The goal of the inquiry is to see
whether and to what extent the terms receive different interpretations in both of these writings.

Furthermore, given these two elements--acceptance of
a theory of different authorship and comparison of the two
writings in terms of ἀγάπη / ἀγαπᾶν --the present study seeks
above all to test the theory of a redaction of the Gospel by
either the author of I John or someone in the same life situation. In particular, it seeks to test J. Becker's theory that
15:1-17 and 15:18-16:15 (plus 13:34-5) were inserted into the
present context by someone whose life situation was the same
as that of I John. The choice of the methodology outlined
above, specially the choice of the theme ἀγάπη / ἀγαπᾶν, was
highly influenced by the high incidence of the terms in the
sections in question. Thus, the study seeks to determine not
only and to what extent the terms are interpreted differently
in the Gospel and in I John (as indeed they are), but also to
see whether the meaning of these terms in certain sections of
the Gospel--sections which have been attributed to a redactor
by Becker--lies closer to the one manifested by I John, thus
presupposing and demanding a similar *Sitz im Leben*.

Although several studies have appeared over the years
on the question of ἀγάπη in the Johannine literature, none has
really, in my opinion, approached the issue from this particular perspective. And yet, it is a perspective that must be
explored minutely, given the emerging theory--subscribed to in
one way or another, as I have pointed out above, by Georg
Richter, Hartwig Thyen, Jürgen Becker, and Rudolf Schnacken-
burg--that a redaction of the Gospel did take place and that
such a redaction is to be associated with I John. Before I proceed to outline the rationale of the thesis, I should like to

24   Love Relationships in John

consider briefly the main works that have appeared on the
question of ἀγάπη in the Gospel and in I John.

Overview of Past Studies on Love in
the Johannine Literature

These main works may be chiefly divided into two major
categories which are, moreover, related to the chronology of
the publication of these works (with one exception).[141] The
first division, and the earlier, consists of a number of massive works on the theme of love in the New Testament as a whole,
so that the Johannine literature forms but one part, one chapter, of the entire work. These works are: (a) James Moffatt,
Love in the New Testament (1930);[142] (b) Victor Warnach, *Agape.*
Die Liebe als Grundmotiv der neutestamentlichen Theologie
(1951);[143] (c) Ceslaus Spicq, *Agapè dans le Nouveau Testament*
(1958-9).[144] The second and later division consists of a number of works that deal directly--with the exception of V.
Furnish--with ἀγάπη and its derivatives in the Johannine writings. These works are: (a) Jerzy Chmiel, *Lumière et charité*
d'après la première épître de Saint Jean (1971);[145] (b) Victor
Furnish, *The Love Command in the New Testament* (1972);[146]
(c) André Feuillet, *Le Mystère de l'amour divin dans la théo-*
logie johannique (1972);[147] (d) Michael Lattke, *Einheit im Wort*
(1975).[148]

Writing in 1972, Furnish provides a succinct and rather
accurate characterization of the three works that encompass the
first division outlined above, viz., Moffatt, Warnach, and
Spicq. He refers to the tendency of these three writers, above
all Warnach and Spicq, to engage in "an unjustified homogenization of differing perspectives and emphases within the New Testament itself."[149] All three works are after what one might
call the "essence" of *the* New Testament theology of love.

I believe that this similarity in purpose is more or
less bound up with the similarity in *raison d'être* that these
authors provide for their respective works. In all three
instances the point of departure is highly polemical in tone:
because love has been misused and misinterpreted throughout
history and in the contemporary world, it is necessary to
define what Christian love really means. The adverb "really"

is very important, because it refers to the basic presupposition shared by these three men that Christian love is best presented in the New Testament and that such a presentation is
essentially monolithic.

Moffatt, for example, argues specifically against two
tendencies of thought in the England of 1930: (a) the understanding of the phrase "God is love" as either a cosmic principle or an inner light; (b) the belief that brotherly love is
the essence of Christianity.[150] Against these deviations he
argues that a consistent image of love appears in the New Testament, centered around the redeeming death of Jesus Christ.[151]
Warnach is even more widespread in his attack than Moffatt,
lashing out against all kinds of modern doctrines that degrade
love (ranging from S. Freud to certain developments within
Christianity itself).[152] Only in the New Testament, he counter-
acts, is the true idea and example of love presented (and presented "from above," i.e., by the Holy Spirit).[153] Spicq limits
himself to a criticism of theologians who read into the Scriptures their own intellectual conceptions--he isolates Anders
Nygrén as an example.[154] By way of contrast, Spicq argues that
only a correct philological analysis of the New Testament can
reveal what the homogeneous conception of love therein presented is.[155]

This "unjustified homogenization" is definitely present
in their attitudes toward the relationship of the Johannine
writings as well. Moffatt is really the only one who faces the
issue of authorship directly, albeit briefly. The basic position is that it really does not matter who wrote the Gospel or
whether the same person also wrote the First Epistle and the
two smaller Letters (II and III John). The differences among
the four writings, Moffatt argues, may be bypassed entirely on
account of the "common spirit which dominates this outlook on
the Christian faith."[156] Both Warnach and Spicq take for
granted the common authorship of the Gospel and the Letters.[157]

In 1971 a dissertation authored by Jerzy Chmiel and
written under the direction of Donatien Mollatt at the Gregorian
University in Rome was published the goal of which was to establish the meaning of the relationship between "light" and "love"
in I John.[158] Chmiel observed that both terms were predicated

of God (1:5; 4:8, 16) and were also used to describe authentic
Christian behavior (2:10). Thus, he argued that the clarification of this relationship could only lead to a better understanding of the theology of the Letter.

     In a brief explication of the methodology to be used in
the work, Chmiel reveals indirectly his conception of the relationship between Gospel and Letters. Thus, he specifies that
he will use "l'analyse littéraire" to place the relevant formulas of the Letter within their context. Furthermore, he continues, he will cite parallels from the Fourth Gospel only when
the text or meaning of the First Letter is obscure. Clearly,
he favors a common authorship.[159] Yet, curiously enough, he is
more than open to the suggestion that I John may have been
edited at a later time by "disciples" of the author--i.e., the
evangelist--who followed closely his thought and vocabulary.[160]

     A year later, i.e., 1972, Furnish published yet a new
study of the theme of love in the entire New Testament. In the
Introduction to the monograph he justifies its *raison d'être* by
pointing out that the work's goal and method differ considerably
from those of its predecessors, specifically the studies by
Moffatt, Warnach, and Spicq. From the point of view of goal,
Furnish argues that, instead of dealing with all the aspects
of ἀγάπη in the New Testament, he will concentrate primarily
on the love command, i.e., " . . . earliest Christianity's view
of loving one's brother, one's neighbor, and one's enemy."[161]
As far as method is concerned, I have already referred to Furnish's succinct evaluation of his predecessors. By way of contrast, he specifies that he will take into account the "full
context" of the love commandment in all the writings examined,
i.e., how the writers appropriate and interpret the commandment
of love.[162]

     With regard to the Johannine writings, Furnish con-
siders the Gospel apart from the Letters. Although he leans
toward acceptance of the theory of different authorship, he
does not adopt a firm stand, preferring instead to consider
the issue in terms of a quasi-school hypothesis. Thus, for
example, he considers the Letters to be within the "theological
jurisdiction of the Fourth Gospel."[163] Furthermore, in his
presentation of the Gospel it is clear that he accepts the

entire Farewell Discourse to have been written by the same
person and thus proceeds to use the data on ἀγάπη from these
chapters to illumine the evangelist's total conception of this
term.[164]

That very same year André Feuillet published a study of
divine love ("l'amour divin") in the Johannine writings. In
the Introduction to the work, Feuillet declares that it was
originally conceived as the first chapter of a more general
introduction to the whole of Johannine theology, but that it
was being published separately because of the length the one
chapter had already attained.[165] In a very brief paragraph,
Feuillet approaches indirectly the question of authorship. He
states that the similarities that exist between the Gospel and
the Letters far outweigh the differences and concludes that
"ils sont proprement inséparables."[166] The impression that the
reader gathers from the work is that Feuillet presupposes a
common authorship, although he does not say so *expressis
verbis*.[167]

Finally, in 1975 Michael Lattke's dissertation on the
"specific" meaning of ἀγαπᾶν and φιλεῖν in the Gospel of John
appeared. Since I shall have occasion to refer to this work
in the chapters to come, I shall limit myself at this point to
a brief description of the thesis. Suffice it to say that
Lattke stands in a tradition of exegesis that begins with
Martin Dibelius[168] and is continued primarily by Ernst Käsemann.[169] This tradition holds that ἀγάπη in the Gospel of John
refers to a restricted, i.e., exclusivistic, unity of revelation between Father, Son, and the disciples. There are no
mystical or ethical overtones at all in the use of the term by
the evangelist; rather, it connotes a unity in revelation, in
the λόγος.

As the title itself indicates, Lattke is concerned primarily with the occurrences of the three terms in the Gospel
(a quick look at the index of scriptural references shows how
infrequently the author has recourse to the evidence of I John).
Although Lattke does not address himself to the question of
authorship directly, it would appear that he does favor a
theory of different authorship.[170] At the very least, he
states that the understanding of ἀγάπη in the Letters is indeed

quite different from that of the Gospel.[171] However, he does
not raise the possibility of redaction on the part of the latter
author within the Farewell Discourse; rather, he adopts, as I
shall show later, a variation of the transpositional or rearrangement theory.[172]

. Not one of these authors, therefore, considers the
question from the particular point of view that I have outlined
for my own work. Most of these authors seem to favor a theory
of common authorship (Moffatt; Warnach; Spicq; Chmiel,
Feuillet), and those that do not (Furnish; Lattke) see no
redaction within Jn 13-17 and, therefore, no possibility of
associating I John with this redaction. Yet, it is this particular question that stands in need of resolution and this
particular problem that I wish to pursue in detail.

Keeping in mind the methodological restrictions outlined above, I shall proceed as follows. In the second chapter
I shall consider the meaning of ἀγάπη / ἀγαπᾶν in the First
Letter as it stands.[173] The goal is to achieve a basic understanding of the meaning of love in I John and its role in the
author's life situation. In the third chapter I shall turn to
those sections within the Farewell Discourse which J. Becker
assigns to a life situation similar to that of I John.[174] By
means of literary criticism and redaction criticism, I shall
determine whether these sections are literary unities and
whether they may reasonably be assigned to a life situation
approximating that of I John. In the fourth chapter I shall
examine by means of redaction criticism the remaining ἀγάπη
passages in the Gospel in order to see whether the results of
Chapter II and Chapter III differ from the evangelist's conception of love.

This inquiry should, it is hoped, shed further light
on the *Nachgeschichte* of the Johannine community. Furthermore,
on account of the thematic concerns chosen for the comparison
of Letters and Gospel, this inquiry should also shed further
light on the questions raised within the first section of this
chapter: Was the Johannine community a sect? Was the latter
stage of the community even more sectarian and exclusivistic?
Finally, on the basis of this inquiry, I shall approach the
question of the extent of the redaction that may be attributed

to I John by entering into an *Auseinandersetzung* with those
exegetes--Georg Richter and Hartwig Thyen--that favor an
extensive reworking of the original document. These concerns
shall form the body of the final chapter of this work.

CHAPTER II

Ἀγάπη/Ἀγαπᾶν IN I JOHN

In accordance with the methodology outlined at the conclusion of the preceding chapter, I should like to begin this
exegetical study of the terms ἀγάπη/ἀγαπᾶν in the Johannine
tradition with a redaction-critical study of these terms in
I John. Although my primary interest lies in the meaning of
these terms as they occur in I John, I shall consider any pertinent evidence from either II or III John whenever applicable.
Furthermore, given the conflicting views on the common authorship of the three Letters, i.e., I-II-III John,[1] I shall use
such evidence solely for the purpose of comparison rather than
for direct contribution to the redaction-critical quest mentioned above.[2]

To begin with, the noun form ἀγάπη occurs a total of
eighteen times in I John: 2:5, 15; 3:1, 16, 17; 4:7, 8, 9, 10,
12, 16[3], 17, 18[3]; 5:3. It is also found twice in II John
(vv. 3, 6) and once in III John (v. 6). Secondly, the verb
form ἀγαπᾶν occurs a total of twenty-six times in the First
Letter: 2:10, 15[2]; 3:10, 11, 14[2], 18, 23; 4:7[2], 8, 10[2], 11[2],
12, 19, 20[3], 21[2]; 5:1[2], 2. Again, the verb form is also found
in II and III John: twice in the former writing (vv. 1, 5),
and once in the latter (v. 1). Therefore, the combined occurrences of noun and verb forms in the First Letter add up to
forty-four instances of the root.[3]

Given the fact that I John consists of only five rather
brief chapters and constitutes approximately fourteen pages
(out of 895 pages) of the K. Aland edition of the Greek New
Testament, it is clear that the theme of love occupies a very
important place in the First Letter.[4] Furthermore, a comparison of the figures quoted above with the corresponding figures
from the larger corpus of the Gospel is rather revealing:

whereas I John shows eighteen examples of the noun form and
twenty-six examples of the verb form, the Gospel has only two
of the former and twenty-six of the latter (including verses
that use the synonymous verb form φιλέω!)[5] Thus, it seems as
if the idea of love has gained considerably in importance in
that period lying between the Gospel and I John (presupposing,
as I do, that the First Letter follows the Gospel in time of
composition).

One also cannot help but notice the unbalanced distribution of both the noun and verb forms in the body of the
First Letter.[6] The following chart depicts the distribution
of ἀγάπη and ἀγαπᾶν according to the five chapters of I John:

I.	*Chapter 1*	:	0	
II.	*Chapter 2*	:	5	2:5
				2:10
				2:15[3]
III.	*Chapter 3*	:	9	3:1 3:16
				3:10 3:17
				3:11 3:18
				3:14[2] 3:23
IV.	*Chapter 4*	:	26	4:7 4:16[3]
				4:8[2] 4:17
				4:9 4:18[3]
				4:10[3] 4:19
				4:11[2] 4:20[3]
				4:12[2] 4:21[2]
V.	*Chapter 5*	:	4	5:1[2]
				5:2
				5:3

The chart shows that the incidence of the references to love
is most frequent toward the center of the Letter. Thus, chapter 1 shows absolutely no examples, while chapters 2 and 5 contain only a small number (five and four, respectively). In
chapter 3, specifically toward the middle of the chapter
(vv. 3:10ff.), one finds both the noun and verb forms occurring
with greater frequency, a trend which culminates in chapter 4,
where there are, all together, twenty-six examples of the root,
i.e., approximately fifty-eight percent of the total number.
It seems, therefore, that the theme of love becomes paramount
toward the center of I John.

.   *Structure of the Letter*

        Before beginning the exegesis of these references to
love, it is necessary to consider the question of the structure
of I John in order to see how these references fit into that
structure and to develop the exegesis accordingly. Unfortunately, this particular question is not as simple as it may
seem *prima facie*: the structure of I John has proved to be a
crux interpretum for students of the Letter over the years.
Indeed, exegetical opinion has seen two irreconcilable
extremes: some scholars have tended to impose ingenious
structures--all at variance with one another--on the text,
while others have despaired completely of finding any type of
visible structure.[7]

        Among the latter one may certainly classify the works
of J. C. O'Neill and Rudolf Bultmann. In a monograph entitled
The Puzzle of I John,[8] O'Neill proposes that the First Letter
should not be read as a continuous "letter" or argument;
rather, he argues, I John (excluding the Prologue, vv. 1:1-4)
should be seen as a collection of twelve self-contained,
originally independent paragraphs or "prophetic words."[9] There
is simply no particular structure or organization behind this
collection of twelve paragraphs. In his commentary on the
Letter,[10] Rudolf Bultmann divides I John into three quite distinct sections: (1) vv. 1:5-2:27--an originally independent
writing or "first draft"; (2) vv. 2:28-5:12--a collection of
originally independent units which deal essentially with the
same themes of vv. 1:5-2:27;[11] (3) vv. 5:14-21--a later addition designed to bring the work into conformity with ecclesiastical tradition. Although not as extreme in his opinion as
J. C. O'Neill, Bultmann also sees very little visible structure
in the Letter as it stands.

        With regard to those exegetes who impose ingenious, if
not fanciful, structures upon the text, one may turn to the
works of Ernst Lohmeyer and M. Albertz as primary examples. In
an article published in 1928,[12] Lohmeyer claims to have dis-
covered a series of sevenfold groupings within the First Letter:
seven main sections,[13] each of which (except for the Prologue,
i.e., the first section, which has seven themes) contains seven

subsections (and some of these subsections also contain seven
additional parts!). Similarly, Albertz divides the Letter into
two main sections and posits within each section a sevenfold
pattern, so that the two patterns parallel and correspond to
each other.[14] Thus, from the lack of structure observed by
O'Neill and Bultmann one proceeds by a quantum leap to a quite
thorough and deliberate organization of the material as it
stands (and vice versa).

For the most part, however, traditional exegesis (and
certainly recent exegesis) has tried to steer a middle course
between either extreme. Thus, for example, some scholars tend
to emphasize the presence of certain overarching concerns within the Letter--but not to the extent of Lohmeyer and Albertz,
while others presuppose the absence of such concerns and posit
instead a "spiraling" (the term occurs quite frequently in the
literature) type of argumentation which utilizes a complex system of synonymous expressions and provides the structural unity
of the Letter--thus avoiding the solution given by O'Neill and
Bultmann.

Furthermore, if I read the course of traditional exegesis correctly, the choice between these two "emphases" seems
to revolve entirely around the question as to whether there is
in the Letter a succession of largely dogmatic and largely
ethical sections: some accept such a succession and see the
dogmatic and ethical interests as the overarching themes of the
structure,[15] while others do not.[16] This succession of ethical
and christological sections was first proposed, in great detail,
in 1892 by Theodor Häring;[17] since then, the theory has been
regularly adopted (e.g., A. E. Brooke, John Bogart) and has
proved to be a viable one in the exegesis of the Letter. However, later proponents have tended to bypass the detailed outline of Häring's thesis and to stress instead its essential
point: the succession of ethical and dogmatic passages within
I John.

I should emphasize at this point that the choice between
"emphases" need not be an either/or proposition, as it is the
case with the choice between extremes, e.g., it is impossible
to agree with both O'Neill and Lohmeyer. It is possible to
perceive a "spiraling" type of argumentation and to recognize

the succession of ethical and dogmatic concerns as the most
overarching within the spiral itself. This is, in effect, the
position of John Bogart: Bogart accepts the basic outline of
Theodor Häring[18] and, at the same time, perceives the "spiraling" argumentation.[19]

      This is a position to which I am very sympathetic,
since it acknowledges and harmoniously reconciles two basic
elements of the First Letter. On the one hand, it acknowledges
the presence of the "spiraling" type of argumentation. It cannot be denied that from paragraph to paragraph the author seems
to examine and describe the same situation or the same problem
with a different pair of colored eyeglasses: a new set of
synonymous words or expressions may replace, either temporarily
or permanently, a previously used set; one word in a paragraph
may become a major theme in another paragraph; a major theme in
one part of the Letter may disappear altogether in another part.
On the other hand, the position takes into account the inescap-
able presence of successive largely ethical (e.g., 1:5-2:17;
2:28-3:24; 4:7-21) and largely dogmatic sections (e.g., 2:18-
27; 4:1-6; 5:1-12).[20] It seems to me reasonable, therefore,
to accept such a succession as constituting the most overarching theme of the spiral.

      Given the fact that this solution emerges as the most
satisfactory one (avoiding either extreme and incorporating
two stylistic and structural elements of the First Letter), it
still remains to be seen how the references to love in the
Letter fit into this particular conception of its structure,
i.e., into the spiraling argumentation and the succession of
ethical and dogmatic passages. The best way, if not the only
way, to realize this task is to see into what "paragraphs," or
"sections," or "thought-units" of the spiral the references to
love fall. At this point, therefore, I should like to list the
number and extent of such "paragraphs" given by a broad variety
of Johannine exegetes. Such a procedure will provide a good
framework from which this study can operate critically, especially since agreement as to the delineation of such paragraphs
among exegetes is closer than is the case with regard to the
overall structure of the work.[21]

Furthermore, in order to avoid needless confusion, I
have selected the main division of the Letter provided by
Theodor Häring as the framework around which to organize the
other suggested divisions, since his is the earliest adoption
of a succession of ethical and dogmatic passages within the
Letter. In the following chart I place Häring's six divisions
at the very top of the page and proceed to list under each
category (vv. 1:5-2:17; 2:18-27; 2:28-3:24; 4:1-6; 4:7-21;
5:1-12) any subdivisions or "paragraphs" within that category
proposed by any of the chosen authors.[22] (See the following
two pages.)

The chart yields several important results. First of
all, two of Häring's categories--both belonging to the largely
dogmatic type--are almost universally acknowledged, viz., 2:18-
27 and 4:1-6, whether the commentators believe in said succession or not. The former is supported by eight exegetes (with
three minor deviations),[23] while the latter is supported by
nine (with two minor deviations).[24] Secondly, another passage
--also belonging to the largely dogmatic type--receives widespread support, viz., 5:1-12.[25] Thirdly, the three remaining
categories--all pertaining to the largely ethical type--are
variously divided by these eleven commentators, viz., 1:5-2:17;
2:28-3:24; 4:7-21, with the result that no particular "paragraph" (except for vv. 2:12-17, which is proposed by six of
the commentators) is adopted by more than three authors.

Methodology

On the basis of these results, it seems appropriate at
this point to classify the references to love only according
to the succession of largely ethical and largely dogmatic sections of the Letter, i.e., the six categories of Theodor Häring
mentioned above, given the widespread agreement that exists
among exegetes with regard to the delineation of the largely
dogmatic passages.[30] At the same time, it also seems appropri-
ate--given the wide variation that exists with regard to the
delineation of the other paragraphs within the largely ethical
sections--to undertake the classification of the references to

Theodor Häring's Outline

	1:5-2:17	2:18-27	2:28-3:24	4:1-6	4:7-4:21	5:1-12
1. O'Neill	1:5-10 2:1-6 2:7-11 2:12-17	2:18-27	2:28-3:10 3:10b-19 3:19b-24	4:1-6	4:7-18 4:19 ———	5:13
2. Bultmann	1:5-2:2 2:3-11 2:12-17	2:18-27	2:28-3:24	4:1-6	4:7-12 4:13-16 4:17-18 4:19-5:5	5:5-13
3. Lohmeyer[26]	1:5-2:6 2:7-17	2:18-27	2:28-3:1 3:2-6 3:7-12 3:13-17 3:18-20 3:21-24	4:1-3 4:4-6	4:7-10 4:11-13 4:14-16a 4:16b-18 4:19-21	5:1-12
4. Kümmel	1:5-10 2:1-2 2:3-6 2:7-11 2:12-17	2:18-27	2:28-3:6 3:7-17 3:18-24	4:1-6	4:7-21	5:1-12
5. Perrin	1:5-2:17	2:18-27	2:28-3:24	4:1-6	4:7-5:5	5:6-12

Theodor Haring's Outline (continued)

	1:5-2:17	2:18-27	2:28-3:24	4:1-6	4:7-4:21	5:1-12
6. Bogart[27]	1:5-2:11 2:12-14 2:15-17	2:18-27	2:28-3:24	4:1-6	4:7-21	5:1-12
7. Houlden	1:5-2:11 2:12-17	2:18-27	2:28-3:24	4:1-6	4:7-21	5:1-12
8. Dodd	1:5-2:6 2:7-17	2:18-28	2:29-3:10 3:11-18 3:19-24	4:1-6	4:7-12 4:13-18 4:19-5:5	5:6-13
9. Law	1:5-7 1:8-2:6 2:7-17	2:18-28	2:29-3:10a 3:10b-24a	3:24b- 4:6	4:7-12 4:13-16 4:17-5:3a	5:3b-12
10. Schnackenburg[28]	1:5 1:6-2:2 2:3-11 2:12-17	2:18-27	2:28-3:3 3:4-24 (3:4-10 3:11-20 3:12-24)	4:1-6	4:7-5:4 (4:7-10 4:11-16 4:17-18 4:19-5:2 5:3-4)	5:5-12
11. Westcott[29]	1:5-10 2:1-6 2:7-11 2:12-17	2:18-29	3:1-12 3:13-24	4:1-6	4:7-21	5:1-12

love according to such paragraphs in the course of the
redaction-critical study that follows.

In the following chart, therefore, I arrange all the
occurrences of either the noun form ἀγάπη or the verb form
ἀγαπᾶν according to the six categories proposed by Theodor
Häring:

I.	1:5-2:17	2:5			
		2:10			
		2:15[3]		Total:	5
II.	2:18-27	--			
III.	2:28-3:24	3:1	3:16		
		3:10	3:17		
		3:11	3:18		
		3:14[2]	3:23	Total:	9
IV.	4:1-6	--			
V.	4:7-21	4:7[3]	4:16[3]		
		4:8[2]	4:17		
		4:9	4:18[3]		
		4:10[3]	4:19		
		4:11[2]	4:20[3]		
		4:12[2]	4:21[2]	Total:	26
VI.	5:1-12	5:1[2]			
		5:2			
		5:3			

The chart shows that most of the references to love in
I John occur within those sections which I have chosen to call
largely ethical sections (forty instances in all): five in
the first such section (vv. 1:5-2:17); nine in the second one
(vv. 2:28-3:24); and twenty-six in the third (vv. 4:7-21).
Furthermore, the chart also shows that the great bulk of such
references is found toward the center of the Letter, specifically, within the third largely ethical section. By way of
contrast, only one of the largely dogmatic sections--a section
which follows immediately the highest concentration of the term
in the Letter--contains references to love, viz., 5:1-12.

Although it would seem advisable *prima facie* to begin
the exposition of the meaning of ἀγάπη/ἀγαπᾶν in the Letter by
concentrating on the third largely ethical section (vv. 4:7-21),
since it is in that section that one finds the highest number

of examples of the root, it seems more judicious to me--given
the "spiraling" type of argumentation already alluded to above--
to examine the examples in the order in which they occur in the
Letter, i.e., beginning with the five examples of vv. 1:5-2:17
and concluding with the four examples of vv. 5:1-12. One of
the important tasks of this examination will be the delineation
of the "paragraphs" or "thought-units" of the spiral within
which the examples occur.

I should like to make two more comments before beginning this redaction-critical study. First of all, one of the
dangers that faces any commentator of the Johannine Letters is
the possibility of entangling himself in the complex system of
synonymous ideas and expressions which undergirds the spiral.
I shall try to avoid this pitfall by staying as close as possible to the stated goal of this chapter, viz., the redaction-
critical study of "love" in I John. Secondly, it has long been
recognized that I John is a highly polemical writing, i.e.,
that it is designed to counteract certain specific problems and
persons within a particular early Christian community (or
group of communities).[31] In what follows, I shall address
myself to the precise nature of such a polemic only after the
redaction-critical study of the chapter has been concluded.

Exegesis of the Love References

I Jn 1:5-2:17

The chart above shows that this section contains five
examples of ἀγάπη/ἀγαπᾶν: vv. 2:5, 10, 15[3]. It is my opinion
(and the reasons are found below) that this section may be
divided into three paragraphs or thought-units: vv. 1:5-2:11;
2:12-14; 2:15-17. Thus, vv. 2:5, 10 belong to the first paragraph, while v. 2:15 belongs to the third one.

Vv. 1:5-2:11. Of the eleven exegetes quoted in the
chart on the structure of the Letter, only two, J. C. Houlden
and J. Bogart, take vv. 1:5-2:11 to be a paragraph in itself.
The arguments on behalf of this delineation are most convincing.
Thus, for example, Bogar claims that the occurrence of the

contrast "light/darkness" in vv. 1:5ff., and 2:8bff., forms
a clear case of *inclusio* and that the paragraph also contains
a series of six *Grundsätze* (1:6, 8, 10; 2:4, 6, 9) which accurately reveal the alleged position of the opponents of I John
and which are now found surrounded by that author's interpretative comments.[32]

Granted that these arguments are persuasive, it seems
to me that the paragraph betrays an even more complex and
deliberate structure, which is still, nonetheless, organized
around the quotations of the opponents--the *Grundsätze*, as
Bogart terms these quotations. That structure seems to consist
of a series of four characterizations of the opponents' stance,
each of which shows a similar pattern of presentation. Thus,
each characterization begins with a "controlling" statement
which introduces some of the major working concepts within that
characterization (e.g., 1:5, 7b; 2:3, 7-8). Then, two mutually
self-exclusive possibilities are given: first of all, the
incorrect alternative is affirmed and refuted (e.g., 1:6, 8;
2:4, 9); secondly, the correct alternative is affirmed and
those who exercise it are said to be in accordance with the
controlling statement (e.g., 1:7a, 9; 2:5, 10). Since the
working concepts are the same, the alternatives are given in
the form of antithetical parallelisms.[33]

It would be incorrect, however, to see the above structure as a rigid, undeviating plan; rather, it would be better
to regard it as a "bone" structure, which is then filled out--
fleshed out, as it were--by the author. Thus, for example, one
finds major working concepts being drawn from outside the controlling statement;[34] expansions of the incorrect alternative
placed immediately after the delineation of the correct one;[35]
substitutions of the working concepts with synonymous expressions within a characterization;[36] the introduction of parenetical advice;[37] and an expansion of a controlling statement.[38]

Indeed, it is in one of those instances of "fleshing
out" the structure that the first reference to love is found
(v. 2:5). The author begins the third characterization with
the controlling statement of v. 2:3, which is given in definitional form and which introduces these two working concepts:
ἐγνώκαμεν αὐτόν and τὰς ἐντολὰς αὐτοῦ τηρῶμεν.[39] Then, the

first and incorrect alternative is given in v. 2:4, utilizing
these two working concepts: ὁ λέγων ὅτι "Εγνωκα αὐτόν, καὶ
τὰς ἐντολὰς αὐτοῦ μὴ τηρῶν ψεύστης ἐστίν, καὶ ἐν τούτῳ ἡ
ἀλήθεια οὐκ ἔστιν. In other words, there can be no claim "to
know him," i.e., Jesus,[40] if his commandments are not carried
out; the definition of v. 2:3 has ruled out such a possibility.
V. 2:5 provides the second and correct alternative, but in so
doing it replaces these two working concepts with synonymous
expressions. First of all, the expression, "to carry out his
commandments," is replaced by the similar expression, "to carry
out his word." Secondly, the expression, "to know him (Jesus),"
is replaced by and equated with the expression, "to make perfect the love of God": ὃς δ'ἂν τηρῇ αὐτοῦ τὸν λόγον (= τὰς
ἐντολὰς αὐτοῦ τηρεῖν) ἀληθῶς ἐν τούτῳ ἡ ἀγάπη τοῦ θεοῦ τετελείωται (= ἔγνωκα αὐτόν).

Therefore, the author is saying that there can be no
love of God without a corresponding knowledge of Jesus,[41] but
a knowledge of Jesus that is present only when Jesus' commandments or word are carried out. It would appear that some are
claiming otherwise.

The second reference to love within this paragraph is
found in the fourth characterization of the opponents' position
(vv. 2:7-11). As already stated, the controlling statement of
this characterization is found in vv. 2:7-8, where the author
leaves behind the ἐντολαί of vv. 2:3-6 and concentrates specifically on one ἐντολή.[42] However, he does not reveal what the
nature of this commandment is until v. 2:9, so that in this
case the controlling statement introduces the working concept
of the antithetical parallelism that follows only in an indirect way.

One main point of this controlling statement--besides
the structural one of introducing the working concepts φῶς/
σκοτία and anticipating that of the love command--is the contrast that is made by the author between the "ancient" or
"traditional" character of the love commandment (οὐκ ἐντολὴν
καινὴν γράφω) and the "newness" of its applicability (πάλιν
ἐντολὴν καινὴν γράφω). That the commandment is traditional
may be gathered from its description in v. 2:7: the adjective
παλαιός; the prepositional phrase ἀπ'ἀρχῆς;[43] the reference to

the aorist in the expression ὁ λόγος ὃν ἠκούσατε.[44] Similarly,
that the commandment is new or applicable may be gathered from
the description of v. 2:8:   the adjective καινός; the explana-
tory ὅτι-clause.[45]

However, while it is easy to see how this particular
ἐντολή may be considered traditional, e.g., attribution to
Jesus, it is somewhat more difficult to see precisely why the
author insists on its character as "new," and the difficulty
lies to a great extent on the terminology employed by the
author in the ὅτι-clause of v. 2:8. This clause has been
interpreted differently by different exegetes. Thus, for
example, Houlden argues that this "newness" is ultimately
related to the dispensation brought by Jesus Christ, a dispensation in which the disciples share.[46] This eschatological
interpretation is also adopted by C. H. Dodd[47] and R. Bultmann.[48] On the other hand, Schnackenburg argues, man has been
able to possess the light of life and to "walk" in that light.
To say, therefore, that τὸ φῶς τὸ ἀληθινὸν ἤδη φαίνει means
that the realm of good is advancing.[49]

It seems to me that Schnackenburg's incorporation of
the historical process into the ὅτι-clause points in the right
direction. Thus, the commandment about to be described is
"new" or, so to speak, still applicable because of the circumstances in the community, i.e., a conflict between "darkness"
and "light." In such a conflict, the author seems to be saying, the love commandment must be continuously exercised; such
a commandment has been and is vital in the triumph of light
over darkness.

In the antithetical parallelism that follows, the term
"love"--in the verb form--is used for the first time within
the characterization, thus identifying the content of the
ἐντολή in question. The incorrect alternative of v. 2:9
--repeated essentially in v. 2:11--declares that there can be
no claim "to be in the light" if a person "hates his brother"
(καὶ τὸν ἀδελφὸν αὐτοῦ μισῶν); indeed, such behavior is nothing
but "darkness," i.e., the very opposite of the claim. By way
of contrast, the correct alternative of v. 2:10 specifies that
the "love of one's brother" (ὁ ἀγαπῶν τὸν ἀδελφὸν αὐτοῦ) is
indeed "light." Since the controlling statement has already

made clear that the exercise of the traditional ἐντολή is vital
to the emergence of "light" over "darkness," the failure to
carry out that commandment, i.e., "hating one's brother," cannot by definition imply the presence of "light." It would
appear that some are claiming otherwise.

Thus, in the fourth characterization love emerges as
a traditional or "old" commandment, but "new" and applicable
(or even necessary) in the present situation as well. However,
neither the extent--who is the ἀδελφός?--nor the nature--what
does love imply?--of love are described in this section.

Vv. 2:15-17. Whereas two exegetes accepted vv. 1:5-
2:11 as a paragraph or thought-unit, only one--John Bogart--
accepts vv. 2:15-17 as such a paragraph. The majority would
include vv. 2:12-14 within the paragraph, yielding vv. 2:12-17
as a unit (O'Neill; Bultmann; Kümmel; Houlden; Schnackenburg;
and Westcott). However, it seems to me that Bogart's position
is correct: vv. 2:15-17 can and should be separated from the
preceding three verses.[50]

After the fourth characterization of vv. 1:5-2:11, the
author offers a series of reasons for writing the Letter, and
this he does in a clearly delineated structure. Thus, in vv.
2:12-14 one finds the following recurring elements: (1) a
reference to the writing, using either the present or the
aorist tenses (γράφω; ἔγραψα); (2) the use of the dative plural
ὑμῖν, following the verb; (3) the use of three vocatives, given
in double succession (τεκνία/παιδία; πατέρες; νεανίσκοι);
(4) the ὅτι-clause that gives the reason or reasons for the
writing, all of which themes find echoes elsewhere in the
Letter.[51] This structure, however, is not continued in vv.
2:15-17; rather, in those verses the author offers concrete
advice to the community as to the limits of love. Similarly,
such advice ends with v. 17, and in the following verses the
author turns from love to a discussion of the "antichrists."
It would seem advisable, therefore, to look upon vv. 2:15-17
as a separate and self-contained paragraph.[52]

The structure of the paragraph runs as follows: (1) a
warning is given by the author to the community, v. 2:15a;
(2) the reason for this warning is then provided in the

conditional sentence of v. 2:15b and expanded in the ὅτι-
clause of v. 2:16; (3) an assessment of the alternatives concludes the paragraph in v. 2:17. All three examples of either
the verb or the noun form of the root "love" are found in v.
2:15.

In the warning of v. 2:15 the author sets down the
following injunction--μὴ ἀγαπᾶτε τὸν κόσμον μηδὲ τὰ ἐν τῷ
κόσμῳ. In other words, nothing that is "of the world" or "in
the world" should be loved by the community.[53] The conditional
sentence of v. 2:15b provides the foundation for this imperative: ἡ ἀγάπη τοῦ πατρός/ἡ ἀγάπη τοῦ κόσμου are mutually exclusive possibilities. To manifest the latter love is to deny the
former; the choice represents an either/or decision--hence, the
injunction.[54] Similarly, the ὅτι-clause of v. 2:16 basically
repeats the ethical dualism of v. 2:15b: to be "of the Father"
(ἐκ τοῦ πατρός) and to be "of the world" (ἐκ τοῦ κόσμου) are
mutually exclusive possibilities. To belong to the latter is
to deny the former; there is no *via media*.

In the third characterization of vv. 1:5-2:11, the
author equates, as I have shown, the perfect love of God with
the carrying out of Jesus' commands or word. Now, that same
love of God (= of the Father) is equated with an attitude that
disclaims or refuses to love "the world" and all which is "in
it" or "of it."[55] In other words, love of the Father cannot
be said to exist unless the commandments of Jesus are carried
out and unless "the world" is bypassed, not loved or pursued.

In that same ὅτι-clause of v. 2:16, the author provides an indication of what it is he means by "the world" or
"the love of the world," i.e., the kind of behavior that is
to be eschewed by anyone professing to love God, and of what
it is that is occurring in the community. Three attitudes are
mentioned: ἡ ἐπιθυμία τῆς σαρκός, ἡ ἐπιθυμία τῶν ὀφθαλμῶν, ἡ
ἀλαζονεία τοῦ βίου. These would be best translated as immoral
or sexual libertinism;[56] greed or lust;[57] and self-boasting.[58]
This is also most probably the kind of behavior that constitutes "the hating of one's brother" mentioned in the fourth
characterization of vv. 1:5-2:11.

The author concludes the paragraph in v. 2:17 with the
application of what appears to be a traditional aphorism[59] to

the ethical dualism he has drawn between the love of the Father
and the love of the world: neither the world nor its desire
endures; on the other hand, he who does the will of God--that
is a synonymous expression for "he who loves God"--endures forever (εἰς τὸν αἰῶνα).

        Summary of vv. 1:5-2:17. In this first largely ethi-
cal section of vv. 1:5-2:17, the author devotes a great deal of
time to the love of God or of the Father, i.e., precisely what
does it mean to love God? In the third characterization of the
opponents' position, he defines such love as a knowledge of
Jesus, a knowledge which involves the execution of the latter's
commandments. It would appear, therefore, that some are claiming to love God--and to know Jesus--without carrying out the
latter's commands. In the parenetical advice of vv. 2:15-17,
the author further defines such love by differentiating it from
the love "of the world." It would appear, once again, that
some are claiming to love God without abandoning what the
author considers to be "the world." In both cases, therefore,
the author rules out certain kinds of behavior from being considered signs of the love of man *for* God.

        Furthermore, the author also devotes a considerable
amount of time to the love command. In the fourth characterization of the opponents' stance, the author singles out a command which he identifies as the love of one's brother--ὁ
ἀγαπῶν τὸν ἀδελφὸν αὐτοῦ. This command, he states, is both
old and traditional as well as new and still applicable.[60] It
is this commandment that defines the realm of "light"; some,
however, are claiming to be "in the light" without carrying
out the commandment which guarantees that particular claim.
As such, the author presents the claim as false: it is "darkness"; it is really "hatred of the brother." Such "hatred"
probably includes the three attitudes mentioned in v. 2:16.

I Jn 2:28-3:24

        The chart above shows that this second largely ethical
section contains nine examples of ἀγάπη/ἀγαπᾶν: vv. 3:1, 10,
11, 14[2], 16, 17, 18, 23. It is my opinion that the section
should be divided into the following paragraphs: vv. 2:28-3:10;

3:11-18; 3:19-24. According to that arrangement, the examples
of v. 3:1 and v. 3:10 belong within the first paragraph; those
of vv. 3:11, 14^2, 16, 17, and 18, within the second; that of
3:23, within the third.

      Vv. 2:28-3:10. Immediately after the parenetical
advice of vv. 2:15-17, the author inserts the first largely
dogmatic section, viz., vv. 2:18-27, the very first description
of the antichrists.[61] This section comes clearly to an end in
v. 2:27; the author urges the community to abide in that possession which is already theirs: καὶ καθὼς ἐδίδαξεν ὑμᾶς,
μένετε ἐν αὐτῷ. The repetition of the latter imperative in
v. 2:28--μένετε ἐν αὐτῷ--serves as the link to the preceding
paragraph and as a signal that a new paragraph has begun. With
v. 2:28 the author leaves behind the description of the message
of the antichrists and returns to a discussion of themes
already pursued in the first largely ethical section, viz.,
"righteousness" and "sin."[62]

      Of the eight exegetes that, according to the chart,
accept vv. 2:18-27 as a self-contained paragraph,[63] only
O'Neill would end the paragraph with v. 3:10. The other seven
would either not break up the second largely ethical section
at all (Bultmann; Perrin; Bogart; Houlden) or would choose
other points of division (Lohmeyer: 2:28-31, 3:2-6, 3:7-12;
Kümmel:[64] 2:28-3:6, 3:7-17; Schnackenburg: 2:28-3:3, 3:4-24).
However, the two exegetes--Dodd and Law--who end the first
largely dogmatic section with v. 2:28 (rather than v. 2:27)
also see v. 3:10 as the conclusion of the next paragraph. I
myself agree with the position taken by O'Neill, Dodd, and Law:
v. 3:10 is the conclusion of the paragraph.

      Just as v. 2:28 contains a link to the preceding para-
graph, so does v. 3:10 provide a link between two paragraphs.
The link is none other than the verb ἀγαπᾶν which is introduced
unexpectedly in the definition of v. 3:10 and is then developed
subsequently in the verses that follow. Thus, with v. 3:11 the
themes of "righteousness" and "sin" are left behind and that of
"love" amply pursued.[65] As such, it seems reasonable to accept
vv. 2:28-3:10 as the next unit of thought.

The example of the root "love" in v. 3:1 occurs toward the beginning of the paragraph. As such, it is found within a presentation of contrary ethical positions given in vv. 2:29 and 3:4. V. 2:29a provides the introduction to both positions: ἐὰν εἰδῆτε ὅτι δίκαιός ἐστιν, which can only refer to Jesus in the context.[66] Then, v. 2:29b describes the execution of righteousness as a sign that the individual "has been born of God": ἐξ αὐτοῦ γεγέννηται, while v. 3:4 describes the execution of sin as a sign of "lawlessness": καὶ τὴν ἀνομίαν ποιεῖ. Thus, "having been born of God" and "lawlessness" are contrary ethical positions.[67]

In v. 3:1 the author develops and expands the expression "having been born of God" of v. 2:29b by means of the related expression, "the children of God" (τὰ τέκνα τοῦ θεοῦ). It is at this point that "love" is used to show what it means to be a "child of God": v. 3:1 provides the origin, the present status, and the consequences of this childhood of God.

First of all, with regard to the origin and source of the expression, the author states in v. 3:1a that it is the love of God toward men that has made possible the reception of that title--ποταπὴν ἀγάπην δέδωκεν ἡμῖν ὁ πατήρ. The precise nature of such love has received varying interpretations. Thus, for example, Spicq believes that it refers to a communication of the divine nature to man, whereby the latter can call himself a child of God.[68] Houlden speaks vaguely of God's initiative in the plan of salvation.[69] The reference seems to be, however, as H. Balz points out,[70] quite specifically to the redemptive death of Jesus Christ.

This conclusion may be gathered from the paragraph itself: ποταπὴν ἀγάπην is Jesus Christ.[71] There are two references--which must be taken as synonymous--in this paragraph to the coming of the Son of God and to his role or mission which illumine the nature of such love. In v. 3:5, the Son of God is said to have appeared (ἐφανερώθη) in order to take away sins--ἵνα τὰς ἁμαρτίας ἄρη.[72] Furthermore, in v. 3:8 he is said to have appeared (ἐφανερώθη) in order to destroy the works of the devil (which works are clearly labelled as sin in v. 3:8ab)--ἵνα λύσῃ τὰ ἔργα τοῦ διαβόλου. As a result, this coming of the Son of God and his redemptive death define God's

love for man: such love is intrinsically associated with the
removal of sin.

Secondly, with regard to the present status of such
love, i.e., the present beneficiaries of it, it appears that
the author only speaks for part of the community, among whom
he includes himself: the dative ἡμῖν and the first person
plural form κληθῶμεν of v. 3:1a; the declaration καὶ ἐσμέν of
v. 3:1b; the accusative ἡμᾶς of v. 3:1c; and the emphatic
declaration of v. 3:2a, νῦν τέκνα θεοῦ ἐσμέν, are all indications that the title, "the children of God," can only be
claimed by a certain segment of the community. In the light of
the antithetical ethical positions mentioned above, the title
would belong only to those "who have been born of God," i.e.,
those who carry out righteousness and avoid sin.

Finally, with regard to the consequences of such a
title, the author revives in v. 3:1c the dualism of vv. 2:15-17.
It is precisely because of the fact that they are "the children
of God" that "the world" does not know them--οὐ γινώσκει ἡμᾶς.
Just as it did not know Jesus, the Son of God, so now "the
world" does not know the "children of God."[73] In other words,
the love of the Father for his children and the acceptance of
that love exclude a similar love on the part of the world.

The second example of the root "love" in v. 3:10 occurs
at the conclusion of the paragraph. In order to understand its
present position, it is necessary to refer briefly to the progression of thought within the paragraph. Following the antithetical ethical positions of vv. 2:29 and 3:4, one finds two
more statements of antithetical ethical positions, which are
synonymous not only with vv. 2:29 and 3:4, but with each other
as well.

First of all, v. 3:6 bases itself on the conception of
Jesus as sinless and of his mission as a redemptive one given
in v. 3:5 to outline two contrary ways of behavior for men.
Basically, the two alternatives are: "not sinning" (v. 3:6a)--
πᾶς ὁ ἐν αὐτῷ μένων οὐχ ἁμαρτάνει; and "sinning" (v. 3:6b)--πᾶς
ὁ ἁμαρτάνων οὐχ ἑώρακεν αὐτὸν οὐδὲ ἔγνωκεν αὐτόν. He who
"abides in Him," i.e., Jesus,[74] does not sin; he who sins has
neither seen Jesus nor known him (therefore, he does not "abide
in Him").[75]

Secondly, after the warning of v. 3:7a, the second
statement is given in vv. 3:7b-8. This statement of antithetical ethical positions goes beyond the other two insofar as it
emphasizes quite strongly the dualistic framework of the conflict. The position presented by v. 3:7b is remarkably similar to that of v. 2:29: he who executes righteousness is
righteous, as Jesus himself is righteous--δίκαιός ἐστιν.[76]
V. 3:8 takes up the suggestion that the just man is like Jesus
himself and attributes the contrary position to the devil: he
who sins is "of the devil," because the devil has always been
a sinner--ἐκ τοῦ διαβόλου ἐστίν.

Then, after these two further statements of antithetical ethical positions, v. 3:10 clearly sets forth the criterion
for the differentiation of the two ways of living. As such,
the entire paragraph is recapitulated in this definitional type
of sentence.[77] The first part of the definition--that which is
to be defined--uses the dualism of vv. 3:7-8--ἐν τούτῳ φανερά
ἐστιν τὰ τέκνα τοῦ θεοῦ καὶ τὰ τέκνα τοῦ διαβόλου.[78] The
second part--the definition itself--also represents a reprise
of earlier material, e.g., the association of "righteousness"
and being "of God"--πᾶς ὁ μὴ ποιῶν δικαιοσύνην οὐκ ἔστιν ἐκ
τοῦ θεοῦ.[79] It is the third part, however, that is totally
unexpected, viz., the love command--καὶ ὁ μὴ ἀγαπῶν τὸν ἀδελφὸν
αὐτοῦ.

The question of the love of one's brother had not been
considered at all in the preceding verses. Yet now, quite
unexpectedly, it forms part of the criterion that differentiates between the two ways of living--and the two titles--vari-
ously outlined in the paragraph. As such, it is to be considered synonymous not only with the first half of the criterion of v. 3:10, but also with the correct positions delineated in the paragraph which that criterion recapitulates: the
execution of righteousness and having been born of God of
v. 2:29; abiding in Jesus and abstention from sin of v. 3:6a;
the execution of righteousness and being righteous as Jesus
himself is righteous of v. 3:7. Similarly, it is to be considered contrary to all the incorrect positions outlined in
the paragraph: the execution of sin and of lawlessness of

v. 3:4; sinning and not having seen or known Jesus of v. 3:6b;
the execution of sin and being "of the devil" of v. 3:7.

In summary, therefore, in this paragraph the love of
God for human beings is mentioned by the author for the first
time. Such love is defined specifically in terms of the mission of the Son of God and, above all, in terms of the latter's
redemptive death. The author also mentions the love of one's
brothers--ὁ μὴ ἀγαπῶν τὸν ἀδελφὸν αὐτοῦ--as a synonym to the
execution of righteousness which classifies a human being as
"having been born of God" and as a "child of God," i.e., as
one of the beneficiaries of God's love for man.

Vv. 3:11-18. It was mentioned before that with v. 3:11
the themes of "righteousness" and "sin" are abandoned in favor
of the "love" theme introduced in v. 3:10 in the form of the
love command. This theme is then pursued rather systematically
in vv. 3:11-18. The repetition of the noun ἡ ἀλήθεια of v.
3:18 in v. 3:19--ὅτι ἐκ τῆς ἀληθείας ἐσμέν--serves as a signal
that a new paragraph has begun, a paragraph that will concentrate on the theme of confidence before the Lord (παρρησία).[80]
Therefore, it seems reasonable to accept vv. 3:11-18 as a self-
contained paragraph.

The structure of the paragraph runs as follows: (1) a
statement of tradition, v. 3:11; (2) the prototype of false
love, vv. 3:12-13; (3) the prototype of correct love, vv. 3:14-
16; (4) parenetical advice, vv. 3:17-18.

Tradition, v. 3:11. The author begins the paragraph
with an explicit appeal to tradition. In v. 3:11 he provides
the reason for the inclusion of the love command in the definition of v. 3:10: the ὅτι-clause specifies that that command
is from the tradition.[81] (Since v. 3:6b also refers the execution of righteousness to tradition,[82] it is clear that the
author is assigning both criteria of the definition of v. 3:10
to the tradition.)

It should be noted that the author begins this second
mention and exposition of the love command--a command which is
now phrased in terms of the reflexive pronoun ἀλλήλων--in
exactly the same way he introduced the first such mention in

vv. 1:5-2:11. In the fourth characterization of that paragraph, the author stated that the command he was singling out
was both "old" and "from the beginning," i.e., traditional.
Likewise, he now states that that same command, which differentiates the "children of God" from the "children of the
devil," is also "from the beginning." In both cases, therefore, he emphatically assigns the origin of the love command
to tradition.

Furthermore, I believe that the use of the reflexive
in v. 3:11 allows one to determine who the ἀδελφός of v. 3:10
(and also of vv. 2:9-11) is. It appears from the context that
it is the brethren of the community whom the author has in
mind.[83] Thus, for example, the execution of the love command
is what characterizes a "child of God"; similarly, the execution of righteousness--which is synonymous with the execution
of the love command--is what characterizes the one who "has
been born of God"; finally, as a "child of God" and as "having
been born of God," he who loves or is righteous is a beneficiary of God's love as described in v. 3:1. Such a one is not
known by "the world," i.e., there are some in the community
who are not carrying out these commands with respect to the
others and who are thus, despite their claims, revealing themselves as the "children of the devil."

Prototype of False Love, vv. 3:12-13. The author
follows this initial appeal to tradition on behalf of the love
command with an example from the biblical tradition that serves
as a prototype for the kind of behavior taking place in the
community.[84] V. 3:12 provides an example of what the love for
one's brother or for one another does not and should not mean
(ἵνα ἀγαπῶμεν ἀλλήλους οὐ καθώς). Thus, the figure of Cain
represents and anticipates those who do not exercise the love
command, while the figure of his brother, Abel, who is not mentioned by name, can only refer to those who do, i.e., the
"children of God." Likewise, Cain's action toward his brother
symbolizes and anticipates the kind of behavior to which the
"children of God" are being subjected.

Besides presenting a prototype, v. 3:12 also deliberately recalls the dualism introduced in vv. 3:7-8 and employed

in the definition of v. 3:10. Thus, the figure of Cain is
explicitly associated with that of the evil one (ἐκ τοῦ πονηροῦ
ἦν),[85] just as those who do not exercise the love command or
righteousness are called τὰ τέκνα τοῦ διαβόλου. Moreover, the
motive for Cain's action against his brother, given in the ὅτι-
clause of v. 3:12c, is not unlike that attributed to the
"children of the devil": whereas Cain's brother's works were
just (δίκαια), his own were evil (πονηρά). Cain's behavior,
in other words, is in keeping with his status: this is precisely the point of vv. 3:8 and 3:10. Thus, what Cain did is
no different from what the opponents do now, since they are
both inspired by the devil.

        Finally, the action taken by Cain against his brother--
καὶ . . . ἔσφαξεν αὐτόν--introduces a contrast between "life"
and "death" which will dominate, with the exception of v. 3:13,
the next few verses of the paragraph and raises a question as
to the extent that that particular action, which is presented
as a prototype for what is taking place in the community,
accurately describes the actions being taken against the
"children of God," i.e., are they being attacked and killed?
Are the terms "life" and "death" to be understood in the
strictly physical sense?[86] It seems that that action and
those terms are to be taken symbolically. First of all, the
Letter provides no evidence that the community is being per-
secuted or killed. Secondly, the actual concrete offence mentioned in v. 3:17 has nothing to do with "life" or "death" in
the physical sense.

        In v. 3:13 the author applies the lack of love shown
in the prototype of v. 3:12 directly to the actual situation
of the community. Thus, what is implicit now becomes explicit.
(As such, v. 3:13 serves as a confirmation that the ἀδελφός of
v. 3:10 and the ἀλλήλων of v. 3:11 refer to the brethren of
the community.) His position is as follows: given Cain's
behavior toward his brother, a righteous man, the brethren,
who also exercise righteousness, should not be surprised that
"the world" hates them in a similar way. In other words, "the
world" and those who belong to it cannot be expected to execute
the love command that is practiced by those who "have been born

of God"; on the contrary, "the world" will manifest nothing but
hatred for the "children of God."[87]

         This antagonism between "the world" and the brethren is
very much in line with the thought of vv. 2:15-17 and v. 3:1c.
In the former case, the author states that love for the Father
and love for the world are mutually exclusive possibilities.
As a result, the community is not to love the world or anything
thereof. In the latter case, the author declares that "the
world" does not know "the children of God." Thus, the community is accorded the same fate that was accorded to Jesus
beforehand. Indeed, v. 3:16 may be said to represent the apex
of this line of thought: not only are "of the world" and "of
God" mutually exclusive possibilities; not only does "the
world" not know the "children of God"; but also "the world"
actually hates them.

         Prototype of Correct Love, vv. 14-16. As it was men-
tioned before, the next three verses are dominated by the contrast death/life which was raised in the prototype of v. 3:12.
Whereas vv. 3:12-13 concentrate on showing what the opposite
of love entails, vv. 14-16 address themselves to the question
as to what loving one's brother really means. Thus, the author
returns to the love command of v. 3:11.

         In v. 3:14 the author openly declares that the ἀδελφοί
of the preceding verse as well as he himself are the ones who
are in contact with tradition: as the ὅτι-clause indicates,
they are the ones who are exercising the love command--ὅτι
ἀγαπῶμεν τοὺς ἀδελφούς; they are the ones who are putting into
practice this traditional command, given "from the beginning";
therefore, they are the ones who can lay a claim to the title,
τὰ τέκνα τοῦ θεοῦ.

         Furthermore, on account of this observable and identi-
fiable behavior, the author states that the ἀδελφοί as well as
he himself have undergone a transformation--that the transformation is regarded as a past event seems evident from the perfect tense of the verb used to describe it, μεταβεβήκαμεν. It
is this transformation that is phrased in terms of the contrast
life/death: both the ἀδελφοί as well as he himself have gone
from death--ἐκ τοῦ θανάτου--to life--εἰς τὴν ζωήν. In other

words, the execution of the love command is a sign that an
individual has attained "life." By way of contrast, those who
show no love, e.g., "the world," and are therefore not in contact with the original tradition, have not attained such a
transformation; rather, they abide in death--μένει ἐν τῷ θανάτῳ.
The precise nature of this transformation may be ascertained
both from the symbolism of the death/life contrast as well as
from the definitional sentence of v. 3:16.

        First of all, an examination of the term "life"--ἡ
ζωή--in the Letter shows that it consistently refers to the
figure of Jesus Christ.[88] The most obvious example occurs in
the Prologue to the Letter, vv. 1:1-4, where "life" is said to
have appeared and been witnessed--ἡ ζωὴ ἐφανερώθη καὶ ἐωράκαμεν.
Again, in v. 2:25 it is said, as a part of the first largely
dogmatic section (vv. 2:18-27), that the believer that abides
in the correct christological doctrine possesses "eternal life"
--τὴν ζωὴν τὴν αἰώνιον.[89] Similarly, after the correct christological doctrine is identified as the witness of God in
v. 5:9, i.e., within the third largely dogmatic section (vv.
5:1-12), v. 5:11 redefines that witness in terms of "life
eternal"--καὶ αὕτη ἐστὶν ἡ μαρτυρία, ὅτι ζωὴν αἰώνιον ἔδωκεν
ἡμῖν ὁ θεός.[90] Finally, in v. 5:20--within the Postscript of
the Letter (vv. 5:14-21)--the correct christological doctrine
is once again declared to be "eternal life"--'Ιησοῦ Χριστῷ
οὗτός ἐστιν ὁ ἀληθινὸς θεὸς καὶ ζωὴ αἰώνιος. There can be no
doubt, therefore, that the transformation from "death" to
"life" is intimately connected with the person of Jesus
Christ.[91]

        Secondly, given the relationship that exists between
the term "life" and the figure of Jesus in the Letter, the
definitional sentence of v. 3.16 becomes rather important in
determining the meaning of the transformation of v. 3:14.[92]
In this verse the author undertakes to define the term "love"
itself--ἐν τούτῳ ἐγνώκαμεν τὴν ἀγάπην--and in so doing provides a prototype for those who show love, just as he had provided a prototype for the lack of love in the figure of Cain
of v. 3:12. The definition presents the redemptive death of
Jesus as the prototype of all love--ὑπὲρ ἡμῶν τὴν ψυχὴν αὐτοῦ

ἔθηκεν. Thus, whereas Cain killed his brother, Jesus gives up
his own life for others: the contrast is unmistakable.

In the claim to a transformation from "death" to "life"
--a claim which is justified by and a transformation which is
observable in the execution of the love command--the figure of
Jesus Christ and the redemptive nature of his death play a
central role. The categories "life" and "death" are clearly
oriented around that particular event: it would seem, given
the occurrences of "life" mentioned above, that to accept such
an event bestows "life" on an individual. Furthermore, the
sign of such life lies in the execution of the love command;
only by loving his brother does an individual show that he has
attained "life."[93]

Just as v. 3:12 presents the life-taking event per-
petrated by Cain as the prototype of "the world's" behavior
toward the brethren, so does v. 3:16 present the life-giving
event of Jesus' death as the prototype of the brethren's love
toward one another. In v. 3:16b, therefore, the author concludes that the brethren must also give up their lives for one
another--καὶ ἡμεῖς ὀφείλομεν ὑπὲρ τῶν ἀδελφῶν τὰς ψυχὰς θεῖναι--
and, since such is the definition of love, it follows that they
must love one another in precisely the same way that Jesus
loved them.[94]

In the application of this prototype to the brethren,
the question arises once again as to the extent that such language accurately describes the actions expected of the "children of God," i.e., are they actually being encouraged to face
persecution and physical death courageously? Once again, I
would have to say that the Letter gives no indications that
such is the case. The terms "life" and "death" are being presented by the author in a highly symbolical manner.[95] Rather,
given the close association that exists between the term "life"
and the redemptive death of Jesus, I would see the love being
urged upon the brethren in v. 3:16b, a love which is patterned
after Jesus' redemptive death, as including an acceptance of
that redemptive death, an acceptance which has definite ethical
consequences.

From this point of view, the "hatred" of the "children
of the devil" or of "the world" includes a refusal to accept

that redemptive death, a refusal which by definition means
lack of "life"--οὐκ ἔχει ζωὴν αἰώνιον ἐν αὐτῷ μένουσαν--and
"death"--ὁ μὴ ἀγαπῶν μένει ἐν τῷ θανάτῳ. Furthermore, the
brother who thus refuses may, following the prototype of Cain,
be termed a "murderer" (ἀνθρωποκτόνος), because he provides
the possibility of "death" to those who have "life" in them.
Needless to say, such a refusal also has definite ethical consequences.

    Parenesis, vv. 17-18. The author follows this inclu-
sion of the acceptance of the redemptive death of Jesus within
the love command for one another with parenetical advice for
the community. First of all, in v. 3:17 he abandons the death/
life contrast of the preceding verses and provides instead a
very concrete example as to what the "hatred of the world" for
the brethren implies. Secondly, in v. 3:18 the author concludes the paragraph with an exhortation to the community--
τεκνία--to include both the redemptive death of Jesus and concrete ethical behavior within their love for one another.

    The example of v. 3:17, viz., the failure to help a
brother in need,[96] is very similar to the examples provided in
v. 2:16. In both cases "God" and "the world" or "love for God"
and "love for the world" provide mutually exclusive possibilities. Thus, just as in vv. 2:15-17 licentiousness, greed and
boasting served as examples of "the world," so in v. 3:17 the
failure to help one's brother characterizes an individual as
being "of the world"--ὃς δ'ἂν ἔχῃ τὸν βίον τοῦ κόσμου--and as
having no love of God--πῶς ἡ ἀγάπη τοῦ θεοῦ μένει ἐν αὐτῷ.[97]
It is this kind of behavior that characterizes "the children
of the devil."

    V. 3:18 is usually not emphasized very much by commen-
tators of the Letter. I believe, however, that Schnackenburg
points in the right direction when he states that the verse
represents a recapitulation of the author's presentation of
love.[98] The words ἀλλά (ἀγαπῶμεν) ἐν ἔργῳ καὶ ἀληθείᾳ should
not be taken as simply neutral rhetorical terms; rather, they
point to the two aspects of the love command which have been
described in the paragraph: the need to carry out concrete
ethical acts, such as that of v. 3:17 (ἐν ἔργῳ) and the need

to accept the redemptive death of Jesus Christ (καὶ ἀληθείᾳ).[99] By way of contrast, the love which "the world" shows
is λόγος--not carried out in deed; and γλῶσσα--misguided
ecstatic speech.[100]

In conclusion, this second paragraph within the second
largely ethical section presents the love command as having
been handed down by tradition and as being the sign that an
individual has experienced a transformation from "death" to
"life." The paragraph also provides a prototype for each of
these realms: Cain's murder of his brother represents the
example *par excellence* of the absence of love, while Jesus'
death on behalf of others serves as the very definition of
love. Finally, the paragraph includes for the first time the
acceptance of that death as part of "love" and the love command.

Vv. 3:19-24. In the process of delineating the preceding paragraph, it was observed that the repetition of the
noun ἡ ἀλήθεια in a different context in v. 3:19 signals the
beginning of a new unit of thought. This unit of thought comes
to an undisputed end in v. 3:24, since beginning with v. 4:1
the discussion continues with the message and doctrine of the
false prophets.[101] The one example of the root "love" within
the paragraph occurs toward the conclusion, viz., v. 3:23. As
a result, it is necessary to see the progression of thought
within the paragraph in order to understand the position and
meaning of this one example.

This progression of thought, however, which centers
primarily on the themes of the condemnation of the heart--ἐὰν
καταγινώσκῃ ἡμῶν ἡ καρδία--and the possession of confidence
before the Lord--παρρησίαν ἔχομεν--has been notoriously difficult for exegesis.[102] Given the purpose of this study, I shall
limit myself to the bare outline at this point. First of all,
the exhortation to love "in deed" and "in truth" is followed
by a definitional sentence concentrated around the expression,
ἐκ τῆς ἀληθείας ἐσμέν. V. 3:20 would then supply the definition to this expression, i.e., the specification of the ἐν
τούτῳ which introduces the above expression.[103]

In the following two verses, vv. 3:21-22, the author
develops the first ὅτι-clause of v. 3:20, viz., the condemnation of the heart, by declaring that the absence of such condemnation depends ultimately on the execution of God's commands
--ὅτι τὰς ἐντολὰς αὐτοῦ τηροῦμεν. Such behavior gives an individual confidence before God--παρρησίαν ἔχομεν πρὸς τὸν θεόν,
a confidence which is demonstrated by the efficacy of that
individual's prayer. Vv. 3:23-24a seize upon the theme introduced by the ὅτι-clause of v. 3:22, viz., the execution of God's
commandments, and develop it further, explicitly identifying
the commandments of God that bestow such confidence, and such
absence of condemnation, upon the believer.[104]

One of these commandments is the love for another,
i.e., the love command with the reflexive ἀλλήλων as the direct
object of the verb (as in v. 3:11). The other commandment is
that of belief in Jesus Christ.[105] Given the inclusion of both
commands under the single term ἐντολή, I believe that the two
are to be considered to a certain extent synonymous.[106] Thus,
love for one another implies belief in Jesus Christ--and specifically correct belief--and vice versa. Therefore, in this
paragraph the author reiterates in the context of confidence
before God the point he makes in the preceding paragraph: love
of the brethren includes belief in Jesus Christ.

If this twofold command is observed, the believer may
address God directly and confidently and obtain whatever he
wishes (v. 3:22). It is interesting to note, once again, the
emphasis that the author places on tradition whenever he speaks
of the love command; in this case, he claims that this twofold
command is from the tradition as well--καθὼς ἔδωκεν ἐντολὴν
ἡμῖν.[107] The author concludes the paragraph with a reference
to a double abiding: only the one who executes the commandments can abide in God and have God abide in him.[108] The one
who does not, therefore, does not abide in God, regardless of
what his claim may be.

Summary of vv. 2:28-3:24. In this second largely ethical section of the Letter, the author introduces, first of all,
a relationship of love which is not found in the first such
section. That relationship consists of the love which the

Father has for man (v. 3:1). That love is specifically defined
in terms of Jesus Christ and, above all, in terms of his
redemptive death (vv. 3:5, 8). It is that love, and that
event, which makes it possible for an individual to claim that
he "has been born of God" and is "a child of God." That particular event is also presented as the prototype of all love
in one of the author's characteristic definitional sentences
(v. 3:16)--ἐν τούτῳ ἐγνώκαμεν τὴν ἀγάπην.

Secondly, the author specifically addresses himself
once again to the love which men should have for God. In
v. 3:17 he states that a person who does not come to the help
of a brother in need cannot have the love of God abiding in
him; rather, such a person belongs to "the world." Thus, as
he did in vv. 2:15-17, the author is probably refuting a claim
to love God on the part of some within the community by showing the incompatibility of the claim being made and the behavior being exercised. Such behavior points to "the world," he
would answer, not to God.

Thirdly, the author continues to place a great deal of
emphasis on the claim that the love command comes from tradition: in v. 3:11 he refers to that command as "having been
heard from the beginning"--ἣν ἠκούσατε ἀπ'ἀρχῆς, while in
v. 3:23 the twofold command which includes the love for one
another is said to have been handed down by God himself--καθὼς
ἔδωκεν ἐντολὴν ἡμῖν.

Fourthly, the author equates the execution of the love
command with the execution of righteousness: both types of
behavior are presented as the criteria which distinguish the
"children of God" from the "children of the devil." Thus, in
effect, anyone who would claim "to have been born of God," to
be a beneficiary of God's love for man, must show by his
behavior that that claim is justified.

Finally, the author patterns the execution of the
traditional love command after the prototype of love, the
redemptive death of Jesus. In other words, the brethren must
love one another as Jesus loved; they must give up their lives
for one another as he did. In the absence of any signs of persecution or bloodshed within the community, it appears that
the author is urging the brethren to include an acceptance of

that prototype of love within the love command. Thus, in
v. 3:23 he proceeds to include within the one command which
guarantees confidence before God the need for belief in Jesus
Christ and for mutual love as a sign that they are to an extent
synonymous.

I Jn 4:7-21

          According to the chart of the occurrences of ἀγάπη/
ἀγαπᾶν above, this third largely ethical section contains in
all twenty-six examples of the root: $4:7^3$, 8^2, 9, 10^3, 11^2,
12^2, 16^3, 17, 18^3, 19, 20^3, 21^2. It constitutes, as I have
already mentioned, the highest concentration of the root in
the Letter. In my opinion, the section may be further divided
into three self-contained paragraphs, consisting of vv. 4:7-12,
13-16a, 16b-21. As a result, one finds fourteen references in
the first paragraph: $4:7^3$, 8^2, 9, 10^3, 11^2, 12^2; one in the
second, 4:16a; and eleven in the third, $4:16b^2$, 17, 18^3, 19,
20^3, 21^2.

          Vv. 4:7-12. There is no difficulty at all establishing
the beginning of the paragraph: vv. 4:1-6 are almost universally acknowledged as a self-contained unit of thought.[109] The
verses are dominated by the author's definition of the τὸ
πνεῦμα τοῦ θεοῦ and its differentiation from the τὸ πνεῦμα τῆς
πλάνης. However, v. 4:7 leaves behind this definition altogether and reintroduces the theme of love with an exhortation--
'Αγαπητοί ἀγαπῶμεν ἀλλήλους. The linkage between the two paragraphs, and the two sections, is provided by the prepositional
phrase ἐκ τοῦ θεοῦ found in the ὅτι-clause which follows the
exhortation. In vv. 4:1-6 the phrase is used to designate
those that possess the "spirit of God" (vv. 4:4, 6), while in v.
4:7 it is used to modify the noun ἡ ἀγάπη.

          On the other hand, the conclusion of the paragraph does
not enjoy as wide a consensus. Of the nine exegetes that
accept vv. 4:1-6 as a self-contained paragraph and v. 4:7 as
the beginning of a new paragraph, only two--Bultmann and Dodd--
would see v. 4:12 as its conclusion.[110] The remaining seven
exegetes would either not break up the third largely ethical
section at all (Kümmel; Perrin; Bogart; Houlden; Westcott) or

would do so at other points (O'Neill, vv. 4:7-18, 4:19-5:13;
Schnackenburg, vv. 4:7-10, 11-16, 17-18, 4:19-5:2). My own
opinion is that v. 4:12 represents the conclusion of this
first paragraph.

In v. 4:12 the exposition of "love" begun in v. 4:7
comes to a temporary end. The apodosis of the conditional
sentence found in that verse contains the link to the following paragraph: the theme of "abiding" is therein introduced
as a consequence of mutual love--ὁ θεὸς ἐν ἡμῖν μένει. V. 4:13
seizes upon this theme, expands it to a double abiding in definitional form, and abandons the theme of love completely, thus
signaling the beginning of a new unit of thought.

The structure of this first unit of thought within the
third largely ethical section runs as follows: (1) a division
of human beings into two categories, the criterion of which is
love for one another, vv. 7-8; (2) two proofs of God's love,
vv. 9-10; (3) parenetical advice, vv. 11-12.

Exhortation--Division, vv. 7-8. Although the ὅτι-
clause of v. 4:7a, the clause that contains the link to the
preceding section, could prima facie be interpreted as claiming that all love is "of God," such a reading of the statement
would represent a grave misunderstanding of the author's position. It is clear that for the author there is a correct form
of love: the statement of v. 3:18 and the admonitions of
vv. 2:15-17 suffice to bring this point across. V. 4:7a is
no exception: only a certain kind of love is acceptable, and
the paragraph will proceed to delineate it.[111] Indeed, the
whole paragraph seems to be oriented against a false love, i.e.,
"false" in the author's eyes, being claimed by some in the
community.

It is the correct kind of love, of course, that the
author exhorts the brethren to practice--ἀγαπητοί, ἀγαπῶμεν
ἀλλήλους--specifically since the ὅτι-clause provides the reason
for the exhortation.[112] The author then begins to elaborate
what correct love, viz., love "of God," implies by means of
a presentation of mutually exclusive possibilities. These two
alternatives are: (1) πᾶς ὁ ἀγαπῶν ἐκ τοῦ θεοῦ γεγέννηται καὶ
γινώσκει τὸν θεόν, (2) ὁ μὴ ἀγαπῶν οὐκ ἔγνω τὸν θεόν. Thus,

the alternatives are presented in terms of what they signify:
he who loves, i.e., who loves correctly, shows that he "knows
God" and "has been born of God"; and vice versa. Both of these
expressions, it should be recalled, appear in connection with
the root "love" elsewhere in the Letter, providing approximately the same meaning in the paragraphs in question as they
do in these verses.

First of all, "knowledge" is found associated with
"love" in both vv. 2:3-6 and 3:6. In the former case, "knowledge of Jesus" is explicitly defined in terms of the execution
of his commands. Furthermore, as it has been shown, such
knowledge is synonymous with "the love of God" on the part of
men. In the latter case, the sinner--as opposed to the righteous person--is denied any knowledge of Jesus whatsoever.
The difference in direct objects, viz., knowledge of God or of
Jesus, is not that important, given the close relationship
that exists between Father and Son in the Letter.[113]

Secondly, "having been born of God" is found associated
with "love" in vv. 2:28-3:10. In v. 2:29 the author declares
that the execution of righteousness is an indication that an
individual "has been born of God." Then, in v. 3:10 righteousness and the execution of the love command are presented as
synonyms, i.e., as the one criterion that differentiates the
"children of God" from the "children of the devil." Therefore, the execution of the love command is also an indication
that an individual "has been born of God."

Consequently, availing himself of previous argumentation, the author argues in these verses that there can be no
claim "to know God" or "to have been born of God" unless one's
love for the brethren verifies those claims. In the verses
that follow the author proceeds to describe more precisely
what such love, i.e., correct love, implies. V. 4:8b begins
this exposition with a ὅτι-clause that is meant to provide the
reason for the division outlined above: he who loves "knows
God" and "has been born of God" because God himself is love--
ὅτι ὁ θεὸς ἀγάπη ἐστίν. This statement is not to be understood as a definition of God nor as a reference to God's nature
or being, which is then communicated to man and forms, in a
very realistic way, the ground for man's own love.[114] Rather,

the statement should be read within its context, i.e., as a
description of God's activity[115] and specifically of the activity outlined in vv. 4:9-10.

Proofs of God's Love, vv. 4:9-10. God's activity--and
God's love--are described by the author in terms of the sending
of his Son, i.e., the coming of Jesus into the world. The love
of God, he argues, has been made manifest to men solely in
terms of his Son: it is the revelation of the Son alone that
testifies to God's love. It is for this reason that I have
chosen to call the two statements of God's activity of vv.
4:9-10 "proofs" of God's love. It follows, consequently, that
correct love is a christologically oriented love.

The two statements or proofs of vv. 4:9-10 parallel and
complement each other; they should be read together as illumin-
ing one another. First of all, they are parallel in structure,
insofar as both use the familiar definitional pattern employed
by the author, i.e., ἐν τούτῳ . . . ὅτι.[116] Secondly, they are
parallel in content as well, since both employ a "sending" formula centered around the verb, ἀποστέλλω. Finally, they complement each other insofar as v. 4:10 gives specific meaning
to the concluding purpose clause of v. 4:9--ἵνα ζήσωμεν δι'
αὐτοῦ.

The first statement or proof immediately develops the
characterization of God provided in the ὅτι-clause of v. 4:8,
since the latter now becomes the expression to be defined: ἐν
τούτῳ ἐφανερώθη[117] ἡ ἀγάπη τοῦ θεοῦ ἐν ἡμῖν.[118] The love that
God has shown is defined as the sending of his only-begotten
Son into the world--τὸν υἱὸν αὐτοῦ τὸν μονογενῆ ἀπέσταλκεν ὁ
θεὸς εἰς τὸν κόσμον.[119] The first statement concludes with the
purpose for such an action on God's part--that men "might live
through him."

The second statement also proposes to define the characterization of God given in v. 4:8--ἐν τούτῳ ἐστὶν ἡ ἀγάπη.
Such love is defined once again as the sending of his Son--
ἀπέστειλεν τὸν υἱὸν αὐτοῦ--and further specified by emphasiz-
ing above all the redemptive death of his Son--ἱλασμὸν περὶ
τῶν ἁμαρτιῶν ἡμῶν, thus making quite explicit the meaning of

the purpose clause of v. 4:9: "to live" means "to have one's
sins forgiven" by Jesus.[120]

God's love is thus specifically defined in terms of
not only the sending of his Son, but also in terms of the
latter's redemptive death, which was the culmination of that
sending. As such, vv. 4:9-10 recapitulate essentially the
thought of paragraphs 2:29-3:10 and 3:11-18. In the former
case, it was observed that the love of God for man mentioned
in v. 3:1 had to be interpreted in the context of vv. 3:5, 8,
where the redemptive death of Jesus was the main emphasis.
Similarly, in the latter case, v. 3:16 defines "love" exclusively in terms of Jesus' death on behalf of others.

Consequently, correct love is oriented specifically
around the event of Jesus' death. Within v. 4:10, the second
statement or proof of God's love, one finds an explicit differentiation of correct love from incorrect love. In the eyes
of the author, correct love implies a recognition, an acknowl-
edgement, that God has loved first, that he has initiated the
chain of love--άλλ'ὅτι αὐτὸς ἠγάπησεν ἡμᾶς--and that such love,
given the connective καί that joins both ὅτι-clauses, includes
the redemptive death of Jesus. On the other hand, incorrect
love implies a belief that man has loved God first, that he
can bypass the outlined chain of love--οὐχ ὅτι ἡμεῖς ἠγαπήκαμεν τὸν θεόν. It is the execution of the first kind of love
that, according to v. 4:7, can and does verify the claim "to
know God" and "to have been born of Him."

Parenesis, vv. 11-12. The author begins the parenesis
of these two verses with a reprise of the vocative 'Αγαπητοί
of v. 4:7 (and v. 4:1 as well). Then, just as he urges the
brethren in v. 4:7 to love one another according to that love
which is "of God," so now the author, having delineated the
nature of that love, exhorts the brethren once again to love
one another according to that love: εἰ οὕτως ὁ θεός . . . καί
ἡμεῖς.[121] Thus, the community must take that example and that
mode of love specified in vv. 4:9-10 and incorporate it into
its own practice--εἰ οὕτως . . . καί ἡμεῖς ὀφείλομεν ἀλλήλους
ἀγαπᾶν. And, once again, in the absence of any persecution or
bloodshed directed against the brethren, it seems more

reasonable to suppose that such an incorporation by the
brethren means the acceptance of that kind of love, that mode
of love, in their love for one another.

In v. 4:12a the author follows the exhortation and
concrete application of v. 4:11 with a brief and undeveloped
argument against the incorrect love he is attacking in the
paragraph.[122] Given the nature of the claim in v. 4:10--ἡμεῖς
ἠγαπήκαμεν τὸν θεόν--the author argues as follows: how can
anyone claim to love God without the Son, if no one has ever
seen God--θεὸν οὐδεὶς πώποτε τεθέαται--except the Son?[123]
Such love is consequently no love at all and implies no knowledge of God whatsoever (see v. 4:8).

Then, in v. 4:12b the author concludes the paragraph
by referring to the consequences which the execution of correct love--ἐὰν ἀγαπῶμεν ἀλλήλους--entails. Such love means,
first of all, that God abides in that individual and, secondly,
that the love of God is made perfect in him.

The first consequence, ὁ θεὸς ἐν ἡμῖν μένει, represents
a return to the abiding formula of v. 3:24a. In that particular verse, within paragraph 3:19-24, the abiding of God in man
(and vice versa) is presented as a consequence of the execution of the two commands mentioned in v. 3:23, belief in Jesus
Christ and love for one another. Furthermore, since the two
commands are to a certain degree synonymous, it appears that
the very same claim of v. 3:24 is being repeated in v. 4:12b:
in order to have God "abide in us," it is necessary to incorporate belief in Jesus Christ within love for one another.
The second consequence, ἡ ἀγάπη αὐτοῦ τετελειωμένη ἐν ἡμῖν
ἐστιν, represents yet another step in the author's desire to
outline what the love of man for God[124] consists of (see vv.
1:3-6; 2:15-17; 3:17): such love is now said to include an
acceptance of the redemptive death of Jesus in one's love for
the brethren.

In summary, one may say that the main emphasis of the
author in the paragraph lies in the differentiation of correct
love, or love "of God," from incorrect love. Correct love is
presented in terms of God's own love toward man, a love which
cannot be understood apart from the sending of his Son and
from the death that the latter encountered. Thus, correct love

must be patterned after this mode of love in order to classify
as being "of God"; otherwise, there can be no claim to any
knowledge of God or to having been born of him.

Vv. 4:13-16a. In v. 4:13 one of the consequences of
the execution of the love command described in the preceding
verse, viz., the abiding of God in man, is now expanded to a
double-abiding formula and defined in terms of the correct
πνεῦμα--ἐν τούτῳ γινώσκομεν ὅτι ἐν αὐτῷ μένομεν καὶ αὐτὸς ἐν
ἡμῖν.[125] This inclusion of a previous expression in a new
context is a clear signal that a new unit of thought is about
to begin.

The definition of the correct πνεῦμα extends from
v. 4:14 to v. 4:16a, where the noun ἀγάπη is reintroduced by
the author. Then, in v. 4:16b the πνεῦμα is abandoned and the
theme of love is once again systematically developed by the
author. Thus, v. 4:16a should be seen as the conclusion of
this second unit of thought in the section.[126] The occurrence
of the noun ἀγάπη in v. 4:16a represents the only example of
the root in the paragraph; its role in that paragraph is not
hard to ascertain.

In v. 4:14 the author defines the possession of the
πνεῦμα αὐτοῦ, where the latter pronoun refers to God the
Father, in terms of an acceptance--καὶ ἡμεῖς τεθεάμεθα καὶ
μαρτυροῦμεν ὅτι--of the fact that God sent his Son as a savior
to the world--σωτῆρα τοῦ κόσμου. Furthermore, according to
v. 4:15, such an acceptance is tantamount to a belief that
Jesus is the Son of God.[127] The main element of the definition
lies in the designation of Jesus, the Son of God, as the "savior of the world." In the light of the statement of v. 2:2,
this designation can only refer in the Letter to the redemptive death of Jesus. Therefore, the acceptance of that death
signifies the possession of the spirit of God.

V. 4:16a recapitulates the definition provided in the
preceding verses and, in doing so, rephrases it in terms of
the noun ἡ ἀγάπη, i.e., specifically the love that God showed
men--τὴν ἀγάπην ἣν ἔχει ὁ θεὸς ἐν ἡμῖν.[128] Thus, v. 4:16a
stands in direct line with the statements of vv. 3:1, 3:16,
and 4:10-11: God's love cannot be understood apart from the

sending of his Son and from the death which he underwent on
behalf of others. That is the very essence of God's love and
its acknowledgment signifies the possession of the spirit of
God.[129]

   Vv. 4:16b-21. As it has already been stated above,
v. 4:16b seizes on the noun ἡ ἀγάπη of 4:16a and develops it
in a new context altogether, viz., outside the definition of
the "spirit of God." If v. 4:16b is to be taken as the beginning of a new unit of thought, then v. 4:21 represents its
conclusion. Whereas vv. 4:16b-21 develop in a rather systematic way the theme of love, v. 5:1 continues this theme but
subordinates it to that of πίστις, i.e., it employs it in a
new context altogether. As a result, v. 4:21 should be seen
as the conclusion to this third and final paragraph of the
section.[130]
        The paragraph duplicates to a large extent the thought
of vv. 4:7-12. Structurally, it may be divided into two subsections: (1) a description of perfect or correct love, vv.
4:16b-18; (2) a discussion of incorrect love, vv. 4:19-21.

        Perfect Love, vv. 4:16b-18. The beginning of the
paragraph adds nothing new at all to what is presented elsewhere in the Letter concerning love. V. 4:16b simply puts
together the characterization of God found in v. 4:8b--ὁ θεὸς
ἀγάπη ἐστίν[131]--and one of the consequences of man's love for
his brother found in v. 4:12--καὶ ὁ μένων ἐν τῇ ἀγάπῃ ἐν τῷ
θεῷ μένει καὶ ὁ θεὸς ἐν αὐτῷ μένει.[132] In so doing, the verse
serves as a transition from the love of God for man, described
in v. 4:16a, to the love of the brethren for one another.
        This love of the brethren is first described in terms
of "correct" or "perfect" love in vv. 4:17-18, thus taking up
the second consequence outlined in v. 4:12--ἡ ἀγάπη αὐτοῦ
τετελειωμένη ἐν ἡμῖν ἐστιν. V. 4:17 proceeds to define this
consequence in a familiar definitional sentence.[133] However,
the verse as it stands presents difficulties, e.g., what
exactly is the definition of ἐν τούτῳ? There are two possibilities as far as I can see: the first one is to take the
ἵνα-clause as the definition; the other, to accept the

ὅτι-clause as the definition. Both possibilities are in
complete agreement with further usage.[134]

Most commentators accept the ἵνα-clause as the definition and understand the verse as saying: love is made perfect
in the community to the extent that the latter has confidence
in the day of judgment.[135] These commentators also point to
the very similar occurrence of "confidence" in v. 2:28, where
it is found associated with the παρουσία. However, this solution, it seems to me, breaks up the sequence of thought of the
paragraph and goes against the author's repeated definitions
of love in the Letter. He never defines love in terms of any
eschatological expectations, but rather always defines it in
terms of what must be done here and now. I would propose,
therefore, to take the ὅτι-clause as the definition of the ἐν
τούτῳ.[136]

"Perfect" love would then be defined as the following
of God's example of love on the part of the community. As
such, v. 4:17 would constitute a recapitulation of v. 4:16b.
The following diagram makes that relationship clear:

      (4:16b)   (4:17)

ὁ θεὸς ἀγάπη ἐστίν

                             καθὼς ἐκεῖνός ἐστιν[137]

καὶ ὁ μένων ἐν τῇ ἀγάπῃ

                       καὶ ἡμεῖς ἐσμεν ἐν τῷ
                       κόσμῳ τούτῳ

Thus, just as God is love--and this he has demonstrated in
sending his Son to die for the sins of men--so too must the
community be like him, love like him--by accepting the mode
of his love and putting it into practice. It is this acceptance that constitutes "perfect" love. If the ὅτι-clause is
taken to be the definition, then the ἵνα-clause takes on the
character of a result clause.[138]

Once the definition of "perfect" love is given, the
author proceeds in v. 4:18 to describe it in terms of a lack
of fear. This association is made three times in that verse:

(1) φόβος οὐκ ἔστιν ἐν τῇ ἀγάπῃ; (2) ἡ τελεία ἀγάπη ἔξω βάλλει
τὸν φόβον; (3) ὁ δὲ φοβούμενος οὐ τετελείωται ἐν τῇ ἀγάπῃ.
What it is precisely that the author has in mind is not immediately discernible, since the vocabulary employed is, for
the most part, unique to this verse.[139] The most satisfactory
solution would be to take the verse in the light of the ἵνα-
clause of v. 4:17, i.e., the perfection of love results in
confidence on the day of judgment, a confidence that excludes
all fear and, specifically, the fear of punishment. Thus,
both confidence and the exclusion of fear would be simulta-
neous and direct effects of the definition of v. 4:17.[140]

       Incorrect Love, vv. 4:19-21. In the remaining verses
of the paragraph, the author turns from "perfect" love to
incorrect love.[141] First of all, v. 4:19 continues the trend
of thought outlined in vv. 4:16b-17: the love of the brethren
for one another should be grounded completely on the love of
God for man.[142] The specific role of v. 4:19 is to stress the
priority of God's love for man and to do so explicitly. The
reason for this emphasis is the fact that the author now
addresses directly contrary claims.

       In v. 4:20 the contrary claim, i.e., incorrect love,
is first refuted in a manner not unlike that found in paragraph 1:5-2:11.[143] The content of the claim itself is exactly
the same as that of v. 4:10b--ἀγαπῶ τὸν θεόν/ἡμεῖς ἠγαπήκαμεν
τὸν θεόν. The difference lies in the fact that v. 4:20 uses
part of the formula of the antithetical parallelism. Thus,
it provides an actual quotation (ἐάν τις εἴπῃ ὅτι), proceeds
to refute that claim in terms of the behavior that accompanies
it (καὶ τὸν ἀδελφὸν αὐτοῦ μισῇ), and concludes by showing the
actual nature of the claim (ψεύστης ἐστίν).

       In that very same verse the author refutes the claim
with another argument that he introduced very briefly in
v. 4:12, viz., no one has ever seen God. Thus, he argues that
no one can love God directly (οὐ δύναται ἀγαπᾶν), because no
one has ever seen God (τὸν θεὸν ὃν οὐχ ἑώρακεν). Any claim to
love, he continues, must begin with the love of the brethren,
because, unlike God, the brethren are visible. The basic

command to love is clearly developed from having seen and
having known the love of God, i.e., Jesus Christ (vv. 4:10-11).

With v. 4:21 the author adds yet another argument to
his refutation: tradition.[144] The community, he declares,
has received an explicit command to the effect that any claim
to love God must be accompanied by a corresponding love of
the brethren. This is, of course, not a new argument; in the
course of the Letter, as I have pointed out, the author
repeatedly associates the love command with tradition (cf.
vv. 2:7-8, 3:11, 3:23-4).

In summary, therefore, one may say that this third
paragraph of the section, like vv. 4:7-12, concentrates on
differentiating "correct" or "perfect" love from "incorrect"
love. This it does by presupposing the confession of paragraph 4:13-16a—a confession which centers on the redemptive
death of Jesus and which interprets that death in terms of
God's love for man—and by incorporating that confession into
the love that the brethren should have for one another. On
the other hand, he attacks contrary claims by using three
distinct arguments: (1) showing how their actual behavior
negates this claim; (2) arguing that, since no one has ever
seen God, no one can love God directly; (3) appealing to tradition.

Summary of vv. 4:7-21. In this third largely ethical
section of the Letter, the author emphasizes above all a relationship of love which he first introduced in vv. 2:28-3:24,
i.e., the love which the Father showed toward man. The author
once again defines this particular relationship of love in
terms of Jesus Christ, his coming to the world and his death
on behalf of men (vv. 4:9-10, 14-16a, 16b-17).

The remainder of the section is devoted, for the most
part, to a differentiation of correct love from incorrect love.
The former love is based above all on the love of God toward
men; such love becomes the prototype of all love (vv. 4:11,
19). Furthermore, only such love lends credence to the claims
of "knowing God" and of "having been born of him." The latter
kind of love is represented by the author as bypassing this
event, this mode of love, in favor of what appears to be a

claim to love God directly. Such a claim is basically a lack
of knowledge of God; and the one who proposes it, a liar.

I Jn 5:1-12

          It was mentioned on p. 39 above that the great major-
ity of the references to love in I John may be found in the
largely ethical sections of the Letter. As a matter of fact,
there are only four instances of the root outside those sections, and they all occur in the third and last largely dogmatic section. These instances are: $5:1^2$, 2, 3. That v. 5:1
begins a new section is, in my opinion, quite evident from the
fact that πίστις now becomes the main theme of the author and
love becomes a subordinate theme, a link to the former paragraph. As such, the occurrences of love are found at the very
beginning of the new section and immediately follow the presentation of love in vv. 4:16b-21.

          Vv. 5:1-5 present a clear case of *inclusio* within the
section: v. 5:1 presents the confession of Jesus as the
Christ--πᾶς ὁ πιστεύων ὅτι ᾽Ιησοῦς ἐστιν ὁ Χριστός--and v. 5:5,
Jesus as the Son of God--ὁ πιστεύων ὅτι ᾽Ιησοῦς ἐστιν ὁ υἱὸς
τοῦ θεοῦ. These two confessions are then united by a series
of synonymous expressions in the intervening verses. Thus,
v. 5:1a declares that anyone who accepts Jesus as the Messiah
"has been born of God" (ἐκ τοῦ θεοῦ γεγέννηται).[145] V. 5:4a
further declares that such a person (πᾶν τὸ γεγεννημένον ἐκ
τοῦ θεοῦ) conquers the world (νικᾷ τὸν κόσμον). Verse 5:4b
defines such a victory solely in terms of faith--ἡ πίστις
ἡμῶν. Finally, v. 5:5 gives the content of that faith as
belief in Jesus as Son of God. Therefore, he who believes
that Jesus is the Christ and the Son of God shows that he "has
been born of God" and "conquers the world."

          The four occurrences of love are interspersed among
these synonymous expressions. First of all, v. 5:1b rephrases
the command attributed to tradition in v. 4:21 in terms of the
theme of γεννάω. In so doing, the verse clearly and explicitly
identifies "the brother" or "the brethren" as those who possess
correct belief. The following diagram shows the parallelism:

            (v. 4:21)   (v. 5:1b)

    ἵνα ὁ ἀγαπῶν τὸν θεόν   πᾶς ὁ ἀγαπῶν τὸν γεννήσαντα
    ἀγαπᾷ καί   ἀγαπᾷ καί
    τὸν ἀδελφὸν αὐτοῦ   τὸν γεγεννημένον ἐξ αὐτοῦ

Thus, anyone who would claim to love God (see vv. 4:10-12, 20)
would also have to show love toward the community (which
believes the tenets of vv. 5:1 and 5).

        In the following two verses, the author specifies once
more what it is that constitutes "correct" love. This he does
by defining,[146] first of all, what the second part of the command given in v. 5:1b implies--ἀγαπᾷ καί τὸν γεγεννημένον ἐξ
αὐτοῦ--and, secondly, what the first part of that same command
requires--ὁ ἀγαπῶν τὸν γεννήσαντα. In so doing, the author
repeats positions he has already taken elsewhere.

        In v. 5:2 he concentrates on the second element of
the command, i.e., the love of the brethren.[147] Such love consists basically of the love of God and the execution of his
commands. In v. 5:3 the author concentrates on the first element of the command, i.e., the love of God. Such love consists of the execution of God's commands. To that extent,
verse 5:3 is a virtual repetition of v. 5:2 as well. There
can be no love of God--and no love of the brethren--without
the execution of God's commands. Thus, given the definition
of God's commands in v. 3:23, it is clear that love of the
brethren must begin with belief in Jesus and continue with the
praxis that such belief involves. It is this combination that
represents a clear victory over the world.

Summary

        In accordance with the plan of action outlined in the
introduction to the chapter, the preceding pages have presented
the redaction-critical study of the terms ἀγάπη/ἀγαπᾶν in
I John not only in terms of the succession of largely ethical
and largely dogmatic sections, but also, and most importantly,
in terms of the "paragraphs" or "units of thought" into which
these sections may be divided and which form the basis for the
spiraling type of argumentation employed by the author in the

Letter. The result of this redaction-critical investigation
has been to reveal the presence of a number of relationships
of love which occur repeatedly in the Letter. In what follows
I should like to gather together the information provided in
the several "paragraphs" and present a summary of what those
relationships entail.

First of all, I should like to begin with the love of
God toward men. This particular relationship, which is first
encountered in paragraph 2:28-3:10, is presented by the author
in strictly historical terms, i.e., as an event of history.
In vv. 3:1 (which is to be taken in conjunction with vv. 3:5
and 8b from the same paragraph), 4:9-10, and 4:14-16, this
event--and this love of God--is described solely in terms of
the mission of his Son and of his death on behalf of men's
sins. The author does not address himself directly to any
other aspects or indications of God's love for men.

Secondly, in this definition of the love of God toward
men, it is implied, but never pursued explicitly as such, that
the Son of God in carrying out his mission and specifically in
dying for men also manifested love toward men. It is he who
forms the necessary link between God and man and, as such,
partakes of that relationship of love as well. Thus, for
example, v. 3:16 defines the noun ἡ ἀγάπη by itself, i.e.,
without mention of the love of God, also in terms of the Son
of God's redemptive death.

Thirdly, the author devotes considerable attention to
a definition of what love for God on the part of man implies
and entails. Furthermore, such a definition, it is fair to
say, is developed by the author in a polemical fashion, i.e.,
he attempts again and again to differentiate between the "correct" and "incorrect" love of God on the part of man. The
verses in question are: vv. 2:5, 15-17; 3:17; 4:10-12a, 20-21;
5:2-3.

According to these verses, "correct" love of God may
be characterized as follows: (1) a knowledge of Jesus which
requires the execution of his commands (v. 2:5); (2) a complete
exclusion of all love for the world (vv. 2:15-17; 3:17); (3) an
acceptance of the fact that God has loved men first through his
Son (vv. 4:10, 19-20); (4) a corresponding love of one's

brother (v. 4:21); (5) the execution of God's commands--which,
according to v. 3:23, include belief in Jesus Christ and love
for one another--(v. 5:3). By way of contrast, "incorrect"
love may be described as follows: (1) a failure to execute
Jesus' commands (v. 2:5); (2) an adoption of the ways of the
world--such as licentiousness, greed or lust, self-boasting
and a failure to help a brother in need (vv. 2:15-17; 3:17);
(3) a claim to love God directly (vv. 4:10, 20); (4) a corresponding hatred of the brethren (v. 4:20); (5) a failure to
execute God's commands (v. 5:3).

Fourthly, it is fair to say that the author concentrates for the most part on the love command, i.e., love of
"the brother" or "of one another." Furthermore, as in the
case of the former relationship of love--of which love for the
brother forms an integral part--this particular relationship
is also developed in a polemical fashion, i.e., the author
attempts to differentiate between "incorrect" and "correct"
love of the brethren. The texts in question are: vv. 2:9-11;
3:10, 14-16, 24; 4:7-8, 11-12; 5:2.

According to these verses, love of the brethren implies:
(1) an abiding in "the light" (v. 2:10); (2) the execution of
righteousness (v. 3:10); (3) a transformation from "death" to
"life" (v. 4:14); (4) an incorporation of the mode of love
which God showed man into one's own love (vv. 3:16, 24; 4:11,
19); (5) abiding in God and vice versa (vv. 3:24; 4:12, 16b);
(6) a knowledge of God and birth from him (vv. 4:7-8); (7) a
love of God through the execution of his commands (v. 5:3).
Again, by way of contrast, "incorrect" love--or "hatred"--shows
the following characteristics: (1) a being "in darkness"
(vv. 2:9, 11); (2) the execution of sin (vv. 3:4, 6b, 8);
(3) an abiding "in death" (vv. 4:14-15); (4) a lack of knowledge of God (v. 4:8b); (5) a lack of love of God (vv. 4:20;
5:2); (6) a failure to execute his commands (v. 5:2).

As I have shown in the redaction-critical study undertaken above, these characteristics of "correct" love of God
and of the brethren (as well as of "incorrect" love) are to a
large degree synonymous expressions, all of which describe the
same reality from different angles. Indeed, even the last two
relationships of love are to a certain degree synonymous,

insofar as "correct" love of God entails love of the brethren
--see #4 and #5 under that category--and "correct" love of the
brethren also entails the love of God--see #7 under that category. The same observation would apply, of course, to "incorrect" love as well.

If such indeed is the case, then one would do well to
determine what it is that ultimately differentiates "correct"
love from "incorrect" love. It is at this point that the first
two relationships of love, viz., the love of God and the love
of Jesus for men, play a major part. Thus, "correct" love
implies an acceptance of God's love toward man in the person
of his Son and of the latter's redemptive death as well as a
willingness to abide by the latter's commands, which are
ultimately those of his Father. Likewise, "incorrect" love
implies a love of God which bypasses that particular mode of
love which God manifested toward men and which claims freedom
from those commands brought by the Son. This latter love is,
in the eyes of the author, nothing but "hatred" of one's
brother.

Finally, it is clear from the Letter that when the
author speaks of the love of the "brother" or of "one another"
he is not speaking of one's neighbor in general, but rather--
and very specifically--of the members of the community. This
is, without doubt, the central concern of the author. The
brethren must love one another "in truth," i.e., according to
right doctrine, and "in deed," i.e., according to right praxis
(e.g., the opposites of vv. 2:16-17; 3:17). Nowhere is this
identification more evident than in the reprise of the command
of v. 4:21 in v. 5:1b.

Sitz im Leben

I stated at the very beginning of the chapter that I
would postpone any consideration of the precise nature of the
struggle in I John until the completion of the redaction-
critical study of the references to love in their respective
paragraphs. At the present time, it becomes necessary to ask
why the author would exhort the community to love one another
according to the commands of Jesus and of God, commands which
include an acceptance of Jesus' redemptive death as the sign

of the Father's love as well as more practical signs of concern for the brother. The response to this question may be
ascertained from the contemporary view of the *Sitz im Leben* of
I John, a view which the findings described above strongly
confirm.

Unlike the wide disagreements that exist concerning
the structure of I John, it is fair to say that the nature and
character of the *Sitz im Leben* of the Letter have enjoyed--
above all, in recent scholarship--a wide consensus of opinion.
This consensus of opinion has tended to see in the opponents
of the Letter the emergence of a docetic-libertine type of
Christianity which has upset and is upsetting the members of
the community.[148] This is not to say, to be sure, that exceptions to the rule may not be found. Among such exceptions one
may cite the work of Alois Wurm and A. E. Brooke.

First of all, writing in 1903, A. Wurm proposed that
the opponents of I John were Jews who refused to accept Jesus
as the Messiah.[149] In more recent times, J. C. O'Neill has
revived a very similar theory, which is, to a great extent,
dependent upon a singular conception of the composition of
the Letter.[150] Secondly, in his commentary of 1912, A. E.
Brooke calls into question the generally accepted opinion that
the front against which the author of I John is battling is a
single, united front--he mentions A. Wurm's theory as an
example--and proposes instead the theory that the author is
addressing himself to "various forms of teaching."[151] By and
large, however, as I have already mentioned, the basic aim of
the Letter has been taken to be an attack against gnosticizing
Christians who were once members of the community.[152]

Perhaps the most thorough example--and certainly the
most recent one--of this latter approach is the one undertaken
by John Bogart in chapter five of his *Orthodox and Heretical
Perfectionism*.[153] In that particular chapter Bogart lists
consecutively all those groups within the Letter whom the
author seems to be attacking; there are ten such groups or
"identifiable categories" (as he calls them). They are as
follows: (1) the antichrists; (2) the false prophets; (3) the
libertines; (4) the haters of the brethren; (5) the heretical
perfectionists; (6) the faint-hearted; (7) those who claim the

initiative in loving God; (8) the ἀγαπητοί who are influenced
by the callous; (9) those who deny that Jesus came by blood;
(10) the idolators.[154]

Bogart proceeds to dismiss immediately groups #6, #7,
#8, and #10 above as referring not so much to the opponents,
but to vacillating members of the community.[155] Then, in a
comparison of the remaining groups, i.e., #1, #2, #3, #4, #5,
and #9, he comes to the conclusion that all these characteristics may be reasonably attributed to one and the same group of
people. This group he characterizes as follows:[156]

> This means that the chief opponents of the author of I John
> were docetist, libertine, charismatic prophets, and itiner-
> ant teachers, treasuring a secret Χρῖσμα, which they gladly
> imparted to a listening world. They had been members of
> the Johannine community, and perhaps still considered them-
> selves to be so.

From the point of view of this study, their characterization
as *docetists* and *libertines* is extremely important.

The description of both "incorrect" love of God and
"incorrect" love of neighbor confirms without doubt the presence of precisely such a group within the community of
I John.[157] The opponents are twice characterized by the
author as proclaiming a direct love of God, i.e., a love which
bypasses entirely God's love for men (vv. 4:10, 19-21) in the
form of the mission of his Son and of the redemptive death of
Jesus. That particular mode of love would be abhorrent to a
docetist position. Similarly, the opponents are characterized
by the attitudes which they adopt toward or within the community, i.e., they are not keeping the commands of Jesus
(v. 2:4) or of God (vv. 3:23; 5:3); they are practicing a
rather *libertine* behavior, which includes, among other things
to be sure, immorality, greed or lust, self-boasting, and a
refusal to help a brother in need. Theirs is a life of sin
and lawlessness in the author's eyes.[158]

In view of this two-pronged type of behavior within the
community--a type of behavior which the author may term a failure to love one's brother (e.g., 3:10, 14; 4:8, 20) or a hatred
of one's brother (e.g., 2:9, 11; 3:13; 4:20)--the author

develops a two-pronged doctrine of love for the brethren:
against *docetism*, he defines God's love toward man precisely
in terms of the redemptive death of Jesus, his Son, and man's
love for man in terms of an acceptance of that death; against
libertinism, he defines love as an execution of Jesus' commands
(or God's commands) which is tantamount to an execution of
righteousness and an avoidance of sin. In the terminology of
v. 3:18, this is love ἐν ἔργῳ and καὶ ἀληθείᾳ.

Thus, clearly, the author's position on the four
relationships of love and his arguments against the claims of
his opponents may be satisfactorily explained in terms of the
commonly accepted *Sitz im Leben* of I John: (1) given the fact
that Jesus, the Son of God, is the love of the Father for men,
no one can claim to love God without Jesus, to see God without
Jesus; (2) given the fact that in Jesus the commands of God are
made known, these commands are traditional and supersede any
other claim (ἀπ'ἀρχῆς), even those of the spirit (δοκιμάζετε
τὰ πνεύματα, v. 4:1); (3) given the origin of the commands,
no one can go against them and claim to be "in the light," or
"to know God," or "to have been born of God," or "to abide in
God."[159]

CHAPTER III

Ἀγάπη/Ἀγαπᾶν IN JOHN 15:1-17;
13:34-35 and 15:18-16:15

In the preceding chapter I have outlined what the meaning of the terms ἀγάπη/ἀγαπᾶν implies in the First Letter of
John by means of a redaction-critical study of these terms in
the context of the sections and paragraphs that constitute the
spiraling structure of I John. In accordance with the methodology outlined at the conclusion of Chapter I above, I now
turn to a redaction-critical study of those same terms in those
sections of the Gospel of John that the German exegete Jürgen
Becker, has outlined as belonging to the same *Sitz im Leben* as
that of the author of I John, viz., vv. 15:1-17; 13:34-35;
15:18-16:15.[1]

First of all, I propose to situate J. Becker's own
exegetical approach to the Farewell Discourse in its proper
historical perspective, i.e., to place it within the four traditional resolutions of the literary and theological problems
posed by that discourse (section on Traditional Resolutions
below) and also within the course of the most recent exegetical
opinion on these problems (section on Recent Exegetical Opinion
below). This historical perspective will help to clarify the
reason why Becker decides to attribute sections from this discourse of the Gospel to a later hand and a later author.

Secondly, I propose to examine the sections thus outlined by Becker separately (section of Jürgen Becker below)
and to test by means of literary criticism whether they do, in
effect, constitute literary unities and by means of redaction
criticism whether they may reasonably be assigned to the same
Sitz im Leben as that of I John. Given the focus of this work,
such redaction criticism will concentrate for the most part on
the meaning of the root "love" in these sections.

Exegetical Perspective--Traditional
Resolutions

Nowadays hardly any exegete would vigorously maintain
that Jn 13:31-18:1 constitutes a literary unity as it stands.
The clearest and most convincing objection against such a
position lies in the apparently concluding statement of
v. 14:31c: Ἐγείρεσθε, ἄγωμεν ἐντεῦθεν.[2] After the departure
of Judas, the son of Iscariot, in vv. 13:21-30 (ἐκεῖνος ἐξῆλθεν
εὐθύς), Jesus begins his farewell address to the disciples. It
is this address, which is interspersed with a certain amount of
dialogue (e.g., vv. 13:36-38; 14:5, 8, 22), that comes to an
end with the above-mentioned command of Jesus in v. 14:31c.

The problem arises from the fact that Jesus then
launches into a new discourse, which, if taken as a unity, is
far more extensive than the first discourse of vv. 13:31-14:31
(encompassing, as it does, all of chapters 15-17). Furthermore, the beginning of chapter 18 can pick up very well
exactly where v. 14:31c leaves off, both sequentially and con-
textually. From the point of view of context, the narrative
returns to Judas' betrayal (vv. 18:2-9), while, from the point
of view of sequence, the command of Jesus of v. 14:31c is
easily continued by the statement of v. 18:1 concerning Jesus'
movement: ταῦτα εἰπὼν Ἰησοῦς ἐξῆλθεν σὺν τοῖς μαθηταῖς αὐτοῦ
πέραν τοῦ χειμάρρου τοῦ Κεδρών . . . .

Thus, given the clarity of the connection between
vv. 14:31c and 18:1ff., the intervening chapters have to be
explained in terms of their present position in the Gospel.
It is at this *crux* that exegetical speculation begins and different schools (= lines of interpretation) emerge.

Historicizing Approach

The first such school of thought might reasonably be
called the "historicizing" approach. Its proponents would not
only defend the literary unity of the discourse, but would also
presuppose the historicity of the events as such. Therefore,
the evangelist would be construed as presenting reliable data
concerning Jesus' life.[3] In a commentary published in 1881,
B. F. Westcott relies on the theory of a "sympathetic" disciple

of Jesus who commits to memory the latter's words in order to
guarantee the historicity of these words.[4] The command of
v. 14:31c presents no problems whatsoever: the material of
chapters 15-17 must have been uttered before the crossing of
the Kidron valley.[5] Decades later (1955), Louis Bouyer con-
tended that Jesus had probably halted at the porticoes of the
Temple to deliver this last discourse.[6]

Transpositional Approach

        The second school of thought, which one might name
the "transpositional" approach, does not agree with the presuppositions of this latter group at all. Rather, the proponents of this solution attempt to resolve the problem by
rearranging verses and chapters in order to present a more
logical pattern of thought.[7] Perhaps the most important proponents of this approach are, in England, J. H. Bernard and,
in Germany, Rudolf Bultmann.[8]

        In a work published posthumously in 1928, J. H. Bernard
suggests the following rearrangement of the Discourse: 13:1-
30; 15; 16; 13:31-38; 14; 17.[9] First of all, Bernard puts
chapters 15 and 16 ahead of chapter 14--relying both on literary and theological grounds. They are seen as following v.
13:30, because v. 15:2 is construed to be a veiled reference
to Judas Iscariot. Secondly, chapter 17 is seen as following
the concluding statement of vv. 14:30-31--"being offered as
the Lord with the Eleven stood up before they left the house
for Gethsemane."[10] Thirdly, vv. 13:31-38 (the denial of
Peter) follow vv. 16:32-33 (a prediction of the disciples'
abandonment of Jesus) on the basis of the Synoptic pattern
(Mk 14:27-14:28ff.).[11]

        A few years later, Rudolf Bultmann proposed in his
commentary of 1941 another thoroughgoing rearrangement of the
discourse material.[12] Whereas Bernard is rather noncommittal
in explaining why the discourses are found in their present
order, Bultmann favors a theory of an accidental dislocation
of the text, which was then subsequently corrected.[13] Bultmann suggests the following sequence of thought: 13:1-30;
17; 13:31-35; 15; 16; 13:36-14:31.[14] First of all, Bultmann
also places chapters 15 and 16 ahead of ch. 14, but--unlike

Bernard--has the latter chapter begin with v. 13:36. The
reason is simple: vv. 13:36ff. (the denial of Peter) after
vv. 16:32-33 (the prediction of the disciples' failure) preserve the Synoptic sequence. Secondly, Bultmann has vv.
13:31-35--and not v. 13:30, like Bernard--precede vv. 15:1-17.
Again the reason is simple: ch. 15 develops the commandment
of love. Finally, Bultmann places ch. 17 immediately after
v. 13:30, so that v. 14:31, in effect, connects directly with
v. 18:1.[15]

Like the "historicizing" solution set forth above,
this approach has not been widely accepted in recent exegesis.
Although some exegetes have opted for Bultmann's solution,[16]
the overwhelming opinion seems to be that such massive rearrangements are really not very helpful at all and create at
least as many problems as there were prior to the reordering
procedure. While a few of the glaring examples are smoothed
over, other problems are not even touched. Thus, for example,
R. Brown,[17] R. Schnackenburg,[18] B. Lindars,[19] and J. Becker[20]
concur that this is not a satisfactory solution.

Softening Approach

The third school of thought--and here one should
especially read the term "school" with as broad a meaning as
possible--could be designated as the "softening" approach.
The answer does not lie in transpositions or additions, but
rather in a correct reading and understanding of the command
of v. 14:31c. I shall note two of these attempts to attain a
correct reading. The first one, authored by P. Corssen,
appeared in 1907 and was meant as a direct reply to the views
that J. Wellhausen had only recently published.[21] Six decades
later, Heinrich Zimmermann, rejecting both the addition theory
and the rearrangement theory, proposed a novel approach based
on the frequent Johannine device of misunderstanding.[22]

Corssen is of the opinion that the second part of the
Farewell Discourse (15:1-16:33) resumes, interprets, and
develops the first part (13:31-14:31).[23] In other words,
their contiguous position presents no problem at all. The one
problem is v. 14:31c, and this he easily resolves by considering the command to be a later addition. Two presuppositions

are at work in this interpretation: a redactor attempts to
bring this Gospel more in line with the Synoptics, and this
reworking is quite evident in Jn 13-17--v. 14:31c is but one
example of these Synoptic-based additions.[24]

Zimmermann's solution lies above all in a recognition
of how the second part of the discourse relates to the first.
Thus, he proposes that the section 13:31-14:31 speaks of a
time prior to Jesus' departure from the world, while 15:1-
16:33 consider the time after such a departure has taken
place.[25] The latter section shows exactly what the life of
the disciples will be like after the ὑπάγειν of the Lord.
V. 14:31c simply expresses this movement from teaching to
reality by means of the literary device of misunderstanding:
the two terms, ἐγείρεσθε and ἄγωμεν, refer to Jesus' departure
as applied to the disciples.[26]

Neither solution really addresses itself to the other
problems of the discourses. The two authors relate both parts
of the Farewell Discourse too easily, without explaining or
even taking into consideration the numerous agreements and/or
disagreements contained in these chapters. Moreover, both
views fail to take into account the concluding character of
vv. 14:27-14:31.[27]

Redactional Approach

The fourth school of thought is the one that has
carried the day in recent and contemporary exegesis: the best
description for it is to call it the "redactional" approach.
The problems of Jn 14-17, this view holds, can be resolved
through a theory of additions--whether by the evangelist or
by a later redactor--to the original document, which was
roughly composed of vv. 13:31-14:31. The main division of
views within this school, especially from the point of view
of my own interests in the development of the section, is that
between those exegetes who propose a single addition and those
who postulate a number of additions. It seems fair to say
that the great majority of adherents subscribe to the first
category.

The beginnings of the single addition theory may be
traced to the work of Julius Wellhausen, who published two

studies on the Fourth Gospel at the beginning of the century.[28]
Wellhausen's main argument is literary in nature: vv. 14:31c
and 18:1 clearly belong together and should follow one another.
This argument he considers to be in and of itself sufficient
for the adoption of the addition theory.[29] Wellhausen also
presents theological arguments which confirm, in his opinion,
what could be held solely on literary grounds.[30] The conclusion he reaches, therefore, is that chapters 15-17 represent
a later addition by a redactor. This proposal was adopted by
two early adherents: E. Meyer[31] and W. Bauer.[32]

On the other hand, the beginnings of the multiple
addition theory are to be found above all in the work of the
Dominican exegete, M.-J. Lagrange, who proposes a series of
three separate discourses in section 15:1-16:33.[33] The evangelist, Lagrange argues, assembles at this point--the very
moment of Jesus' farewell to his disciples--teaching which had
occurred at another time and in another place. In so doing
the evangelist engages in a redactional procedure not unlike
that displayed by the evangelists Matthew and Luke.[34] John
is thus seen as preserving the primitive teaching of Jesus
and, at the same time, coloring it with his own accentuation.
Lagrange describes these three additions as follows: (1) the
first part (15:1-17) deals with the union of the disciples and
Jesus and parallels the Synoptic sending of the disciples on
their first mission (Mk 10 parr.); (2) the second part (15:18-
16:4a) dwells on the theme of the hatred of the world for the
disciples and parallels the Synoptic eschatological discourse
(Mk 13 parr.); (3) the third part (16:4b-33) is a complement
to chapter 14 ("un complément des premiers souvenirs").[35]

Exegetical Perspective--Recent
Exegetical Opinion

Of the four schools of thought--or lines of interpre-
tation--presented above, it seems to me that the second (the
"transpositional") and the fourth ("the redactional") have been
by far the approaches most frequently utilized by exegetes.[36]
I shall now proceed, having described the origins and major
developments of each school, to summarize the directions which
recent studies involving the Farewell Discourse have taken,

since these are the works that are, at the present time,
determining the pattern of Johannine scholarship: Rainer
Borig (1967); Georg Richter (1965-67-68); Raymond Brown (1970);
Barnabas Lindars (1972); Rudolf Schnackenburg (1975); and
Michael Lattke (1975).

Rainer Borig (1967)

          First of all, therefore, in 1967 a study of Jn 15:1-10
by Rainer Borig appeared under the title, *Der Wahre Weinstock*.[37]
This work, written under the direction of Rudolf Schnackenburg,
was submitted in 1964 as the *Inaugural-Dissertation* to the theological faculty of the University of Würzburg. The work is
roughly divided into three parts: (1) In the first part, Borig
undertakes an exegetical analysis of vv. 15:1-10. (2) Next--
and this is by far the largest section of the work--Borig
approaches the symbolism of the vine from a history-of-
religions perspective, devoting particular attention to the
Mandaean texts. (3) Finally, he turns his attention to the
theological content of the verses.

          Borig addresses himself to the question of the literary
problems of the Farewell Discourse at the very beginning of the
first section.[38] His own position may be described as follows:
on the one hand, he states, it is clear that Jn 15-17 represent
an alternative version of Jn 13:31-14:31; on the other, it is
just as clear that the material contained in the second version
is to be attributed to the evangelist as well. The disciple-
redactor ("eine Schüler-Redaktion") responsible for the addition, he continues, showed the utmost reverence for the text of
his master.[39] Thus, Borig's research is to be located within
the school of thought categorized above as the "redactional"
approach.

Georg Richter (1965-67-68)

          Secondly, at approximately the same time that Borig's
dissertation was published,[40] Georg Richter was producing a
number of studies on Jn 13-17. In 1965 Richter published what
amounts to a summary and an anticipation of the larger work
published in 1967, which was the same year that Borig's study
appeared.[41] Richter's article dealt with theological tensions

which he perceived within the Washing of the Feet pericope
itself (Jn 13:1-20). The thesis was presented in much greater
detail in *Die Fusswaschung im Johannesevangelium* (1967), the
main part of which was devoted to an examination of the history of the interpretation of the passage in question.[42]
Then, in an article published in 1968, Richter turned his
attention to the entire Farewell Discourse.[43]

In an exegetical study of Jn 13:1-20, Richter comes
to the conclusion that the passage contains two separate and
independent narratives of the Washing of the Feet episode.
Not only can these two narratives be delineated by means of
literary criticism, but also by means of theological tensions
existing between them.[44] The first narrative, 13:6-10a, is
quite in keeping with the expressed purpose of the Gospel
(v. 20:31): it is to be interpreted as one of Jesus' many
sēmeia, the purpose of which is to defend Jesus' Messiahship
against current objections, specifically the one based on the
nature of his death (Jn 12:34).[45] The second narrative, 13:13-
17, deviates from this apologetical intent of the first narrative. It is no longer a *sēmeion*, but rather an example of
humble service which is to be imitated by Jesus' disciples.[46]

The conclusion he reaches is that someone added this
second version of the episode to the first at a later time.
The purpose of such an addition, he argues, is to interpret
vv. 12-17 in terms of Jesus' death: an act of love which
serves as an example to be reenacted. Richter posits a further
step: just as vv. 13:12-17 shift the focus of vv. 13:6-10a, so
in the same way chapters 15-17 shift the focus of vv. 13:31-
14:31. Moreover, there are close agreements between vv. 13:6-
10a and 13:31-14:31 as well as between vv. 13:12-17 and chs.
15-17; there are also differences between vv. 13:6-10a and
chs. 15-17 as well as between vv. 13:12-17 and 13:31-14:31.[47]

Therefore, not only is section 13:1-20 a combination
of two originally independent and theologically divergent narratives, but Jn 13:31-17:26 shows exactly the same combination
of divergent elements. Unlike Borig, Richter denies that all
this material comes from one and the same author; it simply
could not have.[48] Thus, Richter also subscribes to the 'redactional' theory, but interprets the redaction as being in

tension with the *Grundschrift*. Like Borig, however, he does
see the second Farewell Discourse as a unity and as the work
of a disciple-redactor, but a man whose reverence for the
original work displayed itself in a different manner than the
one postulated by Borig--he would not change the wording of
his Master's original work.[49]

In the article published in 1968, Richter proceeds to
examine in much greater detail the nature and the origin of
the redaction that shifts so noticeably the perspective of the
Grundschrift (v. 20:31). Thus, he draws out the implications
of his earlier allusions to the redaction. On the one hand,
he finds a consistent shift of emphasis in the later material:
there is an evident movement from soteriology to ecclesiology,
from faith in Jesus to love for Jesus.[50] This shift of emphasis is a direct result of a change in the situation of the
community: new problems and dangers have arisen.[51] On the
other hand, he now identifies the redactor as the author of
I John, since that Letter betrays the same concerns as those
witnessed in the passages of the redaction.[52]

Raymond Brown (1970)

It was only two years later (1970) that the second
volume, dealing with chapters 12-21, of Raymond Brown's massive commentary on the Gospel of John was published.[53] The
approach which he takes to the problem of the Farewell Discourse in this second volume relies totally on the theory of
composition of the Gospel which he outlined in the first volume.[54] Five stages are therein posited in the formation of
the Gospel: (1) the existence of a body of traditional material, independent of the Synoptic tradition, pertaining to
Jesus; (2) the development of this material in Johannine patterns mostly through oral preaching and teaching;[55] (3) the
formation of a consecutive Gospel, i.e., the first edition of
the Fourth Gospel as a distinct work;[56] (4) a secondary edition by the same man of stage #3, designed to answer new
problems; (5) a redaction of the entire work by a person other
than the evangelist.[57]

This redactor is very important from the point of view
of the structure of the Farewell Discourse. The material that

he brings to the second edition of the Fourth Gospel is basically of two kinds: some of it goes back to the evangelist
himself, e.g., vv. 6:35-50; 3:31-36; 12:44-50; chs. 15-17; 11;
12. Some of it goes back to fellow preachers of the evangelist, e.g., ch. 21 and the Prologue. In both cases, therefore, the material that is added is taken from the second
stage of the formation. Whether that material goes back to
the evangelist or to his fellow preachers, a certain similarity of style and vocabulary is preserved on account of the
"school" hypothesis that determines Brown's conception of that
early stage.

        Thus, the material of chapters 15-17 was added to the
work of the evangelist by the redactor. In volume II of his
work, Brown explains the development of these chapters.[58]
Originally, he argues, traditional sayings of Jesus (stage 1)
were woven together into thematic units that utilized the form
of a discourse. These units of speech were then woven into
larger compositions (stage 2). All the traditional sayings
that were thus assembled were taken out of their original context and colored by the motifs of the Last Supper. As a result,
"several independent last discourses" were in existence.[59]

        In the first edition of the Gospel (stage 3), the
evangelist included roughly the section 13:31-14:31, although
not all the material which is found therein in the work as we
know it need be considered an original component of that first
edition. This discourse was composed of an introduction (vv.
13:31-38); a main body (ch. 14); and a conclusion (v. 14:31c).
In the redaction of the Gospel (stage 5), genuine Johannine
material was attached to the end of the first discourse (i.e.,
vv. 15:1-17:26).

        Brown holds that this later addition can be divided
into originally independent parts ("subdivisions"): 15:1-17;
15:18-16:4a; 16:4b-33. These parts, taken from the body of
material of stage 2, were then carefully united to form one
discourse.[60] At the end, the originally independent prayer of
chapter 17 was provided as a climax.

        This theory is much closer to that of Borig than to
that of Richter. For example, it assigns the material incorporated by the redactor for the most part to the evangelist

himself, to stage 2 of the process. It also conceives of
this redactor as a disciple of the evangelist, i.e., a person
other than the evangelist, but who knew him well nonetheless.
A major difference would be that Brown allows for subdivisions
within the added discourse, whereas Borig does not raise the
issue. Contrary to Richter, Brown would posit no tension
within the Farewell Discourse as it stands and does not connect the redaction with the author of I John.

Barnabas Lindars (1972)

Approximately two years after Brown completed his
commentary (1972), Barnabas Lindars published his own commentary on the Gospel for the revised edition of The Century
Bible.[61] This large work was preceded in publication (1971),
but followed in writing, by a brief study summarizing the main
lines of that other work.[62] Lindars' view of the formation of
the Fourth Gospel is not altogether unlike that of R. Brown.

For example, Lindars rejects all extensive source
theories--be it a miracle source[63] or an *Offenbarungsreden*
source[64]--in favor of what he calls "the lines of Synoptic
criticism."[65] At the very beginning of the Johannine tradition,
one finds some written work as well as fixed oral traditions,
encompassing both narratives and sayings. This tradition,
Lindars continues, is parallel to, but independent of, the
Synoptic material. This beginning is very similar to that
first stage postulated by Brown.[66]

This original body of traditional material is then
given a "Johannine" form of expression. This expression takes
the form of homilies which the author delivered--possibly
during the Eucharist--to Christian assemblies. As it might be
expected, these homilies were numerous and their contents
varied from occasion to occasion.[67] Once again, the similarity
of this stage of the process to stage 2 of Brown is evident.
One major difference would be that whereas Brown stresses the
school hypothesis, Lindars emphasizes above all the role of
this one man, the evangelist.[68]

Finally, this one man is also responsible for several
editions of the written work itself. In compiling this written
work, he uses for the most part his own homilies, which he

divides in order to form a connected gospel, but also other
pieces specially composed for the occasion which contained
fragments of his homilies. The abrupt transitions and disloca-
tions within the Gospel are best explained by subsequent
revisions of the original document. This stage of the formation clearly parallels stages 3, 4, and 5 of R. Brown's work,
with the singular exception that Lindars allows no room for
a redactor other than the evangelist himself.

In the case of the Farewell Discourse, Lindars sees
vv. 13:31-38 as the conclusion to the narrative of the Last
Supper and as an introduction to the themes of the following
discourse.[69] In the first edition of the written work, ch.
14--the first discourse--followed vv. 13:31-38 and developed
the themes presented therein.[70] In another edition of the
Gospel, the evangelist added an "alternative version" of this
discourse in the form of chapters 15-16. They too summarize
and develop the themes of vv. 13:31-38. Whereas ch. 14 seems
to be orderly and unified, chs. 15-16 consist of homiletic
pieces which have been welded together by the evangelist.[71]

It is evident that Lindars' hypothesis is close to
those of R. Brown and R. Borig. The main difference is that
Lindars assigns all activity within the Gospel to one author,
who is thus responsible for the hardness of the text. This
man--the evangelist--was simply not overly concerned with
internal unity or logical sequence.[72]

Rudolf Schnackenburg (1975)

Three years after the publication of Lindars' commentary (1975), Rudolf Schnackenburg's third volume of his commentary on the Gospel appeared, exactly a decade after the
first volume had been published.[73] As in the case of Raymond
Brown, the solution offered by Schnackenburg to the literary
critical problems of the Farewell Discourse had already been
presented *in nuce* in the Introduction to the first volume.[74]
The process of formation of the Gospel was therein outlined
as follows:(a) the evangelist had various traditions from
which to choose; some of these were already found in written
form, but most were still in the oral stage. This latter
group constituted a very distinctive layer of material.[75]

(b) the evangelist organized these traditions into connected narratives. Some of the materials that he composed were not incorporated until later into the Gospel (e.g., vv. 3:13-21, 31-36; chs. 15-17). (c) a final redactor.[76]

In the later work of 1975, Schnackenburg shifts his position slightly with regard to the composition of that discourse material which was only later incorporated into the Gospel. His first stance was to uphold the authorship of these chapters by the evangelist; the later position holds open the possibility that, although at times using material that stemmed from the evangelist's hand, these chapters were composed and then added to the Gospel by a disciple-redactor ("Schülerredaktion"). This redactor could also have been responsible for certain minor additions to the original discourse (13:31-38; 14:1-31).[77]

With regard to the structure of chapters 15-17, Schnackenburg proposes the following breakdown. Chapter 15, extending from v. 15:1 to v. 16:4a is to be considered a literary unity; its subsections, vv. 15:1-17 and vv. 15:18-16:4a, are united to one another in structure and content. The chapter was written by a disciple-redactor who availed himself of material stemming from the evangelist.[78] Chapter 16, extending from v. 16:4b to v. 16:33, is also a literary unity and constitutes what might be called a "relecture" or even "eine Variante" of chapter 14. This chapter was also written by a disciple-redactor, who quite clearly used material from chapter 14 for his own purposes. Both of these compositions concern themselves with the situation of the disciples in the world.[79] Chapter 17 also presents a literary unity. It too stems from a disciple-redactor who, no doubt, used existing material from the hand of the evangelist.

Schnackenburg's first position--that outlined in the first volume of 1965--was indeed quite close to that of Borig, Brown, and Lindars, i.e., material which the evangelist had composed was later incorporated in a redaction of the original document. The Farewell Discourse represented one of these later additions. The position taken in the volume published in 1975 is much closer to Richter's own theory: this material was composed to a large extent by the later redactor(s). This

addition betrays a new community situation, one that is not
reflected in vv. 13:31-14:31.[80]

Michael Lattke (1975)

Finally, the last work to be mentioned is the dissertation by Michael Lattke dealing with the meaning of love in
the Johannine Gospel. This *Inaugural-Dissertation*, written
under the direction of Anton Vögtle and Alfons Deissler, was
submitted to the theological faculty of the University of
Albert Ludwig in 1973 and was published in 1975.[81] A large
part of the study is devoted to the occurrences of "love" in
the Farewell Discourse.[82]

Lattke is the only one of these exegetes to propose
a revival of the "transpositional" approach, rejecting the
attempt to attribute chapters 15-17 to a later redaction of
the Gospel. The main reason he gives for his acceptance of
a dislocation theory lies in the thoroughly "Johannine" character of these chapters; the theology contained therein, he
maintains, is truly and essentially Johannine theology.[83] In
a dialectic with Bultmann's rearrangement of these chapters,
Lattke proposes the following sequence as "die wesentlich
einfachere Möglichkeit": 13:1-31a; 15-17; 13:31b-14:31.[84]

Chapter 15 would be tied directly to Judas' departure,
while vv. 13:31b-14:31 would take up the theme of glorification introduced in chapter 17. Furthermore, through this
rearrangement certain difficulties would be avoided: (1) the
established Synoptic sequence of prophecy of the disciples'
failure and Peter's denial would be preserved in vv. 13:31b-
38; (2) the question of Peter in v. 13:36 would follow, not
precede, that of Jesus in vv. 16:29f.; (3) the discourse of
vv. 15:1ff. would have as an introduction the words of
v. 13:31a, λέγει 'Ιησοῦς. After the dislocation of the text
took place--an event the nature of which he sees as being
impossible to ascertain--a person other than the evangelist
developed the sequence now present in the text.[85]

Summary

It is evident, therefore, that recent studies of the Farewell Discourse have gone in the two traditionally most popular directions, i.e., either a "transpositional" or a "redactional" theory is offered to account for these literary and theological problems. Michael Lattke is the sole representative of the former option, while R. Borig, G. Richter, R. Brown, B. Lindars, and R. Schnackenburg all opt for the latter approach (with the corresponding variations).

From the point of view of authorship, Borig, Brown, and Lindars would hold that this material which was inserted into the original Gospel stems from the hand of the evangelist. Schnackenburg's first position would also concur with this judgment. The material thus inserted represents material left over from an earlier stage. G. Richter and the later Schnackenburg, on the other hand, would subscribe to a theory of different authorship.

From the point of view of the structure of the additions, the single addition theory is held by R. Borig and G. Richter. Raymond Brown would offer a compromise: originally independent discourses have been welded together into one discourse and have thereby become "subsections" of this latter discourse. Both B. Lindars and R. Schnackenburg would see a plurality of self-contained units. The latter would preserve the integrity of chapter 15 (15:1-16:4a), while the former would not.

Finally, it should be observed that all those adherents to the redactional theory who distinguish between the redactor and the evangelist (all but B. Lindars) characterize this redactor as a "disciple" or a "student" of the evangelist. The concept of a "school," therefore, is consistently used to explain this process of addition or redaction. Thus, the redactor is a disciple either because he incorporated material from the evangelist himself (Borig; Brown) or because he used his master's work as a vehicle for his own compositions (Richter; Schnackenburg).[86]

It is also rather interesting to see that both Borig and Brown (as well as Lindars and the early Schnackenburg) adopt their respective positions on account of what they

consider to be the clearly Johannine character of these chapters. Indeed, both Brown and Lindars expressly consider their
theories as validating the insights of E. Schweizer and E.
Ruckstuhl.[87] Richter is quite aware of the possible objections emerging from stylistic considerations of the chapters
in question; however, he adopts the position that style and
word count are simply inadequate in and of themselves to call
into question his theory of redaction. A "school," he argues,
could basically employ the same style and vocabulary with different theological accents and emphases.[88]

Jürgen Becker

Becker's article appeared in 1970;[89] as a result, it
followed the studies of Borig and Richter; was published at
the same time that Brown's second volume appeared; and preceded the works of Lindars, Schnackenburg (vol. III), and
Lattke. His position within this history of scholarship is
not hard to determine. As it has already been stated, he
divides the Farewell Discourse into an original discourse
(Jn 13:31-14:31) and a second discourse (Jn 15:1-16:33). This
second discourse he subdivides further into three originally
independent discourses, viz., 15:1-17; 15:18-16:15; 16:16-33,
and assigns them to more than one author (the role of the
evangelist--the author of the original discourse--as the author
of any of these discourses is completely ruled out.)[90]

As such, Becker clearly subscribes to the "redactional"
approach first proposed by J. Wellhausen and, within that
approach itself, takes a position not unlike that of M.-J.
Lagrange. Thus, he would agree with those exegetes who ascribe
the material to someone other than the evangelist--thus he is
to be distinguished from R. Borig, R. Brown, and B. Lindars.
He would also agree with those exegetes who divide the material into originally independent sections--thus he is to be
distinguished from G. Richter.[91] Perhaps the closest parallel
to the solution offered by Becker is that of the later Schnackenburg: both claim different authorship; a variety of discourses; and attribution to a school.[92] The main difference

between the two lies in their respective delineations of the
different units of the second discourse, i.e., chs. 15-16.

Having traced J. Becker's exegetical approach to the
Farewell Discourse within the course of modern and contemporary
Johannine exegesis, I now turn, in accordance with the plan
outlined at the beginning of this chapter, to those verses or
sections which he assigns to a hand other than that of the
evangelist and which betray interests and concerns closer to
those of I John than to those of the Gospel. I shall examine
these sections (vv. 15:1-17; 13:34-35; 15:18-16:15) as follows:
(1) determine whether these sections may be considered literary
unities; (2) determine whether there are any clear subdivisions
within the literary unities; (3) examine the theological *Akzent*
of the respective literary unities--primarily through a
redaction-critical study of the terms ἀγάπη/ἀγαπᾶν--and compare that *Akzent* with that of I John outlined in the previous
chapter in order to see whether they could be reasonably
assigned to the same *Sitz im Leben*.

Jn 15:1-17--The Vine and the Branches

Demarcation of the Passage. Becker is certainly not
alone in choosing vv. 15:1-17 as a self-contained unit.[93] On
the one hand, he sees the beginning of the unit, the *Bildrede*,
as being totally unexpected after the end of the discourse in
v. 14:31c.[94] Indeed, only those exegetes who adopt an "historicizing" or a "softening" solution find no real break between
v. 14:31 and v. 15:1. On the other hand, Becker posits a similar break between vv. 15:17 and 15:18 for the following reasons: (1) the parenesis concerning the love commandment is
not continued in vv. 15:18ff.; (2) the hatred of the world,
which becomes the primary element in vv. 15:18ff., is not
anticipated in any way whatsoever within vv. 15:1-17.[95] On
both counts I believe Becker is correct: vv. 15:1-17 emerge
as an originally independent discourse.[96]

One must keep in mind at all times the views of those
exegetes--Richter and Schnackenburg--whose positions are quite
close to that of Becker. Richter may be disregarded at this
point, since he fails to differentiate among subsections of

the one discourse ("die zweite Abschiedsrede"). On the other
hand, Schnackenburg enters into full dialogue with Becker:[97]
Becker is incorrect in associating vv. 15:18-16:4a with
vv. 16:4b-15. Rather, Schnackenburg argues, vv. 15:18-16:4a
should be connected with vv. 15:1-17 both from the point of
view of structure and of content.[98]

First of all, with regard to structure, Schnackenburg
points out the presence of a formal linking element in the
expression, ταῦτα λελάληκα ὑμῖν (vv. 14:25; 15:11; 16:1, 4, 6,
25, 33). This expression, he argues, marks the end of a discourse in vv. 14:25 and 16:33 as well as the end of a subsection in v. 15:11 ("eine Redeeinheit"); therefore, its occurrence in vv. 16:1 and 4 should also be construed as the formal
end of vv. 15:1ff.[99] However, in my opinion, this argument is
not sufficient by itself to claim unity for vv. 15:1-16:4a.
The expression may point to v. 16:4a as a conclusion', as indeed
it does, but it need not include all the material that has followed the last use of the expression, as indeed it does not.
Besides, chapter 17 does not end with a similar expression, so
that exceptions are possible.

Secondly, with regard to content ("Verbindungslinien
und Klammern"), Schnackenburg points out the following important contacts: (1) the common union of love and hatred (Jn
3:19-20; I Jn 2:9-11; 3:13-15; 4:19-21);[100] (2) the opposition
between the world and the disciples (the argument is hard to
grasp here since κόσμος is not present in vv. 15:1-17);
(3) the choosing of the disciples occurs in both v. 15:16 and
v. 15:19;[101] (4) other links, such as τὰς ἐντολὰς τηρεῖν or
τὸν λόγον τ. (15:10, 20) and δοῦλοι (15:15, 20). The strongest
proposed contacts seem to be #1 and #3: the latter could very
well be considered a redactional link; the former is subject
to Becker's observation that hatred is not anticipated in
vv. 15:1-17 nor love pursued in vv. 15:18ff. Thus, the
division 15:1-17 is, in my opinion, much more plausible than
the one proposed by Schnackenburg. (Further theological arguments will confirm this judgment.)

Division of the Passage. Becker further divides this
self-contained unit into three main sections. The first section covers vv. 15:1-8, i.e., the *Bildrede* proper. Its tone
is basically parenetical: the community is required to abide
in Christ and, thus, to bear fruits. The second section leaves
behind altogether the imagery of the vine and the branches and
turns instead to the love of Christ and the execution of his
commandments (vv. 15:9-11). Finally, the third section clari-
fies what the content of the commandment is, i.e., the command
to love one another (vv. 15:12-17).[102]

Once again, Becker is certainly not alone in separating
vv. 15:1-8 as a subsection within the one discourse; most
exegetes that adopt that position base their reasoning on the
abandonment of the imagery of the vine by the author after
v. 8.[103] This, it seems to me, is the most logical division
within this section: (1) with v. 15:8 the imagery is indeed
left behind; (2) and ἀγάπη comes into its own as an explanation of that imagery. One should notice above all the reprise
of the command given in v. 4 (μείνατε ἐν ἐμοί) in v. 9 (μείνατε
ἐν τῇ ἀγάπῃ τῇ ἐμῇ); the change of themes is thus clearly indi-
cated--ἀγάπη now opens and closes the rest of the discourse.

As one might expect, many other solutions have been
suggested: vv. 15:6 and 15:10 have been proposed as the end of
the *Bildrede* section.[104] Schnackenburg proposes the following
division: 15:1-11; 12-17. His reasons are as follows:
(1) the expression ταῦτα λελάληκα ὑμῖν clearly indicates an
end within the Farewell Discourse;[105] (2) with verse 10 the
μένειν ἐν disappears altogether (but this would seem to argue
of itself for 15:10 as the dividing point);[106] (3) the theme
of χαρά, full joy, also points to the nature of the verse as a
conclusion (as in v. 16:24); (4) vv. 12 and 17 constitute a
clear case of *inclusio*.[107]

In my opinion, however, it is the introduction of the
noun ἡ ἀγάπη in v. 15:9 that constitutes the most significant
deviation from the preceding verses, so much so that it should
be regarded--with Becker--as the dividing point. Whether a
further division is necessary between vv. 15:11 and 12, as
Becker suggests, is debatable.[108] Such a division would bring
into focus the *inclusio* of vv. 12-17, but it would also

interrupt the development of the controlling motif of these
verses, viz., ἡ ἀγάπη. As a result, I would prefer to read
vv. 15:9-17 as the second subsection of the discourse.

    Theological "Akzent" of vv. 15:1-17. In contrast with
the first discourse of 13:31-14:31, Becker observes a significant shift of emphasis in this independent unit of 15:1-17:
whereas the first discourse had been concerned solely with
soteriology, the second discourse is primarily parenetical in
tone. From the *solus Christus* doctrine of vv. 13:31-14:31 one
may now see a shift toward ethical behavior as a necessary
condition for "abiding in Christ."[109]

    This shift may be clearly observed according to him in
verses such as 15:7, 8, 10, 11, 14, where the community is
enjoined to behave in a specific manner in order to maintain
and preserve its union with Jesus Christ. Any failure to obey
such commands will result in a rejection of Jesus, as v. 15:2
indicates. On the basis of this series of exhortations and
imperatives, Becker proceeds to outline a *Sitz im Leben* for the
passage. The community being addressed, he argues, is in very
real danger of abandoning its Lord on account of its peculiar
behavior.[110] This was a circumstance which was not present at
the time the first discourse had been written, but had come to
the fore later on. As a result, the author preserves the image
of Jesus as the enthroned Lord ("der Heilspräsenz Christi") of
vv. 13:31-14:31, but now applies it to the situation in his own
community.

    Vv. 15:1-17 should, therefore, be considered an eccle-
siastical addition. It is to be placed within the life situation of the First Letter of John, where the very same problems
concerning ethical standards and behavior are disrupting the
community. Indeed, Becker argues that I Jn 3:17 may provide
the closest parallel to Jn 15:1-17.[111]

    Becker's thesis is clear: both I John and Jn 15:1-17
can, in effect, be differentiated theologically from the Gospel
by means of their ethical demands upon the community. This, I
believe, is a correct observation: ethical behavior now
becomes absolutely necessary for "abiding" in Jesus Christ.
However, if the same *Sitz im Leben* is posited for both writings,

then one would expect in vv. 15:1-17 some mention--whether
explicit or implicit--of the other part of the controversy in
I John, i.e., the christological aberration of the opponents,
in Jn 15:1-17.

    I have shown in the previous chapter that the ἀγάπη
defense of the author of I John was twofold in nature: it
involved a correct christological confession as well as a
corresponding ethical behavior based on that confession. In
order to posit a similar *Sitz im Leben* for vv. 15:1-17, one
must search for both sides of the ἀγάπη argumentation. And,
indeed, both sides are to be found in vv. 15:1-17. Thus, what
I propose to do in what follows is to show that Becker's attribution is essentially correct, but that it requires a more
specific, and therefore tighter, criterion for said attribution.[112] I will be concerned, first of all, with the figure
of the vine and the branches and, secondly, with its development in terms of ἀγάπη.

    Exegesis of Jn 15:1-8. This first subsection of 15:1-
17 may be further divided into four different parts: (1) the
introduction to the discourse, vv. 1-2; (2) an aside concerning the status of the believer, v. 3; (3) the introduction of
the expression μένειν ἐν, vv. 4-7; (4) the climax of the subsection, v. 8.

    Introduction, vv. 1-2. At the very beginning of the
discourse, one finds four identifications being made--two
explicit, two implicit--between the figures of viticulture,
on the one hand, and the community situation on the other.
V. 1ab provides the two explicit examples: a typically Johannine ἐγώ εἰμι saying identifies Jesus as the true vine (ἡ
ἄμπελος ἡ ἀληθινή), while the Father is described as the gar-
dener (ὁ γεωργός).[113] V. 2ab provides the two implicit
examples: the disciples are seen as the branches (πᾶν κλῆμα)
and their work as one of bearing fruit (τὸ καρπὸν φέρον). This
type of comparison and the development thereof have been classified by R. Borig as a *Bildrede*, i.e., neither a parable nor an
allegory, but a form which incorporates both parabolic and
allegorical elements.[114] Already within these two verses there

are clear indications as to the underlying problems behind
the discourse.

First of all, all those being addressed are believers
in Jesus Christ (and verse 3 will confirm this observation);
there is no hint whatsoever of an ongoing dialogue or controversy with the synagogue. The traumatic experience of separation from the synagogue described elsewhere in the Gospel is
totally absent from this discourse.

Secondly, it is clear that the problem that does exist
is taking place within the Christian congregation (or group of
congregations): some believers are behaving as if they were
not believers. In terms of the figure itself, some believers
are not doing what they are supposed to be doing, viz., "bearing fruit." V. 15:2 provides two mutually exclusive possibilities available to the believers (πᾶν κλῆμα ἐν ἐμοί). It also
utilizes the figure of the Father from v. 15:1b and assigns
him a judgmental role with regard to the disciples. On the
one hand, the branch may bear fruit; in that case, the Father
will prune it (καθαίρει) that it may bear more fruit (ἵνα
καρπὸν πλείονα φέρῃ).[115] On the other hand, if the branch does
not bear fruit, the Father will cast it aside, remove it
(αἴρει).[116] There is simply no *via media* in this conception.

Thirdly, v. 15:1a may very well reveal what bearing
fruit means in the situation of the community, i.e., the
nature of the problem that is taking place. Jesus is therein
called not only the vine (ἡ ἄμπελος), but also the "true" vine
(ἀληθινή). The emphasis is clearly on the adjective. One
therefore has to ask why the author employs this specific
qualification. The usual answers have to do with research
into the origin of the figure itself. Thus, for example, if
the origin is seen as being rooted in the Old Testament, the
adjective will be taken to differentiate Jesus from Israel.[117]
If the origin, on the other hand, is sought in the Mandaean
texts, then the adjective will be taken as differentiating
Jesus, the divine vine, from any vine the "world" might
offer.[118]

Yet, neither of these explanations is really satisfactory, since the problem is not that of a contrast with
Israel or, for that matter, with the world (not directly,

anyway). The addressees are Christian believers who have
already made their decision. In its present context, the
adjective demands a different interpretation.[119] Thus, one
must separate--as Schnackenburg correctly points out[120]--the
Sitz im Leben of the tradition from that of the present discourse.[121] Whatever the latter may have been, the adjective
still has to be explained from within the context of an inner-
Christian controversy. It would seem, therefore, that some in
the community are questioning Jesus' position as the *true* vine.
Their status as Christians would seem to favor a different
interpretation of Jesus Christ rather than a total denial of
him. "Not bearing fruit" would have to characterize that
particular position.

Although the adjective is employed twice in the Gospel
with direct reference to Jesus (vv. 1:9; 6:32),[122] it is only
in I John that one finds it within an inner-Christian controversy. In I Jn 2:8, i.e., the controlling statement of the
fourth characterization of the opponents' position in paragraph 1:5-2:11, the author points to a conflict between "darkness" and "light" and declares that the "true" light is emerging as triumphant. Furthermore, it is the exercise of the
love command that is responsible for this outcome, a love command which includes a correct christological confession (i.e.,
the "true" light). Similarly, in v. 5:20 the adjective, used
as a substantive, is applied to the correct christological
confession: καὶ ἐσμὲν ἐν τῷ ἀληθινῷ, ἐν τῷ υἱῷ αὐτοῦ ᾿Ιησοῦ
Χριστῷ. The verse then ends with a declaration to the effect
that this Jesus is the "true" God.[123]

Status of the Believer, v. 3. As I have already
remarked above, v. 15:3 confirms the fact that the addressees
are Christian believers: the vocative ὑμεῖς and the second
person plural form of the verb "to be," ἐστε, make such a conclusion inevitable. Despite its clear connection to v. 15:2b
by means of the link καθαίρω, the verse has proved rather controversial in the history of interpretation. Some exegetes
would assign it to the redaction by the evangelist,[124] while
others would see it as part of the tradition being employed
by the author, i.e., the *Bildrede* itself.[125] I believe that

the first view is the most plausible, since the language of
the figure is therein abandoned except for the clear redactional link of the verb "to cleanse."

The question that must then be asked is what role does
this expansion play in the discourse as it stands. The verse,
in my opinion, constitutes a transition from the figure of
vv. 15:1-2 to the exhortations of vv. 15:4ff. In the former
verses, the author has outlined the alternatives open to the
believer, while in the latter verses his message becomes one
of exhortation: abide in me, i.e., abide in the vine. V. 15:3,
therefore, sets down the common foundation of all believers,
i.e., the origin of the believers' status as believers. Those
who have believed, who have heard,[126] the word of Jesus have
already been made clean: the word of Jesus was the instrument
whereby that cleansing was achieved.[127]

But such an event is not final or conclusive; v. 15:2
has already shown that. Not every one who has heard the word
keeps it, i.e., not every branch of the vine abides in it.
The origin may be the same, but the *dénouement* is indeed quite
different. V. 15:3, therefore, should be seen as a statement
concerning origins, the power of which, to be sure, endures or
should endure throughout the believers' lives.[128]

"Abide in," vv. 4-7. From the descriptions given in
vv. 1-3 of the identical original status of all believers and
of the failure of some believers to bear fruit, the author now
turns toward exhortations and commands; from the indicative
of vv. 1-3 one now proceeds to the imperative mood. Yet, to
be sure, the imperative was already contained *in nuce* in the
use of the indicative, given the alternatives of v. 2.[129] In
other words, the status of being believers must be actively
pursued at all times; there must be an actual attempt to
execute what such status entails.

Thus, the second person plural imperative of v. 15:4a
--μείνατε ἐν ἐμοί--definitely sets the tone for the following
few verses. Indeed, μένειν ἐν dominates thematically through
v. 7 (and it emerges once again in v. 9): v. 4b, which reintroduces the figure of the vine, uses it in the form of a
conditional sentence;[130] v. 5, in the form of a participial

phrase; vv. 6-7, again in the form of conditional sentences.
Throughout these verses, and specifically in v. 15:6, the
possibility of ceasing to "abide in Jesus" is constantly maintained.

     (a). One should, first of all, examine the command
itself of v. 15:4a--μείνατε ἐν ἐμοί, κἀγὼ ἐν ὑμῖν. Above all,
attention must be paid to the following elements: (1) the
object of the preposition ἐν;[131] (2) the reciprocal nature of
the formula.[132]

     With regard to the former, it should be mentioned that,
in addition to the imperative itself, there are seven other
occurrences of the expression within vv. 4-7. Of these seven,
six have either the personal pronoun ἐμοί as an object (five
in all) or the figure of the *Bildrede* (one), i.e., ἡ ἄμπελος.
Not only is the faith content of these verses emphasized thereby, but also the dogmatic or theological nature of the controversy in the community.[133] As v. 1 has already intimated,
these verses also indicate that the center of the problem is
"the vine," i.e., Jesus Christ.

     With regard to the second element above, the conjunc-
tion καί should not be understood as a simple consecutive
καί.[134] Nor should it be understood in terms of a καθώς, i.e.,
as a comparison.[135] The occurrence of the formula in v. 15:7
with τὰ ῥήματα as the subject precludes both of these interpretations. Rather, the conjunction presents two sides of the
same coin.[136] The purpose of the reciprocal formula is really
twofold: it serves to underscore the duty which the disciples
have as disciples as well as their utter dependency on Jesus
and his λόγος or ῥήματα.[137] The disciples are disciples insofar as they have received ("heard") the word. The disciples
remain disciples insofar as they abide in Jesus (i.e., his
word), which also means that his "word" abides in them. They
must abide in that which they already have. If they do not so
abide--and this is precisely the problem--they cease to be
disciples altogether.[138]

     It has already been observed above (see n. 131) that
the expression μένειν ἐν as used in these verses finds no
counterpart in the Gospel. However, a parallel usage may be

found in I John--indeed this is one of Becker's most important arguments.[139] Not only does the phrase appear with
reference to the disciples, as in vv. 2:24; 3:24; 4:13, 15,
16,[140] but one may also discern the dialectic outlined above
between "having received" (v. 15:3) and double abiding (v.
15:4) in the first largely dogmatic section of the Letter,
viz., 2:18-27: the "having received" may be found in vv. 20
and 27a; the double abiding in v. 2:24.[141] Furthermore, the
context is that of an inner-church struggle.

(b). Secondly, attention should be directed as well
to the alternatives open to the believers in vv. 5-6. After
a repetition of the ἐγώ εἰμι saying[142] and the first *explicit*
identification of the branches as the disciples (ὑμεῖς τὰ
κλήματα), the basic thought of v. 2 is repeated. Thus, just
as v. 15:2--the delineation of the options--follows v. 15:1
--the identification of the figure, so now vv. 15:5b-6--a
delineation of the options--follow v. 15:5a--the identification of the figure. These verses, therefore, make explicit
once again the controversy that exists in the community: some
believers are not abiding in Jesus, i.e., they are acting as
if they were not believers.[143]

V. 5b recapitulates v. 2b: the branch that does abide
bears much fruit.[144] On the other hand, v. 6 recapitulates
v. 2a: the branch that does not abide is cast aside and
burned.[145] Once again, there is no *via media* at all in this
conception of discipleship: it is an either/or proposition.
Unfortunately, the verses shed no additional light on the
nature of the controversy.[146]

(c). Finally, in v. 7 the author turns his attention
to one of the options delineated in vv. 5-6--that of the
branch that produces fruit--and attaches to it a definite
reward or recompense. The verse begins with a variation of
the reciprocal formula of v. 15:4a and v. 15:5b. The most
important element of the variation is the substitution of τὰ
ῥήματα for ἐγώ as the subject of the second half of the formula;[147] as I have already remarked, the simultaneity of the
two halves of the formula is thereby clearly affirmed: if

the disciples abide in the λόγος, then the λόγος or the
ῥήματα abides in them.

The consequence, or the reward, of such an abiding is
given in terms of the fulfillment of all petitions or prayers.
Whatever the disciples wish shall be granted to them. In
v. 15:16--and again in reference to a fruit-producing branch--
this fulfillment of petitions is once more promised by the
author.[148] Once again, a connection with I John may be
established. On the one hand, I John presents several
instances of "something" belonging to or having to do with
God abiding in the disciples.[149] On the other hand, this
dialectic of abiding and fulfillment of petitions is also to
be found in the First Letter.[150]

Climax of Subsection, v. 8. With the conclusion of
v. 7, the reward promised to the good branch, the expression
"abiding in" is temporarily abandoned by the author. In
v. 15:8 the proper activity of the disciples--that of producing fruit--is interpreted in the context of the glorification
of the Father.[151] The verse employs one of those construc-
tions that are quite familiar in I John: a demonstrative
followed by a clause substituting for an epexegetical infinitive.[152] Thus, the glorification of the Father is defined in
terms of the proper activity of the disciples (ἵνα καρπὸν
πολὺν φέρητε), that very activity which grounds them as
disciples (καὶ γενήσεσθε ἐμοὶ μαθηταί).[153]

Verse 15:8 constitutes, in effect, the climax of
vv. 15:1-7: the epexegetical ἵνα-clause is a summary of the
message presented in vv. 15:1-7. If the disciple chooses to
abide in Jesus and produce fruit--and some are choosing other-
wise--then the Father will manifest his glory in their activity as well, the very same Father who causes the good branch
to bear much fruit and who fulfills the requests of those who
do produce fruit.[154]

An examination of this first subsection has shown that
there is a burning issue within the community, an issue which,
in the eyes of the author, allows for two alternatives with no
via media at all. This issue is basically, *pace* Becker, one

of faith, and, as it emerges from v. 15:1, not so much one of
apostasy, but rather one of aberration.

   Exegesis of Jn 15:9-17. As already mentioned above,
ἀγάπη becomes the dominant theme of the second subsection of
15:1-17.[155] After the climax of 15:8, ἀγάπη opens the section
in the form of a comparison (καθὼς ἠγάπησέν) and closes it in
the form of a commandment (ἵνα ἀγαπᾶτε ἀλλήλους). The subsection may be further subdivided as follows: (1) the relationship of Jesus to the Father as constitutive for that of
the disciples to Jesus, vv. 9-10; (2) an aside on the joy of
the disciples, v. 11; (3) an exposition of the commandment of
love, vv. 12-17.

   Constitutive Relationship, vv. 9-10. In his exegesis
of Jn 15:1-17, Bultmann sees the second subsection of 15:9-17
as a development of the first subsection, 15:1-8. Whereas the
first subsection urges constancy of faith on the part of the
disciples, the second subsection presents the commandment of
love as the "essential element" of that faith.[156] Moreover,
Bultmann argues, from the point of view of structure, that the
second subsection runs parallel to the first.[157]
   That a certain degree of parallelism is present between
both subsections cannot be denied;[158] it may be observed, first
of all, in the beginning of both sections. Thus, just as
vv. 15:1-17 introduce the *Bildrede* by immediately identifying
the figures of the Father and the Son, so also vv. 15:9-17
present these two figures in terms of their relationship of
love. Furthermore, in both cases the figure of the disciples
is intimately tied in with the other two figures: in v. 2
they are also given a role in the *Bildrede*, while in v. 9 they
form part of this relationship of love. This relationship of
love establishes a hierarchical order of love, a hierarchy
which the comparative conjunction καθὼς itself serves to
establish:[159] just as (and "because") God the Father loved
Jesus, so Jesus loved the disciples. The hierarchy is: God
the Father--Jesus--the disciples.[160]
   The parallelism may also be observed, as Bultmann
correctly points out,[161] in the derivation of the imperative

μείνατε from a preceding indicative, from an existing *status
quo*. Thus, just as the imperative of v. 4 follows upon the
condition of the believers as believers described, above all,
in v. 15:3, so now, the imperative of v. 9b follows upon the
condition of the believers as "beloved" described in v. 15:9a.
Just as the believers are urged to abide in the λόγος which
they have accepted, so now they are urged to abide in the
ἀγάπη which they have experienced. The two imperatives are
clearly related. Moreover, the same situation described in
v. 4 (and specifically in vv. 2 and 6) should be presupposed
in v. 9--there are some who are not abiding.[162] The question
of the specific meaning of "love" and "abiding in love" becomes
paramount at this point.

It should be pointed out, first of all, that the author
does not describe the mode of love or the form of love that
Jesus experienced from the Father. This aspect of the hierarchy he leaves out altogether. Instead, he turns his attention to the other aspect of the hierarchy, i.e., the mode of
Jesus' love for the disciples *and* the corresponding duty of
these disciples. Thus, in a sense, the expression ἐν τῇ ἀγάπη
τῇ ἐμῇ is both objective--it describes the manner of Jesus'
love--and subjective--it specifies the duty of the disciples
in the realm of ἀγάπη.[163]

In v. 10 the author turns to the subjective aspect of
the imperative and patterns the duty of the disciples after
Jesus' own behavior with respect to the Father. The relationship of Jesus to the Father becomes constitutive, becomes an
exemplar, for the relationship of the disciples to Jesus.
First of all, v. 10a defines the commandment of v. 9b--the
concept of abiding in Jesus' love--by means of a conditional
sentence. The definition revolves around the further concept
of "executing" Jesus' commandments (ἐὰν τὰς ἐντολάς μου τηρήσητε): whoever fulfills his commands is the one who abides in
his love. Secondly, v. 10b grounds this definition in Jesus'
own behavior toward the Father (also by means of the comparative καθώς):[164] because he, Jesus, fulfilled the commands of
the Father (τὰς ἐντολὰς τοῦ πατρός μου τετήρηκα), he abides in
the Father's love.

Thus, the objective hierarchy of love can only be preserved if each participant, each member of the hierarchy,
abides in it. The Father loved Jesus, and the latter corre-
sponded by executing the Father's commands. Jesus loved the
disciples, and the latter should correspond in a similar way,
i.e., by executing the commands of Jesus. The fact that an
imperative is used implies quite clearly that some are not
keeping Jesus' commands.

If the mode of God's love for Jesus receives no explanation in vv. 15:1-17,[165] in I John it is not even mentioned.
Yet, the hierarchy (God the Father--Jesus--the disciples) is
nevertheless preserved prominently in the Letter. The centrality of Jesus, Messiah and Son of God, in the chain of love
is strongly affirmed. This centrality may be observed in sections 4:7-12 and 4:16b-21. For example, the declaration of
v. 4:8b ὅτι ὁ θεὸς ἀγάπη ἐστίν, is explained in vv. 4:9-10 in
terms of his sending the Son as a redemptive sacrifice. Likewise, the declaration of v. 4:16b, ὁ θεὸς ἀγάπη ἐστίν, is
explained in terms of vv. 4:14-16a, again by means of the Son's
mission as Savior of the world. In both instances, I John
makes it clear that the love of the Father can only be known
through the Son.[166]

Similarly, the definition of ἀγάπη in terms of the
execution of the commands finds strong echoes in I John.[167]
For example, in the course of the third characterization of
the opponents in paragraph 1:5-2:11 (vv. 2:3-6), one finds a
substitution of the controlling concepts introduced in v. 2:3.
The practical effect of this substitution is to equate the
phrase τὰς ἐντολὰς αὐτοῦ τηρεῖν with the possession of a perfect love of God, ἐν τούτῳ ἡ ἀγάπη τοῦ θεοῦ τετελείωται.[168]
One should also remember that the ἐντολαί refer specifically
to Jesus' commands. Likewise, the definition of v. 5:3
repeats this thought of vv. 2:3-5: the love of God is manifested in the execution of his commands (ἵνα τὰς ἐντολὰς αὐτοῦ
τηρῶμεν).[169]

The Joy of the Disciples, v. 11. In the introduction
to the exegesis of vv. 15:9-17, I decided to call v. 11 an
"aside" on the theme of joy. The reason for this particular

designation is the fact that the verse seems to interrupt the
flow of thought from v. 10 to v. 12.[170] Thus, once the abiding of the disciples has been defined in v. 10 as the execution of Jesus' commands, the author proceeds to focus specifically on the nature of these commands in vv. 12ff. However,
in the midst of this progression of thought one finds an
unexpected reference to the joy of the disciples. As a result,
the meaning of this aside, of this interruption, has to be
explained.

I believe that the verse itself provides two indications as to the reason for its present position in the subsection. The first hint lies in the introductory formula of the
verse, ταῦτα λελάληκα ὑμῖν, the formula which is found
repeatedly throughout the Farewell Discourse as it now stands
(vv. 14:25; 15:11; 16:1, 4, 33; 17:13).[171] The second hint
lies in the content of the verse itself; one finds therein a
reference to Jesus' own joy (ἡ χαρὰ ἡ ἐμή) as well as a reference to the disciples' joy (ἡ χαρὰ ὑμῶν).

With regard to the formula itself, it is clear that
the demonstrative always refers to what has preceded it.[172]
The question then becomes: how far back does ταῦτα extend in
this particular verse? And it is at this point that exegetical
disagreement begins.[173] This question may be resolved, I
believe, in terms of the second hint mentioned above: the contents of v. 11 would seem to summarize the thought of vv. 9-10
(as Lagrange argues). This is precisely the purpose of v. 11,
the "aside." Jesus' joy would thus refer both to the position
that he occupies in the hierarchy of love (v. 9a) and to the
fact that he abides in that position because he has kept the
commands of the Father. Likewise, the disciples' joy would
also refer to their position in the hierarchy (v. 9a) as well
as to their duty to abide in that position by executing Jesus'
commands.

The use of the purpose clause[174] and the reference to
the fulfillment of the disciples' joy stresses the fact that
the disciples must continue to abide in Jesus' commandments if
they are to possess the fullness of joy. To that extent, v. 11
also summarizes the imperative of v. 9b. Jesus' relationship
to the Father--a relationship which constitutes his own χαρά--is

constitutive for the relationship of the disciples to Jesus--
their χαρά is dependent on how well they preserve the relationship.

      J. Becker sees this usage of χαρά with the verb πληρόω
(ἵνα . . . ἡ χαρὰ ὑμῶν πληρωθῇ) as an indication of the close-
ness of this section to I John.[175] I believe his observation
is correct. Although χαρά itself is not connected again with
love in either the Gospel or the Letters, its occurrence in
I John is much closer to v. 15:11 than any of the examples
from the Gospel. The other usages of χαρά--with or without
πληρόω--in the Gospel are not concerned with the idea of
"abiding in"; they do not presuppose a situation where some
are clearly not abiding.[176] Only I Jn 1:4 betrays a similar
situation; furthermore, the verse also stresses quite clearly
the centrality of Jesus in the lives of the believers. Vv. 1-3
present the message about Jesus in terms of a dialectic between
tradition and present preaching, a dialectic which creates
fellowship between those who pass on and those who accept.
This fellowship is then said to be specifically centered
around both the Father and his Son.[177] Then, v. 4 describes
the handing on of this tradition as an attempt to perfect the
χαρά of the community.[178]

      Exposition of the Commandments of Jesus, vv. 12-17. As
I have already mentioned, v. 12 continues the trend of thought
of v. 10 quite well. V. 10 describes the subjective aspect of
the imperative of v. 9b and presents Jesus' relationship to the
Father as an exemplar for the disciples' own relationship to
Jesus. Whoever fulfills the commands of Jesus is the one who
abides in Jesus' love. V. 12--as well as v. 17[179]--continues
to develop the subjective aspect of the imperative by concentrating on the one commandment of love and reintroduces as
well the objective aspect of the imperative at the end (for
further specification in v. 13).

      Vv. 12 and 17 almost reproduce one another, using
slightly different forms of the definitional pattern found in
v. 15:8 (the use of a demonstrative with a following epexegetical clause). V. 12 begins with αὕτη ἐστίν and proceeds to
define the commandment of Jesus--ἡ ἐντολὴ ἡ ἐμή, thus changing

the plural form of v. 10 to a singular.[180] V. 17 begins with
ταῦτα followed by the verb form ἐντέλλομαι and proceeds to
define the content of this "commanding."[181] In both cases the
content is exactly alike: ἵνα ἀγαπᾶτε ἀλλήλους, i.e., the
verb ἀγαπᾶν followed by the reflexive pronoun.

Thus, the most important part of abiding in Jesus'
love--and this will turn out to be the main difference between
this section and the Gospel--is the mutual love that the
disciples are enjoined to manifest toward one another. Therefore, returning to the hierarchy of v. 15:9, the disciples can
abide in that hierarchy if and only if they love one another.
The implication, of course, is, once again, that some disciples
are not abiding in this way, are not--in the eyes of the
author--fulfilling the commandment of mutual love.

The previous chapter has disclosed several instances
of this command to love one another--or its synonymous expression, to love one's brother--in I John.[182] Moreover, in
several of these examples the command is not only associated
with tradition (e.g., vv. 2:7-11; 3:11, 23; 4:21),[183] but
also presented in terms of the same definitional pattern of
Jn 15:12 and 17, i.e., a demonstrative followed by an epexegetical ἵνα-clause (e.g., vv. 3:11, 23; 4:21).

Thus, v. 15:12 continues the presentation of the subjective aspect of the imperative, μείνατε ἐν τῇ ἀγάπῃ τῇ ἐμῇ,
by focusing on the one commandment of mutual love. The verse
reintroduces the objective aspect of that imperative as well,
i.e., the mode of Jesus' love for his disciples, by means of
the καθώς clause at the end.[184] In so doing it is clear that
the author grounds this command to love one another--the execution of which is in keeping with Jesus' own relationship to
the Father and thus allows the disciples to preserve their
position in the hierarchy of love--on the specific mode of
Jesus' love for the disciples. The disciples are to love one
another as Jesus loved them. It is this objective mode of
love that is then specified in v. 13.

In an article written in 1927, Martin Dibelius calls
into question the position of vv. 13-15 in this section.[185]
From a literary point of view, he finds these verses to be
disburbing the sequence of thought in the section: vv. 15:1-12

present a unified structure with which vv. 15:16-17 connect
quite well.[186] From the point of view of content, he also
finds two thoughts that are not explicitly connected with
either the death of Jesus or with Jesus' disciples: (1) "Whoever loves, dies for his friends"; (2) "You are my friends."
Therefore, Dibelius concludes that the evangelist has appro-
priated a traditional saying (v. 15:13) and has turned it into
the *Hauptsache* of the passage.[187]

That v. 15:13 might originally have been a common saying cannot be disputed; that possibility must be granted.[188]
However, if the verse is interpreted as having once been an
independent logion, one must admit all the same that it has
been thoroughly reworked and given a "Johannine" ring.[189] On
the other hand, that vv. 15:13-15 interrupt the sequence of
thought and present themes quite foreign to that sequence cannot be granted.[190] V. 15:13 fits in quite well within the
sequence of thought, insofar as it follows and explains the
reintroduction of the objective aspect of the command in v.
15:12 and presupposes the sequence of love outlined in v. 15:9a.

The reference is clearly to Jesus' death on the cross:
this is the mode of love that Jesus showed toward the disciples.
In turn, this mode of love becomes the *exemplar* of love for the
disciples: they are to love one another as Jesus loved them.
The disciples must incorporate into this love for one another--
and consequently, into their love for Jesus, of which loving
one another is an ἐντολή--the mode of Jesus' love for them. At
this point the similarity to I John becomes quite obvious.

As I have shown in the previous chapter, the author of
I John defines the Father's love for man strictly in terms of
the redemptive death of his Son, a mode of love which the community itself must incorporate into its own practice of love.
First of all, in I Jn 3:11-18 two kinds of love are presented:
that of Cain, which is really death, and that of Jesus, which
is really life. In v. 3:16a the latter love is described in
terms of Jesus' redemptive death.[191] V. 3:16b follows this
prototype of love with an injunction addressed to the disciples:
you too must die for one another. In other words, the love of
the disciples for one another must imitate that of the Master
for them.

Again, in paragraph 4:7-11, a section which begins
with the exhortation, 'Αγαπητοί, ἀγαπῶμεν ἀλλήλους, the love
of God for man is defined in vv. 9-10 in terms of Jesus'
redemptive death. V. 4:11, taking this particular mode of
love into account, then enjoins the disciples to love one
another in the same way (εἰ οὕτως ὁ θεὸς . . . καὶ ἡμεῖς
ὀφείλομεν ἀλλήλους ἀγαπᾶν). Finally, vv. 4:16b-21 define God's
love for man in terms of vv. 14-16a, i.e., the redemptive death
of Jesus. V. 4:19 then bases the love of the disciples for one
another on this definition of love.

It was also determined in the previous chapter that
such language--the incorporation of Jesus' death for the
disciples into the love of the disciples for one another--
should not be read literally, but rather symbolically, since
there was no evidence of persecution or bloodshed in the community.[192] The situation of Jn 15:1-17 is very similar to that
of I John: the dispute, as vv. 15:1-8 clearly indicate, is an
inner-Christian one, and the language employed in the section
betrays no sign of persecution, bloodshed, or carnage--situa-
tions which would force one to take a more literal view of the
love command.

In the verses that follow, vv. 14-16, the term φίλοι
of 15:13 is further developed.[193] Their main purpose is to
specify who these φίλοι--these "friends" or "beloved"--are.
The verses really add nothing new to the contents of the section; rather, they parallel not only the first subsection, as
Bultmann points out,[194] but also vv. 9-10 as well. And, in
doing so, they explicitly give expression to the exclusiveness
of the object of love.

First of all, vv. 15-16a, with their emphasis on the
present status of the believers, parallel both vv. 15:3 and
15:9. The latter verse had posited a hierarchy of love which
included the disciples as the lowest rung of that hierarchy;
the former had referred to a "cleansing" of the disciples by
Jesus' word (ὁ λόγος). Now, vv. 15-16a speak of a revelation
made to the disciples which has lifted them from the category
of δοῦλοι to that of φίλοι.[195] In all three cases, therefore,
a certain status is conferred upon those who believe.[196]

Secondly, v. 14, with its emphasis on the ongoing duty
of the disciples, parallels quite clearly vv. 15:4a and 15:9b.
The latter verse states by means of an imperative that the
hierarchy of love must be maintained; the former, likewise,
indicates that Jesus' word must be preserved. Now, v. 14 makes
it very clear that the status of being φίλοι is dependent upon
certain obligations.[197] In all three cases, therefore, the
conferred status of the believers is not final or everlasting;
it has to be adhered to faithfully by those who possess it--
indicating at all times that there are some who are not doing
so and who, in the eyes of the author, can no longer claim to
be φίλοι.

As I have already mentioned, it emerges very clearly
from these verses who the φίλοι are: they are the ones who
accept the revelation and preserve it. These are the ones who
have benefited from Jesus' death and are now bound to keep the
commands and to love one another. The single commandment of
mutual love--love for one another--extends only to fellow-
believers who continue as fellow-believers, who abide in what
they believe. The exclusiveness of the object of love could
not be more clearly outlined. This very same exclusiveness
appears in I Jn 5:1-2: against the background of those who
claim to love God directly but ignore their brother (vv. 4:10,
20), the author claims that love of God (ὁ ἀγαπῶν τὸν γεννήσαντα) must include love of the believer (ἀγαπᾷ καὶ τὸν γεγεννημένον ἐξ αὐτοῦ).[198]

The second subsection ends in parallelism with the
first subsection. Just as v. 15:7 provides a reward for those
who abide (v. 15:4), so v. 15:16 provides a reward for those
who execute Jesus' commandments (v. 15:14).[199] In both cases,
the faithful believer is assured that his petitions will be
heard and granted. Finally, in v. 15:17 the commandment of
v. 15:12 is repeated, as it has already been pointed out, form-
ing an *inclusio*. Since v. 15:16b takes up the thought of
v. 15:14, the author emphasizes in this conclusion to the subsection the one command to which all others can be reduced
(from the ἐντολαί to the ἐντολή): the love command.

Summary and Conclusion. I began this exegesis of
vv. 15:1-17 with the one objective in mind of determining
whether the passage could reasonably be attributed to the
author of I John or, in a more modest and realistic claim, to
an author whose life situation duplicated that of I John.
J. Becker, as I have shown, espoused precisely such a claim,
but based it entirely on the ethical concerns of the section,
concerns which, in his opinion, paralleled the similarly
ethical interests of the First Letter. I felt, however, that
such an attribution bypassed a very central concern of the
Letter, i.e., the christological doctrine of the opponents.
If the section does indeed belong to a *Sitz im Leben* resembling
that of I John, surely one would find either hidden or open
references to this other side of the struggle as well. It is
my opinion that such concerns do indeed surface in vv. 15:1-17.

    As Bultmann remarks in his *Commentary*, vv. 15:9-17 do
seem to develop vv. 15:1-8:[200] in addition to the parallelism
that exists between both subsections, it is evident that the
aorist imperative of v. 15:9b--μείνατε ἐν τῇ ἀγάπῃ τῇ ἐμῇ--does
indeed take up and develop the aorist imperative of v. 15:4a
--μείνατε ἐν ἐμοί, κἀγὼ ἐν ὑμῖν. In each case the object of
the preposition ἐν, viz., ἐμοί or τῇ ἀγάπῃ τῇ ἐμῇ, dominates
thematically the verses that follow. The question, therefore,
becomes: what is the relationship between the two subsections
of 15:1-17? Bultmann himself interprets the relationship in a
rather abstract manner, paying more attention to the strictly
theological relationship between πίστις and ἀγάπη than to the
implied *Sitz im Leben*.[201] Thus, he sees the command of love
as the essential element in constancy of faith; faith is authentic only when it results in love.[202] When a man becomes a
believer, Bultmann continues, he not only accepts the word that
he hears, but he also "anticipates the concrete decisions called
for by the claims of his brother in everyday life."[203] The
juxtaposition of vv. 15:1-8 and vv. 15:9-17 gives expression to
this fundamental unity. Such a solution, however, sheds very
little light, if any, on the *Sitz im Leben* of the discourse.

    This issue of the relationship of the two subsections
has proved to be rather interesting really. It has become a
battleground for πίστις and ἀγάπη, a sort of head-on meeting

for exegetes of both the "redactional" and the "transpositional" schools who accept vv. 15:1-17 as a unity and v. 15:9
as the beginning of a subsection. For example, Jürgen Becker,
who subscribes to the redactional theory, denies any role whatsoever to πίστις in vv. 15:1-17; it is as if the second imperative (v. 15:9b) totally recapitulated the first (v. 15:4a).[204]
Likewise, J. Heise and M. Lattke, both of whom subscribe to
the transpositional theory, place all the emphasis of the passage on πίστις; again, it is as if the first imperative totally
recapitulated the second one.[205] Yet, on the basis of the exegesis above, a *via media* suggests itself as the most plausible
solution.

First of all, the subsection 15:1-8 is concerned
directly with the issue of faith. The constant exhortations
of the author "to abide" are indicative of this concern. Moreover, the contrast presented is not one of faith versus unbe-
lief--as it would be the case in a conflict with the synagogue;
rather, the contrast is one of faith versus loss of faith. The
people who are being addressed by the author are believers,
Christians (v. 15:3), who are, in the eyes of the author, in
danger of losing this belief. Thus, the object of these exhortations, the object of the expression μένειν ἐν, is, for the
most part, Jesus himself: (ἐν ἐμοί) 15:4[2], 5, 6, 7; (ἐν τῇ
ἀμπέλῳ) 15:4. Some have either abandoned Jesus or are in
danger of doing so, or both. Furthermore, the use of the adjective ἀληθινός in v. 15:1 to modify ἡ ἄμπελος indicates that
this loss of faith should be construed as an "aberration" of
faith; the contrast being presented would thus be correct faith
versus incorrect faith. There are some who are presenting a
view of Jesus which is not the "true" one, and this misunderstanding is, in the eyes of the author, tantamount to an
abandonment of Jesus.

Secondly, the subsection 15:9-17 is unquestionably
concerned with the issue of ethical behavior. The author's
elaboration of the subjective aspect of the aorist imperative
of v. 9b in vv. 10, 12-13, 14, 16b, 17--i.e., what it is that
the disciples must do--gives an indication of the problem at
hand. In view of vv. 10 and 14, it would seem that some
believers (15:15-16a) are not keeping Jesus' commands; in view

of vv. 15:12-13, 17, it would seem that these Christians are, above all, not manifesting the love for one another which succinctly summarizes the commands of Jesus.

The problem in the community which underlies 15:1-17 is a dual one: it involves πίστις, *pace* Becker, and it involves ἀγάπη, *pace* Lattke and Heise. I would suggest, therefore, that this dual problem in the community reflects a situation very much like that of I John. The following similarities should be taken into consideration: (1) the juxtaposition of the themes of faith and love is quite characteristic of the structure of the Letter itself: the Letter, as shown in the preceding chapter, presents a succession of largely ethical and largely dogmatic sections;[206] (2) the inner-Christian character of the controversy--rather than Jewish versus Christian--removes vv. 15:1-17 from the immediate problems of the Gospel and thrusts them into the thought-world of the First Letter, where an inner-Christian struggle also prevails; (3) the multiple terminological and theological affinities which both writings share and which have been described in the course of the chapter, indicate that the problems underlying both writings are extremely similar.[207]

I would take this line of argumentation a step further. It was argued in the preceding chapter that the love command in I John includes--besides certain concrete ethical norms--the espousal and confession of the correct christological formula outlined in the Letter, i.e., to believe correctly was to show love for the brethren; not to do so amounted to hatred.[208] It is my opinion that the same situation may be reconstructed in Jn 15:1-17 and that such a reconstruction explains the relationship between the two subsections as well. The process of reconstruction is not as simple as it is in I John--and that proved difficult enough--on account of the genre being employed by the author, viz., a discourse uttered by Jesus.[209]

First of all, one finds the possibility that a believer may cease to "abide in Jesus," a possibility which is to be construed as a misunderstanding of who Jesus is, viz., a "false" vine. Secondly, one also finds the possibility that a believer may cease to abide in the love of Jesus, a possibility which is presented in terms of the failure to execute Jesus' commands

and, specifically, the command to love one another. Finally,
one also finds a "grounding" of the love command in the mode
of love which Jesus showed toward his disciples (καθὼς ἠγάπησα
ὑμᾶς), a mode of love which is described in v. 15:13 in terms
of Jesus' redemptive death.

I would argue, therefore, that this καθὼς clause of
v. 15:12b--and its elaboration in v. 15:13--provides the key
not only to the relationship between the two subsections of
Jn 15:1-17 with their respective emphases on "faith" and "love,"
but also to the *Sitz im Leben* of the entire discourse.

First of all, the need to ground the love of the disciples for one another on the mode of Jesus' love for them,
viz., his death on their behalf (τὴν ψυχὴν θεῖναι ὑπὲρ ἡμῶν),
and the absence of any evidence that such a sacrifice is being
demanded from members of the community in a literal way indicate that what such a "grounding," such an "incorporation,"
entails is the acceptance of that mode of love, of Jesus'
redemptive death, on the part of the disciples. In this
respect, the καθὼς clause of v. 15:12b sheds light on vv.
15:1-8 and, specifically, on the nature of the "true" vine:
belief in Jesus as Christ and Son of God implies a belief in
his death as Christ and Son of God. A denial of that death,
i.e., the development of a "false" vine, would seem to point
to the existence of a docetic understanding of Jesus Christ in
the community.

Secondly, the inclusion of such an acceptance or belief
within the love command clearly indicates that correct belief
is a form, and indeed the highest form, of mutual love. But
there are other forms. Mutual love also includes other commands of Jesus, the execution of which may also be characterized as "loving one another." In this respect, the καθὼς
clause also sheds light on vv. 15:9-17: in accepting the "true"
vine, the believer also accepts the accompanying ἐντολαί and
acts in accordance with them. A denial of these commands, i.e.,
a failure to observe them, would seem to point to the existence
of a "libertine" understanding of Christian ethics and Christian behavior (the author does not provide any clues in this
brief section as to the exact relationship between docetism

and libertinism other than the acceptance of the one involves
the adoption of the other).

Thus, vv. 15:9-17 may be interpreted as developing
vv. 15:1-8 in three ways: (1) insofar as the nature of the
"true" vine in which all believers must "abide" is clearly
specified in vv. 12b-13; (2) insofar as belief in that "true"
vine, i.e., correct belief is incorporated into the love command itself--love for one another begins with correct belief
in Jesus; (3) insofar as implications of that belief--most
probably concrete ethical practices--are introduced and incorporated into the love command as well. Unfortunately, the
author does not describe any such practice in detail.

Therefore, as in the case of I John, the love command
of Jn 15:1-17 implies and demands correct belief--against a
docetic understanding of Jesus as the Christ and the Son of
God; and correct praxis--against a libertine type of behavior,
apparently characterized by a bypassing of Jesus' commands.
As such, the author attacks with one main sweep the two main
"deviations" within the community and allows no *via media*:
the branch that does not "produce fruit" is "removed" by the
Father (v. 15:2) and also "cast aside and burned" (v. 15:6).[210]
In conclusion, given the similarities in structure, background,
terminology and theology that vv. 15:1-17 have in common with
I John, it is possible to answer the initial question of this
chapter in a positive manner--Jn 15:1-17 may very reasonably
be assigned to a life-situation paralleling or duplicating
that of I John. I would certainly concur with Becker's judgment on this matter, but for reasons which include but go
beyond--and *must* go beyond--his own argumentation.

Jn 13:34-35--A New Commandment

Demarcation of the Passage. In contrast to the considerable amount of time devoted to Jn 15:1-17 as well as to
the other sections comprising the second discourse, Becker
does not spend much time on Jn 13:34-35. Yet, these verses
are, in my opinion, rather important with regard to the above
section, Jn 15:1-17, since they reproduce almost *verbatim* the
love commandment of that section. His position, however, can

be reconstructed from the different comments he makes on the
verses throughout the article.

First of all, he is of the opinion that these two
verses interrupt the smooth progression of thought which
exists in the context.[211] That progression may be outlined
as follows: upon Judas' departure from the scene (v. 13:30),
Jesus launches into what constitutes the first Farewell Discourse of the Gospel (vv. 13:31-14:31). The discourse begins
with a comment on the imminent glorification of the Son, thus
anticipating the hour of Jesus' death and departure from this
world (vv. 13:31-32).[212] In view of this departure, Jesus
addresses the disciples, telling them that they cannot come
with him at this time: ὅπου ἐγὼ ὑπάγω ὑμεῖς οὐ δύνασθε ἐλθεῖν,
καὶ ὑμῖν λέγω ἄρτι (v. 13:33). This saying then gives way to
a dialogue with Peter (vv. 13:36-38), which centers on the
theme of ὑπάγειν.[213] The problem lies in the fact that vv. 34-
35 clearly interrupt the progression of thought, the theme of
ὑπάγειν.

Furthermore, not only do they interrupt that particular theme, but their own thematic concern is quite removed from
that of its context.[214] This concern also deviates, Becker
continues, quite clearly from the situation of an imminent
departure.[215] The conclusion that Becker comes to is that
vv. 13:34-35 represent an addition to their present context.[216]
On both counts I agree wholeheartedly with his proposal: vv.
13:34-35 are indeed a later addition and do not belong in the
context. One must therefore attempt to trace the origin of
these two verses.

Theological "Akzent" of vv. 13:34-35. Becker himself
alludes to the origin of these two verses in a rather minor
remark made in the course of his comments on Jn 15:1-17.
Therein he observes very concisely that Jn 13:34-35 belong
"sachlich" to vv. 15:1-17 and that both passages can be differentiated from the Gospel.[217] Presumably, although he does
not say so *expressis verbis*, the two verses were written by
the same hand that produced Jn 15:1-17. In this conclusion
he is also not alone: both Richter[218] and Schnackenburg[219]
would concur with this judgment, and all three would further,

given their already stated positions on the nature of the
redaction, bring these verses into the sphere of I John and
its life situation. That Jn 13:34-35 either stands or falls
with Jn 15:1-17, i.e., it is either part of the Gospel or part
of the redaction depending on the judgment passed on the latter
section, may be demonstrated by the parallelisms that exist
between them. Furthermore, that both belong to the sphere of
I John follows both from the above analysis of Jn 15:1-17 and
from the content of these verses by themselves. The following
points should be taken into consideration:

(1) First of all, from the point of view of terminology, v. 13:34 employs the same word for "command," i.e.,
ἐντολή, that the other two expressions in vv. 15:12, 17 use
--the latter, of course, in verbal form. Moreover, its singular form is parallel to that of v. 15:12 and should be seen
as a particular stress on the basic character of this commandment.[220]

(2) From the point of view of grammatical structure,
v. 13:34 is also very close to vv. 15:12, 17, insofar as it
too presents the commandment of love in the form of an epexegetical ἵνα-clause, although in this case the preceding demonstrative pronoun is not to be found.[221]

(3) Also from the point of view of terminology, it
should not go unmentioned that the commandment itself, as in
vv. 15:12, 17, employs the reciprocal pronoun, as the object
of the verb, ἵνα ἀγαπᾶτε ἀλλήλους. Moreover, these are the
only three occasions in the Gospel that the reciprocal pronoun
acts as the direct object of ἀγαπᾶν.[222]

(4) V. 13:34b proceeds to ground this commandment to
love one another upon the mode of Jesus' love toward his disciples. The disciples are to love one another both because
and as Jesus loved them.[223] This instance of a καθώς clause
modifying an epexegetical ἵνα-clause is duplicated in v.
15:12.[224] However, in contrast to the latter verse and its
sequence in v. 15:13, v. 13:34b does not elaborate on the mode
of Jesus' love.

(5) V. 13:35 defines the discipleship of Jesus' followers in terms of their execution of the commandment of love.
The grammatical structure of this verse is once again the

familiar one of a demonstrative pronoun followed by an epexegetical clause, which in this case begins with the conditional
particle ἐάν. Furthermore, the verse introduces the demonstrative pronoun with the expression γινώσκειν ἐν, which, as
Schnackenburg observes,[225] is quite common in the Letter, but
foreign to the Gospel.[226]

(6) This definition of discipleship (ὅτι ἐμοὶ μαθηταί
ἐστε) in terms of the commandment of love—which is now given
in the form of a conditional sentence, ἐὰν ἀγάπην ἔχητε ἐν
ἀλλήλοις—[227] finds an indirect parallel in v. 15:8. Although
the theme of being recognized or acknowledged by all (πάντες)
is missing in that verse, one does find an association of discipleship (γενήσεσθε ἐμοὶ μαθηταί) and behavior particular to
such discipleship (καρπὸν πολὺν φέρητε). Moreover, this
behavior includes both an abiding in correct belief (vv. 15:2,
5) and an abiding in mutual love (v. 15:16), which includes
correct belief.

(7) Finally, v. 13:34 characterizes this command of
Jesus as a "new" command. In this regard, the verse is quite
close to I Jn 2:7-11 where the command of love is also termed
a "new" command.[228]

The conclusions that follow from these observations
are inevitable. On the one hand, given the great similarities
in terminology, structure, and theological content, it seems
clear that whoever wrote Jn 15:1-17 also wrote Jn 13:34-35.
On the other hand, it must be granted as well that these two
verses belong to the sphere of I John not only because of their
relationship to Jn 15:1-17, but also on the basis of their own
content as well. I am thinking primarily at this point of
those observations outlined in points #5 and #7 above.

From a theological point of view, Jn 13:34-35 represents what one might call the essence or nucleus of the larger
section, Jn 15:1-17. Despite its brevity, one is able to find
in these two verses traces of that relationship between "faith"
and "love" postulated of Jn 15:1-17. For example, the need to
ground the love of the disciples for one another on the mode
of Jesus' love for them should be taken as a demand for the
acceptance of that mode of love on their part—thus arguing
against a docetic interpretation of Jesus as the Christ

and the Son of God. Similarly, the emphasis on the love command should be seen as going beyond the inclusion of correct
belief within that command to comprehend certain ethical norms
or rules also ascribed to Jesus--thus arguing against a libertine interpretation of Christian ethics and Christian behavior.[229] Once again, therefore, the author attacks with one
main sweep the two main "deviations" within the community.

In conclusion, I would argue that it is possible to
answer the initial question of the chapter in a positive manner: Jn 13:34-35 may also very reasonably be assigned to a
Sitz im Leben paralleling or duplicating that of I John. As
in the case of Jn 15:1-17, I would concur with Becker's judgment on the matter, but would make the main criterion for such
a judgment much more specific.

Jn 15:18-16:15--The Hatred of the World

Demarcation of the Passage. I would like to begin
this section by observing that neither ἀγάπη nor ἀγαπᾶν is
to be found within it.[230] Nevertheless, its opposite, μισεῖν,
occurs a total of seven times (one of which is a quotation
from Ps 49:5). On account of the heavy concentration of this
verb in this one section--compared with five other times in
the Gospel (3:20; 7:7[2]; 12:25; 17:14)--and of the attribution
of the passage to the life situation of I John by Becker, I
have decided to consider it briefly.

The demarcation of the beginning of this section was
already alluded to in the isolation of the self-contained unit,
Jn 15:1-17. What constitutes and grounds the end of the one
section also marks the beginning of a new section, a new discourse: with v. 15:18 a new theme takes over altogether.[231]
This new discourse, Becker argues, has been artificially connected to the former one by means of two redactional devices:
(1) the inherent antithesis between ἀγαπᾶν and μισεῖν;[232]
(2) the remarks of vv. 15:19b-20a. The first remark, 15:19b,
develops the theme of "choosing" introduced in v. 15:16, ἀλλ'
ἐγὼ ἐξελεξάμην ὑμᾶς ἐκ τοῦ κόσμου, while the second remark
recalls a saying of Jesus from v. 13:16, οὐκ ἔστιν δοῦλος
μείζων τοῦ κυρίου αὐτοῦ.[233]

As far as the demarcation of the end of this independent discourse is concerned, Becker is one of the few exegetes
who presents v. 16:15 as the end.[234] Most exegetes would not
extend the discourse that far.[235] First of all, he divides
this long tract into two main sections: vv. 15:18-16:4a,
which deals with the hatred of the world, and vv. 16:4b-15,
which deals primarily with the Paraclete "und bringt einen
ungestörten Ablauf."[236] Secondly, he sees v. 16:16 as the
beginning of a new discourse, which is artificially connected
to the former one by means of v. 16:17c--ὅτι ὑπάγω πρὸς τὸν
πατέρα (thus recalling vv. 16:5, 10).[237]

     At this point I would have to disagree with Becker's
outline of the discourse and accept the position that this
independent unit concludes with v. 16:4a. In view of the
argumentation which may be marshalled in its favor, the latter
view is a much more reasonable position. First of all, the
opposition and persecution of the world described in vv. 15:18-
25 find their climax--and concretization, as Becker himself
argues[238]--in vv. 16:1-4a. With these verses, moreover, the
theme of persecution comes to an end. Secondly, it is only
with v. 16:4b that the theme of departure explicitly enters
into the picture. Vv. 15:18-16:4a may, like vv. 15:1-17, be
termed a discourse, but not a Farewell Discourse.[239] Thirdly,
the theme of vv. 16:4bff. deviates considerably from that of
vv. 15:18-16:4a; all of a sudden, one finds a development of
the figure of the Paraclete (quite independently of vv. 15:26-
27). Moreover, the role of the Paraclete in vv. 16:8-11 vis-à-
vis the world is not really connected at all with the theme of
hatred.[240] Fourthly, Raymond Brown has traced in detail the
parallelisms that exist between vv. 13:31-14:31 and 16:4b-
33.[241] Finally, one may also adduce the apparently concluding
character of the phrase ταῦτα λελάληκα ὑμῖν.[242]

     Division of the Passage. If one leaves out of con-
sideration vv. 16:4b-15--what Becker considers to be the second
major portion of 15:18-16:15[243]--one finds three subsections:
15:18-25; 15:26-27; 16:1-4a.[244] For the purposes of this study,
this threefold division is satisfactory (whether a fourth section is to be posited or not is relatively unimportant). With

regard to the first subsection, Becker follows Bultmann in
positing an underlying source which has been commented upon
by the author;[245] he does not, however, address himself to the
purpose of this source. In the second subsection Becker sees
an interruption of the progression of thought and concludes
that the verses "sind kontextfremdes Gut, das illegitimerweise
seinen jetzigen Platz eingenommen hat."[246] The third subsection represents the concretization--and this is to me a very
accurate interpretation--of the hatred described in the first
subsection.

   Theological "Akzent" of vv. 15:18-16:15. As in the
case of Jn 15:1-17, Becker observes a significant shift of
emphasis in this section as well. In contrast to the original
Farewell Discourse of 13:31-14:31 and the Gospel itself, one
finds in these verses a movement away from soteriology and
Christology toward ecclesiastical concerns.

   Becker cites three primary indications of this movement or shift. First of all, one notices in these verses the
emergence of an ecclesiastical dualism ("verkirchlichte Dualis-
mus"). The term ὁ κόσμος is now defined solely as opposition
to and hatred toward the community; there can exist no possibility of communication between the two spheres--"world" and
community.[247] Secondly, as part of this ecclesiastical dualism
one also notices the corresponding connotations in the terminology employed therein. For example, the term ἡ ἀλήθεια
refers no longer to Jesus alone, but to his doctrine as
well.[248] Finally, the exalted Jesus is no longer the "Christus
präsens" of vv. 13:31-14:31. The exalted Jesus is now portrayed as having sent his Paraclete, who brings to the community his [Jesus'] doctrine.[249]

   On the basis of these three observations, Becker concludes that vv. 15:18-16:15 should also be understood as an
ecclesiastical addition to the Gospel. As in the case of
vv. 15:1-17, these verses are to be placed within the life
situation of the First Letter, where the very same emphasis
on doctrine becomes rather prominent.[250] It is my opinion,
however, that this is really an unwarranted judgment. First
of all, the last two indications leading to this judgment stem

solely from the third Paraclete saying, i.e., Jn 16:12-15, and
these verses form part of that section which is to be separated
from the independent unity of vv. 15:18-16:4a, i.e., vv. 16:4b-
15. Thus, all one is left with is the first argument: the
emergence of an ecclesiastical dualism. Secondly, therefore,
one must ask, is this argument sufficient to warrant the attribution of a *Sitz im Leben* to it which duplicates that of
I John? Several arguments militate against this step.

(1) As in vv. 15:1-17, one would expect to see in this
section as well a reference of some sort to the possibility
that Christian believers, members of the community, may "abandon" their faith (or have indeed already done so). The problem within Jn 15:1-17--and within I John as well--was shown to
be an inner-Christian, inner-community, controversy. Vv. 15:18-
16:4a do not betray any signs at all of such a struggle. The
conflict, as Becker himself points out, is one of complete
dualism between community (believers) and world (unbe-
lievers).[251] The conflict may have been ecclesiastical in
character, but the *ecclesia* therein portrayed shows no signs
of rupture.

(2) An overview of the term μισεῖν in the First Letter
yields a very similar argument. Exegetes have pointed out the
similarities that exist between Jn 15:18-25 and I Jn 3:13--μὴ
θαυμάζετε, ἀδελφοί, εἰ μισεῖ ὑμᾶς ὁ κόσμος.[252] It should be
kept in mind, however, that the κόσμος alluded to in I Jn 3:16
includes the false brethren or teachers (see I Jn 2:19; 4:1;
II Jn 7--these people have gone forth "into the world").
Therefore, given the situation in the community, this hatred
of the world takes on the characteristics, in the eyes of the
author, of the behavior exhibited by the false teachers.[253]
By way of contrast, the κόσμος of Jn 15:18-16:4a does not
include and probably does not even know of such a group. The
community is still struggling with the Jewish synagogue.[254]

(3) This last argument introduces the present one: the
nature which the μισεῖν of the world displays in vv. 15:18-
16:4a is in no way that of I John. As I mentioned previously,
vv. 16:1-4a represent the climax and concretization of vv.
15:18-25; therein the ἀλλὰ ταῦτα πάντα ποιήσουσιν of v. 15:21
are given in detail.[255] "Hatred" takes on the following

modes: (a) exclusion from the synagogue (ἀποσυναγώγους ποιήσουσιν ὑμᾶς); (b) persecution to the point of death (πᾶς ὁ
ἀποκτείνας ὑμᾶς). These verses are crucial to J. L. Martyn's
view of the *Sitz im Leben* of the Gospel, viz., troubled by the
number of defections from within, the *Gerousia* of a Hellenis-
tic Jewish community adopts severe measures against the defec-
tors, including a synagogal ban and, in some cases, assassina-
tion.[256]

As mentioned in the previous chapter (and affirmed of
vv. 15:1-17 as well), I John shows absolutely no signs of persecution or bloodshed. The theme of hatred is confined to the
christological aberration which has emerged from within the
community and to the libertine behavior which such an aberration entails and encourages. This may be seen quite readily
in the use of the verb μισεῖν in the Letter. Aside from
v. 3:13, in all four remaining instances (2:9, 11; 3:15; 4:20)
the verb is used in conjunction with the noun ἀδελφός, indicating thereby the contrary of that which is meant in the
Letter by the expression ἀγαπᾶν τοὺς ἀδελφοὺς αὐτοῦ.[257]

It is my opinion, therefore, that vv. 15:18-16:4a cannot by any reasonable standards be assigned to a life situation paralleling that of I John. The problems and concerns
of the author are quite removed from those of I John and
indeed quite close to those of the Gospel, given the Jewish
controversy which dominates the entire passage. If the passage is not to be assigned to the evangelist,[258] then it
belongs to a period where the concerns of the evangelist were
still very much alive and where the rupture of the community
reflected in I John and Jn 15:1-17 had not yet occurred.
Becker's attribution is quite unwarranted.

Concluding Comments

In the preceding pages I have dealt with those sections
of the Farewell Discourses that J. Becker assigns to a *Sitz im
Leben* paralleling that of I John, i.e., 15:1-17; 13:34-35;
15:18-16:15. In doing so, I have had two main objectives in
mind: (1) to determine by means of literary criticism whether
these sections represent literary unities as they were outlined

by Becker; and (2) to determine by means of a redaction-
critical study of the terms ἀγάπη/ἀγαπᾶν within these sections
whether they could be reasonably assigned to the life situation of the author of I John.

The results may be summarized as follows:

(1) I believe that Becker was correct in identifying
vv. 15:1-17 as a self-contained literary unity. Within the
second discourse, i.e., chs. 15-17, this section stands as an
originally independent unity. I also believe that Becker was
correct in assigning the verses to the *Sitz im Leben* of I John;
however, I did find his criterion for so doing--the danger that
members of the community would relinquish their status because
of certain ethical problems--to be insufficient, since he
failed to take into account both the other side of the ἀγάπη
controversy in I John, i.e., the christological aberration of
the opponents, and the "faith" content of vv. 15:1-17 themselves. In my own redaction-critical study of the passage, I
found the verses to contain very definite references to this
other side of the struggle as well and, on that basis, found
it reasonable to assign them to a *Sitz im Leben* duplicating
that of I John.

(2) I also believe that Becker was correct in identifying vv. 13:34-35 as an addition to the original Farewell
Discourse (vv. 13:31-14:31), in associating these verses with
Jn 15:1-17, and in ascribing them as well to the life situation of the First Letter. Besides their clear association
with and relationship to Jn 15:1-17--a relationship which
demands common authorship--I found that these verses, despite
their brevity, contained traces of that double ἀγάπη defense
that the author of I John employs against his opponents and,
on that basis, found it reasonable to assign them to that life
situation as well.

(3) Finally, I believe that Becker was incorrect in
the demarcation of the third section, vv. 15:18-16:15. It is
my opinion that vv. 16:4b-15 form an independent literary
unity and should not be connected with vv. 15:18-16:4a.
Furthermore, I find it impossible to see this last section as

coming from the life situation of I John: its interests and
concerns were found to be a lot closer to those of the Gospel
--specifically in terms of the synagogal opposition--than to
those of the First Letter.

CHAPTER IV

'Αγάπη AND 'Αγαπᾶν IN THE FOURTH GOSPEL

Granted that certain sections or verses within the
Farewell Discourse of the Gospel of John, viz., vv. 15:1-17
and 13:34-35, may be reasonably assigned to a *Sitz im Leben*
paralleling that of I John on account of the many terminological, grammatical, and theological affinities, it remains to be
seen from a methodological point of view whether such an understanding of ἀγάπη/ἀγαπᾶν can be differentiated from that
exhibited in the remaining chapters of the Fourth Gospel. It
is the purpose of this chapter, therefore, to uncover the meaning of ἀγάπη/ἀγαπᾶν in those sections of the Gospel the authenticity of which no one has questioned.[1]

If one excludes Jn 13:34-35 and 15:1-17 (as well as
chapter 21), one is left with the following occurrences of
ἀγάπη: 5:42; 17:26; and of ἀγαπᾶν: 3:16, 19, 35; 8:42; 10:17;
11:5; 12:43; 13:1[2]; 13:23; 14:15, 21[3], 23[2], 24, 28, 31; 17:23,
24, 26; 19:26. From this list, however, two classes of
examples may be left out of consideration: (1) the first
class consists of references to the figure of the Beloved
Disciple (vv. 13:23; 19:26). The problem of the identity of
this disciple and his importance for the Gospel and its tradition may be separated altogether, without damage, from the
immediate concern of this study;[2] (2) the second class consists of those verses where Jesus is said to love a particular
individual (v. 11:5).[3] This latter usage does not bear that
same theological weight of the other passages (they represent
what Lattke calls "das nicht-charakteristische Vorkommen dieser
Begriffe.")[4]

Besides these examples one must also consider the
other term used by the Fourth Gospel to convey the idea of
love, i.e., the verb φιλέω (5:20; 11:3, 36; 12:25; 15:19;
16:27[2]; 20:2). Although this particular term does not occur

133

in I John, one is justified nonetheless in including it along-
side ἀγαπάω, since the two verbs are synonymous in the Gospel
(e.g., vv. 3:35 and 5:20).[5] However, one must also excise
from the above list any examples of the two classes mentioned
above: references to the Beloved Disciple (v. 20:2) and to
particular individuals (vv. 11:3, 36).

    In the following chart I shall distribute the remain-
ing instances of ἀγάπη, ἀγαπάω and φιλέω according to the following division: (a) section I represents the first twelve
chapters of the Gospel, viz., the so-called Book of Signs;
(b) section II, the Washing of the Feet episode, which is
highly problematical in itself; (c) section III, the original
Farewell Discourse (minus a few minor additions); (d) sections IV and V, independent literary units within the Farewell Discourse; (e) section VI, the prayer of Jesus; (f) section VII, the Passion and Resurrection narratives.

I.	Jn 1-12	Chapter 3	3:16, 19, 35		3
		" 5	5:20, 42		2
		" 8	8:42		1
		" 10	10:17		1
		" 12	12:25, 43		2
					9
II.	Jn 13:1-30		$13:1^2$		-2
III.	Jn 13:31-14:31		$14:15, 21^4, 23^2$		
			24, 28, 31		-10
IV.	Jn 15:18-16:4a		15:19		-1
V.	Jn 16:4b-33		$16:27^2$		-2
VI	Jn 17		$17:23, 24, 26^2$		-3
VII.	Jn 18-20				-0

    A cursory reading of the chart indicates that the
heaviest concentration of the three terms--and it should be
pointed out that only variations of ἀγαπᾶν are to be found in
the section--takes place in section III, i.e., the original
Farewell Discourse of the Gospel. In the brief space of
slightly over a chapter (and excluding vv. 13:34-35), one
finds ten instances of the verb "to love." By way of contrast,
Jn 1-12 present a combined total of nine examples, while Jn
18-20 contain no examples at all. Finally, the other remaining sections--13:1-30; 15:18-16:4a, 16:4b-33; 17--provide a

total of eight occurrences. However, because of the association of these sections with the redaction one must be specially
careful when considering the evidence presented therein.

On the basis of this evidence, therefore, I propose to
examine the meaning of ἀγάπη/ἀγαπᾶν (and the synonymous φιλεῖν)
in the Fourth Gospel by taking the original Farewell Discourse
as the point of departure, i.e., Jn 13:31-14:31. Furthermore,
since the discourse presents four relationships of love, I
propose to examine this section in terms of these four relationships. These relationships are: (1) the love of the disciples for Jesus (vv. 14:15, 21, 23a, 28); (2) the love of the
Father for the disciples (vv. 14:21b, 23b); (3) the love of
Jesus for the disciples (v. 14:21c); and (4) Jesus' love for
the Father (v. 14:31). The selection of this particular point
of departure, aside from the high incidence of the term in
question, will facilitate a comparison with vv. 13:34-35 and
15:1-17, given their contiguity and inclusion within the same
discourse.

I also propose to consider those examples of ἀγάπη/
ἀγαπᾶν (and the synonymous φιλεῖν) that qualify in terms of
these four relationships of love given in vv. 13:31-14:31.
The following chart shows to what extent these relationships
are mentioned in the remainder of the Gospel:

I.	Love of disciples for Jesus	8:42, 12:43, 16:27
II.	Love of Father for disciples	16:27, 17:23
III.	Love of Jesus for disciples	_____
IV.	Love of Jesus for the Father	3:35; 5:20; 10:17

Since this procedure does not account for all the remaining
examples of these three terms, I propose to consider these
individually (3:16; 3:19; 5:42; 12:25; 13:1; 15:19) in order
to see whether they shed any further light on the meaning of
love in the Fourth Gospel.

I should like to begin this exegesis of the love passages, therefore, by considering the structure of the point of
departure, i.e., the original Farewell Discourse, Jn 13:31-
14:31.

Structure of Jn 13:31-14:31

In the examination of vv. 13:34-35 in the last chapter, it was shown that J. Becker's excision of these two verses as a later addition was not an uncommon exegetical position[6] and that one of the main reasons given for the excision is the intrusive character of these two verses, i.e., they seem to interrupt the smooth flow of thought in the context.[7] The "context" presupposed by this exegetical opinion and the "context" meant in my own acceptance of that position is constituted by vv. 13:31-38. Furthermore, it is this "context," these verses, that are also frequently suggested as the introduction to the original Farewell Discourse. The suggestion has much to commend itself.

It is clear, on the one hand, that with v. 13:31 a new major section begins. Judas leaves the company of the disciples at the urging of Jesus (v. 12:27), and the latter then turns to the circle of the disciples for instruction. This instruction has to do--from the point of view of the story--with the anticipated death of the Son of Man and his return to the Father. The theme of mutual glorification in vv. 13:31b-32 sets the tone for the entire discourse: as he is about to depart from the hostile "world," the Son of Man turns to the circle of true disciples--now that Judas has left--and their situation in this "world."[8]

On the other hand, the first section, i.e., the introduction, of this discourse concludes with v. 13:38. At this point the dialogue with Peter (which consists of two question and answer cycles) comes to an end, and Jesus from now on addresses the disciples as a body, i.e., using the second person plural form of the verb: μὴ ταρασσέσθω ὑμῶν ἡ καρδία.[9] Furthermore, the imperative of v. 14:1a, which is a word of comfort, is almost exactly reproduced in v. 14:27c,[10] indicating a clear case of inclusion which must be separated from vv. 13:31-38.

As an introduction to vv. 14:1-31, the role of these verses is quite clear. Not only do vv. 13:31-32 place this entire discourse within the perspective of Jesus' departure, but vv. 13:33, 36-38 begin to address themselves to the

situation of the disciples after the coming glorification of
the Son of Man. These verses, therefore, present the problem
and begin to offer a solution, a word of comfort, to it.
These two sides of the same event will recur again and again
throughout the discourse.

With only a few exceptions, and most notably Rudolf
Bultmann,[11] scholars have consistently pointed out the introductory character of these verses (including or excluding
vv. 13:34-35, as the case may be).[12] Scholarly disagreement
lies not so much in the question of the extent of the introduction, but rather in the selection of the chapters to which
these verses provide an introduction, i.e., are they an introduction to vv. 14:1-31, or are they an introduction to chapters 14-17? The answer will depend to a great extent on the
literary critical perspective the exegete adopts with regard
to Jn 13-17.[13] Given what I consider to be the composite
nature of Jn 15-16 and the absence of the "farewell" theme in
sections of Jn 15-17, it is much more reasonable to see vv.
13:31-38 as the introduction to vv. 14:1-31, i.e., as part of
the original Farewell Discourse of the Gospel.

In the delineation of this introduction, it was
pointed out that vv. 14:1a and 14:27c form a clear case of
inclusion. This observation not only helps in fixing v. 13:38
as the conclusion to the introduction, but also clearly distinguishes v. 14:27 as the beginning of the concluding paragraph, vv. 14:27-31. Furthermore, the occurrence of the customary extension of peace in v. 14:27a--εἰρήνην ἀφίημι ὑμῖν,
εἰρήνην τὴν ἐμὴν δίδωμι ὑμῖν--serves to confirm the concluding
character of v. 14:27 (as well as of the following verses).
With v. 14:31 the discourse comes to an end: vv. 14:29-31b
anticipate the passion of Jesus and the command of v. 14:31c
is only taken up in ch. 18. Thus, Jn 14:27-31 represents the
conclusion to the original Farewell Discourse.[14]

Just as it was the role of vv. 13:31-38 to introduce
the problem of the approaching departure of Jesus and to begin
to address the question of the situation of the disciples after
the departure, so now vv. 14:27-31 assemble together and summarize the major themes of the main body of the discourse,
i.e., vv. 14:1-26, including the overarching theme of Jesus'

departure and his return to the disciples.[15] Thus, for
example, v. 14:28a recalls vv. 14:2-3--Jesus' coming and
going; v. 14:28b recalls both the love of Jesus (vv. 14:15,
21, 23, 24) and Jesus' relationship to the Father (vv. 14:6-11);
v. 14:30 recalls vv. 13:33, 14:19, 25--the theme of "a little
while" and related declarations; vv. 14:31 and 14:27 recall
the motif of vv. 14:15, 19, 22.

Whereas hardly anyone questions the extent of the
introduction to the discourse, there is far more disagreement
concerning the extent of the conclusion. Many Johannine commentators prefer to begin the conclusion with v. 14:25 rather
than with v. 14:27 (regardless of whether they take that conclusion to refer to chapters 13-17[16] or to chapter 14[17]). The
main reason usually given for this choice is the occurrence of
the expression ταῦτα λελάληκα ὑμῖν at the beginning of v.
14:25,[18] an expression which is seen as bearing concluding
overtones throughout the chapters that constitute the present
Farewell Discourse.[19] However, it has already been pointed
out in the preceding chapter that the phrase does not always
imply a conclusion, e.g., vv. 15:11, 16:25, so that the argument in and of itself is not sufficient.[20] Furthermore, the
clear case of inclusion between v. 14:1 and v. 14:27 would
seem to rule out that particular interpretation in this
instance as well.

With the delineation of the introduction (vv. 13:31-
38) and the conclusion (vv. 14:27-31) of the discourse, it
becomes clear that vv. 14:1-26 constitute the main body of
the discourse. It remains to be seen now how that material
is structured and developed. It has been customary to posit
a natural break between v. 14 and v. 15, so that vv.
14:1-14 are regarded as concentrating on the theme of
belief or faith, while vv. 14:15-25 (or 27, as some would
have it) emphasize the theme of love.[21] Although I would agree
with a division between vv. 14 and 15, I would hesitate to
make πίστις and ἀγάπη the overarching themes of the two sections. Rather, I tend to agree with J. Becker's position that
the overarching themes are Jesus' departure and return respectively.[22] Thus, Becker argues that vv. 14:1-3 present the

themes of ὑπάγειν and ἔρχομαι, while the following verses
develop them sequentially.[23]

I see three very strong arguments on behalf of this
opinion. First of all, both within the introduction (vv.
13:31-38) and the conclusion (vv. 14:27-31) one finds references to the themes of departure (vv. 13:31-32, 33, 36-38;
14:28, 30a) and return (v. 14:28), thus anticipating and summarizing the main concerns of the discourse. By way of contrast, neither πίστις nor ἀγάπη is to be found in the introduction (excising vv. 13:34-35 from the context). Secondly,
an examination of the distribution of the different terms used
for the themes of departure and return throughout the discourse shows a clear division of presentation within vv. 14:1-
26. The following chart will make this division clear:

A.   *13:31-38* --The verb ὑπάγειν is used three times
                  with respect to Jesus' departure.
B.   *14:1-3*   --The verb πορεύομαι is used twice of
                  Jesus' departure, while ἔρχομαι is used
                  once for his return.
C.   *14:4-17*[24]--Jesus' departure is alluded to three
                  times: once with πορεύομαι; twice with
                  ὑπάγειν.
D.   *14:18-26* --There are no references to Jesus' depar-
                  ture, but two references to his return:
                  ἔρχομαι occurs twice.
E.   *14:27-31* --Jesus' departure is mentioned twice:
                  once with πορεύομαι; once with ὑπάγειν.
                  Likewise, his return is mentioned once
                  by means of the verb ἔρχομαι.

In conclusion, the chart demonstrates that whereas Jesus'
departure is mentioned three times in vv. 14:4-17, it is not
mentioned at all in vv. 14:18-26.[25] Likewise, whereas Jesus'
return is mentioned twice in vv. 14:18-26, it is not to be
found at all in vv. 14:4-17.[26] The third argument concerns
the figure of the Paraclete. Jesus' return is clearly interpreted in terms of the coming of the Paraclete in vv. 14:16-17

and v. 14:26. The combination of these three arguments makes
J. Becker's position very plausible indeed.

Granted, therefore, that the two major sections of
vv. 14:1-26 are organized around the themes of the departure
and return of Jesus and that all other themes are subordinate
to these--including those of πίστις and ἀγάπη, it remains to
be seen at what point the first section ends and the second
one begins. Becker has chosen v. 14:17 as the end of the
first section and v. 14:18 as the beginning of the second section, largely on the occurrence of ἔρχομαι for the first time
since v. 14:3 in v. 14:18: οὐκ ἀφήσω ὑμᾶς ὀρφανούς, ἔρχομαι
πρὸς ὑμᾶς.[27]

However, it is my opinion that v. 14:15 represents the
beginning of the second section (the theme of ἔρχομαι) and,
consequently, v. 14:14 stands as the end of the first section
(the theme of ὑπάγειν or πορεύομαι). Several arguments may be
advanced on behalf of this proposed division. First of all,
from a structural point of view, the second major section
(vv. 14:15-26) would constitute a clear case of inclusion:
the section would begin and conclude with a reference to the
Paraclete (vv. 14:15-16 and 14:25-26). Secondly, the inclusion of vv. 14:15-17 as part of the larger section vv. 14:15-
26 would place these verses within the theme of Jesus' return.
This is, in my opinion, a correct interpretation of the Paraclete sayings: it is a way of describing the return of Jesus
to the disciples. Thus, in effect, if one were to unite vv.
14:15-17 to vv. 14:4-14, one would be making the theme of
return subordinate to that of departure, thus breaking down
the criterion for the structure of the main body of the discourse.

Thirdly, from the point of view of structure and context, the addition of vv. 14:15-17 to the second section would
help to preserve a threefold series of subordinate themes
within that section. Two of these themes are very closely
connected to one another. Thus, one finds in vv. 14:15, 21a,
and 23a (with an antithesis in v. 14:24a) grammatically different but theologically synonymous definitions of the love
that the disciples must have for Jesus. Each of these definitions is then followed by a statement of reward or recompense

accruing to the disciple. Thus, in vv. 14:16-17a another
Paraclete is promised, who will stay with the disciples forever; in v. 14:21b the disciples will be loved by both the
Father and Jesus, and the latter will reveal himself to the
disciple; in v. 14:23b the Father is said once again to love
the disciple, and both the Father and the Son will come and
abide in him. In each case a different aspect of Jesus'
return is described following the definition of love.[28]

Fourthly, yet another threefold series of a particular
theme may be observed in the proposed arrangement. Although
its relationship to the other two themes is not as close as
that existing between promise and reward, this theme is nevertheless connected to the other two. The theme in question is
that of the opposition that exists between the world and the
disciples (ὁ κόσμος/ὑμεῖς).[29] The theme appears for the first
time as part of the first Paraclete saying (14:17bc). It
reappears in v. 14:19, following the promise of a return given
in v. 14:18, and is expanded in v. 14:20 (ὑμεῖς δὲ θεωρεῖτε/
γνώσεσθε ὑμεῖς). Finally, it occurs once again after vv.
14:21a and b, introducing--by means of the literary device of
Judas' question--the antithesis of vv. 14:23a and 14:24a.

Thus, the theme of opposition follows the pattern of
promise and reward in the first case, while in the latter two
cases it introduces the pattern. The arrangement may be
depicted as follows:

A. *Sequence* *I* --14:15   Love of Jesus
                  14:16-17a   Reward
                  14:17b-c   Opposition between
                                    ὁ κόσμος and ὑμεῖς

B. *Sequence* *II* --14:18-20   Opposition between
                                    ὁ κόσμος and ὑμεῖς
                  14:21a   Love of Jesus
                  14:21b   Rewards

C. *Sequence III* --14:22   Opposition between
                                    ὁ κόσμος and ὑμεῖς

    antithesis ⌜ 14:23a   Love of Jesus
                  │ 14:23b   Reward
                  ⌞ 14:24a   No love of Jesus
                    14:25-26   Reward

The final sequence would be expanded by the inclusion of the
contrary of v. 14:23a in v. 14:24a and a repetition of a

promised reward to the disciples, which forms the inclusion
with the first reward.[30]

It is interesting to see what Becker does with this
threefold series of themes, since he posits the division of
the main body of the discourse at v. 18, leaving out the first
sequence altogether. In effect, what he does is to eliminate
that first sequence by declaring that one of its essential
components--the definition of the love of Jesus--is out of
context in its present position and should be removed.[31]

On the one hand, Becker argues, v. 14:14 unnecessarily
repeats a promise which has already been made quite clear in
the preceding verse (v. 13: ὅ τι ἂν αἰτήσητε ἐν τῷ ὀνόματί μου
τοῦτο ποιήσω/v. 14: ἐάν τι αἰτήσητέ με ἐν τῷ ὀνόματί μου ἐγὼ
ποιήσω).[32] On the other hand, Becker continues, both vv.
14:14 and 15 interrupt the progression of thought that exists
from v. 14:13 to v. 14:16. Thus, in the promise of the Paraclete to the disciples given in v. 14:16, Jesus is indirectly
called a Paraclete as well (καὶ ἄλλον παράκλητον δώσει ὑμῖν).
And, Becker argues, this is precisely the role that Jesus
assumes in v. 14:13.[33] Furthermore, v. 14:16 also helps to
ground the promise made in v. 14:12 to the effect that it is
the coming of the Paraclete that will enable the disciples to
perform greater "works" (καὶ μείζονα τούτων ποιήσει) than
those of Jesus.[34] As a result of these arguments, Becker
adopts the position that vv. 14:14-15 should be removed in
order to keep vv. 14:13 and 16 next to each other.[35]

In addition to the serious objections already indicated,[36] the fact remains that the threefold sequence of
thematic concerns is overlooked and destroyed by such a
theory.[37] By way of contrast, Schnackenburg, who follows
Becker in the selection of v. 18 as the dividing point, does
not adopt this line of thinking at all. Verse 14, Schnackenburg argues, can make perfect sense in its context,[38] and
v. 15 provides a condition for Jesus' activity on behalf of
the disciples.[39] Nevertheless, Schnackenburg ends up elimi-
nating the threefold sequence as well.[40]

Yet a fifth and final argument may be proposed on
behalf of the thematic unity of vv. 14:15-26. This argument
does not proceed so much from the context, the structure, or

the grammar of the section under consideration, but rather
from the structure of the first section, viz., vv. 14:4-14.
A brief consideration of that section shows that v. 14 provides a suitable climax for the overarching theme of departure
(ὑπάγω; πορεύομαι). Thus, the question posed by Thomas in
v. 5 introduces the subordinate theme of the relationship
between Jesus and the Father (vv. 6-7). This theme is further
amplified by means of Philip's question in v. 8 (v. 9). As a
part of this amplification, the subordinate theme of belief is
introduced in v. 10 and continued in v. 11.[41] Vv. 12-14,
which begin with a solemn ἀμὴν ἀμήν saying, then provide a
statement of reward for those who do believe (ὁ πιστεύων), consisting of a promise of "greater" works and an assurance that
all petitions will be granted.[42] As such, these three verses
provide a fitting climax for that section.

On the basis of these five arguments, therefore, it
seems reasonable to believe that the division of the main body
of the discourse should be seen as encompassing vv. 14:4-14
on the one hand and vv. 14:15-26 on the other. This division
may satisfactorily be made under the rubrics of Jesus' departure and return, which form, without doubt, the criterion for
the division of the discourse.[43] The first section would
include subordinate themes such as the relationship between
the Father and the Son and faith, while the second section
would include other subordinate themes, such as the love of
Jesus, the rewards that accrue to that love, and the opposition between the world and the disciples.

Before proceeding to consider in particular the subordinate theme of the love of Jesus (as well as all other
manifestations of ἀγάπη in the discourse), it is necessary to
raise briefly the question of the *Sitz im Leben* of the discourse as presented by J. Becker, since that *Sitz im Leben* is
closely related to the arrangement of the discourse that he
proposes.[44] Thus, not only do vv. 1-3 present the double
scheme that serves as a criterion for the arrangement of the
main body of the discourse (i.e., vv. 14:5-17; 18-26), but
these verses manifest as well a theological *Tendenz* radically
different from that exhibited in the main body of the discourse. The two divisions of that main body, i.e., vv. 14:5-17

and vv. 14:18-26 would have as their purpose the correction of the *Tendenz* of 14:2-3.[45]

Becker argues that the revelatory saying of vv. 14:2-3 (*Offenbarungswort*) has been taken by the author from the Johannine tradition.[46] This *Offenbarungswort* may be distinctly separated from the work of the evangelist both from a terminological point of view[47] and a theological point of view.[48] The latter presents a Jesus whose main purpose in returning to the Father is to prepare "dwellings" for the disciples and who will then return a second time to take his disciples with him. Thus, the community is at present awaiting anxiously the return of the Lord: their sole goal is to be united with him in heaven.[49]

By way of contrast, Becker sees the evangelist as correcting the spatial understanding of Jesus' πορεύομαι as presented in v. 14:2 by means of an understanding of Jesus as the ὁδός here and now (vv. 14:4-17).[50] Likewise, the spatial understanding of Jesus' ἔρχομαι presented in v. 14:3 is corrected by the evangelist in terms of a continued condition of salvation in the present community (vv. 14:18-26).[51] As a result, the original Farewell Discourse emerges as a polemical attack carried out by the evangelist against those in the community who would posit a futuristic eschatology, the essence of which may be found in the *Offenbarungswort* of vv. 14:2-3.[52]

Although I wish to pursue the question of the *Sitz im Leben* of the discourse in greater detail later on, I find it necessary to make some critical remarks with regard to J. Becker's theory at this point, given my adoption of the general structure he proposes for vv. 13:31-14:31. Even if one were to dispense with R. Schnackenburg's textual, linguistic, and theological[53] arguments brought to bear against J. Becker's position--arguments which I find very persuasive indeed--one would still find serious difficulties with the proposed *Sitz im Leben* of the discourse. On the one hand, Becker fails to connect the *Sitz im Leben* with the rest of the Gospel: is the same polemic exhibited by the remainder of the Gospel, or is such a polemic unique to vv. 13:31-14:31? Serious objections could be raised against either position. On the other hand, the theory fails to enter into dialogue with other theories concerning the origin and situation in

life of the Gospel, i.e., to what extent does this study confirm or reject present trends of Johannine research?[54] One
cannot operate *in vacuo.*

I should like to turn at this point to the exegesis
of the passages on love, using, as already explained above,
the original Farewell Discourse as the matrix for such an
enterprise, i.e., a consideration of the four relationships
of love alluded to in vv. 13:31-14:31 and related passages
throughout the Gospel.

Exegesis of the References to Love in
Jn 13:31-14:31 and Related Passages

It would be well to begin this section by reflecting
upon the distribution of the four relationships of love according to the structure of the discourse adopted in the previous
section. That structure consists, once again, of an introduction (vv. 13:31-38), a main body (vv. 14:1-26) which may be
broken down into three main components (vv. 14:1-3; 4-14; 15-
26), and a conclusion (vv. 14:27-31). One finds, first of
all, no examples of any of the four relationships of love in
the introduction. Secondly, one finds one example of the love
of the disciples for Jesus and the only example of the love of
Jesus for the Father in the conclusion (vv. 14:28 and 31,
respectively). All other examples are found within the main
body of the discourse and indeed within the third component of
that main body, i.e., vv. 14:15-26.[55] On the basis of the
evidence, therefore, I propose to begin this exegesis by taking vv. 14:15-26 as the point of departure.

The next point to be resolved concerns the development
of ἀγαπᾶν within the section, i.e., is there a relationship of
love which emerges as primary or which grounds the others and
which, as a result, should control the exegesis? All those
exegetes who posit a triadic pattern in vv. 14:15-24 (or 26,
as the case may be) point to the centrality of the love of
Jesus within each pattern: such love is followed in each case
by the promise of divine presence in the community.[56] Although
this particular relationship of love need not be the first
element of each pattern,[57] nevertheless there is no doubt as
to its centrality in the section. Indeed, the other two

relationships are grounded upon this particular one: they
follow upon this one as promises. As a result, it would be
more reasonable to begin with the condition rather than with
the promises.

Love of the Disciples for Jesus
  (vv. 14:15, 21a, 23a, 24a)

First of all, from the point of view of grammatical
structure, it is clear that all four statements of this relationship vary slightly from each other. Thus, for example,
v. 14:15 employs a simple conditional sentence.[58] V. 14:23a
is quite close to this usage, except for the introduction of
the indefinite pronoun τις and a corresponding change to the
third person singular forms of the verbs in question. By way
of contrast, v. 14:21a eliminates the conditional sentence and
employs instead the participial form of the verb.[59] V. 14:24a
also follows this usage, except for the elimination of the
copulative verb and the conversion of the second participial
form into an active form of the verb. However, despite the
variations, they may all be considered synonymous: they are
providing definitions of what it means to love Jesus.[60]

Secondly, from the point of view of terminology, variations may also be found. Such variations include: (a) the
addition of the verb ἔχειν to τηρεῖν in v. 14:21a; (b) a change
from the ἐντολαί of vv. 14:15 and 21a to the λόγος of v. 14:23a
(c) a shift from the singular λόγος of v. 14:23a to the plural
λόγοι of v. 14:24a. However, one does not get the impression
from the text that these terminological variations bear theological implications.[61] Thus, once again, the verses may be
considered synonymous: they are providing definitions of
what the love of Jesus implies.

Given the position that these verses are synonymous
and that they do provide definitions of the love of Jesus, it
remains to be established exactly what it is that is meant by
keeping Jesus' commandments (τηρεῖν τὰς ἐντολάς μου) or Jesus'
words (τηρεῖν τὸν λόγον, τοὺς λόγους μου), i.e., what is it
that constitutes the love of Jesus on the part of the disciples? Although the definitional statements are rather
terse, one may extract some light on the question from the

usage of either ἔχειν or τηρεῖν with either λόγος or ἐντολή in
the remainder of the "original" Gospel.[62]

The only undisputed occurrence of τὸν λόγον τηρεῖν
takes place in the acrimonious debate between Jesus and the
Jews in Jn 8.[63] Toward the end of the exchange (vv. 8:48-59),
the expression is used three times: twice with respect to the
Jews (vv. 8:51-52); once with respect to Jesus (v. 8:55).[64]
In v. 8:51--after having been accused by the Jews of being
possessed by a demon--Jesus declares that unless someone keeps
his word (ἐάν τις τὸν ἐμὸν λόγον τηρήσῃ), he will not possess
eternal life.[65] From the flow of the debate it is quite clear
that Jesus' λόγος is his claim: his identity and his origin
(vv. 8:14, 18-19, 25-27, 28-29). It is also quite clear from
the other occurrences of λόγος in ch. 8 (vv. 8:31, 37, 43)
that the Jews do not and cannot accept this λόγος. Furthermore, the argument continues, since only Jesus knows the
Father (v. 8:55), the Jews show that they have another Father
when they reject Jesus (v. 8:44).

A very similar interpretation of λόγος--this time with
the verb ἔχειν[66]--is found in Jn 5 (v. 5:38). Following
J. L. Martyn's arrangement of the material at this point,[67] I
see ch. 5 as consisting of a traditional healing story (vv.
5:1-9b), a dramatic expansion of that story (vv. 5:9c-15),
and a sermon addressed to the Jews by Jesus (vv. 5:19-47).[68]
In v. 5:38, within the body of the sermon, Jesus tells the
Jews that they do not have the word of God abiding in them
(καὶ τὸν λόγον αὐτοῦ οὐκ ἔχετε ἐν ὑμῖν μένοντα), precisely
because they do not believe in him (ὅτι ὃν ἀπέστειλεν ἐκεῖνος
τούτῳ ὑμεῖς οὐ πιστεύετε). Therefore, it is quite clear, once
again, that the recognition and acceptance of the identity and
origin of Jesus constitute the λόγος of the Father which is
revealed by Jesus (e.g., vv. 5:19-24, 26-27, 30, 36-37).
Furthermore, as in ch. 8, this λόγος constitutes eternal life,
e.g., vv. 5:24a, 40.[69]

These two instances of τὸν λόγον τηρεῖν and τὸν λόγον
ἔχειν clearly indicate that the λόγος concept--whether attributed to the Father or to the Son--focuses on the person of
Jesus, his origin and identity. Acceptance of that λόγος
means belief in Jesus (vv. 5:38; 8:24), while rejection

--attributed directly to the Jews in both cases--signifies
the loss of eternal life as well as the absence of any knowledge of the Father.[70] An examination of the usage of ἐντολή
in the Gospel, above all its double occurrence in vv. 12:44-
50, tends to confirm this general line of interpretation.[71]

At the end of ch. 12, one finds a discourse of Jesus
which is occasioned by the coming of some Greeks ("Ελληνές
τινες) to see Jesus (vv. 12:20-21). This discourse comes to
an end in v. 12:36a, and then vv. 12:36b-43 pretty much summarize the reception accorded to Jesus in the first half of
the Gospel (v. 37b, οὐκ ἐπίστευον εἰς αὐτόν). As a result,
the occurrence of a brief discourse by Jesus (vv. 12:44-50)
immediately following these verses and preceding the Washing
of the Feet episode is quite unexpected[72] and has led countless exegetes either to doubt its presence in the original
Gospel[73] or to posit a dislocation somewhere along the line.[74]

In vv. 12:49-50 the evangelist has Jesus raise the
familiar theme of not speaking on his own account, but rather
of conveying the Father's message (ἀλλ' ὁ πέμψας με πατήρ
αὐτός μοι ἐντολὴν δέδωκεν τί εἴπω καὶ τί λαλήσω), of carrying
out the Father's ἐντολή. Clearly, the essence of that ἐντολή
is revelation and, as such, eternal life (v. 12:50a). Thus,
as in the previous two cases, two types of response are possible: (1) acceptance, which means belief in Jesus (vv.
12:44-45), i.e., recognition of his origin and identity; or
(2) rejection, which means judgment and loss of eternal life
(vv. 12:47-48).[75]

On the basis of these findings, it would appear that
the definitions of the love of Jesus provided in Jn 14:15-26
--definitions which revolve around the concepts of ἐντολαί and
λόγος--are to be interpreted in terms of belief. In other
words, the love of Jesus can only be expressed in terms of a
belief in his role, an acknowledgment of his origin and identity, a recognition that he has been sent by the Father.[76]
The same conclusion may be reached from the perspective of the
Farewell Discourse itself.

The first indication to this effect lies, I believe,
in vv. 14:4-14, i.e., prior to the development of the threefold series of themes outlined above.[77] Not only is the

question of belief one of the main subordinate themes of the
section (beginning with v. 10), but there is reason to believe
that the pattern, attitude of disciples toward Jesus/reward or
promise, found in vv. 14:15-16, 21, 23 is grounded in a similar pattern contained in vv. 12-14. Thus, in v. 12a the
attitude of belief (ὁ πιστεύων εἰς ἐμέ) is followed by the
promise of greater works than those of Jesus, because Jesus
himself hears the prayers of the believers (vv. 12b-14).
Vv. 14:15-16 (as well as 14:21 and 14:23) clearly pick up this
pattern and develop it further in terms of love of Jesus. In
so doing, however, they should not be seen as adding anything
on to the element of belief, but rather as interpreting that
belief in terms of love.

        The second indication that the love of Jesus in
vv. 14:15-26 means basically faith in Jesus is found in
v. 14:24b. After the third definition of the love of Jesus is
given in v. 23a (along with the promise of v. 23b) and its
antithesis spelled out in v. 24a, v. 24b specifies clearly the
character of the λόγος--and, therefore, the character of all
four statements--which lies at the basis of the love of Jesus:
this λόγος is the revelation of the Father conveyed by Jesus.
Thus, once again, it represents an acceptance and recognition
of Jesus' origin and identity (as in vv. 8:48-59 and 5:19-47
above).[78]

        Thus, the evidence from within the discourse itself
points in exactly the same direction as the evidence from the
remainder of the Gospel: the love of Jesus is nothing other
than faith in Jesus. Many a commentator has stressed as well
the ethical implications of this love for Jesus on the part of
the disciples. Barrett, for instance, declares that John never
allows love to become a feeling or an emotion, but rather presents love as "revealed in obedience."[79] Dodd sees vv. 13:34-
35 as central to the teaching on love of Jn 14, i.e., the keeping of Jesus' commandments includes mutual love.[80] Similarly,
Lagrange separates love from faith as an additional require-
ment.[81] The evangelist, however, gives no indications whatsoever that this is indeed the case, i.e., that love entails
something other than or added to faith.[82]

Before proceeding to examine the three other examples
of the relationship of love between the disciples and Jesus
(vv. 8:42; 12:43; 16:27), it would be well to take into consideration the occurrence of this theme in vv. 14:27-31. It
has already been mentioned that it is the purpose of these
verses, as conclusion, to bring together and summarize both
the major themes and some of the subordinate themes of the
main body of the discourse: the love of the disciples for
Jesus is no exception.[83] Thus, in v. 14:28b--immediately
following the repetition of the two major themes of the discourse, viz., Jesus' ὑπάγειν and ἔρχομαι--one finds the theme
of love for Jesus in conjunction with the theme of rejoicing
as part of an unreal condition: εἰ ἠγαπᾶτέ με ἐχάρητε ἄν,
ὅτι . . .

The idea of love expressed by this unreal condition is
really no different from that of vv. 14:15, 21, 23, viz., faith
in Jesus constitutes love of Jesus,[84] but the emphasis is now
somewhat different. Whereas in vv. 14:15-26 the emphasis was
on the definition of the concept, in v. 14:28 that definition
is presupposed and the emphasis is placed instead directly on
the themes of departure and return.[85] The context itself
indicates this shift: on the one hand, v. 14:27b recalls the
statement of v. 14:1, i.e., the distress which befalls the
disciples on account of Jesus' impending departure; on the
other, v. 14:28a recalls the themes of vv. 14:2-3, i.e., the
departure will be followed by a return (ὑπάγω καὶ ἔρχομαι πρὸς
ὑμᾶς). In view of this assurance of a return, the attitude of
distress is not the proper one; rather, "rejoicing" should pre-
vail, since only by going to the Father can the promise of
vv. 14:12-13, 16, 23b be effected.

The usage of the verb χαίρω in Jn 20:20, i.e., within
the narrative of Jesus' appearance to the disciples, serves to
confirm this line of thought.[86] When Jesus does return after
his death and imparts the promised spirit to his disciples
(v. 20:22, Λάβετε πνεῦμα ἅγιον), the attitude of the disciples
is precisely one of rejoicing: ἐχάρησαν οὖν οἱ μαθηταὶ ἰδόντες
τὸν κύριον. Yet, despite the shift in emphasis, it is quite
clear that in order to have this correct attitude one must
believe that Jesus is going to the Father and has come from

the Father, which is precisely the import of the definitions
of vv. 14:12a, 15, 21a, 23a.[87]

In keeping with the methodology outlined above,[88] I
now turn to other examples of the love of Jesus in the Gospel:

Jn 8:42. The first such example may be found in the
debate between Jesus and the Jews of ch. 8, a debate which,
beginning with v. 31, focuses on the contrast between Abraham
and Jesus. This section, viz., vv. 8:31-59, may be divided
into the following subsections: vv. 8:31-36, 37-47, 48-59;[89]
thus, the statement concerning the love of Jesus is found
within the second subsection. The theme of this subsection is
the contrast between the alleged Father of the Jews--a claim
made in v. 8:33 and repeated in v. 8:39--and their real Father
i.e., Abraham and the devil.

It has already been stated above[90] that in ch. 8 Jesus'
λόγος means his identity and origin and that the Jews do not
and cannot accept this λόγος (vv. 8:31, 37, 43). If one now
concentrates on this second subsection, one finds the argument
that a true child of Abraham would not seek to kill Jesus
(vv. 37-40), but rather love Jesus (8:42), precisely because
of his identity and origin (ἠγαπᾶτε ἂν ἐμέ, ἐγὼ γὰρ ἐκ τοῦ
θεοῦ ἐξῆλθον καὶ ἥκω). It would seem, therefore, that in this
chapter, as in chapter 14, love for Jesus and belief in Jesus
are synonymous concepts. The only difference between the two
chapters is that whereas ch. 14 concentrates on the positive
aspect of such love--those who accept him, ch. 8 stresses the
negative aspect--those who reject him.

Jn 12:43. I have already remarked, with reference to
the brief discourse of Jn 12:44-50, that vv. 12:36b-43 represent a succinct summary of Jesus' ministry to the Jews: οὐκ
ἐπίστευον εἰς αὐτόν.[91] In vv. 42-43 the evangelist acknowledges that some Jews, even from the ranks of the Jewish author-
ities, believed in Jesus, but did not confess him openly,
because they were afraid of being banned from the synagogue.[92]
His judgment with regard to this attitude is rather severe:
ἠγάπησαν γὰρ τὴν δόξαν τῶν ἀνθρώπων μᾶλλον ἤπερ τὴν δόξαν τοῦ
θεοῦ. Such belief, in his opinion, is no belief.

Although Jesus' name is not mentioned *per se* in conjunction with v. 43, the direct object τὴν δόξαν τοῦ θεοῦ does,
in my opinion, refer to him directly and is to be differentiated from the first δόξα, specially if one takes v. 12:41 into
account. In this last verse it is said that the prophet
Isaiah beheld the glory of Jesus (εἶδεν τὴν δόξαν αὐτοῦ)[93] and
wrote about it. Furthermore, the concept of δόξα has been
associated elsewhere in the Gospel with the figure of Jesus
(cf. vv. 1:14; 2:11; 5:44). Thus, in v. 12:43 the evangelist
may be construed as providing a deliberate equivocation:
these half-hearted Jews loved more the "opinion" of men than
the "glory" of God, i.e., Jesus.[94]

This reference, therefore, confirms the association of
love and faith presented in chapters 8 and 14 and indeed goes
a step further: true belief--and thus true love--cannot be
hidden; it must be expressed openly, regardless of the consequences. For the evangelist there is no compromise.

Jn 16:27. Vv. 16:4b-33 have already provided a very
close parallelism to an ἀγάπη reference in ch. 14 of the Gospel,
viz., the relationship between love for Jesus and the attitude
of rejoicing (16:20-24). Keeping in mind the methodological
restrictions placed on all evidence derived from the second
part of the Farewell Discourse (vv. 15:18-16:4a; 16:4b-33; 17),
this example of love for Jesus provides yet another such
parallelism and, indeed, fits quite well into the pattern
established by the other two examples from the Gospel, i.e.,
vv. 8:42; 12:43.

In v. 16:26 Jesus repeats the promise of vv. 16:23-24
to his disciples: at the time of his return, the disciples
will be able to ask the Father whatever they wish and it will
be granted. The following verse, 16:27, then provides the
reason for this assurance: the disciples loved Jesus and
believed in him.[95] Thus, one finds side by side the two concepts of love for Jesus and belief in Jesus, clearly meant to
be synonymous here as well. Therefore, v. 16:27 preserves
the close association between love and faith found in vv. 8:42
and 12:43 and is in a certain sense closer to ch. 14, since it

describes the love for Jesus from its positive standpoint--the standpoint of those who accept him.

One may conclude from an examination of these three instances--and, above all, from the evidence of vv. 8:42 and 12:43--that the understanding of love for Jesus outside of ch. 14 is no different from the understanding of that same relationship as presented in ch. 14. In both cases it is quite clear that the evangelist equates such love with belief in Jesus' origin and identity. The evangelist gives no indications at all that such love means anything other than belief. At this point, one perceives immediately a difference between this understanding of love and the one presented in Jn 13:34-35, 15:1-17, and I John.

First of all, the relationship of love for Jesus on the part of the disciples, while present in Jn 15:1-17 and presupposed in I John, does not play the same central role that it does play in vv. 13:31-14:31 and related passages of the Gospel. That central role is assumed in the former instances by a hierarchy of love that proceeds as follows: God the Father--Jesus--the disciples. The emphasis is placed not so much on what love of Jesus means, but rather on how Jesus loved the disciples and what they in turn must do to abide within that hierarchy of love.

Secondly, although Jn 13:34-35, 15:1-17, and I John define the love for Jesus also in terms of τὰς ἐντολὰς αὐτοῦ τηρεῖν,[96] they go well beyond Jn 13:31-14:31 insofar as they include within those ἐντολαί very clearly the one command of mutual love, viz., love "for one another" and "for one's brother." For example, in Jn 15:10 love for Jesus is phrased in terms of τὰς ἐντολάς μου τηρεῖν; then, in v. 12 the author focuses on the one command of love: ἵνα ἀγαπᾶτε ἀλλήλους. Similarly, in I Jn 2:3-5 the love for God is defined in terms of Jesus' commands, τὰς ἐντολὰς αὐτοῦ τηρεῖν; then, in vv. 2:7-11 the one command of love is singled out and developed in the fourth characterization of the opponent's position: ὁ ἀγαπῶν τὸν ἀδελφὸν αὐτοῦ. As such, they no longer preserve the equation of the Gospel (love for Jesus = belief in Jesus), but rather proceed to include ethical demands as part of those ἐντολαί--as well as the need for *correct belief* in Jesus.[97]

Love of the Father for the
  Disciples (vv. 14:21b,
  14:23b)

          This particular relationship of love--as well as the
following one, i.e., love of Jesus for the disciples--stands
to the first relationship as a promise to a condition. Therefore, this relationship goes into effect only when the first
relationship is already a fact, an existing condition. Whoever loves Jesus (= whoever believes in Jesus' origin and
identity) can rest assured that the Father himself will love
him in return; on the other hand, he who does not so believe
is not loved by the Father.

          This love of the Father toward the disciples occurs
only in the last two of the promises made within the discourse;
it is absent *expressis verbis* from vv. 14:12b-13 and 14:16-17.
In v. 14:21b, the third promise, the love of the Father is
expressed in terms of the future passive form of the verb:
ἀγαπηθήσεται ὑπὸ τοῦ πατρός μου.[98] Subsequently, the promise
abandons the figure of the Father and turns to that of the
Son. In v. 14:23b, the fourth promise, that same love is
expressed in terms of the active voice: καὶ ὁ πατήρ μου
ἀγαπήσει αὐτόν.[99] The remainder of the promise, however, does
include the Father directly: he will come with Jesus (ἐλευσόμεθα) and abide in the believer (μονὴν παρ' αὐτῷ ποιησόμεθα).

          That this action of the Father is associated with the
period of Jesus' return and, indeed, with that return itself
cannot be denied. V. 14:23b is quite clear in saying that
the Father will come with Jesus (ἔρχομαι).[100] Furthermore,
from the point of view of the present form of the original
discourse,[101] such a return seems to be ultimately associated
with the figure of the "other" Paraclete, i.e., the different
expressions of the divine presence in the community seem to
converge primarily upon this one figure. Thus, I would suggest that in order to understand the meaning of the Father's
love one must understand his role in the sending of the Paraclete, a role which is given in the second promise of vv.
14:16-17.

          In v. 14:16 the reader is told that it is the Father
(at the request of his Son) who sends the Paraclete to his
disciples (δώσει ὑμῖν)--a theme which is repeated once again

in the conclusion to the discourse, viz., v. 14:26. This is
the Paraclete who will stay with the disciples forever (εἰς
τὸν αἰῶνα), taking the place of the first revealer. It would
seem, therefore, that the love of the Father is predicated
upon belief in his Son and is experienced in terms of the
presence of the Paraclete within the community.

I now turn to the other instances of this relationship
in the Gospel, and, since both are derived from the expansion
of the original Farewell Discourse (vv. 15:18-17:26), I use
them solely for the purpose of comparison.

Jn 16:27. Besides providing a parallelism to the love
that the disciples must have for Jesus (= belief in him), this
verse also provides an example of the love that the Father
manifests to the believers.[102] Furthermore, as in the case
of vv. 14:21ab and 14:23ab, this love of the Father is presented as being contingent upon belief in his Son, as the ὅτι-
clause indicates: αὐτὸς γὰρ ὁ πατὴρ φιλεῖ ὑμᾶς, ὅτι ὑμεῖς. . . .
An important difference is that in this section (vv. 16:4b-33)
such love is not associated with the figure of the Paraclete.[103] Rather, it seems that God's love toward the
believers is conceived more in terms of his receiving and
granting the disciples' prayers, since the promise of v. 16:23
is repeated in v. 16:26, immediately prior to the statement
concerning the Father's love.[104]

Jn 17:23. At the end of the discourse contained in
ch. 17 of the Gospel, viz., 17:20-26,[105] the author describes
the love that exists between the Father and Jesus,[106] on the
one hand, and the Father and the disciples, on the other.
These two relationships of love, furthermore, are strictly
subordinated to the controlling themes of this discourse: the
revelation of Jesus and the acceptance of that revelation. In
this chapter and in these verses Jesus' mission is described
in terms of making the Father known (see vv. 17:3, 6-8, 25-26),
and the disciples are those who have accepted this revelation
and have become one with the Father and Jesus (vv. 17:11,
22-23). On account of this acceptance, the disciples now
share fully in the glory of Jesus (v. 17:22), a glory which is

described as having been his before the creation of the world
(see v. 17:24--τὴν δόξαν τὴν ἐμὴν ἣν δέδωκάς μοι/πρὸ καταβολῆς
κόσμου).[107]

    The theme of love seems to be connected directly with
the theme of glory. First of all, it should be mentioned that
the love of the Father for the disciples is based on the love
of the Father for Jesus. Thus, for example, in v. 17:23 it
is stated that the unity of the disciples with Jesus and the
Father should lead the world to realize that God loves *them* as
much as he loved Jesus (ἠγάπησας αὐτοὺς καθὼς ἐμὲ ἠγάπησας).
Similarly, in v. 17:26 the acceptance of Jesus' revelation
leads to the same conclusion: God loves them as much as he
loved Jesus (ἵνα ἡ ἀγάπη ἣν ἠγάπησάς με ἐν αὐτοῖς ᾖ). Secondly, in v. 17:24 this love of the Father for Jesus is
expressed in terms of the glory that the Father gave Jesus in
his preexistence (τὴν δόξαν τὴν ἐμὴν ἣν δέδωκάς μοι), as the
ὅτι-clause that follows indicates (ὅτι ἠγάπησάς με πρὸ καταβολῆς κόσμου). Therefore, in accepting Jesus' revelation
(= in coming to know the Father, see v. 17:3) and in sharing
in Jesus' own glory (= in becoming one with Jesus and the
Father, see v. 17:22), the disciples are in effect loved by
the Father.

    All three examples of this particular relationship
presuppose belief in Jesus' origin and identity as a condition
for the relationship to take place. Thus, the love of the
Father in all three cases is directed toward believers. Furthermore, all three examples conceive of this love in terms
of a post-resurrectional activity, i.e., an ongoing activity
in the community, rather than in terms of a particular event
(or series of events) in history. The major difference would
lie in the conception of this love: Jn 13:31-14:31 concentrates on the Father's role with regard to the Paraclete;
Jn 16:4b-33 stresses instead the Father's role with regard to
petitions; and Jn 17 speaks of a sharing in Jesus' glory while
in the world.[108]

Love of Jesus for the Disciples
 (v. 14:21b)

As in the case of the love of the Father for the disciples, the love that Jesus manifests to his disciples stands
to the first relationship as a promise to a condition. Therefore, the relationship is possible only when the first relationship is already operative. Whoever loves Jesus (= whoever
believes in Jesus' origin and identity) can also rest assured
that Jesus himself, in addition to his Father, will return
that love.

This love of Jesus is mentioned only in the third
promise to the disciples (v. 14:21b). After the love of the
Father is introduced in the passive voice, the author takes
up the figure of Jesus and ascribes to him an attitude similar
to that of the Father--except for the sudden change to the
active voice: κἀγὼ ἀγαπήσω αὐτόν. Furthermore, the author
explains this love of Jesus by means of an epexegetical καί
in the same verse: καὶ ἐμφανίσω αὐτῷ ἐμαυτόν.[109] Thus, the
love of Jesus for the disciples is also intimately tied in
with the idea of his return,[110] which is, one must remember,
the main theme of this entire section.

I have already mentioned in the previous section that,
from the point of view of the present form of the discourse,
Jesus' return seems to be ultimately connected with the figure
of the Paraclete. This is the way I interpreted the coming of
the Father expressed in v. 14:23b, and it is the way I would
like to interpret Jesus' own coming, which is given expression
in v. 14:23b (ἐλευσόμεθα) and in the verse under consideration
(v. 14:21b--καὶ ἐμφανίσω αὐτῷ ἐμαυτόν). Thus, as in the case
of the Father's love, one must look to Jesus' activity vis-à-
vis the Paraclete in order to determine what his love for the
disciples entails. That activity is described in the first
promise of vv. 14:16-17.

It has already been mentioned that, according to v.
14:16, it is the Father who sends the Paraclete to the disciples. Jesus' role, as described in that same verse, is to
ask the Father to send the Paraclete (κἀγὼ ἐρωτήσω τὸν
πατέρα),[111] who will teach the disciples all things and remind
them of all that Jesus himself said. Thus, the Paraclete will

continue the revelatory work of Jesus in the community.[112]
Jesus' love toward the disciples is, therefore, predicated
upon their love for him (= their belief in him) and is experi-
enced--like the love of the Father--in terms of the presence
of the Paraclete within the community. Moreover, such a relationship of love is a post-resurrectional, i.e., ongoing,
activity rather than a precise historical event.

A comparison of the second and third relationships of
love in Jn 13:31-14:31 and related passages from the Gospel
with their counterparts in Jn 13:34-35, 15:1-17, and I John
produces the same results as those attained in the previous
comparison of the first relationship of love: there are major
differences between the two given blocks of material. With
regard to these last two relationships of love--the love of
the Father for the disciples and the love of Jesus for the
disciples--the difference may be described as follows: the
post-resurrectional, ongoing relationships of Jn 13:31-14:31
are presented as historical events in Jn 15:1-17 and I John.

Thus, for example, within Jn 15:1-17, v. 15:9 posits
a hierarchy of love that begins with the Father, continues
with the Son, and ends with the disciples (καθὼς ἠγάπησέν με
ὁ πατήρ, κἀγὼ ὑμᾶς ἠγάπησα). The use of the aorist tense
indicates the historical nature of that hierarchy: this *was*
the way that discipleship was constituted. Furthermore, in
the passage the love of the Father for the disciples is not
explicitly mentioned, but it should be understood in terms of
the love of Jesus for the disciples, a love which, according
to v. 15:13, is described primarily in terms of Jesus' redemptive death, i.e., a pre-resurrectional, historical act.[113]

Similarly, I John also presents a historical hierarchy
of love that begins with the Father, continues with the Son, and
ends with the disciples (e.g., vv. 3:1; 4:9-11; 4:14-16). Furthermore, the love of Jesus for the disciples is never explicitly mentioned in the Letter, but it should be understood in
terms of God's love which is conceived primarily in terms of his
Son's mission and redemptive death (e.g., vv. 3:16; 4:9-10;
4:14; 5:6), i.e., a pre-resurrectional, historical act.[114]

Therefore, in neither Jn 15:1-17 nor I John is either
of these relationships of love associated with the idea of the
presence of the Paraclete within the community.

Love of Jesus for the Father
    (v. 14:31)

        The previous relationships of love are found exclu-
sively--except for the love of the disciples for Jesus
described in v. 14:28b--within the third component of the main
body of the discourse, viz., vv. 14:15-26. This fourth relationship of love is found only in the conclusion to that discourse, viz., vv. 14:27-31, and nowhere else in the Gospel.
These verses have already been characterized as performing
two basic functions: (1) they provide a summary of the manifold themes, both principal and subordinate, raised within the
main body of the discourse; (2) they provide a transition to
and anticipate the passion of Jesus.

        Vv. 14:30-31 clearly manifest this combination of
functions. Thus, on the one hand, they recall the theme of
Jesus' immediate departure (vv. 13:33; 14:19, 25) by means of
the phrase, οὐκέτι πολλὰ λαλήσω μεθ' ὑμῶν, as well as the
κόσμος motif of vv. 14:17, 19, 22. At the same time, the
verses anticipate the coming passion and death of Jesus, as
the approaching encounter with "the ruler of the world"[115]
and the directive of v. 14:31 indicate. It is within the
framework of these two verses that the last relationship of
love is found.

        Jesus' love for the Father, which is briefly expressed
by the words ὅτι ἀγαπῶ τὸν πατέρα, is followed by an epexegetical καί[116] which explains the nature of the relationship.
Jesus' love is constituted and manifested by his execution of
that which the Father commands (καθὼς ἐνετείλατο μοι ὁ πατήρ,
οὕτως ποιῶ).[117] In other words, in carrying out the Father's
commands, Jesus shows that he loves the Father. Moreover,
from the context it is clear that part of that command, if
not indeed its culmination, requires Jesus' death.[118] That
death shall serve as a sign--the sign--to the world of the
bond of love that exists between the Father and Jesus.[119]

        From the point of view of the discourse, Jesus mani-
fests his love toward the Father in exactly the same way that
the disciples manifest their love toward Jesus: through the
execution of the loved one's commandment(s). In the latter
case, the commandments really mean belief in Jesus' origin and

identity; in the former, the commandment involves Jesus'
death, i.e., his willing surrender to "the ruler of this
world." Of the four relationships of love presented in the
discourse, this is the only one that may be considered pre-
resurrectional, since it involves a definite event in Jesus'
life.[120]

A comparison of this fourth relationship of love in
Jn 13:31-14:31 with pertinent passages from Jn 13:34-35,
15:1-17, and I John serves to confirm previous results: major
differences do exist between the latter sections and the former chapter. In this case, Jesus' love for the Father is not
developed at all in I John, but it is in Jn 15:1-17. In this
particular discourse Jesus' love for the Father is described
after the hierarchy of love mentioned above is posited in
v. 15:9. Thus, Jesus is said to abide in that hierarchy by
returning the Father's love.

Such love is described in v. 15:10b as the execution
of the Father's commandments: τὰς ἐντολὰς τοῦ πατρός μου
τετήρηκα. The description given is similar to that in Jn
13:31-14:31 on two counts: (1) both define the love of Jesus
in terms of executing the Father's commandments; (2) both
include Jesus' death as part of that commandment. The main
difference, aside from the hierarchy of love itself, is the
fact that in Jn 15:1-17 Jesus' love for the Father grounds
explicitly (v. 15:10b: καθώς) the love of the disciples for
Jesus and, above all, for one another, so that the mode of
Jesus' love--Jesus' death--becomes constitutive for the love
of the disciples itself.

Although this last example in effect concludes the
analysis of the four relationships of love present in Jn
13:31-14:31 and related passages of the Gospel, I wish to
include at this point those passages that treat this last
relationship of love from the other pole, i.e., the love of
the Father for Jesus, to see whether any similarities do
exist. The verses in question are the following: vv. 3:35,
5:20, 10:17, 17:24-26. I shall concentrate on the first
three examples, since I have already examined vv. 17:24, 26
in connection with the second relationship of love.[121]

Jn 3:35. First of all, it should be noted that this
example forms part of a highly controversial group of verses
within the third chapter of the Gospel, viz., vv. 3:31-36.[122]
As it now stands, the chapter may be divided as follows:
(1) a meeting and a dialogue between Jesus and Nicodemus, a
ruler of the Jews (vv. 3:1-10); (2) a discourse by Jesus following upon the dialogue (vv. 3:11-21); (3) a brief observation concerning the respective activities of Jesus and John
the Baptist (vv. 3:22-24); (4) a dialogue between John the
Baptist and his disciples concerning John's role vis-à-vis
Jesus (vv. 3:25-30);[123] (5) a discourse apparently uttered by
John (vv. 3:31-36). However, serious objections have been
raised against this last attribution:[124] (1) the thematic
interest of vv. 31-36 are not those of vv. 25-30; (2) vv. 31-
36 do repeat many of the themes found in the Nicodemus scene
and reflect as well Jesus' style of speech;[125] (3) the observation of v. 32b disagrees with the comment of v. 26.

As a result, many exegetes either relocate these verses
within the third chapter itself[126] or consider them to be an
originally independent discourse.[127] I myself tend toward the
latter solution on account of the similarities that exist
between these verses and vv. 12:44-50. In either case, the
speaker is taken to be Jesus, not John, and authorship is
attributed to the evangelist, not later tradition.[128] Therefore, despite the literary problems present concerning the
position of these verses in the Gospel, they may be accepted
as having been written by the evangelist and, thus, as being
directly relevant to the topic in question.

The discourse concentrates, for the most part, on the
origin and identity of Jesus: he comes from above (ὁ ἄνωθεν
ἐρχόμενος), v. 31; he bears witness to the things from above
(ὃ ἑώρακεν καὶ ἤκουσεν τοῦτο μαρτυρεῖ), v. 32; he is sent by
God (ὃν γὰρ ἀπέστειλεν ὁ θεός), v. 34; he utters the words of
God (τὰ ῥήματα τοῦ θεοῦ λαλεῖ), v. 34. These are all frequent
Johannine themes which stress the unique position of Jesus
vis-à-vis the Father: he is the Revealer.

It is within this framework that v. 35 declares that
the Father loves Jesus--ὁ πατὴρ ἀγαπᾷ τὸν υἱόν--and has handed
over all things to him.[129] In other words, the love of the

Father for Jesus is manifested directly in the revelatory
activity with which he has entrusted Jesus, since it is he
alone who reveals the Father to the world. He alone makes the
Father known.

Jn 5:20. John 5 has already come under scrutiny with
regard to the expression τὸν λόγον τηρεῖν, and it was mentioned
at that point that the chapter consisted of three main sections:[130] (1) a healing story (vv. 5:1-9b); (2) a dramatic
expansion of that story, centering upon a breach of the
Sabbath (vv. 5:9c-15); (3) a homily preached by Jesus to the
Jews (vv. 5:19-47). Thus, the present reference to the love
of the Father for Jesus occurs at the very beginning of that
homily, immediately after a reference to the effect that the
Jews are seeking to kill Jesus (v. 5:18--μᾶλλον ἐζήτουν αὐτὸν
οἱ 'Ιουδαῖοι ἀποκτεῖναι).

The homily begins with the very common theme that the
Son's works are not his own (οὐ δύναται ὁ υἱὸς ποιεῖν ἀφ'
ἐαυτοῦ οὐδέν), but the Father's.[131] The Son can only do that
which he sees the Father doing. Then, in v. 20 the evangelist
states that the Father shows the Son all that he does (πάντα
δείκνυσιν αὐτῷ) and that it is precisely this attitude on the
part of the Father that constitutes and manifests his love for
the Son. In other words, as in the previous example (v. 3:35),
the Father, as a sign and measure of his love, entrusts Jesus
with the task of revelation to the world.

Jn 10:17. This final example of the Father's love for
Jesus differs somewhat from the other two insofar as it
focuses upon a specific event in Jesus' revelatory activity.
It is said in v. 17 that the Father loves Jesus because the
latter is willing to lay down his life in accordance with the
Father's command (διὰ τοῦτο . . . ὅτι ἐγὼ τίθημι τὴν ψυχήν
μου).[132]

In summary, therefore, one may say that this particular
relationship of love is conceived by the evangelist as a pre-
resurrectional relationship, i.e., it is confined to that
period preceding Jesus' death and departure from the world.
The five texts in question stress three different aspects of

that love: (1) vv. 17:23, 26 are concerned with the love of
the Father prior to Jesus' coming into the world. Such love
is associated with the glory bestowed upon the pre-existent
Son. (2) vv. 3:35, 5:20 focus on the revelatory activity of
Jesus in the world: it is the Father's love that entrusts
Jesus with the mission. (3) v. 10:17 deals with one specific
instance of that activity: Jesus' willingness to lay down
his life in accordance with the Father's command. The evangelist is not concerned at all with the relationship of the
risen Jesus to the Father.

As one might expect, given the fact that the two relationships are really opposite poles of the one and same relationship, the love of the Father for Jesus closely resembles
the love of Jesus for the Father both in the meaning of that
love and in its character as a pre-resurrectional relationship. As far as the meaning is concerned, the following
correspondence may be observed: if Jesus shows his love for
the Father through the execution of the latter's commandments,
the Father shows his love for Jesus by entrusting him with
those commandments; if Jesus shows his love for the Father
above all by laying down his life, it is said that the Father
loves him precisely because Jesus is willing to carry out that
commandment. As far as its nature is concerned, it is clear
that the relationship centers on Jesus' mission to the world,
Jesus' ministry in the world. As a result, these three texts
--Jn 3:35, 5:20, and 10:17--may be regarded as confirming the
evidence presented in the fourth relationship of love in Jn
13:31-14:31.

A comparison of these passages with Jn 13:34-35,
15:1-17, and I John shows, once again, that major differences
do exist between the two blocks of material. First of all,
I John does not even mention the love of the Father for Jesus;
he is not concerned at all with this particular relationship.
Secondly, Jn 15:1-17 does mention it (v. 15:9--καθὼς ἠγάπησέν
με ὁ πατήρ), but fails to develop it in any way whatsoever.
Clearly that relationship has ceased to be a matter of interest,
a matter of concern, to these two writings. This fact is, in
my opinion, directly related to the difference in *Sitz im Leben*
of the two blocks of material.

Exegesis of References to Love
Outside Jn 13:31-14:31

A consideration of the four relationships of love presented in Jn 13:31-14:31 and all related passages accounts for
all but six of the love passages in the Gospel of John. The
remaining six are: vv. 3:16, 19; 5:42; 12:25; 13:1; 15:19.
However, of these six examples three may be eliminated from
further consideration at this point or in this study for various reasons.

First of all, v. 15:19 is part of that mass of material the authenticity of which has been recently questioned.[133]
Therefore, from the point of view of the methodology of this
study, I will use the evidence presented in that verse only
if such evidence directly agrees with or contradicts evidence
presented by undisputed passages from the Gospel (which was
the *modus operandi* of the previous section.)[134] Secondly,
both Hartwig Thyen and Georg Richter--exegetes who have
approached the question of redaction in the Gospel primarily
through the exegesis of John 13 and have gone on to assign all
of chapters 15-17 to the redactor as well[135]--take v. 13:1 as
the introduction to the redaction within that chapter.[136]
Thus, I prefer to leave v. 13:1 out of consideration at this
point and discuss it in the next chapter (in the context of an
Auseinandersetzung with both of these authors). Finally,
v. 12:25 is a Synoptic-like saying in which the theme of love
(φιλεῖν) does not seem to carry any precise theological meaning.[137]

Therefore, in this section I shall focus on the two
occurrences of chapter 3 (3:16, 19) and on Jn 5:42.

Jn 5:42

Toward the end of the homily preached by Jesus to the
Jews in ch. 5 (vv. 19-47), one finds this statement concerning
the Jews in v. 5:42: you have no love of God in you (τὴν
ἀγάπην τοῦ θεοῦ οὐκ ἔχετε ἐν ἑαυτοῖς)! This severe accusation
made against the Jews by Jesus resembles very closely the accusation of v. 5:38: the word of God does not abide in you (καὶ
τὸν λόγον αὐτοῦ οὐκ ἔχετε ἐν ὑμῖν μένοντα):[138] In both cases,

therefore, the evangelist is denying the Jews any contact
whatsoever with God the Father; v. 5:37b is quite clear in this
regard: the Jews have never heard (φωνὴν αὐτοῦ πώποτε ἀκηκόατε)
or seen God the Father (οὔτε εἶδος αὐτοῦ ἑωράκατε).

The central point of this homily and the underlying
reason for these accusations is that the Jews do not believe
in Jesus; they refuse to accept his origin and identity. Furthermore, since Jesus is the one who has been entrusted with
revealing the Father (vv. 5:30, 36, 37a, 43), a denial of that
role (= lack of belief in him) results in complete ignorance
about the Father as well. Thus, when the evangelist states
in v. 5:38 that the Jews do not possess "the word of God" and
in v. 5:42 that the Jews do not "love God," the basic accusation being made is that they do not believe in Jesus.

Should one compare this statement of v. 5:42 with
those texts that specify what love for Jesus implies, it
becomes evident that what is being denied of the Jews is being
asserted of the disciples. In vv. 14:15, 21, 23 it is said
that the disciples love Jesus because they execute his commandments (= because they believe in him).[139] In v. 5:42 the
Jews are said not to love God precisely because they manifest
no belief in Jesus.[140] Thus, even though the object of love
is different in the former verses--vv. 14:15, 21, 23 and 8:42
focus on the Revealer; v. 5:42 focuses on the Father being
revealed--the result is the same as in v. 5:42: belief in
Jesus is the determining factor in love. He who believes,
loves Jesus and the Father; he who does not, loves neither one.

Jn 3:16, 19

I have already referred above, in the context of the
love of the Father toward Jesus, to the basic structure of
chapter 3 as it now stands in the Gospel as well as to the
controversial nature of some of its components.[141] According
to that basic structure, vv. 3:16, 19 are both to be found
within the discourse of Jesus (vv. 3:11-21) that follows his
dialogue with Nicodemus (vv. 3:1-10). From the point of view
of literary criticism, recent exegesis has tended to regard
both the dialogue and the discourse, i.e., vv. 3:1-21, as a
literary unity within the original Gospel.[142] However, since

some dissenting voices have been heard, I should like to begin
by considering the point of literary unity.

The dissenting voices have been of two kinds. First
of all, some exegetes have tended to see the discourse (vv.
3:11-21) as being more of a reflection or a meditation on the
part of the evangelist: some begin this reflection with v. 13;
others, with v. 16.[143] This approach is, to a great extent,
based on the presupposition that an exegete can distinguish
passages that convey the original voice of Jesus from passages
that betray the evangelist's own viewpoint.[144] However, since
the advent of redaction criticism such a task has become
increasingly fruitless, if not indeed completely impossible.

Secondly, other exegetes have chosen to break up the
present discourse and either redistribute parts of it to other
points in the Gospel[145] or consider such parts to be later
additions to the original Gospel.[146] In either case, however,
it is the evangelist who is said to have been responsible for
the authorship of the separated section, so that, from the
point of view of the present study, any evidence presented in
that section--specifically vv. 3:16, 19--may still be used in
an examination of the Johannine (= Gospel) concept of love.

Therefore, the suggestions of the dissenting voices
--suggestions which I myself do not follow--do not immediately
affect the present study. With this background in mind I proceed to consider the evidence presented in vv. 3:16, 19 in
terms of its present context, i.e., vv. 3:1-21.

In Jn 3:16 one finds a relationship of love which is
not mentioned elsewhere in the Gospel and is, therefore,
uncharacteristic of the author's thought: ἠγάπησεν ὁ θεὸς τὸν
κόσμον. Indeed, if one recalls the four relationships of love
of Jn 13:31-14:31 and the threefold series of subordinate
themes of Jn 14:15-26, the declaration of Jn 3:16 would seem
to be totally unexpected and surprising, because one of those
subordinate themes of vv. 14:15-26 is the distinction that
exists between the disciples on the one hand and the κόσμος on
the other.[147] It is the disciples (= those who believe) that
God loves, not the world. Thus, Jn 3:16 seems to provide a
different view altogether.

I should like to begin this discussion, therefore, with the position of Jn 3:16 in the theological stance of the Gospel, i.e., is Jn 3:16 contrary to or compatible with the other references examined so far? Many exegetes do not hesitate to take the latter approach, i.e., to affirm compatibility and indeed to describe the statement of v. 3:16 in rather glowing terms. Thus, for example, Lagrange speaks of "un acte d'amour extraordinaire par où les choses célestes se sont mêlées à celles de la terre";[148] Spicq refers to it as follows: "Aucun texte de l'écriture ne donne davantage de lumière sur la 'charité'. . . c'est l'infini de l'agapè divine que l' Apôtre saint Jean veut suggérer à ses lecteurs."[149] On the other hand, other scholars prefer to see in Jn 3:16 an old Christian tradition that the evangelist has adopted and transformed completely.[150]

Before passing a judgment on these positions, I believe it necessary to determine from the context the precise meaning of the verb ἀγαπᾶν in Jn 3:16. That meaning may be ascertained first of all by examining closely the statements of vv. 3:16b and c. It is clear that the statement of v. 3:16a is defined in v. 3:16b; the οὕτως[151] points forward to the ὥστε-clause[152] and may be translated as follows: "Thus . . . in the fact that . . ." Thus God showed that he loved the world in the fact that he gave (ἔδωκεν) his Son. Furthermore, v. 3:16c explains the reason for this giving: that the believer might possess eternal life.

The primary key to the meaning of ἀγαπᾶν in Jn 3:16 would seem to be the meaning of ἔδωκεν in v. 3:16b.[153] Those exegetes that regard v. 3:16 as a summary of the Johannine message and the Johannine conception of love interpret that aorist in terms of the Pauline aorist παρέδωκεν, i.e., as a sacrifice, and tend to see in the verse a reflection of the Isaac episode as well (Gen 22): God showed his love by having his Son die for the sins of the world.[154] On the other hand, those exegetes who see the evangelist as transforming the original meaning of v. 3:16 interpret the verb in terms of the ἀπέστειλεν of v. 3:17 and the Johannine theme of "sending."[155] I believe that the context of v. 3:16 confirms the latter

position and that such a position is quite compatible with the
position on love that the Gospel presents.

First of all, the idea of a sacrifice is totally
absent from the context of v. 3:16, viz., vv. 3:11-21. On the
other hand, one finds several references to the mission with
which the Father has entrusted the Son: (1) Jesus speaks of
the things he has seen and known, v. 11; (2) these things are
τὰ ἐπουράνια, v. 12; (3) Jesus has come down from heaven,
v. 13; (4) his mission involves his death, v. 14; (5) the
Father himself has sent him, v. 17. It would seem more reasonable, therefore, to see in the ἔδωκεν of v. 3:16b--and consequently in the ἠγάπησεν of 3:16a--a reference to the whole
extent of Jesus' mission, i.e., all that which testifies to
his origin and identity (including his death).

It is precisely such a concept of love that is compatible with the other love passages in the Gospel and not the
love of a sacrifice for sins. The latter idea of love is mentioned nowhere in the Gospel. The former idea, on the other
hand, is present not so much in what I have called the post-
resurrectional relationships of love, but rather in the pre-
resurrectional relationships, i.e., the love of Jesus for the
Father and the love of the Father for Jesus. Furthermore,
such a presence, such a parallelism, is not surprising at all,
because--as the aorists ἠγάπησεν and ἔδωκεν indicate--v. 3:16ab
refers to a pre-resurrectional event, not a post-resurrectional
possibility or attitude.[156]

Thus, for example, the love that Jesus had for the
Father is specified in v. 14:31b by means of the following
epexegetical καί: such love is manifested by Jesus' execution
of the Father's command. Moreover, from the context it
becomes evident that Jesus' death is a part of that command.
Similarly, the love that the Father had for Jesus involves
above all the willingness to entrust him with the mission of
revelation, and part of that mission, once again, consists of
Jesus' death. As a result, the love of the Father for the
world is expressed in terms of those elements which are constitutive of the Father-Son relationship of love: such love
is manifested by Jesus' mission in general and by his death
as the end and culmination of that mission in particular.

Although I have agreed with those exegetes that read
the ἔδωκεν of v. 3:16--and, therefore, the ἠγάπησεν as well--
in terms of the ἀπέστειλεν of v. 3:17, I do not believe it
necessary to hold, as most of them do, that v. 3:16 represents
an original Christian tradition ("die übliche christliche
Bedeutung")[157] the meaning of which has been changed by the
evangelist.[158] At the heart of this latter position lies the
conviction that such an understanding of κόσμος is totally
unthinkable in the Fourth Gospel, because for John the world
"ist Widerpart Gottes, des geoffenbarten Heils Gottes und
aller, die daran teilhaben."[159] On the contrary, I believe
that v. 3:16 is, once again, quite compatible with the other
ἀγάπη passages.

This compatibility may be affirmed primarily on the
basis of the distinction observed above between pre-
resurrectional relationships of love and post-resurrectional
relationships. V. 3:16 is certainly incompatible with the
latter: the threefold sequence of κόσμος versus disciples in
vv. 14:15-26 alone establishes that fact. However, v. 3:16
is not incompatible with the former. At this stage the κόσμος
may have a more neutral meaning than that of vv. 14:15-26.[160]
However, as the κόσμος increasingly manifests the rejection of
Jesus, it takes on a more and more negative image (completely
the opposite of the disciples): in other words, the κρίσις
begins to unfold. At the stage of the post-resurrectional
relationships, the κρίσις has taken place and the world is
now excluded from the Father's (and Jesus') love.

In conclusion, therefore, I would say that Jn 3:16 is
indeed uncharacteristic of the author's thought, but no more
so than Jn 14:31 / 3:35; 5:20; 10:17, i.e., those passages
that testify to the Father-Son relationship of love. The
reason these references are all uncharacteristic is that the
evangelist is more concerned with the post-resurrectional
situation. Thus, Jn 3:16 need not be and is not incompatible
with the other ἀγάπη references, unless one interprets that
love in terms of a sacrifice for the sins of the world.

This view of God's love for the world is quite different from that presented in both I John and Jn 15:1-17.
I John, for example, clearly interprets Jesus' death as a

sacrificial death: in v. 2:2 he is said to be a ἱλασμός . . .
περὶ τῶν ἁμαρτιῶν ἡμῶν; in vv. 4:9, 10 the Father sends Jesus
into the world (εἰς τὸν κόσμον) as a ἱλασμὸν περὶ τῶν ἁμαρτιῶν
ἡμῶν.[161] Similarly, Jn 15:13 speaks of Jesus' mode of love as
a death for his beloved (ὑπὲρ τῶν φίλων αὐτοῦ); ὑπέρ is the
preposition used in any interpretation of Jesus' death as a
sacrifice.[162]

The second reference to ἀγαπάω in 3:11-21 could have
been considered in the context of the first relationship of
love described above, but I have chosen to examine it at this
point on account of its proximity to v. 3:16. As in the case
of Jn 12:43,[163] v. 3:19 does not mention the name of Jesus
per se, but does employ a term--like the δόξα of v. 12:43--
that is associated with the figure of Jesus both in vv. 3:11-
21 itself and elsewhere in the Gospel. Thus, the statement
of v. 3:19a, τὸ φῶς ἐλήλυθεν εἰς τὸν κόσμον, can only refer
to Jesus in the light of vv. 3:16b, 17, and the noun τὸ φῶς
is also repeatedly used of Jesus in the Gospel (vv. 1:4, 5, 7,
8, 9; 8:12; 12:35, 46).

V. 3:19a states that "men" (οἱ ἄνθρωποι) loved darkness
more than the light (= Jesus). This particular statement must
be interpreted in terms of vv. 3:16c, 18, i.e., the coming of
the only son leads to a κρίσις: some believe in him and
possess eternal life; others do not and stand judged, lost
(ἀπόληται). Thus, love in v. 3:19 is once again equated with
belief: love of the light (= of Jesus) means essentially a
belief in his origin and identity. V. 3:19, therefore, exem-
plifies the reaction of the world to the ἔδωκεν of v. 3:16b
in the terms of vv. 14:15, 21a, 23a, 24a; 8:42; 12:43; 16:27.
Once again, the evangelist gives no indications that the love
of Jesus means anything other than belief.

Summary of Two Preceding Sections

Before turning to the very important question of the
Sitz im Leben of the Gospel in the light of the above research,
I proceed to give a brief summary of that research. Since the
latter was focused for the most part on the four relationships

of love mentioned in Jn 13:31-14:31, I shall employ those very
same categories in the summary that follows.

Love of the Disciples for Jesus

The exegesis of all those passages which speak either
directly (e.g., vv. 14:15, 21, 23, 28) or indirectly (e.g.,
vv. 3:19; 5:42; 12:43) of the love for Jesus has shown that
such love means essentially belief in Jesus' origin and identity. The author gives no indications whatsoever that ethical
considerations form a part of this love. Furthermore, this
relationship of love is primarily a post-resurrectional relationship; its central position in vv. 14:15-26 verifies this
emphasis. A comparison with Jn 13:34-35, 15:1-17, and I John
has also shown that this particular relationship loses significance in the latter texts, yielding instead to a well-defined
hierarchy of love, and that the equation, love for Jesus =
belief in Jesus, is not preserved in those same texts.

Love of the Father for the Disciples

This particular relationship of love has been shown
to be based upon and to follow as a consequence of the first
relationship of love, i.e., the Father loves those who love
Jesus (= believe in him) and expresses this love by sending
the Paraclete to the believers. This relationship is exclusively a post-resurrectional relationship: the Paraclete succeeds Jesus.

Love of Jesus for the Disciples

As in the case of the last relationship, this third
relationship stands to the first as a promise to a condition:
Jesus will manifest his love toward those who love him
(= believe in him). Likewise, this love is expressed by means
of the figure of the Paraclete: it is Jesus who asks the
Father to send the Paraclete to the believers. As such, this
relationship is also exclusively a post-resurrectional relationship: the Paraclete succeeds Jesus and continues his
work. A comparison of these two relationships with Jn 13:34-
35, 15:1-17, and I John has shown that: (1) these ongoing,

post-resurrectional relationships are presented as historical
events in the latter texts; (2) the love of the Father for the
disciples is understood exclusively in terms of Jesus' love,
specifically his redemptive death; (3) neither relationship
is associated with the figure of the Paraclete.

Love of Jesus for the Father

An examination of the texts that deal with the love
of Jesus for the Father (v. 14:31) or the love of the Father
for Jesus (vv. 3:35; 5:20; 10:17) has also demonstrated that
such love is intimately connected with Jesus' mission of
revealing the Father, a mission which includes and culminates
in his death. In contrast to the first three relationships
of love, this particular one is clearly pre-resurrectional,
viz., confined to Jesus' mission. A comparison of the two
poles of this relationship with Jn 13:34-35, 15:1-17, and
I John has pointed out that: (1) Jesus' love for the Father
is developed only in Jn 15:1-17, where it clearly grounds the
love of the disciples for Jesus and for one another; (2) the
Father's love for Jesus is mentioned only in Jn 15:1-17 but
not developed at all.

Finally, an exegesis of those passages that lie outside the four categories has shown that such passages are in
fundamental agreement with the other passages. Thus, both
v. 5:42 and v. 3:19 present the same equation described in the
first relationship: love of Jesus is synonymous with belief
in Jesus; likewise, v. 3:16 presents God's love for the world
using the categories of the second and third relationships:
Jesus' mission of revealing the Father. The latter verse
would be exclusively pre-resurrectional; the former two verses,
essentially post-resurrectional.

"Sitz-im-Leben" of the Gospel as Indicated
by the References to Love

The issue of the *Sitz im Leben* of the Gospel has
already been broached briefly with respect to Jürgen Becker's
theory concerning the theological revision of the *Offenbarungs-*
wort of Jn 14:2-3 in the main body of the discourse that

follows, i.e., vv. 14:4-26.[164] I now turn more fully to the
central question of the immediate purpose of the Gospel, specifically from the point of view of the evidence accumulated
above from the exegesis of the love passages in the Gospel.
As one might expect, this immediate purpose has received quite
varied interpretations over the years.

        One of the great services rendered to Johannine
research in the recent past has been the publication of a
study--authored by Robert Kysar--that deals exclusively with
the history of contemporary scholarship on the Fourth Gospel.[165] Kysar manages to bring a certain degree of order into
the chaos that comprises such scholarship by approaching his
subject thematically; each chapter represents, therefore, a
brief history of the scholarly positions on a particular
theme. Since one of these chapters deals with the *Sitz im
Leben* of the Gospel,[166] I shall draw in what follows on the
information presented therein.

        According to Kysar, scholarly opinion on the purpose
of the Gospel changed drastically from the early 1960s to the
late 1960s and the early 1970s. In the year 1959 three studies
were published all of which interpreted that purpose to be a
missionary one: the Gospel was written to make converts among
the Jews of the Diaspora.[167] This view, he continues, seemed
to hold its own for a while, but gradually yielded to four
other currents of thought: (1) the Gospel arose out of a
violent dialogue with the synagogue; (2) the Gospel's main
concern was to combat the emergence of docetism; (3) the Gospel came from an anti-Judean, Samaritan Christian church;
(4) the Gospel represents a universal appeal to all Christians.

        Of these four theories, Kysar concludes, the first
one--the serious dialogue with the synagogue--"seems steadily
to be gaining an increasing degree of consent among critics
of the fourth gospel."[168] The work around which most of this
mounting consensus seems to coalesce is J. L. Martyn's *History
and Theology in the Fourth Gospel*, a work which I already have
had occasion to mention several times. Modern Johannine scholarship has seen the formation of a veritable Martyn band-
wagon.[169] I believe that my own work with the love references
of the Gospel leads to an affirmation of Martyn's proposed

Sitz im Leben. However, before outlining my reasons for such
a conclusion, I should like to present an outline of Martyn's
theory concerning the Johannine purpose.

First of all, Martyn's basic presupposition is that
the Fourth Gospel is operating at all times on two distinct
levels of action.[170] The first level is what he terms the
einmalig level, which deals primarily with events in Jesus'
earthly lifetime; the focus of this level is thus primarily
historical.[171] The second level, on the other hand, concentrates on the contemporary problems of the Johannine church
and communicates these problems through the characters of the
einmalig level.[172] The evangelist, he continues, moves from
one level to the other almost unconsciously,[173] and, therefore,
it is the task of the exegete to differentiate between the two
levels.[174]

It is precisely this latter task that Martyn undertakes with regard to chapters 5-11 of the Gospel. Therein he
finds two series of events which duplicate each other closely
and which deal for the most part with the situation of the
community.[175] That situation emerges as one of violent debate
with a local synagogue over the issue of belief in Jesus as
the Messiah.[176] The synagogue has taken stringent steps to
preserve the unity of the community and to stifle the apparently rapid growth of defections--these steps include the
excommunication of those members that profess belief in Jesus
as well as the trial and execution of those Jewish-Christian
preachers who, after excommunication, continue to evangelize
among the Jews. The atmosphere, therefore, is one of definite
tension and one which leads to outright reprisals on the part
of the synagogue.

It is against this general framework of rejection and
persecution that the references to love in the Gospel are best
understood, above all those references that deal with post-
resurrectional relationships of love. Such references have
been shown to be the backbone of the concept of love not only
in the discourse of vv. 13:31-14:31, but also in the remainder
of the Gospel.[177] However, it is in the Farewell Discourse
that the references *explicitly* and *overtly* refer to the present stage of the community at the time of writing.[178] Thus,

once again, I should like to begin the exposition of the *Sitz
im Leben* implied by the love references by concentrating first
of all on Jn 13:31-14:31 and then passing on to the other
related passages.[179]

In the Farewell Discourse there are three main indications that the Christian community is engaged in a serious
dispute with another group:

(1) First of all, it has been shown above that vv.
15-26 consist of a threefold series of three subordinate themes
and that one of these themes--the definitions of what it means
to love Jesus--is the central one, since the other themes are
based upon it. Furthermore, it has been shown that such love
is synonymous with belief in Jesus' origin and identity. In
the third series of the subordinate themes (vv. 22-24), one
finds an antithesis of the definition of love for Jesus: if
such love means the execution of his "word," i.e., belief in
him, then the lack of such love is clearly the failure to
execute his "words," i.e., a refusal to believe in him. Therefore, there are some who believe and some who do not, and the
two groups are being explicitly differentiated from one
another.

(2) Secondly, it has also been shown above that one of
the three subordinate themes of vv. 15-26 is the opposition
that exists between the world (ὁ κόσμος) and those who believe.
In sequence (1) (vv. 14:15-17), those who believe are promised
the gift of another Paraclete, but "the world" will not receive
or see or know him. In sequence (2) (vv. 14:18-21), those who
believe are assured of Jesus' return--a return that is
described in 14:21b--but "the world" will never see him again.
In sequence (3) (vv. 14:22-26), those who believe are once
again assured that they will see Jesus--a vision which is
described in v. 14:23b--but "the world" will never receive
such a revelation. Thus, everything that is promised to those
who believe (= the return and the love of Jesus and the Father
in the figure of the Paraclete) is denied to those who do not
believe. The explicit differentiation of point (1) above is
continued and expanded by means of the term ὁ κόσμος: the
consequences of such a differentiation are spelled out in
black and white terms.

(3) Finally, it has been shown above as well that
vv. 13:31-38 form the introduction to the Farewell Discourse
and, as such, introduce the themes of departure and return.
V. 13:33 places the disciples on the same level as "the Jews":
they cannot follow him; the separation must take place. However, with a beginning word of comfort in v. 13:36, this parallelism ceases, and the contrast between the two groups
becomes starker and starker: the disciples will see Jesus
again; "the Jews" will not (see vv. 14:19 and 7:33-36). Thus,
the differentiation noted above in points (1) and (2) becomes
more specific in point (3): the immediate representatives of
the ὁ μὴ ἀγαπῶν με of v. 14:24 and of the κόσμος of vv. 14:15-
26 are the οἱ Ἰουδαῖοι of v. 13:33.

This differentiation between those who believe and
those who do not and the further specification that the latter
are to be seen as the οἱ Ἰουδαῖοι are confirmed by an examination of the following love references in the Gospel:

(1) The first example is Jn 8:42, which is the first
reference outside the Farewell Discourse to the relationship
of love for Jesus. The context is that of a rather virulent
debate between Jesus and the Jews, a debate the conclusion to
which portrays the Jews as picking up stones to throw at Jesus
(see v. 8:59).[180] In vv. 8:31-59 the debate centers on the
contrast between Jesus and Abraham, and in vv. 8:37-47 the
specific issue is that of the identity of the real Father of
the Jews, i.e., Abraham or the devil. In v. 8:42 Jesus tells
the Jews that if their father were indeed God, they would show
love for him and not seek to kill him, as they are doing
(v. 8:40). Furthermore, v. 8:42 defines in no uncertain terms.
what such love entails: ἐγὼ γὰρ ἐκ τοῦ θεοῦ ἐξῆλθον καὶ ἥκω·
οὐδὲ γὰρ ἀπ᾽ ἐμαυτοῦ ἐλήλυθα, ἀλλ᾽ ἐκεῖνός με ἀπέστειλεν.
Such love is nothing other than belief.

Therefore, not only is the equation, love for Jesus =
belief in Jesus, preserved in v. 8:42, but also the identification of those who do not love (because they do not believe) as
the οἱ Ἰουδαῖοι (see v. 8:31). The atmosphere is one of
rejection as well as one of persecution, as the references to
seeking to kill Jesus and wishing to stone him clearly indicate.

(2) The second example is Jn 5:42, which is the first
reference in the Gospel that does not allude to any of the
four relationships of love mentioned in the Farewell Discourse.
Following Martyn's study,[181] v. 5:42 forms part of the homily
against the Jews which is found in the first series of events
of chapters 5-7 and, as such, points well beyond the *einmalig*
level. In this particular verse Jesus tells the Jews that
they do not have the love of God in them, i.e., they have no
contact whatsoever with God the Father (see v. 5:37). The
reason for such a statement is, as v. 5:43 indicates, that the
Jews do not believe in Jesus (ἐγὼ ἐλήλυθα ἐν τῷ ὀνόματι τοῦ
πατρός μου καὶ οὐ λαμβάνετέ με) and, since Jesus reveals the
Father, in rejecting Jesus they reject the Father as well.

In this case, belief in Jesus is equated with love of
the Father, and the Jews are once again presented as those who
do not believe and are, as a result, denied any contact with
the Father. The atmosphere is certainly one of rejection as
well as one of persecution (see vv. 7:1, 20, 25-27, 30).

(3) The third example of this association between the
lack of love for Jesus (= the refusal to believe in him) and
the Jews is found in Jn 12:43, a verse which forms part of a
succinct summary of Jesus' ministry to the Jews provided by
the evangelist prior to Jesus' turning to his disciples (Jn
12:36b-43). In v. 37 it is said that the Jews did not believe,
while in v. 42 it is said that some believed (ἐκ τῶν ἀρχόντων
πολλοί), but failed to confess it openly.[182] To the evangelist such belief is no belief at all. This last attitude is there presented in terms of love: such people loved
human opinion (ἡ δόξα τῶν ἀνθρώπων) more than Jesus himself
(τὴν δόξαν τοῦ θεοῦ). In other words, correct love demands
belief and confession: to have the former without the latter
is no belief at all; it is rejection.

(4) Finally, I should like to mention in this regard
the evidence adduced above with regard to the defining terms
of ἀγαπάω in vv. 14:15, 21, 23, i.e., the combination of the
verbs ἔχειν or τηρεῖν with the nouns λόγος or ἐντολή.[183] The
first combination is found in vv. 8:48-59, i.e., within the
context of the acrimonious debate already mentioned, while the
second combination takes place in v. 5:38, i.e., within the

homily addressed to the Jews in that first series of events
outlined in chs. 5-7. In both cases the expressions have been
shown to mean nothing other than belief in Jesus, and also in
both cases it is said that the Jews do not accept this λόγος,
i.e., do not believe in Jesus.

I began this exposition of the *Sitz im Leben* implied
by the love references in the Gospel by presenting the theory
that such references were best understood against a general
framework of rejection and persecution by Jews, a framework
such as the one J. L. Martyn reconstructs in his study. I
believe that the evidence presented above warrants and justifies the adoption of such a theory. First of all, the relationships of love from Jn 13:31-14:31 indicate that the community is seriously engaged with a group from which it seeks
to disassociate itself and also that this group is the οἱ
'Ιουδαῖοι. Secondly, the references from outside Jn 13:31-
14:31 confirm this position by repeatedly associating those
characteristics assigned to the other group in Jn 13:31-14:31
--above all, lack of love and refusal to believe--with the
Jews. Furthermore, these references (and specifically Jn 5:42
and 8:42) indicate that the tension that exists is not simply
one of rejection, but also one of persecution.

The situation of the community should therefore be
seen as one of definite and delicate tension. From such a
perspective, the promises made to the believers in vv. 14:12-
14, 16-17, 21b, 23b would serve to strengthen the beliefs of
the beleaguered community by assuring them of this unique and
privileged position with regard to Jesus as well as God the
Father and by absolutely denying any similar status to the
opposition.

Although I have concentrated in this last section on
the post-resurrectional relationships of love, the pre-
resurrectional relationships would find a very definite purpose
within such a context as well. It has been shown above that
these relationships (or poles of the one relationship) stress
above all the privileged position of Jesus with regard to the
Father: the Father loves Jesus and entrusts him with the
mission of revelation; Jesus loves the Father and carries out
that mission. In a debate with the synagogue, this particular

relationship would serve to affirm the belief in Jesus as the
Revealer of the Father, as the only possible link with the
Father.

I began this chapter with the purpose in mind of
seeing whether the understanding of ἀγάπη/ἀγαπᾶν in both
I John and those sections of the Farewell Discourse which
could reasonably be assigned to the same *Sitz im Leben* as that
of I John (i.e., 13:34-35; 15:1-17) could also be differentiated from the understanding of the same terms in the remainder
of the Gospel. The evidence has shown that such a differentiation is not only possible, but necessary: the author of the
Gospel is dealing with relationships of love that are either
transformed or bypassed in vv. 15:1-17, 13:34-35, and I John.
The evidence has also shown that the reason for this necessary
differentiation is quite simple: the author of the Gospel is
involved in a life situation quite different from that implied
by the other writings; above all, the struggle in the Gospel
is not at all intra-church, but rather church versus synagogue.

CHAPTER V

SUMMARY AND CONCLUSIONS

I began the present study with the observation that
exegetes working with the Johannine literature had developed,
over the years, manifold ways of dealing with the similarities
and differences that exist not only between the Gospel and the
Letters ascribed to John, but also within the Gospel itself
(i.e., the identification of distinct literary layers). Then,
following Culpepper's appraisal of the exegetical situation,
I delineated four common denominators to which the manifold
ways can and have been reduced: (1) the utilization of evidence provided by the Church Fathers; (2) close analysis of
terminology and style of the writings in question; (3) conceptual and theological parallels within the same writings;
(4) the structure and function of contemporary "schools."

I proceeded to state that it was not my goal in the
present study to develop or propose yet a new methodology, but
rather to test and refine an already existing hypothesis, viz.,
that of Jürgen Becker, who claims that the author of I John
(or someone in the same life situation)--to be distinguished
from the author of the Gospel--was actively concerned with and
engaged in the redaction of the Gospel. Although Becker is
not alone in this claim, I chose his position in particular
because it provides the most complex view of that process of
redaction. To recapitulate, it is Becker's opinion that the
Nachgeschichte of the Johannine community involves a redaction
of the Gospel by several persons, one of whom--if not the
author of I John, then someone coming from the same *Sitz im
Leben*--added vv. 13:34-35, 15:1-17, 15:18-16:15 to the original Farewell Discourse.

Furthermore, I proposed to undertake the testing of
Becker's hypothesis by means of a variation of the third common denominator mentioned above. Thus, I proposed to carry out

a redaction-critical study of the terms ἀγάπη/ἀγαπᾶν--follow-
ing the exegetical restrictions imposed upon any comparison of
the Gospel and the Letters by Günter Klein--in I John, in those
sections of the Farewell Discourse attributed by Becker to a
similar *Sitz im Leben* as that of I John, and in the Gospel.
The primary reason for the choice of this root was its centrality as well as high incidence in all the writings or passages involved.

       Now that the proposed enquiry has been completed in
the preceding three chapters, it is time to recapitulate the
results of that enquiry and to return to some of the questions
raised in the introductory chapter. Therefore, I propose to
organize this final chapter as follows: (A) a summary of the
results of the redaction-critical study of ἀγάπη/ἀγαπᾶν in
Chapters II, III, and IV; (B) a reconstruction of the development of the Johannine community on the basis of that redaction-
critical study; (C) a response to two questions prompted by
the results of recent exegesis and raised in the first chapter: Was the Johannine community a sect? Was the latter
stage of the community even more sectarian and exclusivistic?;
(D) a brief dialogue with those exegetes who posit an even
more extensive reworking of the Gospel by the author of I John.

                   Summary of Exegetical Results--
                     Chapters II, III, and IV

"Love" and "To Love" in I John

       The development of the second chapter above may be
divided into three primary stages: (a) an analysis and delineation of the structure of I John; (b) the redaction-critical
quest itself in terms of that structure; (c) an outline of the
Sitz im Leben presupposed by the references to love within the
Letter.

       The Structure of I John. First of all, with regard
to the structure of I John, I decided to avoid the two extremes
that have been proposed in the history of the interpretation of
that structure, viz., the absence of any visible structure
(e.g., O'Neill and Bultmann) as well as the presence of an

extremely involved and detailed structure (e.g., Lohmeyer and
Albertz), in favor of the *via media* that more recent exegesis
has adopted. That *via media* revolves essentially around the
belief that the argumentation of the Letter--and, therefore,
its structure as well--may be best characterized as a "spiral,"
i.e., it utilizes a complex system of synonymous expressions
to proceed from unit to unit, from paragraph to paragraph.

Furthermore, I agreed with those exegetes who see in
the Letter a succession of ethical and dogmatic (or christological) sections and proceeded to integrate that succession
into the "spiral," so that the largely ethical and largely
dogmatic sections were seen as constituting the most overarching themes of the "spiral" itself. This position, not unlike
that of J. Bogart, satisfactorily takes into account two basic
structural elements of the Letter.

As a result, I further decided to develop the redaction-critical study of ἀγάπη/ἀγαπᾶν according to that structure, i.e., in terms of the largely ethical (vv. 1:5-2:17;
2:28-3:24; 4:7-21) and largely dogmatic sections (vv. 2:18-27;
4:1-6; 5:1-12) as well as in terms of self-contained units or
paragraphs within the largely ethical sections (I. *1:5-2:17* =
1:5-2:11, 2:15-17; II. *2:28-3:24* = 2:28-3:10, 3:11-18,
3:19-24; III. *4:7-21* = 4:7-12, 13-16a, 16b-21).

Redaction-Critical Study of "Love" in I John. The
redaction critical study of the root "love" within the spiral
unveiled the presence of four basic relationships of love:
(1) the love of God for the disciples; (2) the love of Jesus
for the disciples; (3) the love of the disciples for God;
(4) the love of the disciples for one another.

(1) The love that God has shown toward the disciples
surfaces directly in paragraphs 2:28-3:10, 4:7-12, and 4:13-
16a. In all three cases that love is conceived not only in
terms of a past historical event, but also specifically in
terms of the redemptive death of Jesus, the Son of God, whom
God is said to have sent. Thus, for example, the statement of
v. 3:1--ποταπὴν ἀγάπην δέδωκεν ἡμῖν ὁ πατήρ--should be understood, within the paragraph, in terms of vv. 4 and 8b: the
removal of sins effected by the Son of God. Similarly, the

two statements of vv. 4:8 and 16b--ὁ θεὸς ἀγάπη ἐστίν--can
only be understood in terms of the activity of God described
in vv. 4:9-10 and 4:14-15 respectively: the sending of the
Son to take away sins.

It is the death of his Son that epitomizes and recapitulates God's love toward the disciples; there is no other
form or channel of this particular relationship described in
the Letter.

(2) The love that Jesus has shown toward the disciples
is not explicitly mentioned in I John, but, given the centrality of Jesus' redemptive death in the definition of God's
love for man, one can only infer that Jesus' own love is
implied in that love of God, i.e., it is epitomized and recapitulated in the redemptive character of his death in the
world. He represents the only link between God and man, and,
as such, he too must partake of that love. V. 3:16 represents,
I believe, an indirect reference to this love of Jesus, since
love (ἐν τούτῳ ἐγνώκαμεν τὴν ἀγάπην) is defined therein in
terms of Jesus' redemptive death and no mention is made of the
love of God for men as such.

(3) Within the spiral structure of the Letter, the
author describes several times what the love of man for God
should entail and, as such, utilizes different sets of symbols
or expressions to characterize that love. Furthermore, he
undertakes the delineation of this third relationship of love
almost entirely from a polemical point of view, i.e., attempting to differentiate what "correct" or "perfect" love means
from "incorrect" or "false" love (= hatred). The paragraphs
in question are: 1:5-2:11; 2:15-17; 4:7-12; 4:16b-21; 5:1-12.

According to the author, the essence of "correct" or
"perfect" love lies in the execution of certain commands (τὰς
ἐντολὰς τηρεῖν) which may be attributed to Jesus (vv. 2:3-5)
or to God the Father (vv. 5:2-3). Therefore, only the one who
carries out these commands may be said to love God. The commands are further identified in v. 3:23 as belief in Jesus'
name (ἵνα πιστεύσωμεν τῷ ὀνόματι τοῦ υἱοῦ αὐτοῦ Ἰησοῦ Χριστοῦ)
and love for one another (ἵνα ἀγαπῶμεν ἀλλήλους) and in vv.
2:7-11 and 4:21 as the love of one's brother (e.g., v. 4:21 =
ὁ ἀγαπῶν τὸν θεὸν ἀγαπᾷ καὶ τὸν ἀδελφὸν αὐτοῦ). As a result,

correct love of God involves a certain dogmatic stance as well
as a certain ethical position.

The polemical nature of the presentation also allows
the reader to discern what, in the eyes of the author, constitutes "incorrect" or "false" love. Basically, such love
indicates a failure to execute the designated commands
(vv. 2:3-5; 5:2-3). On the one hand, it involves a claim to
love God directly (vv. 4:10, 20), thus bypassing the love
which God had for men in Jesus. On the other hand, it also
involves a love "for the world" (vv. 2:15-17; 3:17) which is
characterized by the adoption of certain practices such as
licentiousness, greed, self-boasting and a failure to help
one's brother in need. As such, "false" love of God also
involves a definite dogmatic stance as well as a definite
ethical position.

(4) As in the previous relationship of love, the love
of the disciples for one another is developed by the author
in different sections of the spiral (the paragraphs in question are: 1:5-2:11; 2:28-3:10; 3:11-18; 3:19-24; 4:7-12;
5:1-12) and from a polemical point of view as well.

First of all, the author grounds "correct" love for
one another on the love which God had for man, i.e., the
redemptive death of Jesus (vv. 3:16, 24; 4:11, 17-19). That
death becomes a prototype for the behavior of the entire community. Although it would appear *prima facie* that such a
specific grounding should be taken in a very literal sense,
two arguments militate against this position: (1) the absence
of any signs of persecution or bloodshed within the community;
(2) the highly symbolical meaning of the terms ἡ ζωή/ὁ θάνατος
in the Letter. Therefore, it appears much more reasonable to
interpret such a grounding in terms of an acceptance or confession of the redemptive character of Jesus' death, that is,
to love one another implies belief in Jesus as Son of God and
in his death as redemptive. Secondly, "correct" love of the
brethren also signifies the execution of righteousness (vv.
3:10, 2:29, 3:7) and abstention from sin (v. 3:6). As a
result, "correct" love of the brethren involves a definite
christological position as well as a corresponding ethical
stance.

By way of contrast, "incorrect" love of the brethren
(= hatred) implies a bypassing or rejection of that love of
God (vv. 4:10, 20) as well as a turning to sin and lawlessness
(vv. 3:4, 6, 8). Only he who loves "correctly," the author
argues, may be said to be "in the light"; "to have passed into
life"; "to abide in God" (and vice versa); "to know God"; "to
be a child of God."

In summary, it is evident that "correct" love of God
and "correct" love of the brethren are synonymous and coexis-
tent positions and that the first two relationships of love
are central to the differentiation of "correct" love from
"incorrect" love. The failure to accept the first two relationships precludes *ipso facto*--despite any claims to the
contrary--the proper exercise of the last two.

Sitz im Leben. Finally, the delineation of the *Sitz
im Leben* presupposed by the redaction-critical study of ἀγάπη/
ἀγαπᾶν in I John was found to be in basic agreement with the
view held by a majority of contemporary exegetes concerning
that *Sitz im Leben.* Thus, the description of both "incorrect"
love of God and "incorrect" love of neighbor points, without
a doubt, to the presence of a docetic-libertine brand of
Johannine Christianity, a group which bypasses entirely the
redemptive death of Jesus (in favor of a special claim "to
know" him and a direct love of God) and which has adopted an
ethical stance bordering on antinomianism (while still claiming "to abide" in God). In response to this serious controversy within the community, the author presents a two-pronged
command of love: against docetism, he argues that love must
include the correct christological doctrine; against libertinism, he argues that love must also include the execution of
righteousness. Any claim to the contrary is simply not "truth,"
but "falsehood."

*"Love" and "To Love" in Jn 15:1-17,
    13:34-35, 15:18-16:15*

As in the case of the preceding chapter, the development of the third and present chapter may be divided into
three primary stages: (a) an overview of the different

exegetical theories concerning the structure of the Farewell
Discourse in the Gospel aimed at placing J. Becker's theory in
its proper historical perspective; (b) a literary-critical
analysis of those sections of the discourse assigned by Becker
to the *Sitz im Leben* of I John; (c) a redaction-critical study
of ἀγάπη/ἀγαπᾶν in the proposed sections.

  Exegetical Tradition. The overview of the exegetical
tradition has shown that there have been four major ways of
dealing with the literary and theological problems of the Farewell Discourse as it now stands in the Gospel: (1) an attempt
to explain such difficulties by means of Jesus' physical movements (the "historicizing" approach); (2) the rearrangement of
the verses and chapters in question in order to achieve a more
logical sequence or progression of thought (the "transpositional" approach); (3) the explanation of the difficulties
through outright removal or the discovery of a more symbolical
meaning (the "softening" approach); (4) a theory of later additions to an original Farewell Discourse (the "redactional"
approach).

  Furthermore, the overview also showed that more recent
exegesis had opted for either the "transpositional" approach
(Lattke) or the "redactional" approach (Borig; Richter; Brown;
Lindars; Schnackenburg), with the latter--in one form or
another--emerging as the favorite. Finally, an analysis of
Becker's literary theory in the light of this perspective
showed that he stands very much within the "redactional"
approach first proposed by J. Wellhausen and further developed
by M.-J. Lagrange. Becker's own variation may be characterized as follows: (1) chapters 15-17 represent a later addition to an original Farewell Discourse; (2) those same chapters may be divided into originally independent discourses
(Brown; Lindars; Schnackenburg); (3) these discourses may be
assigned to several authors, none of whom is the evangelist
(Schnackenburg); (4) one of these authors comes from a *Sitz im
Leben* similar to that of I John (Richter; Schnackenburg).

Literary Critical Analysis of Jn 15:1-17, 13:34-35, and 15:18-16:15. The verses or discourses that Becker assigns to the situation of I John are: 15:1-17; 13:34-35; 15:18-16:15. On the basis of a literary critical study of these proposed units, I came to the conclusion that the first two sections could and did represent originally independent units, but that Becker was incorrect in the delineation of the third section, viz., 15:18-16:15.

First of all, in the case of the first section, vv. 15:1ff. are totally and completely unexpected after the concluding command of Jesus in v. 14:31c. As such, v. 15:1 should be regarded as the beginning of a new discourse. Similarly, vv. 15:18ff. may be separated from vv. 15:1-17 on two major counts: (1) the development of the love command is not continued at all in the former verses; (2) there is no anticipation whatsoever of the theme of hatred--the main theme of vv. 15:18ff.--in the latter verses. Therefore, v. 15:17 may be regarded as the conclusion of the discourse begun in v. 15:1.

Secondly, vv. 13:34-35 should be considered a clear interruption of the progression of thought in the introduction to the original Farewell Discourse (vv. 13:31-38) and removed as a later addition to its present context. Thus, the theme of the approaching ὑπάγειν of Jesus introduced in v. 13:33 is clearly continued in the dialogue with Peter of vv. 13:36-38.

Finally, the third section as delineated by Becker is simply too long. Given the position that vv. 15:1-17 represent a literary unity, v. 15:18 also represents the beginning of a new unit or discourse. However, its conclusion lies in v. 16:4a, not v. 16:15. The theme concerning the hatred of the world, introduced by v. 15:18, comes to a climax in vv. 16:1-4a, where the specific channels of that hatred are enumerated and concretized. Furthermore, with v. 16:4b the theme of departure explicitly enters into the picture once again (while that of hatred is abandoned).

Redaction-Critical Study. From the point of view of the redaction-critical study of ἀγάπη/ἀγαπᾶν in the literary unities delineated above, i.e., 15:1-17; 13:34-35; 15:18-16:4a,

I came to the conclusion that Becker was correct in assigning
the first two sections to a *Sitz im Leben* paralleling that of
I John (although I found his reasons for such an attribution
to be insufficient *per se*) but incorrect in a similar attribution of the last section--which he sees as a subdivision of
the larger unit, 15:18-16:15.

(1) First of all, vv. 15:1-17 were divided into two
largely parallel sections: vv. 15:1-8, which begin with the
Bildrede of the vine and which concentrate almost exclusively
on the theme of πίστις, and vv. 15:9-17, which begin with a
hierarchy of love and concentrate almost exclusively on the
theme of ἀγάπη. The division is most clearly observed in the
reprise of the imperative of v. 4 in v. 9b.

Within the first section of the discourse, viz.,
vv. 15:1-8, I found the paramount issue to be one of belief.
Thus, for example, the object of the expression μένειν ἐν,
which dominates thematically vv. 4-7, is, for the most part,
either the personal pronoun ἐμοί (vv. 15:4[2], 5, 6, 7) or the
main figure of the *Bildrede*, τῇ ἀμπέλῳ (v. 15:4), i.e., Jesus
himself. Some "branches" or believers have either abandoned
or are in the process of abandoning Jesus. Furthermore, the
use of the adjective ἀληθινός to modify the noun ἡ ἄμπελος in
the *Bildrede* indicates that such an abandonment should be construed not so much as a total loss of faith, but rather as an
aberration of correct belief: some "branches" or believers
are acting as if they were not believers by presenting a view
of Jesus which is not the "true" one.

The second section of the discourse, viz., vv. 15:9-17,
indicates likewise that the community is having problems with
the ethical behavior of some of its members; the paramount
issue, therefore, is one of love. Furthermore, correct love
is developed in terms of five basic relationships of love:
(a) love of the Father for Jesus; (b) love of Jesus for the
disciples; (c) love of Jesus for the Father; (d) love of the
disciples for Jesus; (e) love of the disciples for one another.

(a) The love of the Father toward Jesus--a love which
is not mentioned at all in I John--is introduced at the very
beginning of this section, within the hierarchy of love
posited in v. 15:9a. It is that love which commences the

hierarchy itself: καθὼς ἠγάπησέν με ὁ πατήρ; however, the
author does not describe or expand upon the nature of that
love.

(b) The love of Jesus for the disciples--a love which
is only implicitly mentioned in the First Letter as part of
the love of God for men--constitutes the one and major link in
the hierarchy of love in v. 15:9a: κἀγὼ ὑμᾶς ἠγάπησα. Furthermore, unlike the first relationship of love mentioned
above, the love of Jesus for the disciples is very clearly
amplified in v. 15:13, immediately after the reintroduction
of the comparative conjunction καθὼς in v. 15:12 (καθὼς
ἠγάπησα ὑμᾶς). Such love is described exclusively in terms
of a past historical event (although still outstanding from
the point of view of the discourse), viz., Jesus' death on
behalf of the φίλοι (ἵνα τις τὴν ψυχὴν αὐτοῦ θῇ ὑπὲρ τῶν φίλων
αὐτοῦ).

(c) Given this hierarchy of love of v. 15:9a (God the
Father--Jesus--the disciples), the author proceeds to show how
each element or link of that hierarchy "abides" in it. First
of all, Jesus returned the love of the Father by executing
the Father's commands, among which no doubt the event of
v. 15:13 is included (ἐγὼ τὰς ἐντολὰς τοῦ πατρός μου τετήρηκα).
As in the case of the first relationship, this third relationship is not developed at all in I John.

(d) This definition of the love of Jesus for the Father
then becomes the exemplar for the love that the disciples *must*
manifest toward Jesus. Just as Jesus carried out the Father's
commands and abode in the chain, so must the disciples execute
Jesus' commands (ἐὰν τὰς ἐντολάς μου τηρήσητε) and thus abide
in the chain. This is the only way in which the disciples can
manifest their love for Jesus. Furthermore, vv. 12-17 make
it very clear that the central command to be kept (ἡ ἐντολὴ
ἡ ἐμή) is that of mutual love or love for one another.

(e) The fifth and final relationship of love is that
which must exist among the φίλοι--those who have received
revelation from Jesus and have believed--for one another.
That love is grounded by the author specifically on the death
of Jesus on their behalf: the φίλοι are to love one another
because and as Jesus loved them; they are to incorporate that

mode of Jesus' love, i.e., the second relationship of love, into their own love for one another.

I then proceeded to examine the relationship between these two sections, between vv. 1-8 and 9-17, between πίστις and ἀγάπη, in terms of the "grounding" mentioned above. It seemed to me, given the absence of any signs of persecution or bloodshed in the discourse, that such a grounding of the disciples' love for one another was to be interpreted symbolically: it means the acceptance of that mode of love, of Jesus' redemptive death, on the part of the believer. A corresponding denial of that death, on the other hand, points to the existence of a docetic understanding of Jesus Christ in the community. Furthermore, that acceptance implies as well the execution of Jesus' other ἐντολαί, and a corresponding failure to execute them points to the presence of a libertine understanding of Christian behavior in the community.

As a result, I interpreted vv. 9-17 as developing vv. 1-8 in three major ways: (1) insofar as the nature of the "true" vine is clearly specified in v. 15:13; (2) insofar as belief in that true vine is incorporated into the love command itself; (3) insofar as implications of that belief, in the form of ethical norms or demands, are introduced into the love command as well.

Finally, on the basis of these results, I came to the conclusion that the *Sitz im Leben* of the discourse duplicated that of I John: against a docetic understanding of Jesus as the Christ and the Son of God, the author included correct belief within the love command; similarly, against a libertine interpretation of Christian behavior, the author included correct praxis as a part of that same love command. Thus, once again, one finds a two-pronged love command designed to meet and counteract a two-pronged deviation consisting of docetism and antinomianism.

(2) Secondly, I found that vv. 13:34-35 could also be reasonably assigned to the *Sitz im Leben* of the First Letter both on the basis of their relationship to Jn 15:1-17 and their relationship to I John. Thus, for example, a comparison of the two verses with Jn 15:1-17 shows that the two sections have many terminological, grammatical, and theological

features in common, thus pointing not only to a similar community situation (that situation also betrays signs of the
presence of a docetic-libertine group which the author proceeds to counteract by stressing the execution of the love
command and by grounding that command in the mode of Jesus'
own love for the disciples), but also to a common authorship.
This association between vv. 13:34-35 and 15:1-17 is sufficient
per se to thrust the former verses into the sphere of thought
of I John. However, this judgment is further strengthened by
certain features which the two verses have directly in common
with I John: (1) the use of the introductory formula, ἐν
τούτῳ γινώσκειν, in v. 13:35; and (2) the characterization of
the love command as a "new" command (καινός) in v. 13:34.

        (3) Finally, I found it impossible to connect vv.
15:18-16:4a with the *Sitz im Leben* of I John. Despite the
absence of the terms ἀγάπη/ἀγαπᾶν in the discourse, a study
of the use of the verb μισεῖν in the section shows that the
nature of such "hatred" as given in vv. 16:1-4a includes
(1) the expulsion of believers from the synagogue and (2) persecution to the point of death. However, a study of I John
has already shown that the community is not under persecution
or in danger of death, and, furthermore, that the struggle is
not one of church versus synagogue, but rather correct belief
versus incorrect belief. As a result, the discourse lies much
closer to the concerns and interests of the Fourth Gospel.

"Love" and "To Love" in the Fourth
  Gospel

        Like the other two chapters, the development of the
fourth chapter may be divided into three main stages: (a) a
delineation of the structure of that section where most of the
references to love are found, i.e., Jn 13:31-14:31; (b) the
redaction-critical study itself in terms of that structure;
(c) an outline of the *Sitz im Leben* presupposed by the results
of that redaction-critical quest.

        The Structure of Jn 13:31-14:31. An arrangement of
all the eligible references to love in the Gospel according to
seven major sections (Jn 1-12; 13:1-30; 13:31-14:31; 15:18-

16:4a; 16:4b-33; 17; 18-20) showed that the highest concentration of these references occurs in the original Farewell Discourse of the Gospel, viz., Jn 13:31-14:31. Within the short
space of a chapter, one finds ten of the twenty-seven eligible
references.

　　　Furthermore, I followed for the most part J. Becker's
proposed structure of the Farewell Discourse. That structure
may be delineated as follows: (1) an introduction consisting
of vv. 13:31-38, the purpose of which is to place the entire
discourse within the perspective of Jesus' departure and to
address itself to the situation of the disciples "in the
world" after Jesus' departure. (2) the main body of the discourse, consisting of three main divisions (vv. 14:1-3, 4-15,
16-26). The first division introduces the overarching themes
of the discourse: Jesus' πορεύομαι and ἔρχομαι; the second
develops the one theme of his departure (πορεύομαι/ὑπάγω); the
third takes up that of his return (ἔρχομαι). (3) the conclusion to the discourse, vv. 14:27-31, the purpose of which is
to recall not only the overarching themes of the discourse,
but also other subordinate themes as well and to anticipate
the betrayal of Jesus at the hands of Judas in chapter 18.

　　　A distribution of the ten references to love within
this section according to these three divisions (and subdivisions) showed that the majority of them (eight in all) appear
in the third subdivision of the main body of the discourse,
viz., vv. 14:15-26. As a result, I began the redaction-
critical quest by focusing upon these verses as the specific
point of departure.

　　　Redaction-Critical Study. Secondly, since love is
presented in the Farewell Discourse in terms of four relationships of love, I decided to structure the redaction-critical
study of ἀγάπη/ἀγαπᾶν/φιλεῖν according to those four relationships of love, beginning with the three presented in vv. 15-26
--the designated point of departure--and continuing with the
one contained in vv. 27-31. Furthermore, I decided to consider other examples of these relationships outside the Farewell Discourse immediately after the initial exposition of

each relationship within that discourse and concluded by
examining those texts which did not fit into this arrangement.

The four relationships of love are: (1) the love of
the disciples for Jesus; (2) the love of the Father for the
disciples; (3) the love of Jesus for the disciples; (4) the
love of Jesus for the Father (and vice versa).

(1) The central relationship of love in vv. 15-26 is
that of the love of the disciples for Jesus (vv. 14:15, 21a,
23a, 24a); the other two relationships in those verses relate
to this one as promises to a condition. Other indirect references are found in vv. 3:19; 5:42; and 12:43. The love of
Jesus is defined by the author in terms of executing (τηρεῖν)
Jesus' commands (ἐντολαί), word (λόγος), or words (λόγοι),
and a further examination of these combinations in the Gospel
reveals that they mean nothing other than belief in Jesus and
in his origin and identity.

A comparison of the Gospel with Jn 15:1-17, 13:34-35
and I John shows that this particular relationship of love is
present in Jn 15:1-17 and presupposed in I John and that it is
defined in both writings also in terms of τὰς ἐντολὰς τηρεῖν.
However, that comparison also shows that the equation, love of
Jesus = belief in Jesus, is not preserved in those writings;
rather, love for Jesus is made to include ethical demands as
part of these ἐντολαί as well as the need for *correct* belief
in Jesus.

(2) The love of the Father toward the disciples is
presented in vv. 14:15-26 (14:21b, 23b) as a promise made to
those who love Jesus, i.e., who believe in him. Once that
condition is operative, the Father will manifest his love by
sending the Paraclete to take the place of Jesus among the
disciples. As such, the Father's love is portrayed as an
ongoing, post-resurrectional event in the latter writings:
the love of the Father is understood exclusively in terms of
the sending of the Paraclete.

(3) Similarly, the love of Jesus for the disciples is
also presented in vv. 14:15-26 (14:21b) as a promise to those
who love Jesus, i.e., who believe in him. Jesus will manifest
his love for the disciples by asking the Father to send the
Paraclete to the community so that the latter may continue

Jesus' revelatory work in the community. As such, Jesus' own
love is portrayed as an ongoing, post-resurrectional activity.
A comparison of the Gospel with Jn 15:1-17, 13:34-35 and
I John shows once again that this ongoing, post-resurrectional
activity becomes a historical, pre-resurrectional relationship
in the latter writings.

     (4) The final relationship of love within the discourse
is given in v. 14:31, viz., the love of Jesus for the Father.
Such love is described in terms of Jesus' execution of whatever the Father commands, including his own death. The other
pole of the relationship, i.e., the love of the Father for
Jesus, is found in vv. 3:35; 5:20; and 10:17. That love is
also described in terms of Jesus' mission, i.e., the Father
shows his love by entrusting Jesus with the task of revelation
in the world, a task which culminates in Jesus' death. As
such, both poles of the same relationship clearly point to
its pre-resurrectional character.

     A comparison of the two poles of this relationship
with Jn 15:1-17, 13:34-35 and I John brings out two major
differences: (1) the Father's love for Jesus is mentioned
only in Jn 15:1-17, but not developed at all; (2) Jesus' love
for the Father is developed only in Jn 15:1-17, where it
clearly grounds the love of the disciples for Jesus and for
one another, so that the mode of Jesus' love becomes constitutive for the love of the disciples.

    Sitz im Leben. The results of this redaction-critical
study emphasize the differences that exist between the relationships of love described in Jn 15:1-17, 13:34-35 and I John
and those in the Gospel. First of all, the former writings
include a relationship of love which is completely left out of
consideration by the Gospel: the love of the disciples for
one another, a love which demands a correct christological confession as well as the execution of definite ethical norms.
Secondly, the Gospel elaborates a mutual relationship of love
--that of the Father and the Son--which is completely bypassed
in I John and mentioned, but hardly developed, in Jn 15:1-17
and 13:34-35.

Finally, even when the two sets of writings have relationships of love in common, the meaning of these relationships in each set is quite different. For example, both sets
mention a relationship of love from the Father and/or Jesus
toward the disciples. Yet, in Jn 15:1-17, 13:34-35 and I John
such a relationship is described exclusively in terms of a
specific historical event, viz., the redemptive death of Jesus,
while in the Gospel that relationship is focused on the figure
of the Paraclete, viz., an ongoing, post-resurrectional
activity. Similarly, both sets also mention a relationship
of love from the disciples toward the Father and/or Jesus.
Yet, in Jn 15:1-17, 13:34-35 and I John this relationship
includes the love command, which in turn signifies correct
praxis as well as correct belief, while in the Gospel it is
conceived solely in terms of belief in Jesus' origin and identity.

These differences indicate, first of all, that the
meaning of ἀγάπη/ἀγαπᾶν in I John may be differentiated quite
clearly from their meaning in the Gospel (which includes the
synonymous φιλεῖν). Secondly, the differences also indicate
that the meaning of these same terms in Jn 15:1-17 and 13:34-
35 duplicates that of I John and may also be differentiated
quite clearly from their meaning in the Gospel. As a result,
it is not only reasonable to assign Jn 15:1-17 and 13:34-35
to the same *Sitz im Leben* as that of I John, but also absolutely necessary.

On the other hand, the *Sitz im Leben* presupposed by
the relationships of love contained in the Gospel tends to
confirm the theory of a virulent anti-Jewish polemic in the
community most recently advanced by J. L. Martyn's monograph,
History and Theology in the Fourth Gospel. There are indications both within the Farewell Discourse itself and among the
remaining love references in the Gospel that the "love for
Jesus" (= belief in him) and its consequences are being presented in a polemical fashion and that the object of the
polemic are the οἱ Ἰουδαῖοι.

First of all, within the Farewell Discourse itself one
finds the following clues: (1) in vv. 22-24 one finds an
antithesis of the definition of the love of Jesus: if such

love implies the execution of his commands (or other variations), the lack of such love implies a failure to carry out
those same commands, i.e., a refusal to believe in him; (2) in
vv. 15-26 those who love Jesus (= who believe in him) are constantly differentiated from "the world": whereas the former
will receive the promises accruing to such love (or belief),
the latter is completely denied any such favors; (3) in
v. 13:33 the disciples are placed on the same level as the
Jews: they cannot follow Jesus. However, the rest of the
discourse clearly shows that only the disciples will see him
again, and no one else, i.e., the Jews. It appears, therefore, that the Jews incarnate the attitude of non-belief given
in vv. 22-24 as well as that of the term ὁ κόσμος in vv. 15-26.

Secondly, this line of thought is confirmed by the
context of three other references to love in the Gospel, viz.,
vv. 5:42; 8:42; and 12:43. All these references point specifically to the conflict that exists between Jesus and the Jews,
a conflict which is ultimately based on the refusal of the
Jews to accept Jesus and which betrays an atmosphere of rather
intense persecution.

The love references would then point to an attempt on
the part of the Christian believers--who, according to Martyn's
thesis, have been expelled from the synagogue--to differentiate
themselves from the Jews, from the synagogue, on two counts:
(1) they are the recipients of the only true revelation from
the Father; (2) because of their acceptance of this revelation,
they alone have the Father's love, viz., the possession of the
Paraclete.

*Development of the Johannine Community
in terms of the Redaction-Critical
Results Outlined Above*

Given the exegetical results outlined above, I should
like at this point to paint in rather broad strokes the history of the Johannine community that emerges from these
results, i.e., from the community's developing understanding
of ἀγάπη/ἀγαπᾶν. That history may be divided into four stages:
(1) the Gospel stage (since the root "love" offers very little
information concerning the pre-Gospel stages of the community,

I shall begin with the stage of the evangelist); (2) the
emergence of a docetic-libertine group within the community;
(3) the response of I John to this double threat; (4) the
redaction of the Gospel. Furthermore, I shall present each
stage by collecting and enumerating certain important facts
that have emerged as being unique to each stage.

The Stage of the Fourth Gospel

        With regard to the stage of the evangelist, the fol-
lowing results should be kept in mind:
        (a) an emphasis on the relationship of love that
exists between the Father and Jesus, i.e., the role of Jesus
in carrying out the Father's mission or task in the world.
Jesus is the Revealer of the Father and, consequently, the
only way to the Father.
        (b) an explicit definition of the love for Jesus on
the part of the disciples as belief in him, i.e., belief in
his origin (he comes from and is sent by the Father) and
identity (he reveals the Father).
        (c) an explicit and consistent differentiation of
those who love Jesus (= who have believed in him) from those
who do not, who in turn are identified as "the world" or as
"the Jews." In other words, it is the Jews who fail to accept
Jesus' origin and identity and, in so doing, renounce all contact with the Father.
        (d) a complete absence of any love command addressed
to the believers. The relationship among the brethren is
never discussed.
        (e) a coalescing of all promises made to those who
love Jesus (= who have believed in him) around the figure of
the "other Paraclete," who succeeds Jesus and continues the
latter's presence and revelatory work in the community.
        First of all, point (c) above indicates, without a
doubt, the existence of a controversy between Christian
believers--probably Jews who have accepted the Messiahship of
Jesus--and the Jewish synagogue. Points (a) and (b) identify
the reason for the conflict as being exclusively that of the
origin and identity of Jesus: the Jews refuse to accept Jesus'
claims, while those who do deny the Jews any knowledge of or

contact with the Father, i.e., in denying the Father's
Revealer, they in effect deny the Father himself. Point (d)
shows quite clearly that the community of believers is still
a close-knit community, which is not experiencing any tension
at all from within at this point; the only tension that exists
is coming from the outside and holds completely the author's
attention. Point (e) reveals the self--understanding of the
community: since they have accepted Jesus, theirs is a privileged position vis-à-vis the Father, i.e., both the Father
and Jesus are with them and *only* with them (most probably in
the form of a spirit-filled, prophetic community).

The Docetic-Libertine Group

In contrast with the first stage, a study of the
terms ἀγάπη/ἀγαπᾶν reveals very little information concerning
this second stage, i.e., what exactly did the opponents of
I John. mean when they employed these terms. Yet, enough information is available to reconstruct the bare outlines of their
position (although it must be admitted that such a reconstruction is perforce very hypothetical, given the polemical nature
of the presentation).

(a) the constant accusation on the part of the author
of I John to the effect that this group is not "loving their
brother" shows that they are Christian believers, that they
come from within the community itself (cf., I Jn 2:18-19; Jn
15:1-6). All mention of the οἱ Ἰουδαῖοι disappears; indeed,
the epithets which were once levelled at the Jews are now used
to characterize this group, e.g., Jn 8:44: ὑμεῖς ἐκ τοῦ
πατρὸς τοῦ διαβόλου ἐστέ/ I Jn 3:10: τὰ τέκνα τοῦ διαβόλου.

(b) the group lays claim to a certain πνεῦμα
(vv. 4:1ff.), a "spirit," which the author of the Letter proceeds to characterize as "the spirit of the antichrist"
(v. 4:3), "the spirit which is in the world or of the world"
(v. 4:4), "the spirit of falsehood" (v. 4:6).

(c) this spirit leads the group to proclaim, ἀγαπῶ
τὸν θεόν (v. 4:20). This relationship of love is specified,
first of all, in the third characterization of the opponents'
position in vv. 2:3-6. The substitution of the controlling
terms of v. 3 with synonymous expressions in v. 5 shows that

the group conceives of the love of God in terms of a special
relationship with the Son of God, ἔγνωκα αὐτόν. Furthermore,
this is a relationship which seems to bypass the laws or commands which the community takes as a sign of "true" knowledge,
i.e., an antinomian stance. In view of the other statements
of vv. 1:5-2:11, such a knowledge would include the following
claims: κοινωνίαν ἔχομεν μετ' αὐτοῦ (= μετὰ τοῦ θεοῦ), v. 1:6;
ἁμαρτίαν οὐκ ἔχομεν, v. 1:8; οὐχ ἡμαρτήκαμεν, v. 1:10; ἐν
αὐτῷ ἐσμεν, v. 2:5; ἐν τῷ φωτί (ἐσμεν), v. 2:9.

        (d) the arguments used by the author of I John in
vv. 4:7-12 and 4:16b-21 to counteract the claims of point (c)
above (ἀγαπῶ τὸν θεόν) indicate--given their emphasis on the
unique position of Jesus as the only mediator of the Father's
love and on the exclusive centrality of Jesus' redemptive
death within that mediation--that the group's claims to a
special relationship with the Son of God, a special "knowledge"
of him, includes a complete bypassing of the latter's death in
Jesus, i.e., a docetist position.

        It may be gathered from point (a) above that at the
time the docetic-libertine group emerges in the community the
conflict with the synagogue has died down, if not indeed dis-
appeared altogether. The problem about to erupt is a specifically Christian one, a rupture in the ranks of the believers.
Point (b) shows that this group is a pneumatic, charismatic
group and, as such, is in perfect continuity with the Gospel
stage, where the Paraclete, the spirit of truth, is promised
to those who believe. This consciousness of the spirit drives
the group, according to points (c) and (d), to a docetic-
libertine understanding of Jesus and the Christian life: the
group ceases to observe those rules which the rest of the
community considers necessary for Christian living in favor of
a claim to a specific and special knowledge of the Son of God,
a knowledge which implies love of God and a knowledge which
dispenses with such rules and bypasses completely the death
of Jesus.

I John

        The response to the emergence of this docetic-
libertine group in the community in the form of I John

constitutes the third stage of development. The following
points should be kept in mind:

(a) a deemphasizing of the relationship of love that
exists between the Father and Jesus. Neither pole of this
relationship is even mentioned in I John: the question of
Jesus' role, his origin and identity, is no longer a bone of
contention.

(b) an explicit definition of the relationship of love
between men and God in terms of the execution of certain specific commands (sometimes attributed to Jesus, v. 2:4, and
sometimes attributed to God the Father, vv. 3:23, 5:2-3).
Such commands include, according to v. 3:23, belief in the
name of his Son, Jesus Christ, i.e., the correct christological confession, and love for one another.

(c) a great deal of emphasis on the love which the
disciples--those who have been born of God (vv. 5:1-2)--must
have for one another. Furthermore, this relationship of love
is grounded on the mode of Jesus' love toward the disciples.

(d) a redefinition of the nature of God's and Jesus'
love toward the disciples: such love is no longer presented
in terms of the sending and abiding of the Paraclete to and
within the community; rather, such love is now presented
exclusively in terms of a historical event, Jesus' redemptive
death. Indeed, the author admits of distinctions among the
πνεύματα: only one πνεῦμα may be said to be ἐκ τοῦ θεοῦ
(vv. 4:1-2a), viz., the one who confesses the correct christological doctrine (vv. 4:2-3).

(e) a consistent differentiation of those who exercise
God's (and Jesus') commands from those who do not. The latter
are said to have gone forth into "the world" (v. 4:1b), to
possess "the spirit of the world" (v. 4:4), to be "of the
world" (v. 4:5), and, since the world is governed by the devil
(v. 5:19), they may rightly be called "the children of the
devil" (v. 3:10). All mention of the οἱ 'Ιουδαῖοι has dis-
appeared altogether.

As it was the case in the second stage, points (a)
and (e) reveal the fact that the controversy with the synagogue has ceased. As a result, it is no longer necessary to
define the relationship that exists between the Father and

his Son: all parties involved have accepted the role of
Jesus as Revealer of the Father; they are all Christian
believers.   The bone of contention now becomes the precise
definition of Jesus as the Son of God and the implications of
that definition for everyday Christian life, viz., it becomes
an intra-church controversy.   Given the pneumatic and charismatic self-understanding of the docetic-libertine group,
point (d) shows how the author of I John can no longer hold
that all believers possess the Paraclete, the spirit of truth,
but rather is forced to distinguish among "spirits":   there
can only be one spirit "of God."   Furthermore, he proceeds to
define that spirit in terms of the correct christological doctrine and ultimately in terms of tradition (vv. 1:1-4); thus,
tradition replaces the spirit as the criterion of truth.

    Points (b) and (c) show specifically how the author
combats the positions of the dissenting group: there can be
no love of God unless one loves one's neighbor through the
execution of certain specific commands and unless one believes
in the correct christological doctrine (unless the disciple
loves his fellow disciples as God [and Jesus] loved him).
This is the *only* way to God, and whoever chooses otherwise is
not "of God"; indeed, such a person has neither "seen" nor
"known" God (v. 3:6).   Such a one is "of the world" and, as
such, not to be loved by the community (v. 2:15).

The Redaction of the Gospel

    This last stage of the community could be considered as
a part of the third stage described above, but for analytical
purposes I have decided to consider it by itself.   At some point
along the line, either the author of I John or someone who
shared his exact situation (an ultimate decision on this point
is impossible to make) decided to incorporate his specific point
of view into what appears to have been an already redacted form
of the Fourth Gospel (e.g., vv. 3:31-36; 12:44-50).

    No doubt convinced of the rightness and traditional
nature of his position, this individual inserted vv. 13:34-35
and 15:1-17 into their present context in the Gospel.   The
reasoning behind this specific location is not hard to ascertain: (1) beginning with the departure of Judas in v. 13:30,

the hour of Jesus' glorification, i.e., the hour that signals
the end of his mission in the world and his return to the
Father, is said to have arrived. The death of Jesus is now
imminently anticipated from the point of view of the story as
presented by the evangelist. (2) as a result, Jesus turns to
the remaining disciples, the faithful disciples, and talks
about the circumstances that will ensue after his approaching
departure from their midst--circumstances which are no doubt
operative at the time of the composition of the discourse.

The redactor, therefore, first placed vv. 13:34-35
immediately after Jesus' directive to the effect that the disciples cannot follow him now: ὅπου ἐγὼ ὑπάγω ὑμεῖς οὐ δύνασθε
ἐλθεῖν, i.e., within the introduction to the discourse. Given
this situation, the redactor has Jesus in effect promulgate a
"new" command, the love command, and argue that such a command
is to be observed from that point (= the hour of his death) on.
Furthermore, the redactor has Jesus base the "new" command on
his own mode of love for the disciples--a mode of love which
is yet to be manifested in the story.

Similarly, the redactor placed vv. 15:1-17 immediately
after the conclusion to the original discourse. Thus, after
all the definitions of the love of Jesus are given in vv. 15-26
and after all the promises concerning Jesus' return to those
who show love for Jesus are made, the redactor further clari-
fies what is meant by belief in or love of Jesus in terms of
the situation that is now present in his community.

Viewed in this fashion, vv. 13:34-35 and 15:1-17 are
designed to make explicit the nature and character of Jesus'
approaching death, i.e., Jesus' conception of his own death
from the point of view of the story, and to show quite clearly
that he also commanded the disciples to love one another after
his own departure from the world. As such, the insertions
clearly take the rug from under the opponents' feet (i.e., the
docetic-libertine group): Jesus himself explicitly argued
against a position such as theirs before his own death. Therefore, not only does tradition become an all-powerful weapon
--ὃ ἦν ἀπ' ἀρχῆς, ὃ ἀκηκόαμεν, ὃ ἑωράκαμεν τοῖς ὀφθαλμοῖς
ἡμῶν, ὃ ἐθεασάμεθα καὶ αἱ χεῖρες ἡμῶν ἐψηλάφησαν κτλ.--but also
any claims to "know" Jesus or to be free of his ἐντολαί are
completely invalidated.

Sectarianism and the Johannine Community

In the overview of recent studies concerning the
nature and character of the Johannine community conducted in
the first chapter,[1] it was observed that the majority of these
studies did not hesitate to call the community a "sectarian"
community and, furthermore, proceeded to describe the latter
stage of this community, as represented by the Letters of John,
in terms of a "heightened" sectarianism.

That overview also showed that the main criterion used
by these authors for such a characterization (or a denial of
it, as the case may be) of the community was somewhat different in each case, i.e., each exegete had seized upon a different constitutive element of the community as the basis for
his judgment: Meeks emphasized above all the development by
the community of a symbolic language peculiar to itself which
served to reinforce their outlook on the world;[2] Moody Smith
centered on the exclusivistic and totalistic stance adopted
by the community;[3] Cullmann stressed the absence of a polemic
against the larger (= Synoptic) church;[4] Culpepper spoke of a
devotion to the teachings of a founder or adherence to a set
of principles;[5] Bogart isolated the attitude of perfectionism
among the brethren, i.e., the attainment of ethical and/or
spiritual perfection in this world.[6] One wonders, therefore,
whether Culpepper's despair with regard to the looseness with
which the term "school" has been used by Johannine scholars
would not apply to the usage of the adjective "sectarian" in
that same literature.

On the basis of the redaction-critical study of ἀγάπη/
ἀγαπᾶν in the Johannine tradition conducted above, I should
like at this point to address myself to two of the main questions posed by these studies: Was the Johannine community a
sectarian community? Was the latter stage of that community
even more sectarian and exclusivistic? Furthermore, given the
variations that exist concerning the criteria necessary for
such a judgment, it is my opinion that the exegete must have
recourse to sociological theory and to the typology of sects
outlined in that theory in order to begin to answer this type
of question in an informed fashion.[7] In what follows, therefore, I turn to the work of two men who, in my opinion, have

attempted to elaborate precisely such a typology of sectarianism, viz., Peter Berger and Bryan Wilson.

Peter Berger (1954)

In an article published in 1954 entitled "The Sociological Study of Sectarianism," Peter Berger observes that the
study of sectarianism in general, and above all sectarianism
in the United States, up to that point had been characterized
by an amassing of a great deal of empirical data without a
corresponding theoretical orientation.[8] The purpose of the
article, therefore, as he conceives it, is to begin to provide
the necessary theoretical orientation by developing a typology
of sectarianism which, although aimed primarily at the American
scene, is nevertheless applicable both "outside the American
scene" and "outside the field of Christianity."[9]

This typology he begins to develop by entering into a
critical dialogue with previous definitions of "sect" from the
sociology of religion (e.g., Max Weber, Ernst Troeltsch,
G. van der Leeuw, J. Wach, H. Richard Niebuhr, T. Elmer
Clark).[10] Such definitions, Berger argues, have for the most
part failed to define "sect" in terms of specifically religious criteria and have concentrated instead on historical
accidents of their social structure. As a result, Berger proposes the following definition: "a religious grouping based
on the belief that *the spirit is immediately present,*"[11] where
"spirit" simply means the religious object as such. (Italics
his.)

Furthermore, Berger divides this belief concerning the
immediate presence of the spirit that characterizes the sectarian consciousness into three main religious motifs (a
religious motif is "a specific pattern or gestalt of religious
experience that can be traced in a historical development")[12]:
(1) enthusiasm: an experience to be lived; (2) prophecy: a
message to be proclaimed; (3) gnosticism: a secret to be
divulged. Any sect, Berger argues, can usually be placed
within one of these three types. Below I reproduce Berger's
chart showing the three main types and their respective subtypes:

Type	Motif	Attitude toward the World
	I. Enthusiasm	
Revivalist Pentecostal	"fire falling from heaven"	world to be saved
Pietist Holiness	"follow the gleam"	world to be avoided
	II. Prophecy	
Chiliastic	"The Lord is coming"	world to be warned
Legalistic	"a new order"	world to be conquered
	III. Gnosticism	
Oriental	"wisdom from East"	world irrelevant
New Thought	"powers in the Soul"	"
Spiritist	"voices from beyond"	"

As it may be seen from the chart, each general type and/or subtype generates a certain response to the world, a response which in turn determines the social structure of that sect. Each of these positions constitutes in effect a "new world" or "new reality" quite distinct from the others.

Bryan Wilson (1959)

In 1959, five years after Berger's article, Bryan Wilson published a study entitled "An Analysis of Sect Development."[13] Wilson was grappling with the accepted principle that sects tend to become churches or denominations in the second generation of their existence and sought to discover the factors in the organization and circumstances of sects which either promoted or retarded this development. In so doing, he saw the need to abandon the more general concept of "sect"[14] and to look instead for these factors in the different identifiable subtypes of that term, presuming that each subtype possessed factors or combinations of factors peculiar to itself. Although the study is primarily concerned with the types present in American Protestantism,[15] nevertheless its proposed typology is useful for purposes of comparison.

The main criterion used by Wilson to differentiate among subtypes is the "type of mission" undertaken by the

sects, i.e., the response of the sect to the values of the
larger society, to the values of "the world."[16] He argues
that four such types of mission--and, therefore, four subtypes of sects--may be discerned: (1) the conversionist sect,
which seeks to alter men and the world; (2) the adventist
sect, which predicts a drastic alteration of the world;
(3) the introversionist sect, which rejects the world's
values and replaces them with other higher values; (4) the
gnostic sect, which tends to accept the world's values, but
seeks a new and esoteric means to achieve these values.   In
what follows, I proceed to list the empirical correlates of
each of these subtypes:

(1) the conversionist sect: teaching and activity
center on evangelism; extreme bibliolatry; conversion experience and acceptance of Jesus as personal Savior is the test
of admission; hostile to clerical learning; opposed to science;
disdains culture and artistic values accepted in the wider
society.

(2) the adventist sect: overturn of the present
world order; allegorical exegesis of the prophetic books of
the Bible; Jesus is a divine commander; a high moral standard
based on the moral precepts of Jesus; admission is gained by
thorough understanding of necessary doctrine; separation from
the world.

(3) the introversionist sect: attention drawn to the
community and to the members' possession of the Spirit; reli-
ance on inner illumination; an understanding of itself as a
group of enlightened elect; inner values are incommunicable;
eschatological ideas are of little significance; a strong
ingroup morality; withdrawal from the world.

(4) the gnostic sect: special body of teaching of an
esoteric kind; the Bible is allegorical and complements the
gnosis; conventional eschatology is replaced by a more optimis-
tic and esoteric eschatology; Christ is an exemplar of truth;
there are stages in understanding: enlightenment unfolds;
other churches regarded as ignorant or backward; secular knowledge is valid and useful; gnosis is useful for everyday life
in the world.

    A comparison of Wilson's typology with the one pro-
posed by Berger shows the many similarities that exist between
the two. First of all, both agree that a "sectarian" attitude
implies a greater or lesser rejection of the world and its
values. Secondly, both also agree that this rejection may
take different forms or expressions, thus constituting the
different subtypes. Finally, both are rather close in their
respective delineations of these subtypes. Thus, for example,
Wilson's "adventist" model corresponds closely to Berger's
"prophetic" motif; the only difference seems to be the further
division suggested by Berger, viz., "world to be warned" and
"world to be conquered." Similarly, Wilson's "gnostic" model
corresponds very closely to Berger's "gnostic" motif (although
once again Berger would make a further division). Finally,
Wilson's "conversionist" and "introversionist" models correspond to Berger's division of his "enthusiastic" motif, viz.,
the "world to be saved" and the "world to be avoided" categories respectively.

Bryan Wilson (1973)

    Fourteen years after the first publication of the
preceding article and six years after its revision (1973),
B. Wilson published a major work entitled, *Magic and the Mil-
lenium*, the first chapter of which concerned itself once again
with a typology of sects ("Sociological Analysis and the Search
for Salvation").[17] However, whereas the earlier typology was
incidental to the more immediate purpose of determining the
factors that promoted or retarded sect development, the present
study represents a deliberate and self-conscious attempt on the
part of the author to outline ideal types of sects *per se*.[18]
    The point of departure for this later study lies in
Wilson's belief that the sociology of religion has generally
failed to establish adequate generalizations about complex
processes such as sectarianism (a complaint which Berger had
already made in 1954 as he called for much-needed theoretical
orientation) and that, where it has done so, it has tended to
derive concepts solely from the Christian tradition of the
West, e.g., organizational structure and doctrine (again, a
critique which Berger had also made of his predecessors).[19]

As a result, Wilson argues, the typology that has been consistently promoted and adopted has remained rather narrow in applicability, tracing the dynamics of only certain sectarian movements over time in certain circumstances of western society.

Wilson, therefore, proposes a typology which cuts across cultural lines to describe those social processes which are common to different cultures and which provide "a common stock of analytical apparatus capable of extensive application."[20] As such, he goes beyond his own earlier typology to an even more inclusive one which relies not so much on empirical observation as on an exhaustive delineation of all the options available (whether these options are to be found in the empirical world or not). The criterion used for such a differentiation remains essentially the same as that of the earlier typology: the sect's response to the world.[21] Wilson delineates seven basic types or responses:

(1) the conversionist response: salvation lies in an emotional transformation of the self brought about by God.

(2) the revolutionist response: salvation lies in the destruction of the world with its natural and social order.

(3) the introversionist response: salvation lies in the fullest possible withdrawal from the world.

(4) the manipulationist response: salvation lies in learning the right means or correct techniques in dealing with the world.

(5) the thaumaturgical response: salvation lies in deliverance from highly specific evils.

(6) the reformist response: salvation lies in the adoption of supernaturally-given insights about the ways in which social organization should be amended.

(7) the utopian response: salvation lies in the establishment according to divine principles of a new organization in which evil will be eliminated.

A comparison of this typology with the earlier one shows that the first four "responses to the world" are roughly equivalent to the four "missions to the world": (1) conversionist response = conversionist sect; (2) revolutionist response = adventist sect; (3) introversionist response =

introversionist sect; (4) manipulationist response = gnostic
sect. Thus, three more types have been added to the earlier
typology: the thaumaturgical response ("God will grant particular dispensations and work specific miracles"); the reformist response ("God calls us to amend it"); the utopian response
("God calls us to reconstruct it").[22]

     The above presentation and discussion of the studies
by Peter Berger and Bryan Wilson yield three main insights
concerning the phenomenon of sectarianism in modern sociological theory: (1) a "sectarian" attitude or frame of mind may
be characterized as one which rejects to a greater or lesser
extent "the world" and its values;[23] (2) this rejection of or
opposition to "the world" may take different forms or expressions; (3) as a result, different types of sects (along with
their empirical correlates) may be delineated.

*Discussion of the Johannine
  Community*

     I should now like to return to the two questions
raised at the beginning of this section (i.e., Was the Johannine community "sectarian"? Was the latter stage of that community even more "sectarian"?) and to answer these questions
in the light of the redaction-critical study conducted above.
First of all, given the principle that a "sectarian" attitude
may be essentially characterized as a rejection of the world
and its values, I should like to examine the relationships of
love uncovered in the Fourth Gospel in order to see whether
such a rejection may be discerned among these relationships.

     In his study of the myth of the descending/ascending
Revealer in the Fourth Gospel,[24] W. Meeks concludes that the
myth serves to differentiate Jesus, the "one from above" and
the one "not of this world," from the Jews, the "ones from
below" and the "ones of this world." Furthermore, with Jesus
belong the ones who have been chosen by him, viz., who have
believed in him, so that they too have become "not of this
world" ("A small group of believers isolated over against 'the
world' that belongs intrinsically to 'the things below,' i.e.,
to darkness and the devil"[25]). A study of the four main

relationships of love in the Gospel corroborates very strongly
Meeks' conclusion.

One should recall above all the threefold pattern of
three themes present in vv. 15-26 of the Farewell Discourse,
the purpose of which is clearly to differentiate the disciples
of Jesus (those who love him and believe in him) from "the
world" (those who do not love him or believe in him, viz., the
Jews). Within the pattern certain promises are made to the
believers and absolutely denied to "the world": vv. 14:15-17
extend the promise of "another" Paraclete who will be with the
disciples forever; vv. 14:18-21 assure the disciples of the
corresponding love of Jesus and the Father as well as of
Jesus' return; vv. 14:22-26 repeat the promise of the corresponding love of God and assure the disciples that both the
Father and Jesus will return and abide in them. One should
also recall that this differentiation is consistently maintained in the references to love scattered through the Gospel.

It is evident, therefore, that the author is employing
the relationships of love at least partly to separate an elect
community, the chosen brethren, from the world. Thus, the
pre-resurrectional relationships serve to guarantee the nature
of the revelation accepted by the brethren--it comes from God.
The post-resurrectional relationships serve to strengthen the
brethren in the midst of a very hostile world--God and Jesus
are with us through the Paraclete--and to deny that "world"
any knowledge whatsoever of the Father--God and Jesus are with
us and *only* with us.

Given the conclusion that the relationships of love
show very strongly the sectarian nature of the Johannine community, it remains to be seen which ideal sect type this community approximates most closely. I use in this regard Wilson's
second taxonomy, since it is the most inclusive. One may
reject the sixth and seventh responses (the "reformist" and
the "utopian" responses): the community seeks neither to
amend nor reconstruct the world--that world is under judgment
(κρίσις). One may also bypass the second response (revolutionist): there is no immediate end of the world expected.
Similarly, the first and fourth responses do not seem to apply:
the community neither seeks to convert the world nor to learn

the correct techniques in dealing with that world--once again,
the world is under judgment. The fifth response (the "thaumaturgical" response) is certainly present, but it does not
seem to be the paramount one.

It seems, therefore, that the community's response
could best be characterized as "introversionist": the world
is perceived as intrinsically evil (v. 3:16 would not contradict this judgment, since it refers to a stage prior to the
κρίσις) and salvation is to be sought in as complete a separation from this world as possible.[26] A look at the empirical
correlates which usually accompany this particular response
shows that such a group tends to stress "the members' possession of the Spirit,"[27] which is the very focus of the post-
resurrectional relationships of love outlined in the Gospel.

With regard to the second question posed above--was
the latter stage of the community even more "sectarian"?--I
believe that the answer is an affirmative one. The point of
view represented by the author of I John is, in my opinion,
more exclusivistic, more sectarian than that of the author of
the Gospel. The author's rejection of "the world" may be seen
above all in paragraphs 2:15-17 and 4:1-6. In the former
paragraph, the love "of God" is totally differentiated from
the love "of the world"; there is no *via media* at all. In
the latter paragraph, the spirit "of God" is also totally differentiated from the spirit "of the world"; there is, once
again, no possibility of a *via media*.

Furthermore, this "world" is no longer composed solely
of non-believers--as it was the case in the Gospel stage--but
now includes deviant members of the community as well. The
"new" relationship of love, viz., the command to love one
another in a very precise way, now serves as the main criterion
for membership in that community: whoever does not so love
falls outside the given hierarchy of love, goes forth "into
the world" and is not to be loved by the community (v. 2:15).
As a result, the disciples become fewer and fewer in number;
the world, by contrast, larger and larger; and the isolation,
greater and greater.[28]

In conclusion, one can say that the redaction critical
study of ἀγάπη/ἀγαπᾶν confirms the two main lines of

interpretation taken by recent studies of the Johannine community: the community was a sectarian community (approximating
the introversionist type) and became even more sectarian in its
latter stages. I would not want to claim thereby that its
understanding of ἀγάπη should be seen as the main, if not the
sole criterion, for such a characterization. Rather, I prefer
to claim, in the light of recent sociological theory, that
this understanding is simply one of the many empirical correlates that point in that direction. It seems to me that the
looseness surrounding the adjective "sectarian" in the literature may be resolved if the different "criteria" of sectarian-
ism--e.g., the possession of a self-referring set of symbols,
the attitude of perfectionism--are looked upon as empirical
correlates of sects and, above all, of a particular type of
sect. As such, exegesis would be seen as defining and outlining from different angles the complex nature of this particular historical phenomenon.[29]

*The Washing of the Feet and the
Johannine Redaction*

I pointed out in the preceding chapter that there were
several examples of ἀγάπη/ἀγαπᾶν/φιλεῖν in the Fourth Gospel
that had to be omitted from further consideration in that
chapter for various reasons, viz., vv. 12:25; 13:1; 15:19. In
the case of v. 13:1, the specific reason for the omission was
the fact that both Georg Richter and Hartwig Thyen had previously assigned that verse--as well as several others within
the Washing of the Feet pericope--to a later redaction of the
Gospel, the author of which both men identified as the author
of I John.[30]

Furthermore, it was also pointed out in the first
chapter that both of these men went on to assign a large section of the Gospel outside the Washing of the Feet pericope to
the author of I John, i.e., the latter had engaged in a thoroughgoing revision of the original Gospel.[31] In the light of
the exegetical results obtained in this study, I should like
at this point to enter into dialogue with this theory concerning an extensive redaction of the Gospel by the author of

I John. My point of departure shall be the example of ἀγαπᾶν
found in v. 13:1, a verse which, according to both Richter and
Thyen, constitutes the introduction to the redaction within
ch. 13.   A few preliminary remarks are in order. The double
occurrence of the verb ἀγαπᾶν in v. 13:1--ἀγαπήσας τοὺς ἰδίους
τοὺς ἐν τῷ κόσμῳ, εἰς τέλος ἠγάπησεν αὐτούς--presents a relationship of love which is present only once elsewhere in the
Gospel, viz., the love of Jesus for the disciples, v. 14:21c.
However, a comparison of these two verses shows that whereas
v. 14:21c presents that relationship in terms of an ongoing,
post-resurrectional activity centered around the figure of the
Paraclete, v. 13:1 presents a historical, pre-resurrectional
attitude on the part of Jesus which emphasizes the role of his
death as a part of that love (εἰς τέλος). As a result, the
following question presents itself: should v. 13:1 be assigned
to the same hand that inserted vv. 13:34-35 and 15:1-17 into
the Gospel? I should like to answer this question in terms of
the findings of both Richter and Thyen.

Georg Richter

          Since Richter's theory concerning the literary composi-
tion of Jn 13:1-20 has already been described to a certain
extent in the introduction to the third chapter,[32] I shall
limit myself at this point to its essential elements. The
first stage of the theory outlines from the point of view of
both literary and redaction criticism two quite distinct versions of the Washing of the Feet episode.[33]
          According to Richter, the original version of the
Washing of the Feet episode in the Gospel consists primarily
of vv. 3 and 6-11. This version agrees closely with the stated
objective of the entire Gospel (Jn 20:31), viz., to strengthen
Christian communities in their belief in Jesus as Messiah and
Son of God, specifically in the light of certain objections
being brought against this claim on the basis of Jesus' lowly
death (Jn 12:34). As such, the version is one σημεῖον among
many others. The second version, which was added later, consists primarily of vv. 1 and 12-20. Its purpose is no longer
apologetical in nature; rather, the narrative serves to exhort

the community to behave toward one another as Jesus behaved
toward them. Thus, whereas the first version is christological and soteriological in character, the later version presents
parenetical and ecclesiological interests.

It follows, therefore, that v. 13:1 constitutes the
introduction to the second and later version of the episode.[34]
Richter thinks that vv. 12-17 represent in effect an old and
traditional version: the disciples must serve one another.
However, he sees this original meaning as having been completely reinterpreted by the redactor of the Gospel in the
light of the σημεῖον of vv. 6-10. Thus, the Washing of the
Feet as a sign of Jesus' death became an example for the kind
of behavior which the disciples had to show toward one another.
Furthermore, it is in v. 13:1 that this reinterpretation comes
explicitly to the fore: Jesus' death on the cross now becomes
an act of love toward the disciples which is to be imitated by
the latter in their dealings with one another.[35]

The second stage of the theory proceeds from the more
limited study of Jn 13:1-20 to an examination of the Farewell
Discourse and the Passion narrative of the Gospel. The results
are the same: Richter finds in the latter chapters (above all
in the Farewell Discourse) that same combination of christological and soteriological passages on the one hand (vv. 13:31-
32; 14:2, 30; 17:1b, 2, 4, 5; 18:11; 19:11, 28, 30) and parenetical and ecclesiological passages on the other (vv. 13:34-
35; 15:2-3; 16:7, 28; 17:19) that he had uncovered in the
Washing of the Feet pericope.[36] As a result, Richter concludes
that the same redactor who added the second version of the
Washing of the Feet to the first was also responsible for the
insertion of the latter series of passages and their contexts
into the original Gospel,[37] viz., the second Farewell Discourse
to the first.[38]

The final stage of the theory consists in the attribution of all the parenetical and ecclesiological passages in
chs. 13-17 of the Gospel to the author of I John.[39] Richter
argues that the author of I John uses the Gospel in exactly
the same way as the author of the redaction he has uncovered:
both take a sentence or an idea from the Gospel (e.g., the
death of Jesus on the cross) and develop it in parenetical

fashion (e.g., such a death represents an example for the
disciples to follow). Therefore, he concludes, "Wir im Verfasser von 1 Jo auch den Redaktor oder Herausgeber des vierten
Evangeliums zu sehen haben."[40] This man, faced with new problems in the community, wrote I John and expanded the original
Gospel.

Hartwig Thyen

        Following upon Richter's research,[41] H. Thyen also
comes to the conclusion that the present account of the Washing of the Feet contains two originally independent versions
of that event and that these two versions may be identified
and separated through a literary and redaction-critical study
of the verses involved. Thyen identifies the original version
as having been comprised of vv. 1a, 2a, 3, 4-10a, 18-19, 28,
while the latter version included vv. 1b, 2b, 10b-11, 12-17,
20-27.

        Working primarily with vv. 4-10a--a section which he
calls "eine formal und inhaltliche geschlossene Einheit"[42]--
Thyen argues that the original version of the Gospel presented
the Washing of the Feet as a sign of Jesus' death and return
to the Father. As such, this version is in keeping with the
theological tone of the Gospel as a whole, a tone which he
characterizes (in open disagreement with Richter) as a "nicht-
christliches und spezifisch gnostisches Heilsverständnis,"
i.e., an acceptance of the Revealer implies a total denial of
creation and the world.[43] On the other hand, the second version abandons the concept of a sign and presents the Washing
of the Feet as an example for others to follow. Thus, whereas
the first version is dualistic and soteriological in character,
the second version deals with typical ecclesiastical problems.

        As in the case of Richter, v. 13:1b is interpreted by
Thyen as constituting the introduction to the second and later
version. The theme of love introduced in this half-verse is
quite characteristic of the redaction, but not of the original
Gospel. In adding v. 13:1b to the Gospel, Thyen argues that
the redactor explicitly turned the "weltlose Semeion" of the
first version into an act of love on the part of Jesus toward

his disciples, an act which was to be imitated by them in
their dealings with one another.

        Furthermore, Thyen goes on to claim that this ecclesi-
astical redaction is not limited to the Washing of the Feet
episode, but may be found elsewhere in the Gospel, usually--as
in the case of Jn 13:1-20--in the form of an alternative version of the event or discourse involved, e.g., vv. 1:14-18;
5:26-29; 6:48-58; chs. 15-17.[44] Finally, since both the redactional material and the Johannine Letters present the same
ecclesiastical concerns, Thyen concludes that the author of
the Letters was responsible for the redaction of the Gospel
as well.[45]

Summary-Conclusion

        A comparison of these two theories yields the follow-
ing agreements: (1) both men divide on literary and theological grounds Jn 13:1-20 into two distinct versions; (2) one of
these versions, the core of which consists of vv. 12-17, is
assigned to the later redaction of the Gospel; (3) the introduction to this redactional version may be found in v. 1b;
(4) the aim of this redaction in ch. 13 is to present the
death of Jesus as an act of love to be imitated by the community in their dealings with one another; (5) the parenetical
and ecclesiastical concern may be observed elsewhere in the
Gospel, above all in chs. 15-17; (6) since the same concerns
are present in I John, it is reasonable to suppose that the
author of the Letter was responsible for the insertions, as
he wished to solve certain practical problems that had arisen
in the community.

        First of all, I believe that both Richter and Thyen
have provided a satisfactory resolution of the literary problems present in Jn 13:1-20, problems the nature of which is
not altogether different from that of the occurrence of chs.
15-17 immediately after the command of v. 14:31c. Secondly,
I also believe that both men are correct in considering v. 1b
as a part of that redaction: the nature of the relationship
of love posited in that half-verse is not to be found elsewhere in the Gospel, i.e., a pre-resurrectional love of Jesus
for the disciples. Finally, I would concur with their opinion

that those other texts where the death of Jesus is presented
as an example to be followed are also to be assigned to the
redaction.

However, my main difficulty with the two theories lies
in the criterion that both Richter and Thyen use to assign the
redaction to the author of I John. In both cases that criterion is expressed solely in terms of the ethical or parenetical or ecclesiastical concerns of both the Letter and the
redaction. This position is very similar to the one taken by
J. Becker in assigning parts of the Farewell Discourse to the
Sitz im Leben of I John.[46] Yet, it seems to me that such an
attribution--which, in any case, should never be made in terms
of the precise author of I John, but rather in terms of the
same *Sitz im Leben*--completely bypasses the christological
controversy of I John. If the redaction shares the same *Sitz
im Leben* as that of I John, then one would expect to find
either open or concealed references to the christological
aberration of the opponents as well.

Furthermore, it seems to me that such references are
indeed to be found in Jn 13:1-20, specifically within those
verses assigned to the redaction. If one reads v. 13:14 in
the light of the introduction of v. 13:1b, it is clear that
the aorist ἔνιψα in the former verse is a synonym for the
aorist ἠγάπησεν in the latter: Jesus' act of νίπτειν is also
an ἀγαπᾶν. Similarly, the conclusion of v. 13:14 (καὶ ὑμεῖς
ὀφείλετε ἀλλήλων νίπτειν κτλ.) could also be read in terms of
ἀγαπᾶν: καὶ ὑμεῖς ὀφείλετε ἀλλήλους ἀγαπᾶν! Once again, one
finds a directive to the disciples to love one another (i.e.,
to wash each other's feet) which is grounded upon Jesus' own
love toward them (i.e., he washed their feet = he died for
them).

The same type of argumentation used in the third
chapter (Jn 15:1-17; 13:34-35) would apply here as well: the
command to love one another is very common in I John and
implies a situation where some disciples are not practicing
it--a situation far removed from that of the Gospel; the
grounding of this command on Jesus' love for the disciples is
also present in I John and implies a situation where some
disciples are denying the redemptive nature of Jesus' death--a

situation which is also far removed from that of the Gospel. As a result, one may conclude that the second version of the Washing of the Feet is indeed to be assigned to the same *Sitz im Leben* of I John as both Richter and Thyen claim, but for reasons which go beyond--and must go beyond--the ones they advance. Indeed, it is because of the lack of sufficiently strict criteria, specifically the exclusion of the christological controversy from among such criteria, that they have been able to assign the entire Farewell Discourse to the author of I John, even when sections of that discourse are much closer to the *Sitz im Leben* of the Gospel, e.g., vv. 15:18-16:4a.

It appears, therefore, as if the redactor that has been traced to the *Sitz im Leben* of I John has "sprinkled" that part of Jesus' life which immediately precedes his death with insertions designed to assert the centrality of that death in the life of the community and to trace the origin of the love command to the lips of Jesus himself as he prepared the disciples for his coming departure. In so doing, he has hoped, no doubt, to counteract the pneumatic claims of his opponents with the tradition, the doctrine, the message that comes ἀπ' ἀρχῆς--from the beginning, from the Master himself. It would have been interesting to see what the docetic-libertine group did with the *Grundschrift* and also what the outcome of the controversy and of each group was; unfortunately, that part of the *Nachgeschichte* remains a mystery.

CHAPTER I

[1] By "Johannine" literature or writings it is meant the Gospel (with its possible literary layers) and the three Letters traditionally assigned to John. The Book of Revelation plays no part at all in these recent studies.

[2] R. Alan Culpepper, *The Johannine School*, SBL Dissertations, no. 26 (Missoula, Mont.: Scholars Press, 1975), pp. 1-38.

[3] The interest, I suspect, has not been exclusively exegetical. It would appear that dogmatic views, mostly associated with the issue of apostolic authorship, have played a considerable role in the progress--or stultification, as the choice of opinion may be--of the question.

[4] Culpepper, pp. 37, 261.

[5] Ibid., p. 37.

[6] Ibid. The methodology, as he points out, has not been unknown. Among his predecessors he counts: W. Bousset, *Jüdisch-Christlicher Schulbetrieb in Alexandria und Rom: Literarische Untersuchungen zu Philo und Clemens von Alexandria, Justin und Irenäus*, FRLANT, n. F., no. 6 (Göttingen: Vandenhoeck & Ruprecht, 1915); R. H. Charles, *A Critical and Exegetical Commentary on the Revelation of St. John*, ICC (Edinburgh: T. & T. Clark, 1920); Krister Stendahl, *The School of St. Matthew: And Its Use of the Old Testament* (Philadelphia: Fortress, 1968); B. Gerhardsson, *Memory and Manuscript: Oral Tradition and Written Transmission in Rabbinical Judaism and Early Christianity*, trans. E. J. Sharpe, Acta Seminarii Neotestamentici Upsaliensis, no. 22 (Uppsala: C. W. K. Gleerup, 1961). On p. 261 Culpepper also makes the rather strong claim that even a combination of the other three methodologies could not confirm the Johannine school hypothesis; they merely serve to support such a hypothesis.

[7] As such, it presupposes that the authors of the main body of the Gospel and of the First Letter are different individuals and that the latter follows the former chronologically. This is not a unique presupposition; it has, in my opinion, attained the hypothetical certainty of consensus. More will be said on this matter later on in the chapter.

[8]Jürgen Becker, "Die Abschiedsreden Jesu im Johannes-evangelium," *ZNW* 61 (1970), pp. 215-46.

[9]In his own study, Culpepper offers a "Prospect" at the very end of the last chapter, i.e., a view of the areas which future scholarship can and should turn to. One of these areas is said to be "the need for further study of terms, images, and concepts which assumed special meanings or importance in the schools." (See p. 290.) This study seeks to do precisely that with regard to ἀγάπη, although it will dispense with a history-of-religions comparison. The latter task deserves a great deal of attention and remains one of the goals for the future, but at this point it lies well out-side the scope of this study.

[10]W. Meeks, "The Man from Heaven in Johannine Sectari-anism," *JBL* 91 (1972), pp. 44-72. I shall also refer to a later article published in the Morton Smith Festschrift: "'Am I a Jew?' Johannine Christianity and Judaism," in Jacob Neusner, ed., *Christianity, Judaism, and Other Graeco-Roman Cults: Studies for Morton Smith at Sixty*, 4 vols., Studies in Judaism and Late Antiquity, no. 12 (Leiden: Brill, 1975), I, pp. 163-86.

[11]D. Moody Smith, "Johannine Christianity: Some Reflections on its Character and Delineation," *NTS* 21 (1974-5), pp. 222-48. Like Meeks, Moody Smith followed this article with another one in a different Festschrift: "The Milieu of the Johannine Miracle Source: A Proposal," in *Jews, Greeks and Christians. Religious Cultures in Late Antiquity. Essays in Honor of William David Davies*, ed. R. Hamerton-Kelly and Robin Scroggs, Studies in Judaism in Late Antiquity, n. 21 (Leiden: E. J. Brill, 1976), pp. 164-80.

[12]O. Cullmann, *Der johanneische Kreis, Sein Platz im Spätjudentum, in der Jüngerschaft Jesu und im Urchristentum* (Tübingen: J. C. B. Mohr, 1975). An English translation appeared almost immediately: *The Johannine Circle*, trans. J. Bowman (Philadelphia: Westminster, 1976).

[13]See above, p. 1, n. 2. The dissertation was written at Duke University under the direction of D. Moody Smith.

[14]J. Bogart, *Orthodox and Heretical Perfectionism in the Johannine Community as Evident in the First Epistle of John*, SBL Dissertations, no. 33 (Missoula, Mont.: Scholars Press, 1977). The dissertation was written at the Graduate Theological Union in Berkeley, California, under the direction of Edward Hobbs.

[15]The Johannine "puzzle" refers to the unique character of the Fourth Gospel in early Christian literature. R. Bult-mann, "Die Bedeutung des neuerschlossenen mandäischen und manichäischen Quelle für das Verständnis des Johannesevange-liums," *ZNW* 24 (1925), pp. 100-46.

[16]The reaction, briefly summarized, interpreted Johannine christology not as a progression from a gnostic myth,

but rather as a step toward gnosticism. See, e.g., S. Schulz,
*Untersuchungen zur Menschensohn-Christologie im Johannesevange-
lium* (Göttingen: Vandenhoeck & Ruprecht, 1957).

[17]Meeks, "The Man," pp. 46, 49-50; "'Am I a Jew?,'"
pp. 178-79.

[18]Meeks refers to this adopted methodology as one
employed by some contemporary anthropologists to study the
notion of myths in primitive societies. He refers above all
to the work of Edmund Leach, "Genesis as Myth," *Discovery*,
n.s., 23 (1962), pp. 30-35.

[19]The presupposition is, therefore, that the expression of a myth requires a number of "signals" or "examples"
thereof. Only by uniting these different--to an extent, any-
way--expressions of the myth can the interpreter begin to discern the fundamental structure and its meaning. This presupposition has practical consequences for the question of the
literary unity of the Gospel, as Meeks himself is aware. Not
all the *aporias* in the Gospel--"The countless displacement,
source, and redaction theories that litter the graveyards of
Johannine research are voluble testimony to this difficulty"
--need be considered a result of redaction; it may very well
be that these are a part of the method outlined above, i.e.,
the expression of a myth by successive and slightly different
repetitions of that myth. See "The Man," p. 48.

[20]Ibid.

[21]J. L. Martyn, *History and Theology in the Fourth
Gospel* (New York: Harper & Row, 1968). See "'Am I a Jew?,'"
p. 183.

[22]Meeks, "The Man," pp. 58-59.

[23]Ibid., p. 68.

[24]Ibid., p. 70: "One of the primary functions of the
book, therefore, must have been to provide a reinforcement for
the community's social identity, which appears to have been
largely negative. It provided a symbolic universe which gave
religious legitimacy, a theodicy, to the group's actual isolation from the larger society."

[25]Ibid., pp. 70-71. Meeks employs the term "school"
but once, and that usage seems to be synonymous with that of
"sect." See also, p. 48.

[26]Ibid., pp. 49-50. Not only was the sect in existence
"for a considerable span of time," but also its patterns of
language served to communicate and make sense of all the problems, internal and external, which the sect experienced.

[27]Ibid., p. 71: "The dialectic we have suggested
would surely continue, producing a more and more isolated and
estranged group until some disruption occurred. The Johannine
Letters show a progression of that sort . . ."

[28]Moody Smith, p. 222. The genre of the article is very much like that of Meeks' second article mentioned on p. 3, n. 10, viz., "'Am I a Jew?.'"

[29]Ibid., p. 238.

[30]Ibid., p. 224. Thus, whereas Meeks would stress the centrality of a peculiar terminology in the definition of a religious sect, Moody Smith would rely more heavily on the sense of alienation from, and indeed struggle with, the world.

[31]Ibid., pp. 229-30; 238-40; 244-46. In this article, therefore, Moody Smith follows essentially the work of R. T. Fortna on the isolation of a miracle source in the Gospel (*The Gospel of Signs: A Reconstruction of the Narrative Source Underlying the Fourth Gospel*, NTSMS, no. 11 [Cambridge: University Press, 1970])—although he is reluctant to include the passion narrative, as Fortna does, as part of the *sēmeia* source—and on the association of this source with a sectarian Jewish matrix. In a later article (see p. 3, n. 11), Moody Smith strengthens the connection between the source and the polemic against the sect of John the Baptist, deviating as well from the putative sectarian, proto-Gnostic *Sitz im Leben* he had previously accepted. See "The Milieu of," pp. 175-78.

It should be pointed out that on the point of an underlying *sēmeia* source W. Meeks disagrees. See "'Am I a Jew?,'" p. 184.

[32]Moody Smith, "Johannine Christianity," pp. 230-34; 243-44; 246-48. Moody Smith accepts the position that both activities—narrative and Spirit-inspired prophecy—developed at the same time. See, above all, p. 246.

[33]Ibid., pp. 238-39, 246.

[34]In theory, therefore, Moody Smith accepts the point of view taken by J. Becker (and others as well), but he does remain rather distrustful of the approach in general. Ibid., p. 232.

[35]Ibid., p. 234.

[36]Ibid., p. 224. Like Meeks, Moody Smith sees a much more acute sectarian consciousness toward the end of the tradition. He would also see the *Sitz im Leben* of the Letters as involving a control of the Spirit-filled prophecy which characterized the *Eigenart* of the community from its inception.

[37]Cullmann, pp. ix-xi. See, for example, *Early Christian Worship*, trans. A. Stewart Todd and James B. Torrance, Studies in Biblical Theology, no. 10 (London: SCM, 1953); *Le Problème littéraire du roman pseudo-Clementin*, Études d'histoire et de philosophie religieuses, no. 23 (Paris: F. Alcan, 1930).

[38]Cullmann, *The Johannine Circle*, pp. 9-11.

[39]Ibid., pp. 4, 9. See p. 4: "In particular, if an attempt to distinguish different redactions or different sources (a topic which will be discussed later) goes too far,

it comes up against a barrier. For it is beyond question
that a degree of unity can be followed right through the
Gospel: unity of language, unity of style, and indeed unity
of theological purpose."

[40] Meeks, "'Am I a Jew?,'" pp. 171 ff.; Moody Smith,
"Johannine Christianity," pp. 238ff. This sectarian Judaism
is said to contain proto-Gnostic ideas in its formulations.

[41] Among these one finds similarities in christological
confession and liturgical conceptions; an interest in the mission to the regions of Samaria; a common root in heterodox
Judaism. See Cullmann, *The Johannine Circle*, p. 43. Later
on, Cullmann suggests a triangular relationship among the
Hellenists, the Johannine group, and heterodox Judaism (Ibid.,
p. 52).

[42] This group would represent a brand of Christianity
which is quite distinct from that of the Synoptic Gospels,
which Cullmann conceives to be rather monolithic in its way
of thinking. Synoptic Christianity is to be derived ultimately from the Twelve, while Johannine Christianity is seen
as going back to other disciples of the Lord. In the last
chapter, Cullmann suggests that Jesus himself may have
addressed himself differently to Synoptic Christianity--con-
verts from official Judaism--and to Johannine Christianity
--converts from sectarian Judaism (Ibid., pp. 89ff.). I
wonder whether the underlying idea in such a monolithic conception of the rise of Christianity is a preoccupation on the
author's part with the historicity of Jesus' traditions, i.e.,
an underlying dogmatic presupposition concerning the four
canonical gospels.

[43] The centrality of Samaria in the Fourth Gospel had
already been expressed by Cullmann in a previous work:
"Samaria and the Origins of the Christian Mission," in *The
Early Church*, ed. A. J. B. Higgins (London: SCM, 1956), pp.
185-92.

[44] That there is no open conflict may be gathered from
the use of the Synoptic traditions by the evangelist as well
as by the rather positive image of Peter which emerges from
the Gospel, even when that image is subordinated to that of
the Beloved Disciple. Cullmann, *The Johannine Circle*, pp.
55-56.

[45] This monolithic aspect of the theory may be observed
once again in Cullmann's explanation of the contact that the
group experienced with the remnants of marginal Judaism and
its reaction to that contact. Cullmann declares that the
group refused to yield to open syncretism and, indeed, engaged
in polemics with these syncretistic currents. Ibid., pp. 59-
60. It appears as if the group managed to preserve the
entirety of its theological message, which in turn was derived
from the historical Jesus. The group did not "soil" this
message: "In reality, this influence was probably less

important because here the Johannine group was deliberately
reacting in direct polemic against all the elements which were
irreconcilable with its belief in Christ."   Ibid.

[46]It would not be unfair to say that Cullmann is
reacting against the understanding of the term "sect" adopted
by Ernst Käsemann (*The Last Testament of Jesus*, trans. Gerhard
Krodel [Philadelphia: Fortress, 1968]), whom he attacks quite
often (see pp. 13, 15, 40, 55, 58, 61, 103ff.).

[47]Ibid., pp. 62-85. The role assumed by this particular disciple of Jesus is traced by Cullmann to the possession
of a divine authority, a feeling of being under the influence
of the Spirit, which is conveyed above all by the Paraclete-
sayings of the Farewell Discourse (see pp. 7-8, 13ff.).

[48]Ibid., pp. 17, 40, 53-54, 57. On p. 54 Cullmann
asserts that the relationship between the evangelist and the
author of the Letters must have been as close as that between
evangelist and redactor.
    It should be pointed out that Cullmann uses the term
"school" as a synonym for "circle" or "community"--and does
so rather sparingly, e.g., pp. 7, 40.

[49]Culpepper, *The Johannine School*, pp. 1, 34-38. On
pp. 35-36 Culpepper lists the different understandings of
"school": (1) a school of thought; (2) a particular group or
circle, where the latter term may mean a group of individuals,
a group of congregations, or a group of writers; (3) a sect or
conventicle; (4) a ḥaburah; (5) a community or group where
corporate activities include teaching, studying, writing and
worshipping.
    I have already pointed out the meanings of "school"
which the three preceding writers have adopted: Meeks understands the term as a synonym for a sect; Moody Smith follows
Meeks in this regard; Cullmann uses "school" for an ongoing,
consistent brand of Christianity which traces its roots back
to Jesus.

[50]See above, p. 2, n. 6.

[51]Culpepper, p. 38. The nine schools thus selected
were (in the order of presentation): the Pythagoreans; the
Academy; the Lyceum; the Garden; the Stoa; the Qumran community; the House of Hillel; the school of Philo; and the
school of Jesus.

[52]Ibid., p. 248: "In sum, the dissimilarities between
the schools run so deep that the similarities which can be
observed may be used to establish a pattern for the schools
of antiquity." On the preceding page, Culpepper reveals what
he means by "dissimilarities": the different milieux in which
they functioned and the different purposes for which they
existed.

[53]Ibid., pp. 251-57. On pp. 258-59 Culpepper provides
a one-paragraph definition of the term "school" which comprises
all these various elements.

[54]Ibid., pp. 254-55: "The distinguishing activities of the schools were teaching, learning, and writing. Other organizations shared some of the characteristics of the schools . . . but not this preoccupation with teaching and learning."

[55]Ibid., pp. 262ff.

[56]Culpepper examines, first of all, the figure of the Beloved Disciple and his role in the Gospel. He is of the opinion (following recent positions such as that of J. Roloff, "Der johanneische 'Lieblingsjünger' und der Lehrer der Gerechtigkeit," *NTS* 15 [1968], 129-51) that the Beloved Disciple is both a historical figure, whose death is mentioned in Jn 21:23-24, and a symbolic representation of true discipleship. As such, his role would reveal to a large extent the self-understanding of the community, and this role is shown to be primarily one of interpretation and teaching. The Beloved Disciple functions as an exegete of Jesus' sayings (above all in Jn 13:21-30).

Moreover, when the Beloved Disciple died, the community felt helpless and without guidance. Culpepper, again following recent positions (see p. 267, n. 18), believes that the original promise of the Paraclete had been strongly identified with the figure of the Beloved Disciple, so that when the latter died, his role and activity--interpretation and teaching--were grafted onto the remembered promises of the coming Paraclete. This latter figure would also engage in interpretation and teaching.

The community, therefore, believed itself to be following the role of the Beloved Disciple and to be under the guidance of the Paraclete in the execution of the activities central to their life: "teaching, remembering (reminding), 'keeping' what the B. D./Paraclete had taught and witnessing to the world." Ibid., p. 270.

[57]Ibid., p. 274: "The Gospel's reflection of these activities strongly suggests that the Gospel was written within a school." It is not clear to me, however, how much importance is to be attached to the traditions of the founder --for example, on p. 282 Culpepper declares that the Beloved Disciple "taught the community, and the normative teaching of the community was established"--and how much to the activity of the school that gathered about him--for example, on p. 277 one finds the statement that "The evangelist and probably others whose interpretations of the scriptures and the teachings of Jesus found a place in the Gospel . . ." At one time, the role of the founder seems to be emphasized above all, and yet at another time it is the activity of the community that is highlighted. I believe too little time is devoted to a presentation of the consequences of this theory for the composition of the Gospel.

[58]Ibid., pp. 277-79. It is not clear to me whether the same *Sitz im Leben* would apply to the school that formed around the Beloved Disciple.

[59]Ibid., pp. 263, 279-86.

[60]Ibid., pp. 282ff. Culpepper adopts E. Käsemann's theory that the Gospel portrays a quasi-docetic Jesus (see p. 9, n. 46 above) and proceeds to argue that the opponents of I John, possibly appealing to the Beloved Disciple as well, developed this docetism even further.

[61]Ibid., p. 259. As such, it is a synonym for "movement" or "tradition." Thus, school would be differentiated from a sect insofar as it would engage in learning activity; it would be a narrower term.

[62]For example, it has already been pointed out that Culpepper adopts Käsemann's theory of the Johannine community as a conventicle (Ibid., pp. 282-83). Likewise, on p. 287 he describes the community as an "embattled brotherhood, hard-pressed by conflict with the synagogue, rivalled by a Baptist group, and divided by a docetic Christology." Finally, he ascribes to the "school" that element which was fundamental to Meeks' definition of "sect": the development of esoteric language and metaphorical systems which were known only to the members of the school (see p. 262).
    I wonder whether Culpepper has really narrowed down the concept of a school as much as he believes he has. Does teaching activity have to be carried on in a particular way in order to qualify as a "school"? There are so many divergencies among the nine schools with respect to their common characteristics that it makes one wonder whether "school" is such a fast term after all.

[63]Bogart, *Perfectionism*, pp. 1, 7-8, defines perfectionism as "the notion that a person, by whatever means, is capable of achieving ethical and/or spiritual perfection in his present, earthly existence." Ethical perfection is taken to mean moral purity, while spiritual perfection is taken to mean some kind of union with God.

[64]Ibid., p. 1. On account of the starting point, i.e., I John, Bogart spends much more time than the other four authors on the place of the Letter within the history of the community.

[65]Ibid., pp. 2, 90-91. It should also be pointed out that Bogart is not really concerned with redactions of the Gospel of John. He seems to accept the document as it stands as providing a unity of theological purpose.

[66]Bogart does not claim that this attitude as presented in the Johannine literature is to be derived from Jewish apocalyptic literature. Ibid., p. 3. He does claim, however, that both types of literature have two common elements, whose union, he concludes, leads to a perfectionist stand. These two common characteristics are: (1) ethical dualism; and (2) imminent eschatological expectation.
    The latter element is surprising, given the non-eschatological tone of the Gospel in general. Bogart clarifies this ambiguity by stating that "The eschatology, of course, in each is quite different. The Jewish apocalypticists expected

the eschaton soon in the future, whereas the Johannine Christians, in a sense, believed they were already living in the
new age." It is not clear to me how this difference can
yield an essential element called "imminent eschatological
expectation."

[67]It was this group that became the so-called opponents
of the author of I John. In chapter 5 Bogart devotes some time
and space (pp. 123-33) to the identification of these opponents
and their doctrine.

[68]As in the case of O. Cullmann, one can almost detect
a dogmatic presupposition underlying this judgment. This presupposition would see the Gospel of John as being essentially
in accord with biblical faith. For example, speaking of the
lack of gnostic ideas in John, Bogart declares on p. 134: "In
some places it is gnosticizing, i.e., it employs gnostic myth
and language; but it remains consonant with biblical faith."
The presupposition would also see Gnosticism as being a sully-
ing, a perversion, of that biblical faith. For example, on
p. 136 Bogart declares: "Thus we would say that the Gospel of
John does *not* contain within itself the seeds of gnostic heresy,
or even that its gnosticizing tendencies could have naturally
developed into any full-fledged gnostic system. No, it had to
be radically perverted into gnosticism."

[69]Ibid., p. 135. He speaks of a possible influx of
"pre-Gnostic gentiles" who never accepted the "basic biblical
doctrines" of God and man.

[70]Ibid., pp. 2, 136.

[71]Ibid. This gradualism may be detected above all in
the introduction of the doctrine of expiation for sin by the
blood of Christ and a concomitant casuistic system of differentiating between mortal and non-mortal sins. Since Bogart
claims that perfectionism is an absolute term, the emergence
of gradualism constitutes in effect a major deviation from
that traditional attitude (see also, pp. 7-8).

[72]For Käsemann, see above, p. 9, n. 46. Bogart
believes that the gnosticizing element in Johannine christology,
i.e., the picture of a God walking upon the earth, is essentially correct (thus far he accepts Käsemann's theory), but he
does not regard this observation as being sufficient to make
the claim that the community was a sect. Ibid., pp. 136-37.

[73]Bogart quotes a long paragraph from W. Meeks' article,
"The Man from Heaven," that highlights the use of peculiar
language as a basic characteristic of a "sect." Although he
does not directly address himself to Meeks' criterion, it
appears that Bogart would consider such a criterion insufficient. Ibid., pp. 137-38.

[74]Ibid., p. 138.

[75]Ibid., p. 139 (see above, n. 71).

[76]Bogart does not take a position with respect to the authorship of the Letter, declaring that such judgments really lie outside the realm of his thesis. On p. 19 he affirms that what is important is that *"the theological differences between them* (i.e., the Gospel and the First Letter) *are properly discerned."* (Italics his.)

[77]I have difficulties with this position. On the one hand, perfectionist beliefs are said to constitute the essence of sectarianism. On the other hand, Bogart states that this perfectionism is not present in I John, and yet the latter remains sectarian. It seems to me that the definition of sectarianism needs revision. See his statement on p. 140: "It remained alienated from the world and therefore sectarian in that sense; but from the standpoint of Jews and pagans in the early centuries of our era, *all* Christians were sectarians!"

[78]At the same time, it is interesting to note that Bogart does affirm a heightening of the sectarian attitude vis-à-vis the world at the same time that I John was written. Ibid., p. 139.

[79]See, for example, the list of authors assembled by W. G. Kümmel, *Introduction to the New Testament*, 2nd ed., translated by H. C. Kee (New York: Abingdon, 1975), p. 442, n. 2: Bultmann, Dodd, Wilder, Windisch-Preisker, Dibelius, Goguel, McNeile-Williams, Moffatt, Schelkle, Conzelmann, Haenchen, O'Neill, Thüsing, Schottroff, Klein, et al.

[80]Kümmel himself does not believe that the available evidence is sufficient to warrant a different authorship. Ibid., p. 445: "Thus although it is likely that I John was written some time later than Jn and although it cannot be clearly proved that I John was written by the author of Jn, there are no cogent reasons for assuming that I John is to be attributed to another author than Jn." Likewise, B. Vawter, "The Johannine Epistles," in *The Jerome Biblical Commentary*, ed. Raymond Brown et al. (Englewood Cliffs, N.J.: Prentice-Hall, 1968), adopts the position that the "secretary-disciple" of the Apostle John was responsible for the writing of both Gospel and epistles. According to Vawter, the theological differences--and he seems to agree on this particular point with C. H. Dodd--may be explained adequately by a separation in time; indeed, Vawter considers I John to have been written before the Gospel. See Part II, pp. 404-5.

[81]C. H. Dodd, "The First Epistle of John and the Fourth Gospel," *BJRL* 21 (1937), pp. 129-56.

[82]H. J. Holtzmann, "Das Problem des erstens johanneischen Briefes in seinem Verhältnis zum Evangelium," *Jahrbücher für protestantliche Theologie* 7 (1881), pp. 690-712; 8 (1882), pp. 128-52, 316-42, 460-85.

[83]J. Martineau, *The Seat of Authority in Religion*, 3rd ed. (London: Longmans, Green & Co., 1891).

[84]C. von Weizsäcker, *The Apostolic Age of the Christian Church*, trans. J. Millar (New York: G. P. Putnam's Sons, 1899).

[85]Ernest F. Scott, *The Fourth Gospel: Its Purpose and Theology* (Edinburgh: T. & T. Clark, 1906).

[86]H. Windisch, *Die katholischen Briefe*, Handbuch zum Neuen Testament, no. 15 (Tübingen: J. C. B. Mohr, 1930).

[87]J. Drummond, *An Inquiry into the Character and Authorship of the Fourth Gospel* (London: Williams & Norgate, 1903).

[88]R. Law, *The Tests of Life. A Study of the First Epistle of St. John* (Edinburgh: T. & T. Clark, 1912).

[89]A. E. Brooke, *A Critical and Exegetical Commentary on the Johannine Epistles*, ICC (Edinburgh: T. & T. Clark, 1912).

[90]V. H. Stanton, *The Gospels as Historical Documents*, Part III: *The Fourth Gospel* (Cambridge: University Press, 1920).

[91]B. H. Streeter, *The Four Gospels: A Study of Origins* (London: Macmillan & Co., 1924).

[92]C. H. Dodd, *The Johannine Epistles*, The Moffatt New Testament Commentary (London: Hodder & Stoughton, 1946).

[93]W. F. Howard, "The Common Authorship of the Johannine Gospel and Epistles," *JTS* 48 (1947), pp. 12-25; W. G. Wilson, "An Examination of the Linguistic Evidence Adduced Against the Unity of Authorship of the First Epistle of John and the Fourth Gospel," *JTS* 49 (1948), pp. 147-56; A. P. Salom, "Some Aspects of the Grammatical Style of I John," *JBL* 74 (1955), pp. 96-102.

[94]H. Conzelmann, "'Was von Anfang war,'" in *Neutestamentliche Studien für Rudolf Bultmann zu seinem siebzigsten Geburtstag am 20. August 1954*, 2nd ed., BZNW, no. 21 (Berlin: Töpelmann, 1957), pp. 194-201.

[95]Günter Klein, "'Das wahre Licht scheint schon!' Beobachtungen zur Zeit und Geschichtserfahrung einer urchristlichen Schule," *ZThK* 68 (1971), pp. 261-326.

[96]See above, n. 89.

[97]Dodd, "The First Epistle," p. 131.

[98]Dodd considers it very significant that some of the idiomatic expressions common to both the Gospel and the Letter are used to excess by the latter, e.g., the use of the participle with the article as substantive and the articular participle with πᾶς. This, he argues, is a natural procedure for any imitator. Ibid., pp. 134-35.

[99]Ibid., pp. 131-38; *The Johannine Epistles*, pp.
xlix-l.

[100]Ibid., pp. 138-41; *The Johannine Epistles*, pp. l-li.

[101]Ibid., pp. 141-42; *The Johannine Epistles*, pp. li-
lii. Whereas in 1937 Dodd played down the importance of this
observation, thinking that the difference could be explained
by a difference in aim or the use of sources by the evangelist,
in 1946 he emphasized the point strongly, calling it a "for-
midable difference."

[102]Ibid., pp. 141-48. See esp., p. 148: "In these
three points therefore the teaching of the Epistle differs from
that of the Gospel . . . But the three points in question,
Eschatology, the Atonement, and the Spirit, are central to
early Christian belief and doctrine, and divergences on such
points raise serious doubts about unity of authorship." I
should point out that what Dodd means by a "more primitive"
conception of the Spirit is his belief that the Spirit is conceived of in the Gospel in very personal terms, but not in
the Letter.

[103]Ibid., pp. 148-54. Among such elements Dodd counts
the axioms of I Jn 1:4 and 3:2 plus technical terms such as
χρῖσμα and σπέρμα. Dodd believes that the author of I John
is using the terms employed by his Gnostic opponents and con-
verting such terms into weapons by reinterpreting their meaning.

[104]Ibid., pp. 154-56; *The Johannine Epistles*, pp. lv-
lvi. See "The First Epistle," p. 155: "If I may close, as I
began, on a note of mere impressionism, I should say that the
Epistle appears to me, for all its likeness in certain respects
to the Gospel, to reveal a mind which thinks and expresses
itself in significantly different ways; a mind inferior to
that of the Evangelist in spiritual quality, in intellectual
power, and in literary artistry." It is interesting to note
that Dodd in his commentary evokes a contemporary model of a
teacher, Karl Barth, and a number of followers--"an influen-
tial school of theologians"--who depend on and utilize his
ideas while developing them in different directions. See *The
Johannine Epistles*, p. lvi.

[105]Ibid., p. 155, n. 1; *The Johannine Epistles*, pp.
lv-lvi. Dodd grants the possibility of minor additions and
editorial work, but gives no indication as to its extent and
location.

[106]Conzelmann does refer to Dodd's commentary when
speaking of the differences and similarities that exist
between the two writings, but he does not pass judgment on
Dodd's conclusions. Furthermore, he avoids all terminological
or stylistic considerations. Conzelmann, p. 194, n. 1.

[107]Yet even the usage in I Jn 1:1 betrays a significant
difference according to Conzelmann. Whereas in the Prologue to

the Gospel the emphasis is placed on the "person" of the
revelation, in the Letter the use of the neuter ὅ indicates a
shift toward "substance" or "doctrine." Ibid., p. 196.

[108]Conzelmann, p. 197, does refer to a prototype of
this meaning in vv. 6:64; 15:27; 16:4, where the expression
refers to the beginnings of discipleship. However, at this
stage the expression has not yet become a *terminus technicus*.

[109]Ibid., pp. 195, 198-99. The tradition being
invoked is twofold. It consists of the christological kerygma
(v. 2:23f.) and the love commandment (vv. 2:7; 3:11; II Jn 5),
both of which are closely united. Thus, the false teachers
are being attacked on these two fronts at the same time.

[110]Ibid., p. 198: "Man versteht die Ausdrucksweise
des Briefes m. E. nur durch die Annahme, dass der Verfasser
das Johannesevangelium bereits als feste Autorität vor Augen
hat." In another work, *An Outline of the Theology of the New
Testament*, trans. John Bowden (New York: Harper & Row, 1968),
Conzelmann devotes more time to the role of reflection in the
emergence of tradition (see esp., pp. 296-302).

[111]This argumentation is highly dependent on the
interplay of the adjectives "old" and "new" with respect to
the commandment of love in vv. 2:7f. The characterization
"old" betrays the sense of tradition that dominates the
author's thinking, while the characterization "new" refers to
the new historical conception of Christianity. Conzelmann,
"'Was von Anfang War,'" pp. 198-99.

[112]Ibid., p. 198. Conzelmann speaks of the Letter as
a "johanneischer Pastoralbrief."

[113]Conzelmann, *An Outline*, p. 321.

[114]Ibid., pp. 355-56. Conzelmann states that the
Johannine community gives the "appearance" of being a sect,
because of its separation from the world. However, that it is
not a sect becomes apparent from the lack of secret doctrine
--which thus emerges as his definition of a sect. Conzelmann
argues that, on the contrary, the community's doctrine leads
to a public confession of faith.

[115]The methodological considerations may be found in
G. Klein, "Das wahre Licht," pp. 261-69.

[116]Ibid., p. 261.

[117]Among the exegetes that have gone in this direction
Klein mentions R. Gyllenberg, B. Noack, S. Schulz, E. Haenchen,
W. Wilkens, U. Wilckens, J. L. Martyn, and R. Fortna. The
general consensus from this "traditionsgeschichtliche Betrach-
tungsweise" is that the author of the Gospel stood within a
very definite tradition, a very specific circle: "Als den . . .
Exponenten 'eines Kreises . . . der sich gleicher Sprache und
gleicher Vorstellung bediente.'" Ibid., p. 262 (Klein is quot-
ing from E. Käsemann at this point).

[118]Ibid., p. 263.

[119]Ibid.   Klein mentions specifically J. Becker in
this regard.   On p. 264, n. 17, he refers to two temptations
that all exegetes who follow this approach must guard against:
(1) to accept all differences in the text as being contradic-
tions; (2) to bypass all similarities or agreements as presenting no evidence for redaction.   I have already referred to
Moody Smith's guarded approach to this line of argumentation
undertaken by Becker and others (see above, p. 6, n. 34).

[120]Ibid., p. 264.

[121]Ibid., pp. 264-66.

[122]Ibid., pp. 264-65.   Klein argues directly against
E. Schweizer's study of the ecclesiology of the Gospel and the
Letters ("Der Kirchenbegriff im Evangelium und den Briefen des
Johannes," in *Neotestamentica. Deutsche und englische Aufsätze
1951 bis 1963* [Zürich: Zwingli Verlag, 1963], pp. 254-71) and
E. Haenchen's summary article of recent research on the Johannine Letters ("Neuere Literatur zu den Johannesbriefe," *TRu*
26 [1960], pp. 1-43).   The former had argued that the ecclesiology of the Letters showed a more logically advanced stage
insofar as the unity of the church was in danger and new
vocabulary arose to deal with this problem, while the latter,
among other arguments, had posited a basic change from a contrast of faith/lack of faith to correct/incorrect faith.

[123]Klein, p. 266.   But not, by way of contrast, to the
form-critical arguments he had brought to bear against
Schweizer and Haenchen.   Rather, he uses here a more factual
refutation of Dodd's arguments: (1) against eschatology,
Klein argues that Dodd's arguments would count only if the
references to the "day" of vv. 6:39-40, 44; 12:48, were
removed as additions.   Even then one would still have to consider the possibility of a redaction of I John as well.
(2) against soteriology, Klein argues that there are indications of a similar soteriology in the Gospel and, again, that
one would also have to consider the possibility of redaction
in I John. (3) against pneumatology, Klein argues that the
Paraclete conception of Jesus in I Jn 2:1 is preserved in Jn
14:16.

[124]Conzelmann's work, however, is also criticized
methodologically by Klein from the point of view of the
expression selected for comparison, since Conzelmann speaks
of a "gewisses Vorbild" of the ecclesiastical usage of I John
in the Gospel.   Such a view is, in the end, subject to the
same form-critical arguments employed against Schweizer and
Haenchen.   Ibid., p. 268.

[125]Ibid., pp. 268-69.   Klein accepts the common consensus that I John was written later than the Gospel, so that
any shift in perspective is to be seen as proceeding from Gospel to Letter.

[126]Yet, see Kümmel's evaluation on pp. 444-45: "And
against Klein's analytical differentiation is to be said that
Jn may by no means be interpreted 'transchronologically' and
that Jn rather reflects throughout the future 'in the perspective of universal history' too (cf. Jn 5:24; 12:31)."

[127]Klein, pp. 269-91, esp., pp. 280-84. The author
does not abandon altogether the "transchronological" eschatology. Rather, he adopts what Klein calls "eine Zweistufen-
Eschatologie" where one level presents, for example, a chronologically undifferentiated opposition of light and darkness,
but at the other--and this is the innovation--this opposition
is historicized and traditional Christian eschatology introduced. Ibid., pp. 325-26.

[128]Ibid., p. 291. Also, with respect to Conzelmann's
view of a self-realizing eschatology, Klein believes that the
latter has indeed pointed out an aspect of eschatology in the
Letter, but that the whole conception goes beyond this one
aspect. Thus, in terms of the "Zweistufen-Eschatologie," Conzelmann's view of the historicization of "light" and "darkness"
constitutes but one level. See above, n. 127.

[129]See above, p. 17, n. 105.

[130]Klein, p. 263.

[131]G. Richter, "Die Fusswaschung Joh 13:1-20," *MüTZ*
16 (1965), pp. 13-26; *Die Fusswaschung im Johannesevangelium:
Geschichte ihrer Deutung*, Biblische Untersuchungen, no. 1
(Regensburg: Friedrich Pustet, 1967); "Die Deutung des
Kreuzestodes Jesu in der Leidensgeschichte des Johannes-
evangeliums," *BiLe* 9 (1968), pp. 21-36.

[132]H. Thyen, "Johannes 13 und die 'kirchliche Redaktion' des vierten Evangeliums," in *Tradition und Glaube. Festgabe für K. G. Kuhn* (Göttingen: Vandenhoeck & Ruprecht, 1971),
pp. 343-56.

[133]For Richter, see, above all, "Die Fusswaschung,"
pp. 12-18, 24-26; for Thyen, see pp. 345-55.

[134]Richter, "Die Fusswaschung," pp. 22-24; "Die Deutung," p. 26; Thyen, pp. 355-56.

[135]Richter, "Die Deutung," pp. 35-36. (On p. 23 of
his other article, "Die Fusswaschung," Richter speaks in terms
of a disciple-redactor; therefore, he too adopts a variation
of the school hypothesis.) Thyen, p. 350, n. 19.

[136]See above, p. 2, n. 8.

[137]As I shall point out in the third chapter, one has
to be careful with R. Schnackenburg's works, i.e., the three
volumes of the commentary (*Das Johannesevangelium*, 3 vols.,
Herders Theologischer Kommentar zum Neuen Testament, no. 4
[Freiburg: Herder, 1965-75]) because his opinion of the

history of the composition of the work does change in the
third volume. It is this third volume (1975) that I have in
mind here.

[138]Becker, pp. 235-36, 239-41, 246; Schnackenburg, III,
pp. 101-6, 140-43.

[139]Becker, p. 233, n. 66a; Schnackenburg, passim.

[140]For example, in "Die Deutung," pp. 35-36, Richter
names the following exegetes as witnessing to the approach he
himself adopts, i.e., different authorship: C. H. Dodd,
R. Bultmann, H. Conzelmann, E. Lohse, W. Marxsen.

[141]Yet a third category could be said to exist in the
works of Olivier Prunet, *La morale chrétienne d'après les
écrits johanniques* (Paris: Presses Universitaires de France,
1957) and Noël Lazure, *Les valeurs morales de la théologie
johannique*, Études bibliques (Paris: J. Gabalda, 1965). Both
of these works examine, as the titles indicate, the moral
thought or position of the Johannine Gospel and Letters *as a
whole*, so that love constitutes only a part, or perhaps a
chapter, of the entire work. I have chosen to mention them in
a footnote because, unlike the other two categories, love or
its derivatives constitute only one of many other thematic
interests. Furthermore, both of these works, as the titles
also suggest, accept the common authorship of the Gospel and
the Letters: it is their combined evidence that constitutes
the "Johannine" moral position. See Prunet, pp. v-vii;
Lazure, pp. 9-11. As such, they differ radically from the
goal of the present study.

[142]J. Moffatt, *Love in the New Testament* (London:
Hazell, Watson & Viney, 1930), esp., pp. 235-308.

[143]V. Warnach, *Agape. Die Liebe als Grundmotiv der
neutestamentlichen Theologie* (Düsseldorf: Patmos-Verlag,
1951), esp., pp. 150-79.

[144]C. Spicq, *Agapè dans le Nouveau Testament*, 3 vols.,
Études bibliques (Paris: J. Gabalda, 1959). The first
volume deals with the Synoptic Gospels; the second, with the
Pauline literature; the third, with the Catholic Epistles,
Hebrews, and the Johannine Literature.

[145]J. Chmiel, *Lumière et charité d'après la première
épître de Saint Jean* (Rome: Institut Pontifical des Recherches
Ecclesiastiques, 1971).

[146]V. Furnish, *The Love Command in the New Testament*
(New York: Abingdon Press, 1972).

[147]A. Feuillet, *Le mystère de l'amour divin dans la
théologie johannique*, Études bibliques (Paris: J. Gabalda,
1972).

[148]M. Lattke, *Einheit im Wort: Die spezifische
Bedeutung von ἀγάπη, ἀγαπᾶν und φιλεῖν im Johannesevangelium*,
StANT, no. 41 (Munich: Kösel, 1975).

[149]Furnish, p. 19.

[150]Moffatt, p. 5. Moffatt also presents many examples of historical deviations (see pp. 1-9), but these two are uppermost in his mind.

[151]Ibid., pp. 1, 5. See his statement on purpose on p. 8: "It is in such a light that one studies the NT--not to discover a ready-made manual of devotion for love any more than for a church-order or even for Christian philosophy, but to ascertain the cardinal principles apart from which any conception or practice of love in Christianity is unlikely to prove adequate."

[152]Warnach, pp. 11-15.

[153]Ibid., pp. 16-18, 27-30.

[154]The work referred to is *Agape and Eros*, trans. Philip S. Watson (Philadelphia: Westminster, 1953). Along with Gustaf Aulén, Anders Nygrén formed part of the so-called Lund school of theology, which traced certain dominant themes through all of Christian history.
In this study, Nygrén claims that the Johannine conception of love should not be regarded as the climax of the New Testament, because the realm of such love--the persons that such love encompasses--is actually quite limited. Johannine theology, he concludes, is quite particularistic in this regard. See pp. 149ff.

[155]Spicq, I, p. 6.

[156]Moffatt, p. 252. Moreover, this "common spirit" is attributed to the existence of a "group" or "circle" which presumably shows strict adherence to a set of doctrines held in common. Thus, Moffatt adopts a variation of the "school" hypothesis.

[157]Warnach, pp. 150, 163, 171, also adopts the position that the author is John the apostle. Spicq, III, p. 246. Furthermore, Spicq, III, p. 216, also adopts a rearrangement of the Farewell Discourse (following Spitta, Moffatt, and Bernard--see chapter III below) as follows: v. 13:31a; chs. 15-16; vv. 13:31b-38; ch. 14; ch. 17.

[158]Chmiel, pp. 1-6.

[159]Ibid., p. 2: "Nous recurrons largement aux parallèles du quatrième évangile pour éclairer tel ou tel passage plus obscur."

[160]Thus, again, a variation of the "school" hypothesis, Ibid., pp. 3-4, 240-42. For the purposes of his project, however, Chmiel proposes to examine the Letter from the point of view of a complete document: "En analysant le texte de l'Épître, nous l'acceptons tel qu'il se présente a nous dans son état actuel."

[161]Furnish, p. 19.

[162]Ibid., pp. 19-20.

[163]Ibid., pp. 148-49: "Their relationship to the Gospel may indeed be compared to the relationship of the Pastoral epistles to the letters of Paul."

[164]Ibid., pp. 135ff. Furnish does speak of a redaction in the case of chapter 21; however, his position is less than firm: "Although it is doubtful that chapter 21 was an original part of this Gospel or comes from the same hand, . . ."

[165]Feuillet, pp. 1-3.

[166]Ibid., p. 1. Indeed, at times the impression is given that Feuillet has not quite decided the issue of authorship with regard to the Apocalypse, see pp. 1-2.

[167]Ibid., pp. 1-2, passim.

[168]M. Dibelius, "Joh 15:13. Eine Studie zum Traditionsprobleme des Johannesevangelium," in *Festgabe für Adolf Deissmann zum 60. Geburtstag* (Tübingen: Mohr, 1927), pp. 168-86. This article was reprinted in *Botschaft und Geschichte* (Tübingen: Mohr, 1953), I, 204-20.

[169]See p. 9, n. 46.

[170]Lattke, p. 106, n. 2.

[171]Ibid. In the First Letter, Lattke declares, one finds an ethical interpretation of ἀγαπᾶν τοὺς ἀδελφούς. The Letter is concerned with concrete ethical questions.

[172]Lattke does speak of a redaction of the Gospel in terms of ch. 21 and vv. 6:51b-58, but that is the extent of it. Ibid., pp. 5-6.

[173]Scholarship dealing with I John has been directed from its earliest period at the reconstruction of an underlying source. The theory was first elaborated in 1907: E. von Dobschütz, "Johanneische Studien. I," *ZNW* 8 (1907), pp. 1-8. Then, it was considerably expanded by Rudolf Bultmann, "Analyse des ersten Johannesbriefes," in *Festgabe für Adolf Jülicher* (Tübingen: Mohr-Siebeck, 1927), pp. 138-58. It was not until 1951 that the theory was seriously attacked by scholars (and pretty much abandoned since): Herbert Braun, "Literal-Analyse und theologische Schichtung im ersten Johannesbrief," *ZThK* 48 (1951), pp. 262-92; Ernst Käsemann, "Ketzer und Zeuge. Zum johanneischen Verfasserproblem," *ZThK* 48 (1951), pp. 292-311.

[174]In an earlier article ("Aufbau, Schichtung und theologiegeschichtliche Stellung des Gebetes in Johannes 17," *ZNW* 60 [1969], pp. 56-83), Becker argues that a great part of ch. 17 also belongs to the *Sitz im Leben* of I John. However, since the meaning of ἀγάπη/ἀγαπᾶν plays no role in such an

attribution, I prefer to leave it out of consideration in this study, although I shall use it for purposes of comparison in ch. IV below. See below, ch. IV, p. 134; p. 147, n. 62. See also, Schnackenburg, III, p. 230: "Die theologischen Verbindungsfäden zum Ev scheinen mir stärker zu sein als zu den Briefen."

CHAPTER II

[1]For a summary of these views, see Kümmel, *Introduction to the New Testament*, pp. 449-51.

[2]A similar methodological precaution will be taken in Chapter IV below with regard to those sections of the Gospel the authenticity of which has been called into question, specifically those sections within the Farewell Discourse that do not belong to the original discourse (chapters 15-17). The evidence from these chapters--excluding vv. 15:1-17--will be used solely for the purpose of comparison as well.

[3]There are, correspondingly, four occurrences in II John and two in III John.

[4]K. Aland et al., eds., *The Greek New Testament*, 3rd ed. (New York: United Bible Societies, 1975). This is the critical edition of the Greek New Testament to which I shall refer and from which I shall quote in this work.

[5]See below, ch. IV, pp. 133-34.

[6]This unbalanced distribution is also found with respect to other leading themes in the Letter, e.g., the combination light/darkness, which is very important at the beginning of the Letter, does not occur at all after I Jn 2:11. For a fuller account of the distribution of the main themes, see J. L. Houlden, *The Johannine Epistles*, Harper's New Testament Commentaries (New York: Harper & Row, 1973), pp. 22-23.

[7]R. Schnackenburg summarizes it quite well: "In der Frage der Gliederung von 1 Joh stehen sich zwei extreme Auffasungen gegenüber. Die einen wollen einen recht kunstvollen Aufbau entdecken, die anderen vergleichen das Schreiben mehr dem 'Wogenspiel des Meeres.'" See *Die Johannesbriefe*, 2nd ed., Herders Theologischer Kommentar zum Neuen Testament, no. 12:3 (Freiburg: Herder, 1963), p. 10.

[8]J. C. O'Neill, *The Puzzle of I John: A New Examination of Origins* (London: S.P.C.K., 1966).

[9]Ibid., pp. 1-7, 65-67. These twelve paragraphs are: (1) 1:5-10; (2) 2:1-6; (3) 2:7-11; (4) 2:12-17; (5) 2:18-27; (6) 2:28-3:10a; (7) 3:10b-19a; (8) 3:19b-24; (9) 4:1-6; (10) 4:7-18; (11) 4:19-5:13a; (12) 5:13b-21.

This theory proposed by O'Neill is intimately associated with two other working hypotheses that he adopts in his
study. First of all, O'Neill believes that he can separate
a source within each of these twelve self-contained units on
the basis of literary and theological considerations. Secondly, O'Neill sees I John *as it stands* as being directed
specifically against the Jews. The author of I John was a
member of a Jewish sectarian group who, along with many others,
had become a Christian by confessing that Jesus was the Messiah.
In the "tract" that he writes, the author is using twelve
poetic admonitions from the traditional writings of the Jewish
group (source) and enlarging these admonitions by showing how
they find their fulfillment in Jesus (redaction); furthermore,
he is directing this work against those members of the sectarian group that did not become Christians (the Jewish opponents). Ibid.

[10]R. Bultmann, *The Johannine Epistles: A Commentary
on the Johannine Epistles*, trans. R. Philip O'Hara et al.,
Hermeneia (Philadelphia: Fortress, 1973).

[11]It is presumably at this stage that the Prooemium
(vv. 1:1-4) and the conclusion (vv. 5:13-21) are added. Ibid.,
pp. 1-3. See also, R. Bultmann, "Die kirchliche Redaktion
des ersten Johannesbriefes," in *Exegetica*, ed. Erich Dinkler
(Tübingen: Mohr-Siebeck, 1967), pp. 381-82. The article
originally appeared in *In Memoriam Ernst Lohmeyer*, ed. Werner
Schmauch (Stuttgart: Evangelisches Verlagswerk, 1951), pp.
189-201.
    See *The Johannine Epistles*, pp. 43-44: "Attempts to
find a train of thought in 2:28-5:12 are futile. The whole
section 2:28-5:12 is obviously not a coherent organic composition, but rather a compendium of various fragments collected
as a supplement to 1:5-2:27."

[12]E. Lohmeyer, "Über Aufbau und Gliederung des ersten
Johannesbriefes," *ZNW* 27 (1928), pp. 225-63. See esp., pp.
254ff.

[13]The main sections are: (1) "Prolog": 1:1-4; (2) "Das
erste Offenbarungswort": 1:5-2:6; (3) "Das zweite Offenbarungswort": 2:7-17; (4) "Christen und Antichristen": 2:18-3:24;
(5) "Von der Liebe": 4:1-21; (6) "Vom Glaube": 5:1-12;
(7) "Epilog": 5:13-21. Ibid., pp. 231ff.

[14]M. Albertz, *Botschaft des Neuen Testaments*, 2 vols.
(Zürich: Evangelischer Verlag, 1952), I:2, pp. 432-33. The
two main sections are: (1) vv. 1:3-3:10, centered around the
expression, "God is Light"; (2) vv. 3:11-5:21, centered around
the expression, "God is Love."

[15]Thus, Norman Perrin, *The New Testament: An Introduction* (New York: Harcourt Brace Jovanovich, 1974), pp. 274-78;
Willi Marxsen, *Introduction to the New Testament*, trans. G.
Buswell (Philadelphia: Fortress, 1974), p. 261; W. G. Kümmel,
pp. 435-36; Bogart, pp. 15-16.

[16]Thus, J. L. Houlden, pp. 22-24. See p. 23: "Each cycle includes a consideration of the central theme with some subordinate question in mind; or, alternatively, using the great, constant words and ideas for material, it radiates from some new notion or question, introduced or brought into prominence for the first time. In other words, it is like a series of connected, revolving discs, placed side by side, each of which differs from the rest in having a centre of distinctive colour." C. H. Dodd, *The Johannine Epistles*, pp. xxi-xxii. See p. xxii: "The writer 'thinks around' a succession of related topics. The movement of thought has not inaptly been described as 'spiral.'" R. Law, *The Tests of Life: A Study of the First Epistle of St. John*, 3rd ed. (Grand Rapids, Mich.: Baker, 1914), p. 5: "The course of thought . . . is like a winding staircase--always revolving around the same centre, always returning to the same topics, but at a higher level." R. Schnackenburg, p. 11: "So setzt er [the author] zu Belehrungen und Mahnungen an und immer wieder neu an. Dadurch entstehen gewisse grössere Abschnitte, in denen ein Gedanke den anderen hervorruft."

[17]Theodor Häring, "Gedankengang und Grundgedanke des ersten Johannesbriefes," *Theologisches Abhandlungen*, ed. Carl von Weizsäcker (Freiburg im Breisgau: Mohr, 1892). The outline of the theory is conveniently reproduced by A. E. Brooke, *The Johannine Epistles*, 2nd ed., ICC (Edinburgh: T. & T. Clark, 1957), pp. xxxiv-xxxvii.

Häring divides I John into three main sections with their respective dogmatic and ethical subsections. The first section extends from 1:5 to 2:27: the ethical thesis is found in 1:5-2:17; the christological, in 2:18-27. The second section begins with 2:28 and concludes with 4:6: the ethical thesis is found in 2:28-3:24; the christological, in 4:1-6. The third section extends from 4:7 to 5:12: the ethical thesis is found in 4:7-21; the christological, in 5:1-12.

[18]Bogart, p. 16, provides three reasons for accepting Häring's basic outline: (1) it avoids subjective titles; (2) it recognizes the two major concerns of the Letter; (3) it points out the parallelisms of the two sections.

[19]Ibid., pp. 16-17. Thus he argues that a particular theme may be developed at one point more than at another or that it may be expressed in different terms. Furthermore, the sections are said to "flow" into one another, "making the discernment of divisions difficult."

[20]It is not necessary that the dogmatic sections be *exclusively* dogmatic or that the ethical sections be *exclusively* ethical in order to recognize the described succession; it is sufficient that such sections be *largely* dogmatic or *largely* ethical (as they are) in content and emphasis. Furthermore, I am not advocating as rigid a structure as Häring's complete outline would have it; the spiral argumentation is much more flexible, much more malleable (but within it one can recognize a certain succession of ethical and dogmatic concerns).

[21]See e.g., O'Neill, p. 1; Schnackenburg, p. 11.

[22]I should stress that this subordination of the
other authors is simply a very practical step in the process
of comparison. It certainly does not imply that these authors
accept the overall structure proposed by Häring, i.e., the
succession of ethical and christological "theses."

From this point onward I shall use the term "section"
to refer to Häring's six main divisions and the term "paragraph" to refer to any subdivisions of these six divisions.

[23]The supporters are O'Neill, Bultmann, Lohmeyer,
Kümmel, Perrin, Bogart, Houlden, and Schnackenburg. Dodd and
Law would add on v. 2:28; Westcott, v. 2:29.

[24]The supporters are O'Neill, Bultmann, Kümmel, Perrin,
Bogart, Houlden, Dodd, Schnackenburg, and Westcott. Lohmeyer
divides it further into vv. 4:1-3, 4-6, while Law includes v.
3:24b, no doubt because of the occurrence of τὸ πνεῦμα in that
verse as well.

[25]There are in all five supporters: Lohmeyer, Kümmel
Bogart, Houlden, and Westcott. The remaining six exegetes
would begin the paragraph with other verses: (1) v. 4:19--
O'Neill; (2) v. 5:3b--Law; (3) v. 5:5--Bultmann and Schnackenburg; (4) v. 5:6--Perrin and Dodd.

[26]I have decided to include the seven subsections of
two of the main sections--"Christen und Antichristen," 2:18-
3:24, and "Von der Liebe," 4:1-21--because they all comprise
two or more verses. See above, p. 33, n. 13.

[27]I have already mentioned Bogart's acceptance of
Häring's basic outline (see above, p. 35, n. 18). However,
Bogart is not really interested in any subdivisions except
those which are immediately relevant to his study. See p. 17:
"The exact division between major divisions, sections, and
subsections is not directly relevant to the concerns of this
study, except for showing that 1:5-2:11 forms an original
unit."

[28]I include some sections under the larger term
"Abschnitte" because they include as many as nine verses.
These sections have been placed in parentheses in order to
distinguish them from the main sections.

[29]B. F. Westcott, *The Epistles of St. John. The Greek
Text with Notes* (Abingdon, Eng.: Marcham, 1966). This is a
reprint of the third edition of the work published in 1892.

[30]I certainly agree with Häring and the majority that
vv. 2:18-27 and 4:1-6 constitute paragraphs or units of thought.
In the former case, the author leaves behind the contrast of
ἡ ἀγάπη τοῦ πατρός and ἡ ἀγάπη τοῦ κόσμου to a discussion of
the antichrists in v. 4:1. Similarly, v. 2:28 takes up the
expression μένετε ἐν αὐτῷ of v. 2:27 and develops it in another
direction. Furthermore, the section begins with a new address
(παιδία) and ends with an obvious closing (ταῦτα ἔγραψα ὑμῖν).

In the latter case, the author proceeds from a statement concerning what is necessary to achieve confidence (παρρησία)
before the Lord to a discussion of the false prophets in v.
4:1. V. 3:24b seems to be the link between two paragraphs,
preserving the verb μένειν from 3:24a and introducing the
noun πνεῦμα, which is developed subsequently. Similarly,
v. 4:7 picks up the prepositional phrase of v. 4:6, ἐκ τοῦ
θεοῦ, and develops it in another direction.
      I am also in agreement with those exegetes--including
Häring--who read vv. 5:1-12 as a paragraph. V. 5:1 subordinates the primary theme of ἀγάπη from the previous verses to
that of πίστις and thus initiates a section on correct belief.

      [31]From now on I shall call these specific persons
whom I John is combatting "the opponents." This is a term
which has become quite common in New Testament exegesis to
refer to those parties or individuals being fought against by
the respective New Testament writings. See, e.g., J. J.
Gunther, *St. Paul's Opponents and their Background. A Study
of Apocalyptic and Jewish Sectarian Teachings*, NovTSup, no. 35
(Leiden: Brill, 1973).
      I shall also use the singular form "community," with-
out implying thereby that there was only one community and
not several in a geographically circumscribed area. There is
simply no way of knowing the extent of the audience of a particular New Testament writing; therefore, I use "community"
for the sake of convenience.

      [32]Bogart, pp. 16-17, 25ff. The six *Grundsätze* show,
for the most part, the same literary form: (1) an opening
quotation formula; (2) an apparent quotation of the opponents;
(3) a statement concerning the actual behavior of the opponents; and (4) a statement concerning the consequence of that
behavior.

      [33]The basic structure would look as follows:

cont. sta.	1:5	1:7b	2:3	2:7-8
alter. #1	1:6	1:8	2:4	2:9
alter. #2	1:7a	1:9	2:5	2:10

      [34]The first characterization depends partly on the
κοινωνίαν ἔχειν of the Prologue (v. 1:3).

      [35]These expansions occur within the second and fourth
characterizations and add nothing of substance to the original
statement of the incorrect alternative within those characterizations. Thus, the cycles of n. 33 above are expanded as
follows:

cont. sta.	1:7b	2:7-8
alter. #1	1:8	2:9
alter. #2	1:9	2:10
alter. #1	1:10	2:11

      [36]This is most clear in the third characterization as
one proceeds from one alternative to the next. More on this
point below.

[37]See vv. 2:1-2, between the second and third characterizations. This advice is not unrelated to the discussion
since it focuses on the question of sin in the community and
the role of Jesus in the forgiveness of sins, issues which
were introduced in the course of the second characterization.

[38]I read v. 2:6 as an expansion of the controlling
statement of v. 2:3 (although admittedly using quite different
language). One could also read it as parenetical advice, but
its introduction in v. 2:5c--ἐν τούτῳ γινώσκομεν ὅτι ἐν αὐτῷ
ἐσμεν--follows the pattern of the introduction in v. 2:3.
Therefore, I prefer to read it as an expansion of that verse.

[39]This is a type of definition where the ἐν τούτῳ is
given in further detail in the clause that follows. This
clause substitutes for the more common epexegetical infinitive
following a demonstrative pronoun. See F. Blass and A. Debrunner, *A Greek Grammar of the New Testament*, ed. R. W. Funk
(Chicago: University Press, 1961), #394). In I John this construction may be found in vv. 2:5; 3:16, 24; 4:6 (where the
preposition ἐκ instead of ἐν is used), 13; 5:2.

[40]In the present context of the paragraph, the αὐτόν
and αὐτοῦ of v. 2:3 can only refer to "Jesus Christ the
Righteous One" of v. 2:1. It is the closest antecedent. This
point of view is confirmed by the expansion statement of
v. 2:6--he who would claim to "be in him" must *walk* as he did
(a feat which can be achieved only by performing his commandments; the expression καθὼς ἐκεῖνος περιεπάτησεν can only refer
to Jesus. Houlden, p. 65, assumes that the pronouns refer to
God because of the previous reference to the κοινωνία τοῦ θεοῦ.
However, the evidence of vv. 2:1-2 cannot be ignored.

[41]With Dodd, *The Johannine Epistles*, p. 31, I take the
genitive of ἡ ἀγάπη τοῦ θεοῦ as an objective genitive: the
love of man for God as defined by the author, i.e., by the
carrying out of Jesus' commands.

[42]Indeed, the entire paragraph seems to proceed from
the universal to the particular, from a very general description to a more specific one. See, for example, the succession
of correct alternatives: 1:7--"if we walk in the Light";
1:9--"if we confess our sins"; 2:5--"whoever carries out his
word"; 2:10--"he who loves his brother."

[43]This is an instance of the prepositional phrase upon
which H. Conzelmann bases his comparison of the Gospel of John
and the First Letter. See above, ch. I, pp. 17-19. This
particular example is one of those that refer to the beginning
of the church or the historical appearance of Jesus. Indeed,
Conzelmann argues that the author has the original command of
Jn 13:34-35 in mind at this point and that the usage of the
command in the Gospel may be differentiated from its usage in
I John by a shift from eschatology to ecclesiology. See Conzelmann, pp. 198ff. Given the possible redaction of the Gospel
by the author of I John mentioned in the preceding chapter, a
position such as Conzelmann's can no longer be assumed; rather,
it must be proved or disproved.

[44]Such a claim is really no different from others made by the author in the course of the paragraph, e.g., in the first characterization the controlling statement (v. 1:5) is said to be ἡ ἀγγελία ἣν ἀκηκόαμεν ἀπ' αὐτοῦ; in the third, the commandments that exemplify the knowledge of Jesus (v. 2:3) are said to be *his* commandments (τὰς ἐντολὰς αὐτοῦ).

[45]Again, the claim is no different from others made in the course of the paragraph, e.g., the specification καὶ ἀναγγέλλομεν ὑμῖν with regard to the first controlling statement of v. 1:5; the parenetical advice of vv. 2:1-2--γράφω ὑμῖν ἵνα μὴ ἁμάρτητε.

[46]Houlden, pp. 67-68. Houlden, like Conzelmann, presupposes that the author of I John has seen this commandment in the Gospel and preserves the adjective καινός precisely because of that fact.

[47]Dodd, pp. 34-35. Dodd argues that a new age did indeed dawn with Jesus, so that the ὅτι-clause merely echoes a thought that runs through the entire New Testament. The special contribution of the Fourth Evangelist was to transform the original eschatological time-scheme into contemporary philosophical thought, i.e., two orders or planes of reality.

[48]Bultmann, *The Johannine Epistles*, pp. 27-28, sees the terms "light" and "darkness" as designating "not only the essential antithesis of the nondivine and divine spheres, . . . but also the antithesis of the epochs, which have become clear through the eschatological event of the revelation as such."

[49]Schnackenburg, p. 113.

[50]Bogart, p. 16.

[51]For example, *2:12*: 1:9, 2:1, 5:16-17; *2:13a, 14b*: 2:4; *2:13b, 14c*: 4:4, 5:4-5, 19; *2:14a*: 4:12, 20; *2:14b*: 1:1-4, 2:7.

[52]Bultmann, among others, has suggested the possibility that these verses come from the hand of the ecclesiastical redactor (see above, p. 33, n. 11), because they seem, first of all, to interrupt the context and, secondly, to employ terminology which is characteristically different from that of the author. See *The Johannine Epistles*, pp. 30ff. Bultmann's position is not given as final: he leans toward it, but does not fully espouse it. I would argue, however, that the verses do fit in quite well within the context. Just as in the case of vv. 2:1-2 parenetical advice is given which develops the theme of ἡ ἁμαρτία in vv. 1:7b-10, so now in vv. 2:15-17 similar advice is given which develops the theme of the love command. In effect, what the verses do is to make concrete and specific what the concepts "love" and "hatred" (as well as "light" and "darkness") mean. Similarly, the presence of uncharacteristic terminology may be explained by the author's use of traditional expressions. On this last point, see Schnackenburg, p. 127.

[53]The underlying thought is that "the world" is in the power of "the evil one" (see v. 5:19).

[54]There is no indication here that a metaphysical dualism is being posited by the author. Rather, the dualism is basically ethical in character: certain ways of behavior are identified with God because they were made known by his Son; other ways of behavior are identified with "the world" and ultimately with "the evil one" (I Jn 3:8; 5:19) because they are contrary to the commands of Jesus. See Schnackenburg, pp. 133-37: "Exkurz 6: Der 'Welt'-Begriff in 1 Joh 2,15-17."

[55]Again, with Dodd, p. 39, I take the genitive of ἡ ἀγάπη τοῦ πατρός to be an objective genitive. See also, Schnackenburg, p. 127: (1) the author has spoken of "knowledge of the Father" in v. 2:14a; (2) the subjective genitive would not agree with the expression οὐκ ἔστιν ἐν αὐτῷ.

[56]In the New Testament ἐπιθυμία is often used vox media (Lk 15:16; 16:21), but mostly it is to be construed as evil desire. The expression of this evil desire is usually characterized by the genitive that follows. See Friedrich Büchsel, "ἐπιθυμία, ἐπιθυμέω," in the Theological Dictionary of the New Testament, 10 vols., ed. Gerhard Friedrich and Gerhard Kittel, trans. Geoffrey Bromiley (Grand Rapids, Mich.: Wm. B. Eerdmans, 1964-76), III, pp. 168-71. Thus, for example, Paul uses it in Rom 13:14 to refer to those faults listed in v. 13: revelling, drunkenness, debauchery, licentiousness, etc. Likewise, in Gal 5:16ff. the problem that the community is having with the flesh is referred to as "desires of the flesh." On this last point, see Hans Dieter Betz, "Spirit, Freedom, and Law," Svensk Exegetisk Arsbok 39 (1974), pp. 145-60.
     From this point onwards all references to the Theological Dictionary of the New Testament will be presented as "TDNT."

[57]The expression is not to be found elsewhere, but a desire of the eyes implies either a desire for material possessions or sexual possession.

[58]In the Greek tradition the ἀλάζων is that person who claims more for himself than he actually possesses (e.g., Eth. Nic. IV, 13, 1127b). This meaning also appears in the Septuagint (Wis 5:8; Hab 2:5). See G. Delling, "ἀλάζων, ἀλαζονεία," in TDNT I, pp. 266-67. In the New Testament the noun occurs only here and in Jas 4:16, a passage which exhibits the meaning described above (Jas 4:13b-17): those who plan ahead regardless of God's will. I Cl. 21:5 uses it, as in the case of Jas 4:16, in conjunction with καυχάζομαι, implying a definite affinity with the latter term.

[59]Thus, Bultmann, The Johannine Epistles, p. 34.

[60]In II John 5 the author repeats the love command--ἵνα ἀγαπῶμεν ἀλλήλους--and presents it in terms of the same antithesis found in I Jn 2:7: καινός/ἀπ' ἀρχῆς. However, the emphasis is solely on the "traditional" aspect of that command: οὐχ ὡς ἐντολὴν γράφων σοι καινήν.

[61]See above, p. 36, n. 30.

[62]Bultmann, however, attributes v. 2:28 to the ecclesiastical redactor. In "Die kirchliche Redaktion," he proposes the following two excisions: (1) the conditional ἐὰν φανερωθῇ is a later addition; (2) the prepositional phrase, ἐν τῇ παρουσίᾳ, is also a later addition. Thus, originally the noun παρρησία and the verb μὴ αἰσχυνθῆναι, he argues, would have referred to God the Father, not to Jesus. See pp. 388-89. In the later commentary (see p. 44, n. 4) Bultmann suggests that the entire verse was added by the redactor. However, the clear link μένετε ἐν αὐτῷ would seem to militate against this position.

[63]These are, once again, O'Neill, Bultmann, Lohmeyer, Kümmel, Perrin, Bogart, Houlden, and Schnackenburg.

[64]Both Häring and Brooke would choose the conclusion of the first paragraph as taking place in v. 3:6. See Brooke, pp. xxxv-vi, 79. The other paragraphs would be 3:7-18 and 3:19-22.

[65]Dodd, p. 81: "He has been speaking of 'righteousness' and 'sin.' He now makes it clear that the specifically Christian form of righteousness is love, or charity, and the lack or denial of charity is, more than anything else, what Christianity means by sin."

[66]If v. 2:28 is original, the antecedent of δίκαιος can only be Jesus. If v. 2:28 is a later addition, as Bultmann claims, the statements of vv. 1:9 and 2:1 would still compel one to refer δίκαιος to Jesus and not to God the Father. Furthermore, the statement of v. 3:5, which clearly refers to the historical appearance of the Son of God, calls Jesus "sinless"--ἁμαρτία ἐν αὐτῷ οὐκ ἔστιν--which is the equivalent of δίκαιος in the passage.

[67]The combination of ἀνομία (which occurs only here in the entire Johannine literature) and δικαιοσύνη may be found in Mt 13:41--in an eschatological setting; Mt 23:28 (with δίκαιος); Rom 4:7--where Paul quotes Ps 32:1-2 to justify righteousness apart from works; Rom 6:19--where Paul explains that the community has advanced from lawlessness to righteousness; II Cor 6:14; Heb 1:9. Also, lawlessness and sin are equated in the quotation of Rom 4:7 and in Heb 10:17.

[68]Spicq, III, pp. 252-55. See p. 254: "Cette *agapè* est à prendre en son sens chrétien non seulement d'amour temoigné, manifesté et actif, mais de réalité existante en soi et communicable; elle devient un don accordé par le Père aux croyants: ἀγάπην δέδωκεν." Lazure, pp. 234ff., follows a similar line of interpretation, referring to a "demeure de Dieu" in the believer.

[69]Houlden, pp. 88-89.

[70]H. Balz, "Der erste Brief des Johannes," in H. Balz and W. Schrage, *Die "katholischen" Briefe. Die Briefe des*

Jakobus, Petrus, Johannes und Judas, NTD, no. 10 (Göttingen: Vandenhoeck & Ruprecht, 1973), p. 180.

[71]Jesus is called "love" once again in v. 4:16. V. 4:15 contains a confessional formula to the effect that Jesus is the Son of God. V. 4:16 then follows with an affirmation on the part of the author to the effect that "we" have known and have believed in the love which God showed "us." The reference is unmistakably to the coming of the Son of God.

[72]This is precisely the claim of vv. 1:7b and 2:2.

[73]The author is careful to reserve the term "Son of God" to Jesus alone, while employing "children of God" with regard to all those who believe in Jesus as Son of God, even though Christians are called "sons of God" in the tradition (Mt 5:9, 45; Gal 4:5-6; Rom 8:14). In an article written in 1969, Floyd Filson ("First John: Message and Purpose," *Interpretation* 23 [1969], pp. 259-76) argues that the use of the term "little children" betrays the fact that the author is older both in age and in the espousal of the Christian faith. While that may be true, the appellation recalls above all the status of the community vis-à-vis the opponents. It may be an endearing term, but it is a theological term as well.

[74]The antecedent of αὐτός is clearly the Son of God, whose role is described in v. 3:5.

[75]This argument is not unlike that of the third characterization of the opponents' position in vv. 1:5-2:11, viz., vv. 2:3-6. In that characterization the knowledge of Jesus --ἐγνώκαμεν αὐτόν--is defined as the carrying out of his commands. Furthermore, in the expansion of the controlling statement of v. 2:3, i.e., v. 2:6, "abiding in Jesus"--ὁ λέγων ἐν αὐτῷ μένειν--is defined in terms of "walking as he did." In this particular presentation of antithetical ethical positions, the knowledge of Jesus and "abiding in Jesus" are defined as "not sinning." It would appear that some are claiming otherwise.

[76]The main difference lies in the substitution of δίκαιος for the expression, ἐξ αὐτοῦ γεγέννηται.

[77]See above, p. 41, n. 39.

[78]Just as v. 3:1 expands the expression ἐξ αὐτοῦ γεγέννηται of v. 2:29 by means of the related expression τὰ τέκνα τοῦ θεοῦ, so does v. 3:10 follow the reintroduction of ἐκ τοῦ θεοῦ γεγέννηται in v. 3:9 with the same related expression, τὰ τέκνα τοῦ θεοῦ.

[79]The same thought may be found in the claims of v. 2:29a--the association of "righteousness" and "having been born of God"; v. 3:7--the righteous man "abides in" Jesus; v. 3:9a--the righteous man does not sin. Thus, to say that he who does not do righteousness is not "of God" is simply to utilize another combination of synonymous terms to convey the same meaning.

[80]Of the three exegetes that consider 2:28 (or 2:29)-
3:10 to be a self-contained paragraph, two--O'Neill and Dodd--
extend this second paragraph to v. 3:18 as well. The other,
R. Law, makes no division until v. 3:24.

[81]Thus, one finds elements usually associated with
tradition in the Letter: the aorist tense of ἀκούω (1:1, 3,
5; 2:7, 24); the prepositional phrase ἀπ' ἀρχῆς (1:1; 2:7, 24).
Furthermore, the noun ἀγγελία is also used of a tradition to
be handed on in v. 1:5 (with ἀπ' αὐτοῦ).

[82]In v. 3:6b the one who sins--which is tantamount to
saying "the one who does not execute righteousness"--is said
to have neither seen (οὐχ ἑώρακεν) nor known (οὐδὲ ἔγνωκεν)
Jesus. In other words, such a person is not in contact with
the tradition, even though he may claim that he is. Only certain ways of behavior allow a person to be in the tradition,
and one of these is "not sinning" or "executing righteousness."

[83]Thus, Balz, p. 184; Houlden, p. 97; Brooke, p. 90.
Bultmann, on the other hand, believes that "the brother" or
"one another" means simply "one's neighbor." See, e.g., *The
Johannine Epistles*, p. 54: "The meaning is everywhere the
same: love of neighbor is demanded."

[84]This is really the only explicit allusion to the
biblical tradition and to the Old Testament in I John. It is
certainly an indication that the dialogue with the synagogue
has ended; the problem now seems to be a totally different one:
an inner-church struggle.
   The figure of Cain appears in two other late New Testament writings: Heb 11:4 and Jude 11. The latter reference
is very interesting, since Cain (along with Balaam and Korah)
is made to represent the evil ways of the false teachers who
practice licentiousness and deny Jesus.

[85]That "the evil one" has been operative in history
from the beginning may be gathered from v. 3:8--the devil has
been a sinner "from the beginning."
   In the Letter the terms ὁ διάβολος (vv. 3:8^2, 10) and
ὁ πονηρός (vv. 2:13, 14; 3:12^2; 5:19) are synonymous. The
proximity of v. 3:12 to vv. 3:8, 10 alone indicates this.

[86]See Schnackenburg, pp. 195-96, who suggests that the
author may have in mind the persecutions of Domitian.

[87]The hatred of the brethren was also mentioned in the
first exposition of the love command in paragraph 1:5-2:11.
It was stated in the fourth characterization of that paragraph
that there were some who claimed to be "in the light" but who
showed themselves to be "in darkness" because they hated their
brother.

[88]The terms "life" and "life eternal" should be considered synonymous, as their juxtaposition in v. 1:2 shows.

[89]V. 2:24 specifies that if the correct christological
doctrine of vv. 22-23 "abides" in the community, the community

will "abide" in the Father and the Son, and it is this "abiding," this promise (ἡ ἐπαγγελία), which constitutes "eternal life."

[90]V. 5:11c proceeds to identify that "life" as being the Son of God himself--καὶ αὕτη ἡ ζωὴ ἐν τῷ υἱῷ αὐτοῦ ἐστιν.

[91]The only other instances of the noun ὁ θάνατος in the Letter occur in vv. 5:16-17, where it is found three times. The passage is instructive because it concerns the forgiveness of sins. There is one sin, the author states, that cannot be forgiven, viz., the sin "unto death" (πρὸς θάνατον). Given the consistent meaning of the term "life" in the Letter, the sin unto death would seem to signify the sin of doctrinal deviation and, specifically, as I shall show later, the denial that the death of Jesus was redemptive. Such a denial cannot be forgiven, because he who would forgive is no longer an object of belief in his role as forgiver.

[92]On the question of definitional sentences, see above, p. 41, n. 39.

[93]This type of argumentation is also present in v. 3:1. In that verse the execution of righteousness (a criterion which is later equated in v. 3:10 with the execution of the love command) is also presented as a sign that the individual has undergone a transformation, viz., that he "has been born of God" and is now "a child of God." Such a transformation is also clearly associated with the redemptive death of Jesus Christ: it is that death which specifically defines God's love for men and constitutes them "children of God."

[94]All three times that the verb ὀφείλω is used, it refers explicitly to the imitation of Jesus' life on the part of the community. Thus, in v. 2:6 "abiding in" Jesus is clearly defined in terms of "walking as he did." Likewise, in v. 4:11 the mutual love of the brethren is patterned after Jesus' own example in vv. 4:9-10.

[95]I have already mentioned the triviality of the event described in v. 3:17. Furthermore, the passage from "death" to "life" described in v. 14 confirms this symbolical interpretation.

[96]The noun σπλάγχνα can mean either the physical entrails of an animal or a man (e.g., Acts 1:18) as well as the "heart" of a man as the repository of mercy and compassion (which meaning may be extended to God as well). Pauline usages, such as II Cor 6:12, 7:15, Philemon 7, 12, 20, exemplify this latter meaning and are rather close to that of I John. See H. Koester, "σπλάγχνον," TDNT, VII, pp. 548-59.

[97]It would appear that, as in the fourth characterization of vv. 1:5-2:11, some are claiming to love God while exhibiting the kind of behavior described in this verse. For the author such a claim is impossible, given the criterion that distinguishes the "children of God" in v. 3:10, i.e., the love of one's brethren.

[98]Schnackenburg, p. 201.

[99]This interpretation agrees with the meaning of the
noun ἀλήθεια in the Letter, where it repeatedly represents the
correct christological position (see vv. 2:21; 4:6; 5:6).
A very similar usage may be found in both II and
III John. In II John 1 the author of that Letter refers to
the children whom he is addressing as τοῖς τέκνοις αὐτῆς, οὓς
ἐγὼ ἀγαπῶ ἐν ἀληθείᾳ; further on, in v. 3, the author associates once again "love" and "truth"--ἔσται μεθ᾿ ἡμῶν . . . ἐν
ἀληθείᾳ καὶ ἀγάπῃ. Similarly, in III John 1 the author of
that Letter addresses a certain Gaius whom, he says, he loves
in the truth--ὃν ἐγὼ ἀγαπῶ ἐν ἀληθείᾳ.
These references certainly imply that both II and
III John presuppose the existence of a "correct" love, a love
which is "in the truth." Although it is impossible to ascertain what III John means precisely by the term "truth,"
II John is far more explicit. According to that Letter,
"truth" means basically the execution of God's commands (vv.
4-6), which are also Jesus' commands (vv. 9-10). Therefore,
"to love in the truth" is basically--as in the case of I Jn
3:11-18--an acceptance of the figure and role of Jesus Christ,
specifically his redemptive death (v. 7).

[100]This is simply another way of expressing the falsehood which the author ascribes to the incorrect positions of
paragraph 1:5-2:11 (e.g., vv. 1:6, 8, 10; 2:4, 9).

[101]See above, p. 36, n. 24. Only O'Neill and Dodd
present vv. 3:19-24 as a self-contained paragraph.

[102]The precise arrangement of clauses and the precise
progression of thought are notorious difficulties. See Dodd,
p. 88.

[103]Dodd's own reconstruction is plausible: take πεί-
σομεν and γνωσόμεθα as referring back to ἐν τούτῳ, which is
then answered by the second ὅτι-clause of v. 3:20, while the
first ὅτι-clause is accepted as parenthetical. Ibid., pp.
89ff.
See above, p. 41, n. 39 for this aspect of definition.

[104]Just as the movement from vv. 2:3-6 to vv. 2:7-11,
i.e., from the third characterization to the fourth of paragraph 1:5-2:11, involves a change from the plural form, ἐντολαί, to the singular, ἐντολή, so now a similar change is found
from the plural of v. 3:22 to the singular (twice) of v. 3:23
to the plural of v. 3:24. In the former case, the change to
the singular is identified as the "love for one's brother"; in
the latter, the same change is identified as "belief in Jesus
Christ" and "love for one another."

[105]As I shall show later, belief in Jesus and, specifically, *correct* belief in Jesus, is the main object of the
largely dogmatic sections.

[106]An analogous example would be the twofold criterion
of v. 3:10 which distinguishes the "children of God" from the

"children of the devil": the execution of righteousness and
the love for one's brother. The command would also include,
as the author states elsewhere, specific and concrete ethical
actions toward the brethren, but the main emphasis in this
verse is, without a doubt, the inclusion of belief within that
command.

[107]The subject of the verb ἔδωκεν is not the Jesus
Christ of the ἵνα-clause, but the antecedent of the αὐτοῦ in
the expression, καὶ αὕτη ἐστὶν ἡ ἐντολὴ αὐτοῦ. This αὐτός as
well as the preceding ones ultimately go back to the noun in
the following prepositional phrase of v. 3:22, πρὸς τὸν θεόν,
i.e., God the Father.
     The love command *per se* is said to be traditional in
vv. 2:7-8 and v. 3:11. Furthermore, belief in Jesus as the
Christ and the Son of God is also ascribed to the tradition
repeatedly in the Letter (e.g., vv. 1:1-4; 2:24-25).

[108]In the third characterization of paragraph 1:5-2:11,
viz., vv. 2:3-6, "abiding in him," where the pronoun refers to
Jesus Christ, is made to depend also on the execution of Jesus'
commandments or on the way "he walked." Thus, the argument is
the same, but the referents are different. This difference,
however, is insignificant, given the role of Jesus vis-à-vis
God and the claim made on the former's behalf in v. 5:20.

[109]See p. 36 above. Of the eleven exegetes, nine
support such a delineation (O'Neill, Bultmann, Kümmel, Perrin,
Bogart, Houlden, Dodd, Schnackenburg, and Westcott). The
other two--Lohmeyer and Law--introduce minor variations.

[110]Law, who would consider vv. 3:24b-4:6 as the preceding paragraph, does regard vv. 4:7-12 as a self-contained
unit. Lohmeyer, however, who divides vv. 4:1-6 into vv. 4:1-3,
4-6, presents the following arrangement: vv. 4:7-10, 11-13,
14-16a, 16b-18, 19-21.
     Both Häring and Brooke adopt vv. 4:7-12 as a paragraph.
See Brooke, pp. xxxvi, 117.

[111]The use of the linking prepositional phrase ἐκ τοῦ
θεοῦ to modify the noun ἡ ἀγάπη in v. 4:7 points in this
direction as well. In the preceding paragraph the prepositional
phrase is used by the author to differentiate the "correct"
spirit from the "false" one, the "correct" believers from the
false ones (see vv. 4:2-3, 4-5). Similarly, in the present
paragraph it is the love "of God" that is being described.

[112]This is the first time that a statement incorporating the love command--whether the object of the verb be τὸν
ἀδελφόν or ἀλλήλους--is not explicitly ascribed to the tradition by the author. Indeed, the paragraph does not produce
that kind of a claim at all.

[113]See above, p. 59, n. 108. This close relationship
may also be observed in the role that Jesus plays within the
author's definition of God's love toward men (vv. 3:1ff.; 4:9,
16).

[114]Brooke, p. 118, tends in this direction. Spicq, III, p. 271, who calls it the supreme revelation of New Testament love, is also very much within this line of interpretation.

[115]Bultmann, *The Johannine Epistles*, p. 66. Dodd, p. 110, also follows this line of interpretation, but in a much more general way: "If He creates, He creates in love; if He rules, He rules in love; if He judges, He judges in love."

[116]See above, p. 41, n. 39.

[117]The author of the Letter uses φανερόω a total of eight times (vv. 1:2^2; 2:19, 28; 3:2^2, 5, 8). Its different meanings are: (1) it may refer to the second coming of Jesus Christ (vv. 2:28; 3:2); (2) it may refer to a revelation not yet attained (v. 3:2); (3) no specific technical meaning (v. 2:19); (4) it may refer directly to the first coming of Jesus Christ (vv. 1:2^2; 3:5, 8). Finally, the meaning in this verse is rather close to #4 above, since it does refer indirectly to the coming of Jesus Christ; however, its direct and primary signification is the "love from God"; the love of God or from God was manifested in the event of Jesus Christ.

[118]It is not necessary to adopt a restrictive interpretation of this prepositional phrase; it may very well refer to all human beings, since it speaks of a mission prior to decision on the part of a human being. As such, it would anticipate the prepositional phrase εἰς τὸν κόσμον and recapitulate the thought of v. 2:2b. However, only the community of the author would betray an acceptance of that mission. For another opinion, see Brooke, p. 119.

[119]The sending formula is much more frequent in the Gospel than in the Letter, where it appears only three times (I Jn 4:9, 10, 14). The designation μονογενής is equivalent to the Hebrew יָחִיד which means "only" or "beloved." On this point, see Schnackenburg, p. 230. I tend to see a certain polemical reason for the employment of this expression. The *only* Son may refer to the distinction made between the historical Jesus and the Son of God by the opponents; "only" would then affirm unequivocally the unity of these two "persons." On the christological deviation of the opponents, see the section on the *Sitz im Leben* of the Letter at the end of the chapter.

[120]In the exegesis of paragraph 3:11-18, I remarked that the transformation from "death" to "life" being claimed by the author in v. 3:14 on the basis of the execution of the love command was ultimately based on the person of Jesus Christ. It was shown at that point that the term "life" is used by the author to refer to Jesus and to the redemptive nature of his death (vv. 1:1-4; 2:25; 5:11, 20). Thus, the development of the purpose clause ἵνα ζήσωμεν δι᾽ αὐτοῦ in terms of Jesus' redemptive death, ἱλασμὸν περὶ τῶν ἀμαρτιῶν ἡμῶν, is in keeping with similar argumentation found elsewhere in the Letter. See above, pp. 55-57.

^{121}V. 4:11 stands to vv. 4:9-10 in very much the same
way that v. 3:16b relates to v. 3:16a, viz., the death of
Jesus becomes normative for the love of the community. Both
verses, furthermore, employ the verb form ὀφείλομεν: one has
no choice but to love in this way, i.e., the way of vv. 4:9-10
and 3:16a. See above, p. 56, n. 94.

^{122}It should be noted that in this particular paragraph the author provides no concrete examples of this kind
of love as he does in vv. 2:15-17 and 3:17.

^{123}The argument will be taken up again and developed
in the third paragraph (vv. 4:16b-21) of this largely ethical
section. See, e.g., vv. 4:19-20.

^{124}The genitive αὐτοῦ is an objective genitive:
mutual love and all that it entails shows that an individual
loves God (and vice versa). Thus, Dodd, p. 113. Brooke, however, disagrees (p. 120), and Spicq, III, p. 287, calls it a
genitive of quality, i.e., divine love as such.

^{125}V. 4:13 is very similar to v. 3:24b in structure
and terminology. Both verses use the definitional sentence
ἐν τούτῳ γινώσκομεν. In both verses that which is to be
defined is the concept of "abiding," and in both cases that
definition is given in terms of "spirit." Minor differences
are the double abiding of v. 4:13 and the use of the perfect
tense instead of the aorist in that same verse.

^{126}Of those exegetes that accept vv. 4:7-12 as a
paragraph, all but one also accept vv. 4:13-16 as a paragraph
(Bultmann, Law, Häring, Brooke). Dodd represents the only
exception; he prefers to extend the unit up to v. 4:18. See
Brooke, p. xxxvi.

^{127}This belief presents the same consequences that
follow from the possession of the spirit of God, viz., a
double-abiding: God abides in that believer, and that believer
abides in God. As such, it is presented by the author as
another way of formulating the "spirit of God."

^{128}Houlden, p. 116, is far too general in interpreting
this belief in love: "Presumably the sense is that we believe
that God's love is bestowed upon us, or that we have confidence
in this love." Balz, p. 194, sees the point, but does not
develop it: "Damit ist der Aufruf zur Liebe letztlich selbst
ein Bekenntnis."

^{129}The paragraph leaves no doubts as to who the pos-
sessors of the spirit of God are: the author and those in his
community who believe as he does. This claim may be observed
in the progression from v. 4:15 to v. 4:16. The former verse
offers a definition in terms of the indefinite pronoun, ὃς ἐὰν
ὁμολογήσῃ ὅτι; the latter identifies quite clearly who it is
that so confesses: καὶ ἡμεῖς ἐγνώκαμεν καὶ πεπιστεύκαμεν τὴν
ἀγάπην.
      Both of these verbs, it should be recalled, are used
elsewhere with respect to the person of Jesus: γινώσκειν is

thus found in vv. 2:3-6 and 2:28-3:10 (see v. 3:5); πιστεύειν
is found in vv. 3:19-24 (see v. 3:23).

[130]Of the four exegetes that accepted vv. 4:13-16 as
a unit of thought (Bultmann, Law, Häring, and Brooke), only
the latter two present vv. 4:16-21 as a distinctive unit of
thought. Bultmann adopts the following division: vv. 4:17-18,
4:19-5:5, while Law adopts the following division: vv. 4:17-
5:3a. See Brooke, p. xxxvi.

[131]As in the case of v. 4:8b, the characterization of
God as "love" cannot be separated from its context. In both
cases this characterization is directly related to the manifes-
tation of love in the sending of his Son and in the redemptive
death which the latter undergoes. In vv. 4:9-10 one finds the
context for the statement of v. 4:8, while that of v. 4:16b is
found in the preceding verses, viz., vv. 4:14-16a.

[132]One finds minor changes in this reprise: (1) from
the use of the reciprocal pronoun in v. 4:12, the author
switches to the verb μένειν followed by a prepositional phrase;
(2) the abiding of the believer in God is now included as a
consequence, primarily because this aspect of the abiding has
been introduced in v. 4:13; (3) the other consequence of v.
4:12--the perfection of God's love in the believer--is taken
up in the following two verses.
        Also, the relationship of v. 4:16b$_2$ to vv. 4:16b$_1$, 16a,
15, and 14 is very similar to that between v. 4:11 and vv. 4:10,
9, and 8. The principle at work is as follows: "Given the
extent of God's love, then . . . ," i.e., the community must
take that example and mode of love and incorporate it into its
own practice.

[133]See above, p. 41, n. 39.

[134]Although a ἵνα-clause never follows an ἐν τούτῳ
introduction elsewhere, it does follow εἰς τοῦτο in v. 3:8,
which is also a definitional sentence. Brooke, p. 123, also
suggests (but does not adopt himself) the possibility that the
ἐν τούτῳ may recapitulate the preceding thought. This is
highly unlikely, however, and Brooke himself provides the
reason--the definition usually follows the phrase.

[135]Houlden, p. 117; Dodd, p. 119; Brooke, p. 124;
Balz, p. 194; Westcott, p. 150; Spicq, III, p. 293.

[136]Just as he attributes v. 2:28 to the ecclesiastical
redactor (see above, p. 47, n. 62), Bultmann also assigns
parts of v. 4:17 to that redaction. Bultmann, *The Johannine
Epistles*, pp. 72ff. The main step is to remove the prepositional phrase ἐν τῇ ἡμέρᾳ τῆς κρίσεως and substitute in its
place another prepositional phrase from the same verse: ἐν
τῷ κόσμῳ τούτῳ. Two other emendations would be required in
the ὅτι-clause as well: the addition of the phrase ἐν τῇ
ἀγάπῃ τοῦ πατρός to καθὼς ἐκεῖνός ἐστιν and of ἐν τῇ ἀγάπῃ to
καὶ ἡμεῖς ἐσμεν. Aside from the merits of the proposal--which
to me seems just too complicated to be plausible--one would
still find a ἵνα-clause and a ὅτι-clause as possible definitions of the ἐν τούτῳ.

[137]A possible difficulty lies in the usual identification of ἐκεῖνος with Jesus in the Letter (vv. 2:6; 3:3, 5, 7,
16). Thus, Brooke, p. 124; Bultmann, *The Johannine Epistles*,
p. 72. However, the usage is not universal: in v. 5:16
ἐκεῖνος does not refer to Jesus Christ. Given this exception
and the context of v. 4:17, the ἐκεῖνος in this case should be
associated with God the Father.

[138]See Blass-Debrunner-Funk, #391:5. In other words,
the imitation of God's love on the part of the community would
result in "confidence" on the day of judgment.

[139]Neither φόβος nor ἔξω βαλεῖν nor κόλασις occur
elsewhere in the Letter. At the same time, one should avoid
unnecessary psychological observations, e.g., Spicq, III, pp.
296ff.

[140]There is a basis for this identification on the
grounds that some of these terms (ἔξω βαλεῖν; κόλασις) are
interpreted eschatologically elsewhere, e.g., Mt 25:46; II Pet
2:9; Lk 13:28.

[141]As in the case of v. 4:16b, much of the material
contained in these verses has already been presented elsewhere
in the preceding paragraph, 4:7-12. For example, v. 4:19a =
v. 4:11b; v. 4:19b = vv. 4:10, 11a; v. 4:20 = v. 4:12a; v. 4:21
= vv. 4:14, 16.

[142]The elements are simply reversed:

v. 4:17--ὅτι καθὼς ἐκεῖνός   καὶ ἡμεῖς ἐσμεν ἐν τῷ κόσμῳ
        ἐστιν   τούτῳ
v. 4:19--ἡμεῖς ἀγαπῶμεν   ὅτι αὐτὸς πρῶτος ἠγάπησεν ἡμᾶς

[143]See above, pp. 40-42.

[144]The prepositional phrase ἀπ' αὐτοῦ seems to refer
here to God the Father (as it was the case in v. 3:23). There
is no other suitable antecedent. In any case, the agency of
Jesus Christ in conveying the command is presupposed.

[145]It should be recalled that in v. 2:29 that very
same claim--"to have been born of God"--was shown to be true
by the execution of righteousness. Furthermore, in v. 4:7 the
execution of the love command, which was to be understood in
terms of the mission of the Son of God, also gave rise to the
same claim, "to have been born of God."

[146]In both cases he employs the familiar definitional
pattern. In v. 5:2 he uses the phrase ἐν τούτῳ, followed by
ὅταν, while in v. 5:3 he employs the simple demonstrative pronoun followed by a ἵνα-clause. See above, p. 41, n. 39.

[147]The change from τὸν γεγεννημένον ἐξ αὐτοῦ to τὰ
τέκνα τοῦ θεοῦ makes it clear that the latter term refers
explicitly to those who hold the beliefs of vv. 5:1 and 5. In
two previous occasions in the Letter, the author has used the
verb γεννάω as an introduction to the term "the children of
God." First of all, in v. 2:29 he who does righteousness is

said to "have been born of God." The following verse describes
the origin of this status in terms of τέκνα θεοῦ. Secondly,
in v. 3:9 he who is born of God is said not to commit sin.
The following verse differentiates between two groups of people,
the children of God and the children of the devil.
In II Jn 6 the author defines ἀγάπη--the love of the
brethren, since that is its immediate antecedent--in terms of
the execution of God's commands: ἵνα περιπατῶμεν κατὰ τὰς
ἐντολὰς αὐτοῦ. I say "God's" commands because that is the
immediate antecedent of αὐτός (παρὰ τοῦ πατρός, v. 4).

[148]A cursory look at the recent *Introductions* to the
New Testament confirms this judgment of the contemporary exegetical situation. See, e.g., Kümmel, pp. 440-42; Marxsen,
p. 263; Perrin, p. 248.

[149]A. Wurm, *Die Irrlehrer im ersten Johannesbrief*, Biblische Studien, no. 8:1 (Freiburg: Herder, 1903).

[150]See above, p. 33, n. 9.

[151]Brooke, pp. xxxviii-xli.

[152]See Haenchen, "Neuere Literatur," pp. 35-38.

[153]Bogart, pp. 123-41. See also, Schnackenburg, pp.
15-23.

[154]The verses used to describe these categories are
as follows:
     1. vv. 2:18-20, 22, 26-28
     2. vv. 4:1, 2, 3b, 5
     3. vv. 1:6; 2:4, 6, 15-17; 3:4-7, 10
     4. vv. 2:9, 11; 3:12-13, 14b-15, 17-18; 4:8, 20
     5. vv. 1:8, 10
     6. vv. 2:28; 3:1-3, 19-22; 4:17-18; 5:3b, 14
     7. vv. 4:10, 19
     8. vv. 4:11-12
     9. vv. 5:6-11
    10. v. 5:21

[155]This exclusion is not entirely justified in my
opinion. Even if the groups in question represent members of
the community who have remained orthodox, nevertheless the
dangers against which they are being warned are those of the
opponents, and, as such, these groups and the dangers attend-
ing them should not be left out of consideration, but rather
should be seen in conjunction with the other groups. Thus,
for example, Bogart declares on p. 126: "How the persons in
group #7 got the notion that loving God was man's initiative
is unknown." However, as I have shown, the claim is the same
as that of v. 4:20a and is refuted by the author in exactly
the same way.

[156]Ibid., pp. 130-31.

[157]I should also remark that this description by
Bogart does not contain the slightest allusion to persecution

or bloodshed being carried out against the "orthodox" members
of the community by those who have deviated from such "ortho-
doxy." As a result, the interpretation taken above concerning the imitation of Jesus' death as representing basically an
acceptance of such a death by the members of the community is
considerably strengthened.

[158]But certainly not in the eyes of the opponents,
given the claims made within the second characterization of
paragraph 1:5-2:11--ἁμαρτίαν οὐκ ἔχομεν (v. 1:8); οὐχ ἡμαρτήκαμεν (v. 1:10). Indeed, it is probably because of sinless-
ness, past and present, that they are adopting this type of
behavior.

[159]The author devotes most of his time to a description of what love for the brethren, i.e., those who believe
correctly, should imply. He does not, however, emphasize much
the kind of behavior that the believer must adopt toward those
who have fallen away. A glimpse of this attitude may be
gathered from the juxtaposition of the following verses:
(1) in vv. 2:19 and 4:1 the author states that the opponents
had once belonged to the community (ἐξ ἡμῶν ἐξῆλθαν), but had
now gone forth into the world (ἐξεληλύθασιν εἰς τὸν κόσμον);
(2) in vv. 3:1 and 3:13 it is said that the world--in clear
reference to the opponents of the author--does not know (οὐ
γινώσκει) and actually hates (μισεῖ) the brethren; (3) consequently, in v. 2:15 the brethren--ἀγαπητοί--are advised to
"not love" (= hate) the world, implying those who have deserted
the community in doctrine and praxis. However, what this
"hatred" specifically entails is not given in detail.
    II John may provide a glimpse in this direction, inso-
far as the advice of v. 10 is concerned: if someone with a
different doctrine comes (i.e., the doctrine of v. 7a) to a
believer's house, that person must not be received or even
greeted (μὴ λαμβάνετε αὐτὸν εἰς οἰκίαν καὶ χαίρειν αὐτῷ μὴ
λέγετε).

CHAPTER III

[1]See above, ch. I, p. 2, n. 8; p. 21, n. 130; pp.
22-24.
    The proposed context for such additions is not sur-
prising. Indeed, recent research in the Synoptic Gospels has
tended to see in the Apocalyptic Discourse of Jesus (Mk 13
parr.) similar reflections on the status quo of the respective
communities. See, e.g., Theodore Weeden, *Mark--Traditions in
Conflict* (Philadelphia: Fortress, 1971); William G. Thompson,
Matthew's Advice to a Divided Community, AnalBib, no. 44 (Rome:
Biblical Institute Press, 1971); C. H. Talbert, "The Redaction
Critical Quest for Luke the Theologian," in *Jesus and Man's
Hope*, 2 vols., ed. Donald G. Miller and Kikran Y. Hadidian
(Pittsburgh: Pittsburgh Theological Seminary, 1971), I, pp.

171-222. The redactor would have found it most convenient to read his own situation as well into the mouth of the departing Jesus.

[2]Raymond Brown, *The Gospel according to John (xiii-xxi)*, The Anchor Bible, no. 29a (Garden City, N.J.: Doubleday, 1970), pp. 582-83. Brown lists six problems of one sort or another that militate against literary unity: (a) the break between vv. 14:31 and 18:1; (b) disagreements within the discourse (e.g., vv. 13:36 and 16:5); (c) duplications and repetitions (e.g., between vv. 13:31-14:31 and 16:4b-33); (d) similarity of some of the material to Synoptic material that forms part of the public ministry (e.g., vv. 15:18-16:4a and Mt 10:17-25); (e) lack of connection with the theme of Jesus' departure (vv. 15:1-6); (f) a variety of theological outlooks.

[3]See, e.g., B. F. Westcott, *The Gospel according to St. John*, 2nd ed. (London: John Murray, 1903), p. liii: "Neither the apostolical authorship nor the historical trustworthiness of the narrative is affected by the admission that the writer fulfills his work, according to his own words, with an express purpose in view." The first edition of this work was published in 1881.

[4]Ibid., pp. lxiii-lxiv.

[5]Ibid., p. 211.

[6]H. Bouyer, *Le quatrième évangile* (Tournai: Castermann, 1955), p. 202.

[7]R. Bultmann, *The Gospel of John--A Commentary*, trans. G. R. Beasley-Murray et al. (Philadelphia: Westminster, 1971), p. 459. Bultmann dismisses the possibility of secondary additions on the basis of the thoroughly Johannine style of the chapters in question.

[8]Neither man was the first to propose such a hypothesis. Others before them had already rearranged the text, e.g., B. W. Bacon, *The Fourth Gospel in Research and Debate* (New Haven: Yale University Press, 1918); Friedrich Spitta, *Das Johannesevangelium als Quelle der Geschichte Jesu* (Göttingen: Vandenhoeck & Ruprecht, 1910).

[9]J. H. Bernard, *The Gospel according to St. John*, 2 vols., ICC (New York: Charles Scribner's Sons, 1929), I, xx-xxiii.

[10]Ibid., p. xx. Bernard is still preoccupied with "historicizing" presuppositions, although these are not primary.

[11]Ibid., pp. xx-xxi.

[12]R. Bultmann, *Das Evangelium des Johannes*, Kritisch-exegetischer Kommentar über das Neue Testament (Göttingen: Vandenhoeck & Ruprecht, 1941). All references to Bultmann's commentary will be to the English translation of n. 7 above.

[13]See Bultmann, *The Gospel of John*, pp. 459-60, n. 6.

[14]Ibid., p. 461. See also, D. Moody Smith, *The Composition and Order of the Fourth Gospel* (New Haven: Yale University Press, 1965), pp. 168ff.

[15]Moreover, the petition of v. 17:1 that the Father glorify the Son has been heard in v. 13:31, and thus the latter verse should follow, not precede, ch. 17. Bultmann also has v. 13:1 as the beginning of the prayer of ch. 17. Bultmann, p. 461.

[16]H. Becker, *Die Reden des Johannesevangelium und der Stil der gnostischen Offenbarungsrede*, FRLANT, no. 68 (Göttingen: Vandenhoeck & Ruprecht, 1956); J. Heise, *Bleiben. Menein in den Johanneischen Schriften*, Hermeneutische Untersuchungen zur Theologie, no. 8 (Tübingen: J. C. B. Mohr, 1967).

[17]Brown, pp. 584-85. All references to the second volume of Brown's commentary will be listed simply as: Brown. References from the first volume will be explicitly designated as such: Brown, I.

[18]R. Schnackenburg, III, pp. 101-2. All references from this volume in this chapter will be listed from this point onwards simply as: Schnackenburg.

[19]B. Lindars, *The Gospel of John*, New Century Bible (London: Oliphants, 1972), pp. 442ff., 467-68.

[20]J. Becker, p. 216.

[21]P. Corssen, "Die Abschiedsreden Jesu in dem vierten Evangelium," *ZNW* 8 (1907), pp. 125-42. The subtitle itself indicates Corssen's preoccupation with J. Wellhausen's approach: "Mit besonderer Berücksichtigung von J. Wellhausen, Erweiterungen und Änderungen im vierten Evangelium."

[22]H. Zimmermann, "Struktur und Aussageabsicht der johanneischen Abschiedsreden (Jo 13-17)," *BiLe* 8 (1967), pp. 279-90. See p. 282: "Beide Hypothesen . . . haben den unstreitbaren Nachteil, dass sie nicht zum Verständnis des Textes hinführen, wie er überliefert ist. Wenn die Kap. 15-17 als Nachtrag deklariert oder in die Abfolge der Kap. 13 und 14 hineingestellt werden, kann der überlieferte Text nicht eigentlich in der Blick kommen."

[23]Corssen, pp. 126-27.

[24]Ibid., pp. 138ff.

[25]Zimmermann, pp. 288-89.

[26]Ibid.

[27]This is J. Becker's main criticism of this approach, and I believe that he is quite correct in this observation.

See Becker, p. 217: "Sie verkennt zudem ebenso wie Corssen,
dass der Abschnitt 14:27-31 als ganzer Abschluss einer Rede-
komposition ist."

[28]J. Wellhausen, *Erweiterungen und Änderungen im
vierten Evangelium* (Berlin: Georg Reimer, 1907) and *Das
Evangelium Johannis* (Berlin: Georg Reimer, 1908). At the
time that Wellhausen published these works, F. Spitta, B. W.
Bacon, and H. H. Wendt had already advanced their respective
theories of rearrangement. See, e.g., F. Spitta, *Zur Geschichte
und Literatur des Urchristentums*, 2 vols. (Göttingen: Vandenhoeck & Ruprecht, 1893-96); H. H. Wendt, *Das Johannesevangelium*
(Göttingen: Vandenhoeck & Ruprecht, 1900).

[29]Wellhausen, *Das Evangelium Johannis*, pp. 77-80.
P. Corssen refuses to concede this point in his article and
proceeds instead to call into question the other arguments
that Wellhausen considers to be secondary evidence as the
only true evidence that can be summoned on behalf of the additions theory (Corssen, p. 125). In this work of 1908, Wellhausen correctly points out--against Corssen's position--that
the removal of these words does not help the situation all
that much.

[30]Ibid., pp. 77-79; *Erweiterungen*, pp. 7-8. The
theological arguments are: (1) whereas in vv. 13:31-14:31 it
is the Father who sends the Paraclete, in vv. 15:1-16:33 that
role is assigned to Jesus; (2) whereas vv. 13:31-14:31 contain
no mention of the Parousia, vv. 15:1-16:33 do.

[31]Eduard Meyer, *Ursprung und Anfänge des Christentums*,
3 vols., 4th ed. (Stuttgart: J. G. Cotta, 1924), I, p. 313.

[32]Walter Bauer, "Das Johannesevangelium," in *Die
Evangelien*, 2 vols., HNT (Tübingen: J. C. B. Mohr, 1919),
II, p. 142.

[33]M.-J. Lagrange, *Évangile selon Saint Jean*, 4th ed.,
Études bibliques (Paris: J. Gabalda, 1927). Lagrange takes
his inspiration from Durand whom he quotes on p. 398.

[34]Ibid., p. 434.

[35]Ibid., pp. 398-99. In an article written in 1954
("'L'heure' de Jean xvii," *RB* 61 [1954], pp. 392-97), A.
George--invoking the memory of Lagrange and others--adopts a
similar point of view with regard to vv. 15:1-17:26, except
that he would break the entire section into seven fragments
("fragments johanniques"): 15:1-8; 15:9-17; 15:18-16:4a;
16:5-15; 16:16-24; 16:25-33; 17. These fragments would have
as their purpose "servir d'ébauches au discours actuel de
xiii,31 - xiv,31," Ibid., p. 393. Although Becker claims
that George is positing different authors for these fragments
(see Becker, p. 219), this observation cannot be reached from
what George has to say.

[36]Zimmermann, p. 280: "Aus der Vielzahl der Meinungen,
die seither über die Struktur der Abschiedsreden geäussert

wurden, sollen nur zwei Hypothesen herausgegriffen werden,
weil sie auch heute noch die Auffassung über die Abschiedsreden
massgebend bestimmen: die Nachtrags- und die Umstellungs-
hypothese."

[37]R. Borig, *Der wahre Weinstock; Untersuchungen zu Jo
15:1-10*, StANT, no. 16 (Munich: Kösel Verlag, 1967).

[38]Ibid., pp. 19-21.

[39]Ibid., p. 21.

[40]It is interesting to read G. Richter's review of
Borig's work in *MüTZ* 20 (1969), pp. 72-73. Richter takes
Borig to task for presupposing that the evangelist himself
was responsible for the alternative version of chs. 15-17 (the
review, in effect, contains *in nuce* Richter's own solution to
the problem). Such presuppositions, Richter argues, should
not be summarily accepted.

[41]G. Richter, "Die Fusswaschung." See above, ch. I,
p. 21, n. 131, for this and the following two references.

[42]Idem, *Die Fusswaschung im Johannesevangelium.*

[43]Idem, "Die Deutung."

[44]Richter gives due credit to those who were aware of
the literary problems prior to his own exegesis, specifically
to the work of M.-É. Boismard ("Le lavement des pieds," *RB*
71 [1964], pp. 5-24) to which he refers as "die ausführlichste
literarkritische Untersuchung über die Fusswaschung," in "Die
Fusswaschung," pp. 18-20.

[45]Ibid., pp. 13-18. Also "Die Deutung," pp. 24-25.
Richter sees the evangelist as developing a twofold line of
defense: (1) death on the cross was a part of the Father's
plan for salvation. (2) Jesus himself was aware of the
manner in which he would die.

[46]Idem, "Die Fusswaschung," pp. 24-26.

[47]Ibid., p. 23. Also, *Die Fusswaschung*, pp. 309-13.

[48]Idem, "Die Fusswaschung," p. 23.

[49]Ibid.

[50]Idem, "Die Deutung," pp. 30-35.

[51]Ibid., p. 35.

[52]Ibid., p. 36.

[53]See above, p. 82, n. 2. The first volume had
appeared in 1966: R. Brown, *The Gospel according to John
(i-xii)*, The Anchor Bible, no. 29 (Garden City, N.J.: Doubleday, 1966). Just as Richter reviews Borig's work, so also

Brown reviews Richter's work, and in a very favorable way (*TS* 30 [1969], pp. 120-21). See p. 121: "I believe that R. has made a major break-through in the understanding of this diffi- cult passage and would make only some minor qualifications."

[54] Brown, I, pp. xxiv-xxxix. See, however, Brown's latest blueprint: "Johannine Ecclesiology: The Community's Origins," *Interpretation* 31 (1977), pp. 379-93.

[55] Brown, I, xxxv, would also hold that toward the end of this period written forms of these Johannine patterns began to appear. As far as authorship is concerned, Brown allows for a possible number of sources ("the work of more than one man"), but also stresses the role of a dominant source or man. Thus, he combines the concept of "school" and that of a "prin- cipal preacher" within the same school.

[56] Brown takes the "principal preacher" of the last stage as the probable author of this first edition of the Gospel, thus accounting for the basic cohesiveness which he finds in the work. Ibid., pp. xxxv-xxxvi.

[57] Such a person is associated with the "close-knit school" postulated in stage 2, perhaps a "close friend" or "disciple" of the evangelist himself. Brown would also admit that to separate the second edition (fourth stage) from the final edition (fifth stage) is not always possible. Ibid., p. xxxvi.

[58] Brown, pp. 581-604.

[59] Ibid., pp. 585-87.

[60] Ibid., p. 587.

[61] See above, p. 84, n. 19.

[62] B. Lindars, *Behind the Fourth Gospel*, Studies in Creative Criticism, no. 3 (London: S.P.C.K., 1971)

[63] See, e.g., R. Fortna, *The Gospel of Signs*. See above, ch. I, p. 6, n. 31.

[64] See, e.g., R. Bultmann, *The Gospel of John*, pp. 6-9.

[65] Lindars, *The Gospel*, p. 47.

[66] Ibid., pp. 47-48. Lindars sees these Synoptic-type sayings as the starting points of many discourses. These say- ings, usually introduced by the declaration ἀμὴν ἀμὴν λέγω ὑμῖν, are to be found in the Farewell Discourse as well, e.g., vv. 13:38; 14:12, 16:20, 23.

[67] Ibid., pp. 51-54. Also, *Behind the Fourth Gospel*, pp. 43-60.

[68] Idem, *The Gospel*, p. 46.

[69]Ibid., pp. 460-61. Vv. 13:31-35 recapitulate vv. 13:1-20, Jesus as the model of discipleship; vv. 13:36-38 recapitulate vv. 13:21-30, the failure of discipleship.

[70]Ibid., p. 467.

[71]Ibid., pp. 486-87. This proposition is not unlike that made by R. Brown. Lindars identifies some of these "pieces": the Paraclete passages; the allegory of the vine (vv. 15:1-17); the teaching on persecution (vv. 15:18-25; 16:1-3); the exposition of "a little while" (vv. 16:16-22).

[72]Ibid., p. 461.

[73]See above, ch. I, p. 22, n. 137.

[74]See, above all, "Literarkritik am Joh-Ev" and "Tradition und Redaktion," I, pp. 32-60.

[75]Ibid., p. 59: "Für seine besonderen Überlieferungen standen dem Evangelisten mündliche Erzählungen von eigenständiger Originalität zur Verfügung." Also, among these traditions one may find both signs and discourse material. This first stage is comparable to stages 1 and 2 of Raymond Brown's theory.

[76]Ibid., p. 61. The final redactor was responsible for the following elements: (1) the introduction of the discourse material left behind by the author; (2) the addition of ch. 21; (3) the inversion of chs. 5 and 6; (4) a change of vv. 7:15-24 to their present position; (5) the addition of vv. 12:44-50; (6) brief glosses and comments (vv. 4:2 or 4:1-2; 4:44; 6:22-23; 7:39b; 11:2; 12:16). This stage would correspond to stage 5 of the process outlined by R. Brown.

[77]Among these one would find vv. 13:34-35 and "einzelne Worte als Einschübe." Idem, III, p. 54.

[78]Ibid., pp. 103-6.

[79]Ibid., p. 142. Schnackenburg believes that each chapter was written by a different hand: "Man kann es sich so vorstellen, dass ihr Autor die Abschiedsrede des Evangelisten kannte und für seine Absicht benutzte. Er kannte aber auch die Rede von Kap. 15 und knüpfte besonders an ihren zweiten Teil ('Geschiedenheit' von der Welt) an. Im Unterschied zu dieser Rede leitete ihn aber weniger ein paränetisches (auf mahnenden Zuspruch gerichtetes) als ein 'parakletisches' (Trost und Ermutigung intendierendes) Interesse."

[80]Ibid., pp. 231-45.

[81]See above, ch. I, p. 24, n. 148; pp. 27-28.

[82]Lattke, pp. 132-246.

[83]Ibid., p. 133. Lattke does allow for a later redaction with regard to other texts, e.g., ch. 21 and vv. 6:51c-58.

It is interesting to see Lattke quote P. Corssen in this context, since this was the same line of criticism that the latter employed against J. Wellhausen.

[84]Ibid., p. 135: "Auf diese Weise wäre nur eine, wie immer zu erklärende, Vertauschung anzunehmen und entsprechend auch nur eine einzige Umstellung vorzunehmen."

[85]Ibid., p. 137.

[86]One should remember that Schnackenburg begins to point the way toward a number of redactors and not just one. On the problems pertinent to the usage of the term "school," see above, ch. I, pp. 1, 9-11.

[87]Brown, I, p. xxxix; Lindars, The Gospel, p. 47. E. Schweizer, Ego Eimi, die religionsgeschichtliche Herkunft und theologische Bedeutung der johanneischen Bildreden, zugleich ein Beitrag zur Quellenfrage des vierten Evangeliums, FRLANT, no. 38 (Göttingen: Vandenhoeck & Ruprecht, 1939); E. Ruckstuhl, Die literarische Einheit des Johannesevangeliums, der gegenwärtige Stand der einschlagigen Erforschung, Studia Friburgensia, no. 3 (Freiburg: Paulus-Verlag, 1951). The basic point of both these studies was to emphasize the thorough and consistent Johannine style of the entire work.

[88]Richter, "Die Fusswaschung," pp. 23-24; "Die Deutung," p. 34: "Der Inhalt und die Tendenz ein und desselben Wortes und ein und desselben Satzes ist nicht immer derselbe."

[89]A year earlier he had published a study of Jn 17. See above, ch. I, p. 28, n. 174.

[90]J. Becker, "Die Abschiedsreden," p. 229.

[91]Becker and Richter are nevertheless quite close in attributing the material (or, at least, parts of it) to the author of I John. Becker is very much aware of Richter's approach and solutions to the problem, but considers the latter's results much too vague. This is a charge which, I believe, can justifiably be brought against Richter. He has certainly pointed the way, but has not done so in detail. Ibid., p. 231, n. 57.

[92]It should not be forgotten that, from a different perspective, both Lindars and Brown argue for originally independent units of discourse.

[93]See, among others, Bultmann, p. 523; Lindars, The Gospel, p. 486; Brown, p. 665; Heise, p. 81; Lagrange, p. 398.

[94]J. Becker, p. 229: "Joh 15 setzt nach 14:31 hart und abrupt ein mit der 'Bildrede' von Weinstock (15:1-8)."

[95]Ibid., p. 230: "15:1ff. und 15:18ff. lassen sich völlig unabhängig voreinander verstehen."

[96]Becker is reluctant to call this discourse a "Farewell" discourse, since there is no specific or overt treatment
of the theme of Jesus' departure. This is a Jesus who speaks
as an enthroned Lord ("der erhöhte Herr"), not as a Lord about
to depart ("der zum Aufbruch bereite Herr"). Ibid., p. 231.
Heise adopts a contrary position: this is a Jesus who is about
to depart (p. 86).

[97]Schnackenburg, pp. 103-4, argues that both Bultmann
and Becker unite vv. 15:18ff. with vv. 16:5ff. because of the
common theme of the unbelieving world: "Doch dürfte eine
genauere Strukturanalyse diese Entscheidung als falsch er-
weisen."

[98]Wellhausen, *Das Evangelium Johannis*, p. 68, adopts
a very similar structure, although he does not justify the par-
titioning as clearly as Schnackenburg.

[99]Schnackenburg, p. 104.

[100]Brown, pp. 586-87, also remarks upon the connection
of love and hatred, but sees it as an editorial welding of two
originally independent discourses.

[101]Ibid. Again, Brown sees this repetition of the
theme in v. 15:19 as an example of editorial welding.

[102]J. Becker, pp. 229-30. This third section is
clearly delineated by means of an inclusion. V. 12a defines
the commandment as being that of mutual love and v. 17 confirms it.

[103]Thus, Bultmann, p. 529; Lagrange, pp. 400-05; Heise,
p. 89; Bernard, II, 477; S. Schulz, *Komposition und Herkunft
der Johanneischen Reden*, BWANT, no. 81 (Stuttgart: W. Kohlhammer, 1960), p. 84; C. H. Dodd, *The Interpretation of the
Fourth Gospel* (Cambridge: University Press, 1970), p. 411.

[104]Brown, pp. 665-68, is the one who suggests v. 15:6
as the dividing point (J. Wellhausen had already proposed this
division; see *Das Evangelium Johannis*, pp. 68-69). Vv. 15:1-6
and 15:7-17 would be related to each other as vv. 10:1-5 and
10:6-18 are related: the first section would be made up of
figurative sayings, while the second would provide an explanation of such sayings. Indeed, Brown further proposes that
vv. 15:1-6 have been taken from another context and developed
by means of the parenetical section. Borig, p. 19, argues on
behalf of v. 15:10 as the dividing point, since v. 15:11 contains the expression ταῦτα λελάληκα ὑμῖν which recapitulates
the above ten verses.

[105]This is not always the case, however: neither vv.
15:1-17 nor ch. 17 end with the expression. Furthermore, the
expression is not always at the end, e.g., vv. 16:6, 25. It
is interesting to see Borig take the same expression as an
introduction to the next subsection. See above, pp. 97-98.

[106]This is an argument which Borig himself, p. 19, employs.

[107]Lindars' arrangement is very similar.   See *The Gospel*, p. 490.

[108]Bernard, II, pp. 483-90, proposes a similar division: vv. 15:9-11, 12-17.

[109]J. Becker, p. 236.

[110]Ibid., p. 232.

[111]Ibid., p. 233.   In n. 66a of the same page Becker states that it is impossible to claim that the same author wrote both pieces; there is no way of proving the claim at all.

[112]It is interesting to see how Becker denies that the text has any specific interest in the question of faith. This he does against J. Heise's position concerning vv. 15:1-17. (It should be remembered that Heise adopts Bultmann's theory of rearrangement and, therefore, does not consider the possibility of redaction. See above, p. 84, n. 16.)

[113]Other ἐγώ εἰμι sayings may be found in vv. 6:35, 41, 48, 51; 8:12; 10:7, 9, 11, 14. Bultmann, p. 225, n. 3, distinguishes among four forms of the saying: (1) the presentation formula, where the ἐγώ is the subject and replies to the question, "Who are you?"; (2) the qualificatory formula, answering the question, "What are you?"; (3) the identification formula, where the speaker identifies himself with another person or object; (4) the recognition formula, which alone has the ἐγώ as the predicative. It answers the question, "Who is the one that is expected, asked for, spoken to?" The Johannine formulas are to be classified in this last category.

[114]Borig, p. 22. Borig argues that the figure of the vine cannot be termed a parable, because it lacks a narrative form; nor a comparison ("Gleichnis"), because it lacks any particle of comparison; nor an allegory, because, if it were, the ἐγώ εἰμι would be found at the end and because vv. 4 and 6 contain particles of comparison. Bultmann, pp. 529-30, had already advanced pretty much the same arguments. Brown, pp. 668-69, terms it a "mashal."

[115]No specific meaning need be attached at this point to the verb form, καθαίρει, although it may be connected with v. 15:7. It should be seen primarily as another figure of the *Bildrede*.

[116]Bernard, II, p. 479, sees this warning as an "allusion to the failure and doom of Judas," but this view is dependent on his rearrangement of the chapters. Lagrange, p. 401, interprets the contrast in terms of doing good works. Brown, p. 676, sees the possibility of a polemic against Jewish Christians who had not yet publicly professed their faith. He concludes, however, with the following observation: "But

such a reference is very speculative." In that same page,
however, Brown--without passing any judgment at all on author-
ship--also expresses the possibility of a polemic against the
antichrists of I John. Thus, he clearly sees a connection
between the two writings, a connection which he does not
elaborate. Schnackenburg, p. 110, offers a rather similar
suggestion.

[117]Thus, Bernard, II, pp. 477ff., who sees the figure
as pointing consistently to a degenerate Israel, e.g., Ez
15:2; 19:10; Is 5:1; Jer 2:21; Hos 10:1; Dodd, *Interpretation*,
pp. 411-12, who, using Ps 79, would include the Messiah within
the figure of the vine; Borig, pp. 192-94.

[118]Bultmann, pp. 530ff.; E. Schweizer, *Ego Eimi*, pp.
39-41; Lattke, pp. 162-63.

[119]Bultmann, p. 531.

[120]Schnackenburg, pp. 122-23.

[121]Such a position would be quite consistent with the
usual division of vv. 15:1-17 by exegetes into tradition and
redaction. For example, Schnackenburg, pp. 109-10, 123, would
assign vv. 1-2 and v. 6 to the tradition--"eine ältere Gestalt." Its *Sitz im Leben* could very possibly have been
polemical in nature--"ein christlicher 'Mashal'." Likewise,
those who posit an underlying *Offenbarungsreden* source would
assign certain verses to this source. See, e.g., Bultmann,
p. 529, n. 1; Heise, p. 81, n. 169; H. Becker, pp. 119ff.

[122]It is used nine times in all: vv. 1:19; 4:23, 37;
6:32; 7:28; 8:16; 15:1; 17:3; 19:35. It is used directly of
Jesus in vv. 1:9, 6:32, and 15:1. It is used of the Father
in vv. 7:28 and 17:3.

[123]It is interesting to see that neither Brown nor
Schnackenburg, both of whom connect v. 15:2 with the opponents
of I John, interpret the adjective in a similar fashion; not
even overtones are claimed.
    From this point onwards I shall refer--both in the
main text and in the footnotes--to similarities in expressions
and concepts between these verses and I John as well as to dissimilarities between them and the Fourth Gospel. These observations should be considered ancillary to the main argument,
which is centered around the use and meaning of the root "love."

[124]See above, n. 121. Bultmann, p. 534, n. 1;
Brown, p. 676; Schnackenburg, p. 111. Schnackenburg, for
example, states that the *Bildrede* shows a better structure if
one removes v. 3 altogether from it. V. 3, he continues, contradicts somewhat the thought of v. 2: the Father need not
cleanse the disciples because they are cleansed by the word
of Jesus.

[125]Bernard, II, p. 480; C. K. Barrett, *The Gospel
according to St. John* (London: S.P.C.K., 1962), p. 395; Borig,

pp. 41-44. The latter argues forcefully that the Johannine *Bildrede* is not like a Synoptic parable, i.e., it includes commentary as part of its form. Furthermore, there is really no tension between vv. 15:2 and 3; rather, the two verses present different perspectives of the event of purification.

[126]As Borig, p. 43, remarks, the "hearing" of the disciples is already present or understood in the "speaking" of Jesus.

[127]This use of the preposition διά with the accusative is thus very close indeed to that of διά with the genitive. See Bultmann, p. 534, n. 2. For a different opinion, see Bernard, II, p. 480.

[128]I Jn 2:18-19 provides a very similar situation. Those who are now separated from the community were once a part of the community, i.e., had heard and accepted the word of Jesus, but again they did not endure.

The Prologue to the Letter also presents the term λόγος with reference to the original preaching and hearing of the proclamation: as it was then received, so now it is passed on.

Likewise, I Jn 3:1 speaks of being "a child of God" through God's love--a love which is defined in terms of vv. 3:5, 8--but v. 2:29 specifies that such a claim is valid only when a certain condition is met: the execution of righteousness. Thus, once again, reception does not guarantee "abiding." See above, ch. II, pp. 47-51.

[129]Bultmann, p. 534; J. Becker, p. 232.

[130]V. 4 in itself presents an example of *inclusio*, beginning with the imperative, μείνατε ἐν ἐμοί, and concluding with the conditional clause, ἐὰν μὴ ἐν ἐμοὶ μένητε.

[131]The expression μένειν ἐν is found outside of vv. 15:1-17 as a *terminus technicus* (rather than as a simple geographical observation, e.g., vv. 7:9; 11:6) in the following verses: 5:38; 6:56; 8:31; 12:46; 14:10, 17, 25. In contrast to the nine times where the expression refers to the disciples in vv. 15:1-17, only vv. 6:56 and 8:31 present a similar usage elsewhere in the Gospel. In v. 8:31 the context is clearly that of a polemic against the Jews: the object of the preposition is τῷ λόγῳ τῷ ἐμῷ. In v. 6:56 the object is ἐμοί as in vv. 15:1-17, but the context is eucharistic. Furthermore, this latter example forms part of a section which has been assigned to later redaction (vv. 6:51-58) by exegetes, e.g., G. Richter, "Zur Formgeschichte und literarischen Einheit von Joh 6:31-58," *ZNW* 60 (1969), pp. 21-55; "Die Fusswaschung," pp. 24ff. For a contrary position, see P. Borgen, *Bread from Heaven*, NovTSup, no. 10 (Leiden: Brill, 1965); Meeks, "The Man from," pp. 58-59.

In contrast to the three times that the expression refers to Jesus abiding in the disciples (in vv. 15:4, 5 the μένειν is understood in κἀγὼ ἐν ὑμῖν; in v. 15:7, the subject is τὰ ῥήματα), only v. 5:38 presents a corresponding usage.

Again, in a quite polemical passage directed against the Jews, the verse refers to the word of God--καὶ τὸν λόγον αὐτοῦ οὐκ ἔχετε ἐν ὑμῖν μένοντα.
     V. 14:10 is unique insofar as it refers to the relationship of the Father to Jesus: the former abides in the latter. V. 12:46 has "darkness" as a direct object and may thus be taken out of consideration. Finally, vv. 14:17 and 25 use παρά instead of ἐν and do not seem to fit the pattern of the other verses.
     Therefore, the use of μένειν ἐν within an inner-Christian controversy is unique to vv. 15:1-17 in the Gospel.

     [132]This reciprocal formula occurs only in v. 6:56. The content, moreover, is quite removed from that of vv. 15:1-17. If it is to be considered original to the Gospel (see n. 131 above), then it would represent an example where the redactor has utilized expressions from the Gospel for his own purposes. See Schnackenburg, p. 112.

     [133]Bultmann, pp. 534-35, interprets the preposition ἐν as referring to a relationship in which the "one who abides" allows himself to be determined by the other (as in μείνατε ἐν ἐμοί) or determines the other (κἀγὼ ἐν ὑμῖν). The verb μένειν is taken as meaning "persistence in the life of faith; it is loyal steadfastness to the cause only in the sense of always allowing oneself to be encompassed, of allowing oneself to receive." This is what constitutes, according to him, the reciprocity of the relationship.

     [134]See Blass-Debrunner-Funk, #442:2. The consecutive καί is especially frequent after imperatives, e.g., Jas 4:7. Its meaning would then be: "Abide in me, *and then* I will abide in you."

     [135]Thus, Heise, pp. 85-86, who compares it to the καθώς of v. 13:34.

     [136]Borig, pp. 45-46; Brown, p. 678. Yet, both stress the personal aspect of the union or relationship. The repetition of the formula in v. 15:7 would deemphasize this personal aspect in favor of a holding on to τὰ ῥήματα.

     [137]V. 4b makes this dependency clear in terms of the figure of the vine. A branch in and of itself cannot produce any fruits; it needs the vine. In the same manner (καθώς--οὕτως), the disciples (ὑμεῖς) cannot produce fruit in and of themselves; they need Jesus (ἐν ἐμοί).

     [138]The implication would seem to be as follows: one cannot claim "the word"--as some are apparently doing--unless one "abides" in that word. There must be a claim to discipleship which contradicts, in the eyes of the author, the nature of discipleship.

     [139]Becker, pp. 234-35. See also, Schnackenburg, p. 112.

     [140]The different objects of the preposition are:
(1) Jesus: vv. 2:6; 3:6; (2) the χρῖσμα: vv. 2:24, 27;

(3) the Father: vv. 3:24; 4:13; (4) the Father and the Son: v. 4:16.

[141]The dialectic is found once again within paragraph 3:19-24: the element of tradition or "having received" is given by v. 3:23--a tradition which includes both correct belief and love for one another--and that of double abiding is provided by v. 3:24.

[142]The ἐγώ εἰμι saying is found repeated as well within the same discourse or section in ch. 6 (vv. 35, 47, 51) and ch. 10 (vv. 11, 14). The terminology employed in the repetition is not always the same; thus, here, for example, the adjective ἀληθινός is not used at all.

[143]Whereas in v. 2 the metaphor used had been that of "producing fruit," now in vv. 5-6 the metaphor is that of "abiding" or "remaining." The reason is simple: μένειν ἐν has been introduced in v. 15:4. Heise, p. 87, states that these two metaphors should not be regarded as synonyms; rather, "producing fruit" presupposes "abiding." Yet, the two terms are, to a degree, synonymous: "producing fruit" comprehends "abiding." But it also comprehends other activities as well, all of which presuppose this abiding.

[144]The designation of the good branch in this verse bears the reciprocal formula of v. 15:4a--ὁ μένων ἐν ἐμοὶ κἀγὼ ἐν αὐτῷ--thus reinforcing the utter dependency expressed by the renewed identification formula. See Blass-Debrunner-Funk, #468:3. This is an example of a participle continued by a finite verb.

[145]Some of these terms have been employed in the Synoptic tradition with eschatological overtones, e.g., τὸ πῦρ (Mk 9:43; Mt 13:40, 25:41); ἐβλήθη ἔξω (Mt 8:12); καίεται (Mt 13:40). Therefore, exegetes like Brown, p. 679, and Bernard, II, pp. 481-82, do not totally rule out such an interpretation, although neither one adopts it in a systematic way. I think, however, that the punishment should be understood in terms of the figure itself. Thus, Barrett, p. 396; Lindars, *The Gospel*, p. 489; Schnackenburg, p. 114.

E. Hirsch (*Studien zum vierten Evangelium*, Beiträge zur historischen Theologie, no. 11 [Tübingen: J. C. B. Mohr, 1936], p. 111) proposes that ch. 15 should be interpreted from the point of view of an official excommunication. However, this procedure is not to be found in either the Gospel or I John; there is simply no evidence for an official process of excommunication.

The two aorist passives constitute examples of the gnomic aorist, which describes an act which is valid for all time. See Blass-Debrunner-Funk, #333:1. The gnomic aorist is always found in the New Testament in conjunction with comparisons.

[146]Schnackenburg, p. 114, suggests two causes for this division among the disciples: doctrinal deviation and the sin unto death of I Jn 5:16, a sin which, he maintains, cannot be

272   Love Relationships in John

deciphered at all. This sin unto death, however, is basically
that of doctrinal deviation: the imagery of "life" and "death"
in I John and its relationship to the possession of the correct
christological dogma make this equation imperative. See ch. II,
pp. 55-57. Lagrange, p. 404, would soften this absence of a
via media insofar as an image ("seule image") cannot express
all possible aspects of the question.

[147]In v. 15:7 one may also notice a switch from the
participial phrase to a conditional sentence as well as a
return to the second person plural form of address. As
already pointed out above (see p. 105, n. 131), the abiding
of the word in the disciples is found only in Jn 5:38, where
the polemic is clearly anti-Jewish.

[148]This second formulation is much more explicit in
assigning the fulfillment to the Father: τὸν πατέρα becomes
the direct object of the verb αἰτέω. Jesus appears therein as
an intermediary of such a prayer, since the disciples are to
address their petitions to the Father in his name. This function of the Father is probably implied in v. 15:7 as well.
        This mention of the Father in v. 15:16 and his probable
role in v. 15:7 as well constitute the first mention of him
since v. 15:2. Vv. 15:5-6 bypassed completely the judgmental
role of the Father of v. 15:2 (except perhaps for an implied
presence in the passive aorists of v. 15:6). There is no
doubt that this fulfillment of petitions is to be associated
with the umbrella term "producing fruit" as well as with the
expression of v. 15:2, ἵνα καρπὸν πλείονα φέρῃ.
        Brown, p. 680, sees v. 16 as forming an inclusion with
vv. 7-8 on account of the similar imagery.

[149]I Jn 2:14, 24, 27; 3:9, 15, 24; 4:12, 15, 16. Perhaps the closest examples are vv. 2:14, 24; 3:24; and 4:15.
In v. 2:14--which is part of the direct addresses of vv. 2:12-
14--it is said that the λόγος τοῦ θεοῦ abides in the "young
men." Vv. 2:24, 3:24, and 4:15 all present examples of a
double abiding: in v. 2:24 the subject is τὸ χρῖσμα and the
confession it implies; in vv. 3:24 and 4:15 the subject is ὁ
θεός. All other examples present different subjects: v. 2:27
has τὸ χρῖσμα; v. 3:9, τὸ σπέρμα; v. 3:15, ζωὴ αἰώνιος;
v. 4:12, ὁ θεός; v. 4:16, τὴν ἀγάπην ἣν ἔχει ὁ θεὸς ἐν ἡμῖν.

[150]The verb αἰτέω is found twice in I John (vv. 3:22;
5:14). The first instance, a part of vv. 3:19-24, is perhaps
the more significant. Therein the confidence (ἡ παρρησία)
before God that allows a believer to petition and to be certain of the fulfillment of that petition is said to be based
on the execution of the commands of God. Indeed, in v. 3:24
one finds this concept of a double abiding based on these
ἐντολαί: καὶ ὁ τηρῶν τὰς ἐντολὰς αὐτοῦ ἐν αὐτῷ μένει καὶ
αὐτὸς ἐν αὐτῷ. Thus, the execution of the commands, which in
itself constitutes the double abiding relationship, leads to
prayer and to the fulfillment of that prayer. In the second
instance, belief in Jesus precedes and constitutes the confidence which the believer has in prayer (which prayer is also
fulfilled).
        The dialectic is not found in the Gospel, although the
promise of the fulfillment of prayer is, e.g., vv. 14:10-13 and

16:23ff.   In the former instance, faith grants the believer
the privilege of prayer and the assurance of the fulfillment
of that prayer.   Moreover, v. 14:13 presents Jesus as the one
who hears and grants the prayer--καὶ ὅ τι ἂν αἰτήσητε ἐν τῷ
ὀνόματί μου τοῦτο ποιήσω.   See Schnackenburg, p. 115.

[151]The introduction of the theme of glorification at
this point may have been suggested to the author by its occurrence in v. 14:13 where it is found immediately after the
promise of the fulfillment of prayer is extended to the
believers.   The same sequence is present in vv. 15:7-8:   the
fulfillment of prayer and the theme of glorification.   If such
were the case, the differences would indicate that the author
of vv. 15:1-17 has interpreted that sequence liberally.   Thus,
he no longer connects the theme of glorification specifically
with the theme of fulfillment, and he now includes the disciples within the theme of glorification.

[152]See above, ch. II, p. 41, n. 39.

[153]K. Aland adopts the reading γένησθε, a subjunctive
witnessed to by B, D, L, X, Θ, Π, it, vg, et al.   However, the
future γενήσεσθε is to be preferred--ℵ, A, K, Ψ, et al.--as
the lectio difficilior.   The use of the subjunctive is probably
an assimilation to the subjunctive φέρητε.   (It should be
pointed out that Aland gives the reading a very low rating of
[D].)   There are occasions when the future connected by καὶ
does follow a subjunctive with ἵνα; on this point, see Blass-
Debrunner-Funk, #369:3.
        Although the use of the future tense in such a situa-
tion tends to bestow a certain degree of independence on the
καὶ; nevertheless, the future here should not be regarded as
a consequence, since in order to "produce fruit" the conditions
of discipleship must be already in existence.

[154]Richter, "Die Deutung," pp. 31-32, sees this extension of the glorification of the Father to the activity of the
disciples as a basic difference between the redactor and the
evangelist (who speaks only of the activity of Jesus with
regard to that theme).   See also, Brown, p. 680; Schnackenburg,
p. 116.

[155]Although I have differentiated, whenever appropriate,
between the usages of vv. 15:1-8 and those of the Gospel in
general, I will refrain from doing so with regard to the theme
of ἀγάπη.   Thus, from a methodological point of view, I shall
limit my remarks to any similarities that might exist between
vv. 15:9-17 and I John.   The differentiation from the Gospel
will be the aim of the next chapter.

[156]Bultmann, p. 529.

[157]Bultmann, pp. 539-40.   Both subsections begin with
a reference to the Father (vv. 1, 9); both derive the imperative μείνατε from the existence of Jesus for his own (vv. 2-4,
9b); the indicative of v. 3 is paralleled in v. 14; the motif
of v. 4 is paralleled by that of v. 16.

[158]Although parallelism is present, it should not be
emphasized too much, e.g., the Father, while mentioned in
vv. 15:9-17, does not play as large a role as he did in vv.
1-8; the option of not producing fruit does not appear in vv.
9-17. More stress should be placed on the interpretative function of the second subsection than on the parallelism *per se*
(as Bultmann himself argues). See Brown, p. 680.

[159]See Blass-Debrunner-Funk, #453:1, 2. When καθώς
introduces a sentence, it may have something of the meaning
"because," that is, it may provide the reason for the statement that follows. In this case, that statement is introduced
by καί, not οὕτως, which is a perfectly acceptable use of the
correlative. The author of vv. 15:1-17 also employs this construction in v. 4b (with οὕτως); in vv. 15:10, 12; and in v.
13:34b--which, I shall argue, comes from the hand of the
author of Jn 15:1-17.

[160]Unlike v. 15:2, the second subsection attributes
no role to the Father beyond what is stated here in v. 15:9,
except for his role in the hearing and granting of prayers of
v. 15:16. Thus, as it has already been pointed out, the parallelism does have limits.
     The hierarchy of ἀγάπη is expressed in terms of the
aorist: the Father loved the Son (ἠγάπησεν); the Son loved the
disciples (ἠγάπησα). The action is certainly in the past, i.e.,
this is the way that discipleship *was* constituted. The employment of the aorist tense with respect to the love of the Son
anticipates v. 13--the mode of Jesus' love for his disciples.
Borig, p. 166, interprets the aorists in question from the
literary point of view of the departure ("literarisch-
fiktiven"), thus leaving out apparently the mode of Jesus'
death.

[161]See above, n. 157. Yet, the passage is not
from v. 2 to v. 4 (a position he must take because of his
source hypothesis); it also includes v. 3, since it is in that
verse that the original condition of all believers is
described.

[162]The parallelism does not extend to an explicit portrayal of those believers who are not abiding, a portrayal
such as that of v. 2 or v. 5. It is to be presupposed, however, that no *via media* is possible here as well.
     Lattke, pp. 167-68, adopts a quite different point of
view (in keeping with his theory of rearrangement). Thus, he
states that neither v. 15:4a nor v. 15:9b should be understood
as an imperative in the sense of a duty or a law; there is no
comparable use of the imperative in the Gospel. (It is interesting to see Lattke isolate Wellhausen as the proponent of
such a theory, a fact which is not surprising at all, given
the latter's theory of additions.) Rather, Lattke continues,
the imperative should be seen as an invitation issued to the
believer.

[163]Bernard, II, p. 484, insists that even in v. 10,
where the definition is given, it is the love of Jesus *for* the
disciples that is meant by the prepositional phrase ἐν τῇ

ἀγάπη μου. He thus bypasses the dialectic between the hierarchy of love and the need to abide in that hierarchy.

[164]With this use of the perfect tense, τετήρηκα, there begins a series of perfect tenses in vv. 11ff.: λελάληκα; εἴρηκα; ἔθηκα. Their purpose is, as Brown, p. 663, remarks, to give an "air of completed action."
Again, Lattke, p. 167, interprets this relationship between Jesus and the Father in a totally different way. It is not a relationship of obedience at all; rather, it is a statement concerning the unity that exists between the Father and the Son.

[165]Barrett, p. 397, suggests that the aorist with regard to the relationship between Father and Son may point to their "pretemporal" relations. This would certainly seem to be the case here; one might think, for example, of I Jn 1:2-3, where "life eternal" is said to have been with the Father before it was revealed: ἥτις ἦν πρὸς τὸν πατέρα καὶ ἐφανερώθη ἡμῖν.

[166]See above, ch. II, pp. 64-65, 67-68, 76-79. In both cases God's love and its mediation by Jesus are expressed from the point of view of the community as recipients of that love (and not Jesus, as in v. 15:9), e.g., v. 4:9: ἐν τούτῳ ἐφανερώθη ἡ ἀγάπη τοῦ θεοῦ ἐν ἡμῖν; v. 4:16: τὴν ἀγάπην ἣν ἔχει ὁ θεὸς ἐν ἡμῖν. Jesus is the conveyor of that love.

[167]Once again, one finds no parallel to v. 15:10b. Jesus as Son and Messiah is never described from the point of view of his relationship to the Father. This is not the interest of I John. Nor does one find a parallel to the imperative μείνατε ἐν τῇ ἀγάπη τῇ ἐμῇ, although one does find an instance of μένειν ἐν with ἀγάπη in v. 3:17. In that verse there is an argument to the effect that love for God (i.e., obj. gen.) cannot exist in a person who turns away from those in need. Such behavior is not and cannot be love.

[168]See above, ch. II, p. 42.

[169]Although both of the examples in I John speak of the love "of God" and these verses speak of the love "of Jesus," the difference is not as significant as it may seem *prima facie*. In both cases, Jesus is the mediator of the Father's love; he is the Father's love. Indeed, as I have pointed out repeatedly in the previous chapter, the "commands" in I John are sometimes attributed to Jesus, sometimes to the Father.

[170]Brown, pp. 667, 681, classifies the verse as a transition verse between Jn 15:7-10 and 12-17 (one should remember that Brown ends the *Bildrede* with v. 6), but he does not explain what "transition" means at this point. His view that the verse represents a summary of what precedes it is, however, a good observation.

[171]This is the formula which Schnackenburg, p. 104, uses as an argument to see Jn 15:1-16:4a as a literary unity

("ein gewisses formales Gliederungselement") and vv. 15:1-11
as a subsection of that larger unity. See also, J. Schneider,
"Die Abschiedsreden Jesus," in *Gott und die Götter*. *Festgabe
für E. Fascher* (Berlin: Evangelische Verlaganstalt, 1958),
p. 108.
        In v. 16:25 one finds the expression again, but with
the prepositional phrase ἐν παροιμίαις between ταῦτα and λελάληκα.

[172]Bernard, II, p. 485; Bultmann, p. 335, n. 5.

[173]For example, Brown--given his theory of subdivision--
would extend it to v. 7 (i.e., vv. 15:7-10); see p. 681.
Lagrange, p. 406, would see it as encompassing only vv. 9-10.
Schnackenburg, p. 117, and Borig, p. 19, would have it refer
to the whole of the *Bildrede*--given their acceptance of the
Gliederungselement theory.

[174]Purpose clauses also follow this expression in
vv. 16:33 and 16:1, 4.

[175]J. Becker, p. 234. Schnackenburg, pp. 117-18, also
points out that "joy" is to be found both in I John (v. 1:4;
also, II Jn 12 and III Jn 4) and in the Farewell Discourse
(vv. 16:21-22, 24; 17:13) in sections where the community
reflects on its possession of salvation.
        Although ταῦτα λελάληκα ὑμῖν does not occur in I John
--obviously because it is neither a discourse nor a farewell
discourse--one finds rather similar expressions with the verb
γράφω, e.g., I Jn 1:4; 2:1, 26; 5:13.

[176]In v. 3:29 the expression appears in the context of
a polemic against the followers of John the Baptist. In
Jn 16:20-24 both the noun χαρά and the expression with πληρόω
are discussed from the point of view of Jesus' departure and
his eventual return. In v. 24 this perfect joy is associated
with the granting of the disciples' petitions. In v. 17:13
the contrast is made with the world, i.e., the disciples versus
the world.

[177]Thus, the possession of the correct christological
dogma is clearly made a part of that tradition, a tradition
which can be substantiated (as vv. 1-3 indicate).

[178]The choice of readings does not affect the meaning:
if ἡμῶν is to be preferred (ℵ, B, Ψ), then it includes both
the author and the community; if ὑμῶν (A, K, P, it, vg, et al.),
then it refers specifically to the community that has and is
vacillating to some extent.

[179]Vv. 12-17 form an *inclusio*, as many exegetes have
pointed out. See, e.g., J. Becker, pp. 229-30; Schnackenburg,
p. 105; Brown, p. 667.

[180]A very similar progression from the plural "commands" to the singular "command" may be observed in I John.
Thus, for example, from the execution of Jesus' commands in
vv. 2:3-6, the author concentrates specifically on the one

command of love in vv. 2:7-11. Again, in paragraph 3:19-24
the author declares that it is the execution of God's commands
that grants the believer confidence before the Lord and then
proceeds to define the "command" in question--and that command
includes both belief in Jesus Christ and love for one another.
See above, ch. II, pp. 42, 58-59.

The Gospel contains a similar interchange, not with
the term "command," but rather with its synonymous expression,
"the word." For example, in v. 14:23 the love of Jesus is
defined as the execution of the "word" (τὸν λόγον μου τηρήσει);
in the following verse, v. 14:24, the opposite of this attitude
is given, but now in plural form (τοὺς λόγους μου οὐ τηρεῖ).
It should be pointed out that this latter exchange proceeds
from the singular to the plural, contrary to those outlined
above.

[181]The verb ἐντέλλομαι is not to be found at all in
I John, and only twice elsewhere in the Gospel. In v. 8:5 it
forms part of the story of the adulterous woman, which is a
later addition. In v. 14:31, the conclusion to the original
Farewell Discourse, it is used of Jesus' coming to his death
--a command from the Father. This is, therefore, the only
instance where it is applied to the disciples.

[182]This is another one of J. Becker's arguments on
behalf of an association with I John (see Becker, p. 234).
See also, Schnackenburg, p. 124.

Likewise, see Brown's curious remark (p. 680): "Was
the writer of I John the editor who brought the *mashal* into
the context of the Last Discourse and supplied it with an
explanation made up of Last Discourse themes?" This parenthetical remark, however, is not developed at all.

[183]This element of tradition is *ipso facto* built into
the apparent situation of vv. 15:1-17, since these verses
represent a discourse of Jesus prior to his departure.

[184]This καθώς should also, to a certain extent, be
read as "because." See above, p. 108, n. 159.

[185]See above, ch. I, p. 27, n. 168.

[186]Dibelius, pp. 204-5. V. 17 repeats v. 12, and
v. 16 connects quite well with the theme of love in v. 12.
Likewise, v. 16 presents themes which are also present in
vv. 15:1-12, such as the "bearing of fruit" and the granting
of petitions. Dibelius, p. 205, concludes: "Was zwischen
V. 12 und V. 16 liegt, bedeutet also einen *Umweg*, und es fragt
sich, warum er eingeschlagen ist." (Italics his.)

[187]Vv. 15-16 would represent a midrashic development
("eine midraschartige Abschweifung") of the traditional saying
of v. 13. Ibid., p. 206.

[188]Brown, p. 682; Lindars, *The Gospel*, p. 491;
Schnackenburg, pp. 124-25; Bultmann, p. 542, n. 7.

[189]For example, the saying employs the very familiar
use of the demonstrative pronoun (μείζονα ταύτης ἀγάπην) with

an epexegetical ἵνα-clause. The verse also employs a phrase
--τὴν ψυχὴν αὐτοῦ θῇ--which is present elsewhere in the Gospel,
e.g., vv. 10:17-21; 13:37-38. Dibelius does not stress this
assimilation at all. See Schnackenburg, p. 125; Lindars, *The
Gospel*, p. 491.

[190]Dibelius attempts to show in the article that the
thought expressed in v. 13, the concept of love therein
posited, is quite foreign to the concept of love present in
the Gospel. The latter concept, he argues, presents love as
a unity of being by virtue of divine resemblance. The former
concept presents love as an act of heroism. The evangelist
appropriates the traditional saying, but does not accept its
concept of ἀγάπη; this may be shown by the fact that he does
not explicitly apply the saying to Jesus and develops only the
term φίλοι. This position is somewhat ironic: why would the
evangelist accept a saying whose conception of love deviated
from his own, make that saying the *Hauptsache* of the passage,
and fail to develop its meaning at all?

[191]It should be noted that the expression used in
I Jn 3:16-17--ὑπέρ . . . τὴν ψυχὴν θεῖναι--is the same as that
of v. 15:13. Moreover, as in this latter verse, v. 3:16 also
employs the demonstrative with an epexegetical clause (whereas
v. 3:16 uses a ὅτι-clause, v. 15:13 employs a ἵνα-clause. The
variation, however, is not significant).

[192]See above, ch. II, pp. 51-58, 61-71.

[193]Dibelius, p. 206, points out the chain-like effect
of these verses, all the links of which are variations of the
root "love." Becker, p. 230, also adopts the interpretation
of this progression of thought. The links are as follows:
ἠγάπησα (v. 15:12) is continued by v. 15:13a, ἀγάπην. V. 15:
13b introduces φίλων, which is then immediately picked up by
v. 15:14a (φίλοι) and further developed by means of the comparison δοῦλοι/φίλοι in v. 15:15.

[194]Bultmann (see above, p. 108, n. 157) sees a parallel between v. 3 and v. 14 (ὑμεῖς καθαροί ἐστε--ὑμεῖς φίλοι
μού εστε), but v. 14 is more a consequence than a statement
of fact (= v. 15). One also finds the obvious parallel
between v. 7 and v. 16.

[195]This consideration of what it is that makes a
believer (and a friend) is very close to that of
v. 15:3. In both cases the difference is one of *revelation*:
v. 15:3 expresses this revelation in terms of Jesus' λόγος and
its acceptance by the disciples; v. 15:15b expresses this
revelation by means of the verb γνωρίζω and the phrase πάντα
ἃ ἤκουσα παρὰ τοῦ πατρός μου. V. 15:15b goes beyond v. 15:3
insofar as it identifies the ultimate source of such revelation: Jesus obtains what he reveals from the Father himself.
This is a motif which is quite common in the Gospel (vv. 3:32;
5:20; 8:26, 28, 40) and which underlies--but is not primary
in--the First Letter as well (vv. 1:1-3; 5:9-10).
     One should also observe the fact that the Father
appears in all three descriptions of the *status quo*: in

v. 15:1, which goes together with v. 15:3, it is his role to prune the vine; in v. 15:9a, it is he who stands at the very beginning of the hierarchy of love; in v. 15:15, it is he who is presented as the ultimate source of the revelation. Jesus is a mediator, *the* mediator to be sure.

The verb γνωρίζω does not appear in I John, but it is found at the end of Jn 17 (v. 17:26), where the disciples are distinguished from the world precisely because they accept the revelation that Jesus has brought.

[196]V. 15:16a makes explicit a thought which has been implicit all along: the call to discipleship was not a choice on the part of those who became disciples (οὐχ ὑμεῖς με ἐξελέξασθε), but rather a choosing by Jesus (ἀλλ' ἐγὼ ἐξελεξάμην ὑμᾶς). The initiative was certainly his own. Again, this motif occurs elsewhere in the Gospel, e.g., vv. 6:70 and 13:18 (although the latter verse is attributed by Richter, *Die Fusswaschung*, pp. 301-13, to the redactor of the Gospel). I John presupposes this general motif as well, e.g., vv. 3:1; 4:10-12, 20b.

[197]These obligations are described in a fashion that closely parallels that of vv. 15:9-10a. The imperative of v. 15:9b is therein defined as the execution of Jesus' commands (ἐὰν τὰς ἐντολάς μου τηρήσητε). In this particular verse the status of φίλοι is said to be preserved only by carrying out Jesus' commands (again defined in terms of a conditional clause): ἐὰν ποιῆτε ἃ ἐγὼ ἐντέλλομαι ὑμῖν. The use of the relative pronoun in the plural also parallels the τὰς ἐντολάς of v. 15:10a.

[198]V. 5:1 is central to this argument, since it defines the believer in Jesus Christ (the orthodox believer) as "he who is born of God." V. 5:2 then makes love for this believer a prerequisite for the love of God.
See above, ch. II, pp. 72-73.

[199]After the statement on choosing and being chosen of v. 16a, the author repeats in v. 16b the thought of v. 14, i.e., the duty which the disciples have as disciples. This repetition is effected by means of the ἵνα-clause that follows the perfect tense of τίθημι. At this point, the author resurrects the language of the *Bildrede*:
ἐὰν ποιῆτε ἃ ἐγὼ ἐντέλλομαι = ἵνα ὑμεῖς ὑπάγητε καὶ καρπὸν ὑμῖν   φέρητε καὶ ὁ καρπὸς ὑμῶν μένῃ
Thus, just as the terminology of the *Bildrede* preceded the promise of v. 15:7, so now that very same terminology once again introduces the repetition of that promise.

Some exegetes would see in vv. 15:7-8, 16, an understanding of "bearing fruit" that includes missionary activity. Thus, Brown, pp. 680-83; Lindars, *The Gospel*, pp. 489-93; Bernard, II, p. 488. But mission is hardly the interest here; the problem at hand is one of loyalty or faithfulness, of "abiding." See Schnackenburg, pp. 127-28.

[200]Bultmann, pp. 529, 546-47.

[201]Of course, for Bultmann the section is to be attributed to the evangelist, who has once again commented on

the *Offenbarungsreden* source (see p. 529, n. 1). Furthermore,
Bultmann considers vv. 15:1-17 to be a commentary on vv. 13:34-
35 "in the sense that it goes more deeply into the grounds of
the command of love, already briefly defined by καθὼς ἠγάπησα
ὑμᾶς," as well as a commentary on vv. 13:1-20. Ibid. This is
the reason why Bultmann places chs. 15-16 immediately after
vv. 13:31-35 in his rearrangement of the material (Ibid., p.
461).

[202] Ibid., p. 529.

[203] Ibid., p. 547. Faith and love, the hearing of the
word and the execution of it, are not related in the sense of
a temporal succession, i.e., first one hears, then one does.
In hearing, Bultmann argues, one anticipates all future doing.

[204] J. Becker, p. 233.

[205] Heise, pp. 89-91; Lattke, pp. 169-70.

[206] See above, ch. II, pp. 33-36.

[207] Among these affinities one finds: (a) the attribution of the adjective "true" to Jesus; (b) the position that
an original status obtained by a believer must be maintained
by that believer; (c) the concept of "abiding in"; (d) the
dialectic of abiding and fulfillment; (e) the theme of joy.

[208] See above, ch. II, pp. 73-79. In this regard,
Bultmann's remark to the effect that the command of love is
central to the constancy of faith on the part of the believer
is accurate as far as it goes (see above, p. 117).

[209] The genre lacks the specific, detailed arguments
and observations that one finds in the First Letter, which is
specifically and explicitly directed against the existing
problems of the community.

[210] This activity by the Father--clearly enunciated in
v. 15:2 and intimated by the passive verb forms of v. 15:6
(see above, p. 107, n. 148)--may point to a claim similar to
that of I Jn 4:10, 19-20.

[211] J. Becker, p. 220.

[212] Ibid., p. 219. Becker is quite right in pointing
out that this discourse is a "farewell" discourse ("eine
Abschiedsrede"): in view of his imminent departure, Jesus
addresses his disciples--τεκνία, ἔτι μικρὸν μεθ᾽ ὑμῶν εἰμι.

[213] Thus, immediately after Jesus' instruction, Peter
asks him, κύριε ποῦ ὑπάγεις.

[214] It is precisely with this thought in mind that
Bultmann places chapters 15 and 16 after vv. 13:31-35, thus
acting as a commentary on the "new" commandment (see above,
p. 117, n. 201). Interestingly enough, neither Lattke nor
Bernard have this consideration in mind when they suggest their
respective rearrangements.

[215]J. Becker, p. 220.

[216]Ibid. Others have reached a similar conclusion:
Wellhausen, *Erweiterungen*, p. 14, n. 1; *Das Evangelium Johannis*, p. 61; E. Hirsch, p. 103--who considers vv. 13:34-38 to
be an addition, not just vv. 34-35; G. Richter, "Die Deutung,"
p. 30; H. Thyen, p. 354; Schnackenburg, pp. 59-61.
The difficulty that the verses occasion may be observed
in the problem that they present to those who consider them to
be part of the context. For example, Brown, pp. 608ff., refers
to vv. 13:31-38 as being "obviously a composite." Following
the judgment of Loisy, Brown declares that those verses which
contain Johannine themes, viz., vv. 31-32, 33, 34-35, are more
"juxtaposed than connected." Nevertheless, he sees vv. 34-35
as "ensuring the continuance of his (Jesus') spirit among his
disciples."

[217]J. Becker, p. 234.

[218]Richter, "Die Deutung," pp. 30ff.

[219]Schnackenburg, pp. 60-61.

[220]The redactor was most probably aware of the usage
of the plural form in vv. 14:15ff., so that by utilizing the
singular form here he is actually duplicating the exchange
found in Jn 15:1-17 (as well as in I John). See above,
p. 113, n. 180.

[221]Blass-Debrunner-Funk, #394. The demonstrative may
be omitted without making the epexegetical construction impossible. The same construction is used with the command in
I John. See above, p. 113.

[222]See above, p. 113, n. 182.

[223]It should be recalled that καθώς does have the
added connotation of a reason, a ground, e.g., "because." See
above, p. 108, n. 159.

[224]Bultmann, p. 525, n. 5, does not see this second
ἵνα-clause as being parallel to the first and being consequently dependent on ἐντολὴν δίδωμι; rather, he sees it as
stating the purpose of the καθώς clause. This view is dependent on his theory--already mentioned--that with faith, with
the acceptance of the word, the believer accepts as well all
future concrete decisions of love. Thus, he sees the καθώς
clause as indicating this aspect of faith and the following
ἵνα-clause as the fulfillment of that purpose of Jesus' revelation (= love). However, the ἵνα-clause should be taken as a
reprise of that first clause, which is then modified by the
καθώς clause. See Schnackenburg, pp. 60-61.

[225]Schnackenburg, p. 59.

[226]See I Jn 2:3 (with ἐάν), 5; 3:16, 19, 24; 4:2, 9,
13; 5:2. In v. 15:8 one finds a beginning ἐν τούτῳ followed

by an epexegetical ἵνα-clause, but without the expression
γινώσκειν ἐν.
    See above, ch. II, p. 41, n. 39.

[227]This variation of the love command is clearly
intended as a synonym for the one which uses the direct object
ἀλλήλους. The combination of the noun "love" and the verb "to
have" is found in the Gospel (v. 5:42), the First Letter
(v. 4:16), and Jn 15:1-17 (v. 15:13). Of the three examples,
the latter is the closest, since it too (1) presupposes the
mode of love as an exemplar--though not a literal one--for the
disciples to follow; and (2) parallels the above command, ἵνα
ἀγαπᾶτε ἀλλήλους. The author, whom I consider to be one and
the same, may very well have phrased the ἵνα-clause of v.
13:35 with this traditional saying in mind.

[228]Schnackenburg, p. 59. See above, ch. II, pp. 42-43.

[229]Lattke, pp. 206-18, denies the presence of any
ethical concerns in these two verses as well. Once again, he
interprets the command of mutual love solely in terms of
"faith." This command, he argues, represents the last link
in a chain of reciprocal relationships which may be outlined
as follows: Father--Son, Son--Disciples, Disciples--Disciples.
The chain is neither metaphysical nor mystical nor ethical in
nature: it is essentially a chain of revelation; it is the
λόγος communicated from the higher link to the lower link that
constitutes the chain and the preservation of that λόγος that
justifies the existence of the chain.
    Lattke is quite correct in stressing the role of λόγος
in the love command, but that λόγος has now become more specific, and it is also accompanied by definite ethical norms.

[230]The verb φιλεῖν occurs in v. 15:19 as a means of
differentiating the disciples from "the world": if they were
"of the world" (ἐκ τοῦ κόσμου), "the world" would love them
(ὁ κόσμος ἂν τὸ ἴδιον ἐφίλει). Although the hatred of "the
world" for the disciples is mentioned in I Jn 3:13, the
absence of the verb φιλεῖν from the Letter would militate
against such an association without further confirming evidence.

[231]One should recall the reasons for the demarcation
of the passage at this point: (1) the parenesis concerning
the love command is not continued at all in vv. 15:18ff.;
(2) the hatred of the world, which becomes the dominant theme
of these verses, is not anticipated at all in vv. 15:1-17.
J. Becker, p. 230.

[232]It should be recalled that Schnackenburg, p. 104,
sees this antithesis as an argument on behalf of the isolation
of vv. 15:1-16:4a as a self-contained unit. Wellhausen, *Das
Evangelium Johannis*, p. 70, adopts a similar division.

[233]J. Becker, p. 230. Again, Schnackenburg, p. 104,
sees this common theme of "choosing" as an argument on behalf
of the larger unity he proposes.

[234]A. Loisy, *Le quatrième Évangile* (Paris: Alphonse Picard, 1903), p. 778.

[235]Other solutions offered are as follows: (1) v. 15: 25--E. C. Hoskyns, *The Fourth Gospel*, 2nd ed., edited by F. N. Davey (London: Faber & Faber, 1947), pp. 479-81; (2) v. 15:27--Barrett, pp. 399-400; (3) v. 16:4a--Lagrange, p. 415; Wellhausen, *Das Evangelium Johannis*, p. 71; Brown, pp. 691-95; Bultmann, pp. 547-48; Schnackenburg, pp. 103-5; Spitta, p. 311; (4) v. 16:11--C. H. Dodd, *Interpretation*, p. 410.

[236]J. Becker, p. 238. The primary reason for joining vv. 16:4b-15 to vv. 15:18-16:4a is the presentation of the Paraclete in vv. 16:8-11 as the accuser of the inimical world: "Der Paraklet wird das sündige Verhalten der Welt in einem Prozess von kosmischen Ausmass aufdecken so dass der Hass der Welt sein gerechtes Gerichtsurteil bekommt."

[237]Ibid., p. 239.

[238]Ibid., p. 238: "16:1-4a konkretisieren die grund- sätzliche Angaben zum Hass der Welt. Synagogenausschluss und sogar Tötung zur vermeintlichen Ehre Gottes wird dieser Hass zeitigen."

[239]As in v. 15:11, the phrase ταῦτα λελάληκα ὑμῖν does not in itself connote the idea of a departure. Only vv. 15: 26-27 could be considered as an indication of an *Abschiedsrede*, but the loose connection of these verses with their context has forced many exegetes to consider them as an addition. See Schnackenburg, p. 105.

[240]Not one of the ὅτι-clauses of vv. 16:8-11, clauses which explain the accusations brought by the Paraclete against the world, actually develop the themes of hatred (μισεῖ) or persecution (διώξουσιν) or killings (ὁ ἀποκτείνας ὑμᾶς).

[241]Brown, pp. 587-95. Brown also considers vv. 15:18- 16:4a to be a unit because of the parallelisms that these verses have in common with Mt 10:17-25. Ibid., p. 693.

[242]Cf. its use in v. 16:33, which concludes section 16:4b-33. Schnackenburg, p. 104; Borig, p. 19; Schneider, p. 108, have all called attention to this structural link. However, given the other non-concluding examples of the for- mula, this argument is valid only when taken together with all the others.

[243]This is a section which Becker does not subdivide further.

[244]Among the exegetes that accept v. 16:4a as the end of a section, the following accept the threefold structure: Lagrange, pp. 409-17; Wellhausen, *Das Evangelium Johannis*, pp. 70-71. Brown, p. 695, and Bultmann, pp. 550-51, make a further subdivision: the latter, by choosing vv. 15:21-25;

the former, vv. 15:22-25. Schnackenburg, pp. 105-6, eliminates the last section, vv. 16:1-4a, as a later addition, thus regarding v. 16:1 as the original conclusion of the discourse and v. 16:4b as a doublet.

[245]Unlike Bultmann, however, he does not see the source as a part of the hypothetical *Offenbarungsreden* source (see Bultmann, p. 548), but calls it instead a unity in itself and classifies it as an independent *Offenbarungsspruch*. J. Becker, p. 236.
     What the evangelist has added consists basically of the redactional devices of vv. 19b-20 as well as the comments of vv. 21, 23, and 25.
     The question of an underlying source is outside the scope of this study.

[246]J. Becker, p. 238. See above, p. 126, n. 239.

[247]Ibid., p. 239.

[248]Ibid., pp. 239-40. This added connotation may be observed above all in the neuter plural terms of vv. 16:12 (πολλὰ λέγειν); 16:13 (τὰ ἐρχόμενα); and 16:15 (πάντα ὅσα).

[249]Ibid. The presence of Jesus is given in terms of the past, as the perfects and aorists of vv. 15:18-24, 16:1, 4 indicate.

[250]Becker refers several times to Conzelmann's article ("'Was von Anfang war'") with regard to this point. See above, ch. I, p. 15, n. 94.

[251]Ibid., p. 239. See also, Schnackenburg, p. 129.

[252]Brown, pp. 695-97; Schnackenburg, p. 129; Bultmann, p. 548, n. 5. Attention is also given to the similarly dualistic conflict between community and world portrayed in I Jn 4:5-6 (αὐτοὶ ἐκ τοῦ κόσμου εἰσίν/ἡμεῖς ἐκ τοῦ θεοῦ ἐσμεν).

[253]The same observation applies to I Jn 4:5-6. Indeed, this differentiation of the two groups (ἐκ τοῦ κόσμου-ἐκ τοῦ θεοῦ) occurs immediately after the definition of the τὸ πνεῦμα τοῦ θεοῦ in terms of the correct christological confession (vv. 4:1-3).
     See above, ch. II, pp. 76-79; also, pp. 52-58.

[254]That the "hatred" comes from the synagogue may be gathered from vv. 15:21ff. First of all, the argument that all these things carried out against the believers because they (= the persecutors) have not known God--ὅτι οὐκ οἴδασιν τὸν πέμψαντά με--is frequently employed in the debates with the Jews (e.g., vv. 5:37; 7:28; 8:19, 54-55). Likewise, the proofs adduced in vv. 15:22 and 24 on behalf of Jesus' identity--his words and his works--are also used in the disputes with the Jews (e.g., vv. 10:37-38). In this regard, Schnackenburg's evaluation (p. 132) is to the point: "Die Argumentation ist eine Zusammenfassung der Streitreden Jesu mit den

ungläubigen 'Juden' im Joh-Ev, eine gedrängte Apologie des
joh. Christentums gegenüber dem zeitgenössischen Judentum."

[255]Ibid., pp. 138-40. Schnackenburg interprets
vv. 16:2ff. as an addition to vv. 15:18-16:1 (the role of
v. 16:1 is a bit imprecise: on p. 106 Schnackenburg declares,
"Wahrscheinlich schloss die ursprüngliche Rede mit 16:1"; and
yet on p. 140 one also finds the following statement, "Die
ganze kleine Redeeinheit V 1-4a [durch ταῦτα λελάληκα ver-
klammert] ist aus der Bedrängnis, in der die joh. Gemeinde
steht, angefügt") because it attaches the concrete examples
of hatred to a prophecy of Jesus concerning persecutions. The
author is seen as wishing to clarify contemporary events in
the light of prophecy. Given Schnackenburg's literary position on the Farewell Discourse, someone must have added vv.
16:2-4a to the already later discourse of Jn 15:1-16:1. The
question that arises on account of this explanation is, what
stage of the community does this addition represent if it is
twice removed from the Gospel and still alludes to persecutions by the Jews?

[256]Martyn, pp. 18-22, 47.

[257]Its occurrence in v. 3:15 is rather instructive,
following, as it does, the statement of v. 3:13. In this
case, the one who hates (πᾶς ὁ μισῶν τὸν ἀδελφὸν αὐτοῦ) is
called a murderer (ἀνθρωποκτόνος). Then, in v. 3:17 an ethical example of this hatred is given not in terms of killings
or persecutions, but rather in terms of bypassing the needs
of a brother. In other words, "hatred"--though developed by
means of a vocabulary implying death and killing--emerges as
an example of libertine behavior.
See above, ch. II, pp. 51-58.

[258]Schnackenburg, pp. 138-40, is of the opinion that
it does not come from the evangelist, but rather from his
disciples. The connection with vv. 13:31-14:31 may be
observed by the use of v. 13:16 in v. 15:20 and by terminological differences as well. Yet, see the statement on p. 129:
"Der Abschnitt könnte vom Evangelisten stammen."

CHAPTER IV

[1]In addition to vv. 15:1-17 and 13:34-35, one must
also leave out of consideration ch. 21, a body of material
which is generally taken to be the work of a later redactor.
See, e.g., Moody Smith, "Johannine Christianity," p. 235. The
chapter contains four instances of the verb ἀγαπάω (vv. 7, 15,
16, 20) and five instances of the verb φιλέω (vv. 15, 16,
17[3]). In vv. 7 and 20 the reference is to the disciple that
Jesus loved. The other seven instances form part of a dialogue
between Peter and Jesus (vv. 21:15-19). The precise relationship of this chapter to either the Gospel or to I John would

take this study too far afield, but it does remain one of the
author's future projects.

[2]On the question of the Beloved Disciple, see R.
Schnackenburg, "On the Origin of the Fourth Gospel," in *Jesus
and Man's Hope*, I, pp. 223-46; and Culpepper, pp. 264-70.
Lattke, pp. 11ff., also leaves these verses out of consideration.

[3]Lattke, pp. 11ff.

[4]Ibid.

[5]The question as to whether the two verbs are synonymous or not finds representatives on both sides of the issue.
Most recently, C. Spicq, III, pp. 135-36, argues in favor of
such a distinction. Spicq sees ἀγαπᾶν as expressing, in general, respect for someone superior and, in the Fourth Gospel,
spiritual relations; on the other hand, the general meaning of
φιλεῖν he takes to be that of a love among equals and its specific meaning in John that of a natural affection. Others,
like Lazure, pp. 214-15, and Lattke, pp. 11-12, take the two
terms as synonymous. In view of the interchange between
ἀγαπᾶν and φιλεῖν in vv. 3:35 and 5:20, in the Lazarus episode
of ch. 11, and in the questions and answers from the dialogue
with Peter in ch. 21, it seems reasonable to say that neither
the evangelist nor the redactor had different theological connotations in mind when the two terms were employed.

[6]See above, ch. III, p. 122, n. 216.

[7]See above, ch. III, p. 122.

[8]This theme of the glorification of the Son of Man is
first introduced by the author in Jn 12:20-26. Upon hearing
that some Greeks (῏Ησαν δὲ ῝Ελληνές τινες) had come to see him,
Jesus exclaims solemnly in v. 12:23, ᾽Ελήλυθεν ἡ ὥρα ἵνα δοξα-
σθῇ ὁ υἱὸς τοῦ ἀνθρώπου. However, it is not until Judas leaves
and the τεκνία (v. 13:33) are left alone that the actual "hour"
of Jesus' return to the Father begins.

[9]Even when he is interrupted further on in the discourse by individual disciples, Jesus continues to address
them primarily in terms of the second person plural form of
the verb in question. For example, after Thomas' question of
v. 5, Jesus responds first of all in the third person singular
(v. 6b) and then turns to the second person plural form (ἐγνώ-
κατε/γνώσεσθε/γινώσκετε/ἑωράκατε). After Philip's question
of v. 8, Jesus uses the second person singular briefly, but
turns immediately to the second person plural form (πιστεύετε/
λέγω ὑμῖν). Finally, after Judas' question of v. 22, Jesus
responds initially in the third person singular, but then turns
to the second person plural form (ὁ λόγος ὃν ἀκούετε/λελάληκα
ὑμῖν).

[10]In v. 14:27 the imperative μὴ ταρασσέσθω is followed
by another imperative which concludes the phrase, μηδὲ δειλι-
άτω. This latter verb, δειλιᾶν, is a *hapax legomenon* in the

New Testament.   Both the noun and the adjective are found,
however: δειλία occurs once in II Tim 1:7 and δειλός three
times, Mt 8:26, Mk 4:40, Rev 21:8.

[11]In the process of rearrangement, Bultmann, pp. 523-
39, 595-603, breaks up vv. 13:31-38 into 13:31-35 and 13:36-38.
The former division he places immediately following ch. 17--at
the beginning of the Farewell Discourse--so that the theme of
glorification follows the introduction of that theme in ch. 17.
Furthermore, vv. 13:31-35 precede ch. 15, so that the theme of
love in vv. 34-35 is followed by that same theme in ch. 15.
The latter division Bultmann places at the end of the discourse, preceding vv. 14:1-31 and following ch. 16. With vv.
13:36-14:4 the question of discipleship is then raised, first
negatively (vv. 13:36-38) and then positively (vv. 14:1-4).
The rest of the chapter, i.e., vv. 14:5-31, continues this
theme "demonstrating (after the promise has been made in 13:36-
14:4) the inner unity of the promised future in the world
beyond with the present eschatological existence." (Ibid.,
p. 595.) See above, ch. III, pp. 83-84.

[12]Brown, pp. 608-9; Schnackenburg, pp. 53-63; Dodd,
Interpretation, pp. 403-4; Westcott, pp. 196-98; J. Becker,
pp. 219-20; A. Wikenhauser, *Das Evangelium nach Johannes*, 2nd
ed., RNT, no. 4 (Regensburg: F. Pustet, 1957), pp. 260-61.
All references to either Brown's second volume or Schnackenburg's
burg's third volume of their respective commentaries will be
made simply as, Brown; or, Schnackenburg (as in the previous
chapter).

[13]Barrett, pp. 13-15, 375, sees vv. 13:31-38 as anticipating "the themes, and even the form, of chs. 14-16" on two
counts: (1) the introduction of the theme of departure and
glory; (2) the rejection of Peter's offering. Lindars, *The
Gospel*, pp. 460-61, 466-69, presents an even more complicated
picture. On the one hand, vv. 13:31-38 recapitulate ch. 13:
vv. 13:1-20 and 13:31-35 both share in the theme of Jesus as
the model of discipleship. On the other hand, vv. 13:31-38
anticipate the themes of chs. 14-17 in the following manner:
v. 13:36 is taken up in ch. 14; vv. 13:34-35 in ch. 15;
v. 13:35 in vv. 15:18-16:15; v. 13:33 in v. 16:16; vv. 13:31-
32 in ch. 17. Lindars, however, refuses to see this chiastic
correspondence as deliberate; rather, vv. 13:31-38 introduce
both ch. 14 and chs. 15-16. These two sections or discourses
were added in different redactions of the Gospel, but both
have vv. 13:31-38 as their introduction.
See above, ch. III, pp. 91-92.

[14]Dodd, *Interpretation*, pp. 403-6; Lagrange, pp. 392-
400; J. Becker, pp. 227-28; Wikenhauser, pp. 280-83.

[15]Dodd, *Interpretation*, p. 406; Lagrange, p. 392;
J. Becker, p. 228.

[16]This position is taken primarily by those who rear-
range the discourses, placing ch. 14 either at the very end of
the entire series of discourses (Bultmann; Lattke) or immediately preceding the end (Bernard). See, e.g., Bultmann, pp.
625-31; Bernard, II, pp. 552-57.

[17]Brown, pp. 632, 652; Schnackenburg, pp. 63-65;
Lindars, *The Gospel*, p. 483.

[18]Another reason would be that, if vv. 14:25-31 were
to be the conclusion, then the summarizing character of the
concluding paragraph would also include a reference to the
theme of the Paraclete (vv. 14:25-26), which appears in vv.
14:16-17.

[19]Brown, p. 652, states that vv. 14:25-26 could just
as easily be assigned to the main body of the discourse, but
decides against such an alternative solely on account of this
phrase; Lindars, *The Gospel*, p. 483; Schnackenburg, pp. 94,
104. See above, ch. III, pp. 98, 111, 126.

[20]See above, ch. III, p. 126, n. 242.

[21]Brown, pp. 623-24, 642-43. Brown further subdivides
both units as follows: (I) vv. 1-4, 6-11, 12-14; (II) vv. 15-
17, 18-21, 23-24. Bultmann, pp. 603-12. Bultmann subdivides
the last section into vv. 15-17, 18-21, 22-24; likewise, he
considers vv. 14:1-4 together with vv. 13:36-38 (see above,
p. 137, n. 11). Wikenhauser, pp. 261-63, 268. Wikenhauser
subdivides the first section as follows: vv. 1-4, 5-11, 12-14;
and the second section, vv. 15-17, 18-21, 22-24, 25-26.

[22]J. Becker, pp. 219-23.

[23]Ibid., pp. 222-23.

[24]Although Becker proposes v. 14:17 as the end of the
first major section, I tend to see v. 14:15 as the dividing
verse. This position would not affect the distribution of the
themes of departure and return, since neither ὑπάγειν nor
πορεύομαι are found in vv. 14:15-17. I shall return to this
point subsequently.

[25]There are two verbs, ὑπάγω and πορεύομαι, which are
used as synonyms to describe Jesus' departure to the Father.
In all, ὑπάγω is used six times (vv. 13:33, 36[2]; 14:4, 5,
28); πορεύομαι, four times (vv. 14:2, 3, 12, 28).

[26]Jesus' return is expressed solely in terms of the
verb ἔρχομαι (vv. 14:3, 18, 23, 28). It should be observed
that in v. 14:23 the verb is used in the first person plural
of the future tense, thus including both the Father and the
Son.

[27]J. Becker, p. 226. See also, Schnackenburg, p. 86.

[28]Those exegetes mentioned above (see p. 138, n. 21)
who divide the main body of the discourse into a "faith" section and a "love" section do see this last section as consisting of a triadic pattern of love and promise (Bultmann, pp.
612-14; Wikenhauser, p. 268; Brown, pp. 642-43). Thus, each
pattern would begin with a definition of the love of Jesus
and continue with a statement concerning the divine presence

in the disciples. Bultmann, p. 613, would also see an ascending order in the promises of the divine presence: first, the
Paraclete; then, Jesus; finally, Jesus and God.

[29]None of the exegetes who adopt the triadic pattern
sees this theme as being a part of that pattern. Yet, it
seems to me that it has to be considered as an element of
each pattern.

[30]I shall examine in greater detail the different
elements of these sequences when it comes time to concentrate
on the references to love. For the purpose of determining
the structure of the discourse, these remarks are sufficient
at this point.

It should be noted, however, that although the second
instance of the κόσμος theme (v. 14:19) follows directly upon
the first (v. 14:17bc), the two should be separated from each
other. In v. 14:17bc the occasion for the comparison between
"world" and "disciples" is provided by the coming of the
Paraclete, while in v. 14:19 it is the return of Jesus that
occasions the comparison. In v. 14:22 the comparison is
clearly separated from what precedes it by the insertion of
Judas' question.

[31]J. Becker, pp. 224-26, removes vv. 14:14-15. See
p. 224: "Beide Verse sind sperriges Standgut, das auszuson-
dern ist."

[32]Ibid., p. 225: "Der klare Gedanke in v. 13 bedarf
keiner Wiederholung . . . So ist v. 14 störend und überflüssig."
Furthermore, Becker accepts the absence of v. 14 in a number of
manuscripts as confirming the suspicion that it is an interpolation. V. 14 is omitted by X, f[1], 565, 1009, 1010, 1365,
et al. Yet, the fact remains that it is found in the majority
of witnesses, including the most important ones, e.g., p[66],
p[75], ℵ, A, B, D, K, L, W, et al. The omission would be
easier to explain in terms of a later scribal emendation to
avoid the apparent repetition of v. 14:13.

[33]In other words, the sending of the spirit of truth,
of the "other" Paraclete, is clearly a function of Jesus as
Paraclete before the Father: it is his asking the Father--in
accordance with the description of his role in v. 14:13--that
results in the sending of the Paraclete (καὶ ὅ τι ἂν αἰτήσητε
--→καγὼ ἐρωτήσω). However, a serious objection may be brought
against this view. Schnackenburg, p. 84, correctly remarks
that the function of the Paraclete in v. 14:16 is not that of
a heavenly intercessor (as is the case in I Jn 2:1), but
rather that of an earthly comforter. The description of the
"other" Paraclete as the one who will abide with the disciples forever (ἵνα μεθ' ὑμῶν εἰς τὸν αἰῶνα ᾖ) confirms this
view: Jesus is departing, so another Paraclete is sent by the
Father.

[34]The fact remains, however, that the grounding of the
"greater works" is already provided in v. 14:12--ὅτι ἐγὼ πρὸς
τὸν πατέρα πορεύομαι. It is Jesus' return to the Father that
will allow, because of the promise of the fulfillment of

prayers, these works to be performed. Furthermore, there is
no clear indication given in v. 14:16 that the Paraclete is
connected in any way with the greater works. On this point,
see Schnackenburg, p. 80, n. 69.

[35]J. Becker, p. 225. At no point does Becker indicate
a possible reason for introducing vv. 14:14-15 between vv.
14:13 and 16. This proposed interpolation seems to be rather
meaningless.

[36]See above, ns. 32, 33, 34.

[37]Becker is neither the only one nor the first one to
have proposed some type of excision with regard to v. 14:14
and the verses surrounding it. For example, Wellhausen, *Das
Evangelium Johannis*, pp. 64-65, suggests that originally v.
14:13 had the reading ποιήσει, thus presenting the Father as
the subject of the verb. When v. 14:14 was added, the subject
of the verb became ἐγώ, referring to Jesus, and this correction found its way into v. 14:13. Spitta, p. 345, adopts a
rather similar conclusion: neither v. 13b nor v. 14 belonged
to the *Grundschrift*. Furthermore, the redactor deliberately
changed the ποιήσει of v. 13a to ποιήσω. Finally, Spitta
adds v. 14:15 to the interpolation as well. Hirsch, p. 106,
removes vv. 13-15 as coming from the redactor and interrupting
the trend of thought from v. 12 to v. 16.

[38]Schnackenburg, p. 83, argues that if one accepts
the two readings of με as the object of the verb αἰτέω (which
is omitted by A, D, K, L, Π, Ψ, Byz Lect, Diatessaron, Augus-
tine, Cyril, Euthymius, et al.) and ἐγώ as the subject of
ποιήσω (some manuscripts have τοῦτο, e.g., p[75], B, A, et
al.), the verse does make sense in the context. It serves to
accentuate and define the specific role of Jesus as "Gebetener
und die Bitte Erfüllender." Schnackenburg is correct in the
acceptance of these two readings: the variant readings (i.e.,
the omission of με and the substitution of τοῦτο) may be
easily regarded as a scribal attempt to bring v. 14 in line
with v. 13.

[39]Ibid., pp. 80-84.

[40]Ibid., p. 83. Schnackenburg argues against any
attempt to make ἀγάπη the central theme of this second section: "Aber das ist schwerlich ein genügender Grund, einen
neuen Abschnitt zu beginnen, da ab V 18 das Theme von 'Kommen'
Jesu . . . ebenso beachtlich ist." However, to start the
section with v. 14:15 does not mean, as some have argued, that
love is the central theme, but rather that love is one of the
main subordinate themes of that section and must be placed
within it.

[41]V. 14:10b presents the two motives for belief: the
words of Jesus *per se* (τὰ ῥήματα ἃ ἐγὼ λαλῶ ὑμῖν ἀπ᾽ ἐμαυτοῦ
οὐ λαλῶ) and the works (ὁ δὲ πατὴρ ἐν ἐμοὶ μένων ποιεῖ τὰ ἔργα
αὐτοῦ). V. 11 picks up these two motives: πιστεύετέ μοι . . .
εἰ δὲ μή, διὰ τὰ ἔργα αὐτὰ πιστεύετε.

[42]Schnackenburg, p. 79; Lindars, *The Gospel*, pp. 475-76; Bultmann, p. 611.

[43]Yet another division is proposed by Lagrange, pp. 372-78. Lagrange offers vv. 1-11 as the first section of the discourse and vv. 12-26 as the second section. What divides the second section from the first, verse 12 from verse 11, is that beginning with v. 14:12 the emphasis is placed on the work of the disciples. Spicq, III, p. 181, offers a similar solution.

[44]I say "briefly" because I shall take up the question of the *Sitz im Leben* at the conclusion of the chapter, once the love passages have been examined in detail. Since Becker makes no judgment about the implications of his findings for the *Sitz im Leben* of the entire Gospel, it seems more appropriate to mention his position at this point rather than after all the love passages have been examined.

[45]Becker, pp. 222-23. These two divisions are Becker's own divisions.

[46]Ibid., p. 221. On p. 222 Becker reconstructs the original saying, following Bultmann's opinion that the clause εἰ δὲ μή, εἶπον ἂν ὑμῖν ὅτι is to be removed from the original saying and attributed to the evangelist (Bultmann, p. 601). The original saying would run as follows:
- 1a. ἐν τῇ οἰκίᾳ τοῦ πατρός μου μοναὶ πολλαί εἰσιν
- 1b. . . . [καὶ] πορεύομαι ἑτοιμάσαι τόπον ὑμῖν
- 2a. καὶ ἐὰν πορευθῶ καὶ ἑτοιμάσω τόπον ὑμῖν
- 2b. πάλιν ἔρχομαι καὶ παραλήμψομαι ὑμᾶς πρὸς ἐμαυτόν
- 2c. ἵνα ὅπου εἰμὶ ἐγὼ καὶ ὑμεῖς ἦτε

Schnackenburg, p. 66, who adopts Becker's division, is quite adamant on this textual point: "Eine durch nichts gerechtfertigte Gewaltlösung ist es, die Worte εἰ δὲ μή, εἶπον ἂν ὑμῖν als Zufügung zu streichen, um so einen glatten Spruch zu erhalten." Rather, Schnackenburg sees the point of reference of the phrase to be v. 13:33, i.e., after the ὅτι one should read a ὑπάγειν. This very persuasive theory is further strengthened by his comment on Becker's solution: if the evangelist is indeed carrying out a polemic against the point of view represented by vv. 14:2-3, why would he confirm that point of view by introducing these words? (See also, "Das Anliegen der Abschiedsrede in Joh 14," in *Wort Gottes in der Zeit. Festschrift Karl Hermann Schelkle zum 65. Geburtstag*, ed. H. Feld and J. Nolte [Düsseldorf: Patmos Verlag, 1973], pp. 95-110. This article, published prior to the third volume of the commentary, is concerned for the most part with the problematic verses, 14:2-3.)

[47]Becker, p. 222. This is the only example of ἑτοι-μάζειν in the Gospel and the Letters, and it is the only instance in the Johannine literature of this particular meaning of παραλαμβάνειν (see vv. 1:11; 19:16). Likewise, the expressions ἡ οἰκία τοῦ πατρός or μοναὶ πολλαί, referring to heavenly dwellings, are found nowhere else in the New Testament. Schnackenburg, "Das Anliegen," pp. 102ff., once again disagrees with this terminological separation. Thus, for

example, he argues that πάλιν is a Johannine word and that it has no reference to a παρουσία in the context. Likewise, Jn 8:35 already contains three of the themes of v. 14:2--οἰκία; μένειν; ὁ υἰός. Furthermore, παραλαμβάνειν need not be taken as a parousia word; it simply follows the metaphor of οἰκία or μονή.

[48]It should be pointed out that Becker is not alone in this position, as he himself recognizes (Becker, p. 221). Thus, for example, Bultmann, p. 598, n. 6, assigns vv. 14:2-3 (minus the εἰ clause) to the *Offenbarungsreden* source. Other exegetes point to the traditional flavor of these verses, but assert nonetheless that they were written by the evangelist himself. Thus, for example, C. Clemen, *Die Entstehung des Johannesevangelium* (Halle: M. Niemeyer, 1912), pp. 249-50; S. Schulz, *Untersuchungen zur Menschensohn-Christologie*, pp. 159-64, who states that an old tradition has been partly changed by the evangelist. As far as I can see, none of these authors interprets this "reworking" polemically.

[49]J. Becker, p. 222.

[50]Ibid., pp. 223-26.

[51]Ibid., pp. 226-27.

[52]Ibid., p. 228.

[53]Schnackenburg, "Das Anliegen," pp. 106-7, sees the two verses as fitting quite well within the context and as representing "typisch 'Johanneische' Worte." Indeed, he argues, the evangelist's realized eschatology may be seen in these two verses as well: it is customary for the evangelist to take "Ausdrücke . . . die ihm aus der allgemein-urchrist-lichen Tradition bekannt sind" and to read these expressions in terms of his own beliefs. It is this rereading that he undertakes in v. 14:3 with respect to eschatological beliefs. There is no need, therefore, to separate these verses from the rest of the discourse and to assign them to a different author. Although there may be a certain reinterpretation of eschato-logical beliefs, there is no polemic evident in the section. See also, ns. 46 and 47 above.
    I agree wholeheartedly with this trend of thought. Besides, if Becker were correct in isolating theologically and terminologically a saying from the Johannine Gospel, in what sense could this saying be assigned to a Johannine "Gemeinde-tradition"? What would the adjective "Johannine" mean?

[54]I have in mind at this point J. L. Martyn's attempt to compare methodologically different studies of the Fourth Gospel to see whether the lines of research intersect in any way ("Source Criticism and Religionsgeschichte," in *Jesus and Man's Hope*, I, pp. 247-73, esp. pp. 247-53).

[55]The following chart brings out this distribution much more clearly. Let the Roman numerals I, II, III, and IV stand for the different relationships of love mentioned above,

i.e., I = the love of the disciples for Jesus; II = the love of the Father for the disciples; III = the love of Jesus for the disciples; IV = the love of Jesus for the Father.

	13:31-38	14:1-3	4-14	15-26	27-31
I	--	--	--	vv. 15, 21, 23a	v. 28
II	--	--	--	vv. 21b, 23b	--
III	--	--	--	v. 21c	--
IV	--	--	--	--	v. 31

[56] See above, p. 141, n. 28.

[57] If one includes the κόσμος motif in each pattern, then it is that motif that constitutes the final element of the second and third patterns (vv. 14:18-21, 22-27).

[58] Instead of the future form τηρήσετε in the apodosis (a reading which is supported by B, L, Ψ, min, cop [sa, bo], Eusebius, Melitius, et al.), two other readings may be found: the aorist subjunctive τηρήσητε (p[66], ℵ, min, arm) and the aorist imperative τηρήσατε (A, D, K, W, X, Δ, Θ, min, it, vg, syr, eth, Origen, Eusebius, et al.). The future form is to be preferred in view of the use of the future in vv. 14:12, 13, 14, 16, 18, 20, 21, 23.

[59] Furthermore, this particular statement reverses the order of the other three: first, the theme of commands; then, that of love. This inversion leads to the reprise of the second participial form in v. 14:21b--ἐκεῖνός ἐστιν ὁ ἀγαπῶν με. ὁ δὲ ἀγαπῶν με . . .

[60] Bultmann, pp. 612-13.

[61] Some would disagree, e.g., Bernard, II, p. 548, who states that ἔχειν means "to know them and apprehend their meaning," while τηρεῖν means "to keep them, which is a harder thing." However, this exegesis seems somewhat forced; Bernard gives no reasons for the proposed distinction. See also, Barrett, p. 388; Westcott, p. 207.

[62] By "original" Gospel I mean those sections the authenticity of which has never been questioned. All other sections must be handled as follows: (1) any examples in vv. 13:34-35 and 15:1-17 must, from the point of view of this study, be excluded altogether (vv. 13:34; 15:10[2], 12); (2) any examples that form part of the later Farewell Discourse, i.e., vv. 15:18-16:4a; 16:4b-33; ch. 17, should not be used as primary evidence for Johannine usage, but may be used for the purpose of contrast (e.g., vv. 15:20; 17:6).

[63] The combination of ἐντολή (singular or plural) and the verb τηρεῖν is not found elsewhere in the "original" Gospel.

[64] The exchange begins in v. 8:12 with an ἐγώ εἰμι saying of Jesus and focuses on the contrast between Abraham and

294   Love Relationships in John

Jesus in v. 31. This contrast pervades the rest of the debate
(vv. 37, 39, 40, 53, 56, 57, 58). Schnackenburg, II, p. 238,
posits three subsections: vv. 8:30-36, 37-47, 48-59. Brown,
I, p. 361, also sees three subsections, but divides them somewhat differently: vv. 8:31-41a, 41b-47, 48-59.

[65]The saying is clearly directed at the Jews. In
v. 8:52 one finds a typical instance of a complete lack of
understanding on the part of the Jews: they understand Jesus'
saying from a purely physical point of view. The saying is
repeated by the Jews (with minor variations): καὶ σὺ λέγεις,
ἐάν τις τὸν λόγον μου τηρήσῃ.

[66]Although the precise combination of ἔχειν and λόγος
does not appear in Jn 14, I feel justified in considering the
union of these two terms in v. 5:38 as being synonymous with
the different variations of ch. 14. The absence of a fast
and rigid formula in the latter chapter as well as the occurrence of these two terms--even if separate from each other--in
vv. 14:21a, 23a, and 24a more than justify this step.

[67]Martyn, *History and Theology*, pp. 49-50.

[68]These three elements are duplicated in chs. 9-10 of
the Gospel: a traditional healing story (vv. 9:1-7) is followed by a dramatic expansion (vv. 9:8-41) and a homily
delivered to the Jews in Jerusalem (vv. 10:1-18). The first
series, extending from ch. 5 through ch. 7, would exemplify
the statement of Jn 16:2b, while the second series, extending
from ch. 9 through ch. 10, would represent the actions of Jn
16:2a. Ibid.

[69]The combined usage of ἐντολή and ἔχειν is not found
outside of Jn 14:21a. For rabbinic parallels, see A. Schlatter,
Der Evangelist Johannes (Stuttgart: Calwer, 1948), pp. 300-1.

[70]Besides the examples of vv. 8:51, 52, 55, the combination of λόγος and the verb τηρεῖν occurs in vv. 15:20 and
17:6. Although I do not wish to consider ch. 17 on the same
level with the "original" Gospel (see above, p. 147, n. 62),
nevertheless it is important to point out significant parallels
whenever present. After the request on the part of Jesus to
be glorified once more with the glory that was his now that he
has accomplished his work (vv. 17:4-5), Jesus describes this
work (τὸ ἔργον τελειώσας ὃ δέδωκάς μοι ἵνα ποιήσω): he has
revealed the Father's name to the disciples, and they in turn
have kept the Father's word (καὶ τὸν λόγον σου τετήρηκαν).
Vv. 17:7-8 explain this further: in accepting Jesus' words
(τὰ ῥήματα), the disciples acknowledged his role and identity,
his origin and his relationship to the Father. This is precisely the import of both v. 8:51 and v. 5:38.

[71]Aside from vv. 14:15, 21a, the noun occurs in vv.
10:18; 11:57; and 12:49-50. In v. 10:18 the ἐντολή refers
specifically to Jesus' death: it is he who lays down his life
on command from the Father. In v. 11:57 the usage is completely "secular," i.e., not theological in character.

[72]For example, in v. 12:36b one is told that Jesus is now alone; he departs from his disciples. After the summary statement of vv. 12:37-43, he is still alone supposedly; consequently, a discourse beginning with v. 12:44 is completely out of place.

[73]Schnackenburg, II, pp. 513-14; Brown, I, p. 490. Others are aware of the lack of connection between the passage and what precedes it, but do not see it as coming from a later stage, e.g., Dodd, *Interpretation*, pp. 381-82; Wikenhauser, p. 240. In all cases, however, the authorship of the passage by the evangelist is not in question.

[74]Bernard, II, pp. 445-49, places the passage after v. 12:36a so that the ideas of "light" and "truth" are continued in vv. 44-46. Bultmann, pp. 342ff., creates a long discourse on light consisting of vv. 8:12; 12:44-50; 8:21-29; and 12:34-36.

[75]In vv. 12:47-48 Jesus' message from the Father is described as τὰ ῥήματα, rather than αἱ ἐντολαί or ὁ λόγος, but there is really no difference among the various usages. They are interchanged throughout the Gospel, e.g., v. 14:10/v. 14:24a.

[76]Many others have reached a similar conclusion, e.g., Wikenhauser, p. 268; Bultmann, p. 612; J. Becker, p. 227; S. Schulz, *Das Evangelium nach Johannes*, NTD, no. 4 (Göttingen: Vandenhoeck & Ruprecht, 1972), p. 187; Lattke, p. 227.

[77]See above, p. 141.

[78]This description of Jesus' work is quite common throughout the Gospel, especially in the context of anti-Jewish debates, e.g., vv. 7:16; 8:26, 28; 12:49-50.

[79]Barrett, p. 385; R. H. Lightfoot, *St. John's Gospel. A Commentary*, ed. C. F. Evans (Oxford: University Press, 1956), pp. 270-71, also interprets the verses in terms of obedience of Jesus' precepts.

[80]Dodd, *Interpretation*, pp. 405-6. See also, Lindars, *The Gospel*, p. 477.

[81]Lagrange, p. 380. See also, Spicq, III, p. 182.

[82]Both Brown and Schnackenburg posit a *via media* insofar as they accept both faith and ethics to be part of the commands. See Brown, pp. 638, 640-42. Schnackenburg, however, is a bit more cautious: he stresses the element of faith and speaks of ethical norms in terms of the implications of the commands. See Schnackenburg, p. 84.

[83]See above, pp. 137-38.

[84]Lattke, p. 236. Similarly, Schnackenburg, p. 97.

[85]In vv. 14:15-26 the relationship was certainly
present insofar as the theme of return dominated those verses.
In v. 14:28 that relationship is the focus of attention, due
for the most part to the linkage with the theme of rejoicing.

[86]The verb χαίρειν occurs elsewhere, e.g., vv. 3:39;
4:36; 8:56; 11:15; 16:20, 22; 19:3; and the noun may be found
in vv. 3:29; 15:11; 16:20, 21, 22, 24. In vv. 3:29 and 8:56
the χαίρειν or χαρά is associated with the historical appearance of Jesus, not with his departure. Similarly, neither
v. 4:36 nor 11:15 nor 19:3 are of immediate importance in
this regard. Besides Jn 20:20, only Jn 16:20ff. are immediately relevant; however, from a methodological point of view,
one must remember the restrictions placed on evidence taken
from material in Jn 15:18-17:26 (see above, p. 147, n. 62).
        Given the methodological restrictions, it is quite
clear that the examples in vv. 16:4b-33 are quite close to
vv. 14:28 and 20:20. For example, at the very beginning of
the section, in vv. 16:6-7, the theme of distress is raised,
and v. 7 addresses itself to this distress from the point of
view of the Paraclete--συμφέρει ὑμῖν ἵνα ἐγὼ ἀπέλθω. Later,
in vv. 16:20-24 the theme of distress is again raised, and
the disciples are promised--following the parable of v. 21--
that their sorrow will turn to joy when they see Jesus--πάλιν
δὲ ὄψομαι ὑμᾶς, καὶ χαρήσεται ὑμῶν ἡ καρδία. Thus, in all
three cases, i.e., vv. 14:28, 16:20-24, and 20:20, rejoicing
is associated with Jesus' return.

[87]See R. Brown's statement on p. 654: "The Johannine
Jesus represents the Father and leads to the Father, and so in
going to the Father he is accomplishing his life's purpose;
any love that would fail to recognize and respect that is not
real love. Thus implicitly faith and love are closely associated here."

[88]See above, p. 135.

[89]I am following at this point R. Schnackenburg's
division (see II, p. 238) as the most satisfactory one. Many
exegetes designate vv. 48-59 as a subsection, e.g., Brown, I,
p. 161; Lindars, *The Gospel*, p. 331; Lagrange, p. 250; Wikenhauser, p. 182. However, there is much more disagreement when
it comes to separating the first subsection from the second
one: Brown chooses vv. 41b-47; Wikenhauser, vv. 39-47;
Lindars, vv. 39-47. Schnackenburg's division, which has the
second section begin with v. 37, seems more appropriate:
vv. 31-36 would concentrate on the theme of freedom, while
vv. 37-47 move on to the contrast between being children of
Abraham and being children of the devil.

[90]See above, p. 147.

[91]See above, p. 148.

[92]The Gospel has already introduced two examples of
this kind of attitude: Nicodemus, a ruler of the Jews, who
comes to Jesus by night (v. 3:1) and the parents of the man
born blind (vv. 5:19-23).

[93]The reference here is most probably to the temple vision of Is 6. Both Bultmann, p. 453, and Brown, I, pp. 486-87, see the possibility that the evangelist may be following the Targumic tradition of that vision, where it is said that Isaiah saw the *shekinah* of the Lord, rather than either the Masoretic text or the Septuagint, where Isaiah sees the Lord directly. In view of the λόγος concept of the Prologue and the "dwelling" concept of v. 1:14, it is not difficult to see how the evangelist would have applied the vision of Isaiah to the figure of Jesus. It is then because of that vision that the prophet could predict the reaction of the Jews to the λόγος: Jn 12:38b (Is 53:1); Jn 12:40 (Is 6:10).
A rather similar presentation of another Old Testament figure occurs in Jn 8:56, where it is said that Abraham saw "the day of Jesus"--ἵνα ἴδῃ τὴν ἡμέραν τὴν ἐμήν--and rejoiced --καὶ εἶδεν καὶ ἐχάρη.

[94]A very similar equivocation occurs in v. 5:44, i.e., toward the end of the sermon delivered by Jesus to the Jews. In v. 5:43 Jesus declares that the Jews do not accept him despite his proclaimed origin, i.e., they do not believe in him. This situation is then expressed in v. 5:44 in terms of δόξα: the Jews would rather accept "glory" from each other than the "glory" of the only God.

[95]One could consider this particular reason given for the promise of vv. 16:23-24 as yet another parallelism with ch. 14, since in v. 14:12 belief in Jesus is made a condition for the granting of all petitions (vv. 14:13-14). The one difference would be that whereas ch. 14 has Jesus answer the prayers directly, ch. 16 has the Father perform that role (see v. 16:23).

[96]In I John the love of Jesus as such is not developed directly; rather, the author always speaks of the love of God. It is that love which is defined in terms of the expression, τὰς ἐντολὰς τηρεῖν. However, I believe that such love is nonetheless presupposed, since it is Jesus who has brought the ἐντολαί of God to men, to "the world." Thus, for example, in I Jn 2:3-5 the love of God is defined in terms of the execution of Jesus' commands, and in v. 5:3 that same relationship is defined in terms of the execution of God's commands. See above, ch. II, pp. 42, 72-73, 73-75.

[97]See above, ch. II, pp. 40-44, 57-58; ch. III, pp. 112-13, 117-19.

[98]As Bernard, II, pp. 548-49, points out, this is the only instance in the Gospel of ὑπό followed by a genitive of agent.

[99]The difference is really insignificant: there is no reason to suppose a change in meaning. Thus, for example, the future passive of v. 14:21b is followed immediately by ἀγαπάω in the active voice (though the subject of this second form is no longer the Father).

298   Love Relationships in John

[100]Lattke, pp. 231-32, interprets the love of the
Father solely in terms of what follows the two καί of vv.
14:21b and 14:23b: "Das zweimalige epexegetische καί in den
Versen 21 und 23 (καὶ ἐμφανίσω bzw. καὶ πρὸς αὐτὸν ἐλευσόμεθα)
zeigt im engeren Zusammenhang, wie das ἀγαπᾶν durch den Vater
und seinen Gesandten verstanden werden will: als Offenbarung."
However, I believe a certain differentiation is possible among
the different figures associated with the return.

[101]See Brown, p. 643, who allows for the possibility
that the different sayings may have had independent origins.
However, at the time of the composition of the discourse, the
different sayings coalesce around the figure of the Paraclete:
"The sayings about these indwellings have been woven together
into a unit that begins and ends on the theme of loving Jesus
. . . in the final stage . . . all these indwellings were
thought to be accomplished through and in the Paraclete."

[102]Brown, pp. 646-47; Wikenhauser, p. 273. See above,
pp. 152-53.

[103]The reason is partly, no doubt, the fact that in
this section it is not the Father who sends the Paraclete, but
rather Jesus (v. 16:7--ἐὰν δὲ πορευθῶ, πέμψω αὐτὸν πρὸς ὑμᾶς).

[104]Likewise, it is not Jesus who hears the petitions
of the disciples (cf., vv. 14:13-14--καὶ ὅ τι ἂν αἰτήσητε ἐν
τῷ ὀνόματί μου τοῦτο ποιήσω), but the Father (v. 16:23--ἄν τι
αἰτήσητε τὸν πατέρα ἐν τῷ ὀνόματί μου δώσει ὑμῖν).

[105]Both Schnackenburg, pp. 214-15, and Bultmann, pp.
512-22, break up these verses into two subsections: vv. 17:20-
23, 24-26. Schnackenburg further states that Jn 17:20-21
represents a later addition to the discourse.

[106]This relationship of love between the Father and
Jesus, i.e., from the Father toward Jesus, is not mentioned
elsewhere in the Gospel.

[107]This is the glory which, from the point of view of
immediate departure, Jesus is about to regain; see v. 17:5.
This is also the glory that is mentioned in v. 1:14.

[108]At this point I withhold all comparison with either
Jn 15:1-17 or I John until the completion of the presentation
of the next relationship of love. The reason will become clear
at that time.

[109]The verb ἐμφανίζειν does not occur outside of this
discourse in the Gospel, and, although it is found a few times
in the New Testament (e.g., Mt 27:53; Acts 23:15, 22; 24:1;
25:2, 15; Heb 9:24; 11:14), it does not bear this meaning
elsewhere. The adverb is found in Acts 10:40 with reference
to the risen Lord: τοῦτον ὁ θεὸς ἤγειρεν τῇ τρίτῃ ἡμέρᾳ καὶ
ἔδωκεν αὐτὸν ἐμφανῆ γενέσθαι, but this is the only such
instance.
     The verb, however, is used of theophanies in the Old
Testament, e.g., Ex 33:13, 18, where Moses asks God to reveal

himself--ἐμφάνισόν μοι σεαυτόν; Wis 1:2, where the Lord is
said to reveal himself to those that put their trust in him:
ἐμφανίζεται δὲ τοῖς μὴ ἀπιστοῦσιν αὐτῷ.

[110]Barrett, p. 388, suggests that the verb may refer
to one of three things: (1) a resurrection appearance; (2) a
spiritual revelation of Jesus; (3) the Parousia appearance.
From the point of view of the chapter, the third alternative
may be left out altogether (see Wikenhauser, p. 272). I
believe that the evangelist has the resurrection appearance
in mind as part of a return, but above all, it seems to me, he
concentrates on the "spiritual" revelation of Jesus, if by
that adjective one means strictly his revelation through the
Paraclete. In other words, his return is more than just a
temporary one--as the first alternative would imply; it is a
lasting return--as the description of the Paraclete in v.
14:16 specifies (ἵνα μεθ' ὑμῶν εἰς τὸν αἰῶνα ᾖ).

[111]The verb ἐρωτάω is used frequently in the different
sections of the Farewell Discourse to refer to a prayer of
Jesus to God: vv. 16:26; 17:9[2], 15, 20.

[112]Bultmann, p. 626; Brown, p. 644.

[113]See above, ch. III, pp. 108, 119-20.

[114]See above, ch. II, pp. 48-49, 54-57, 64-65, 67-68,
73-76.

[115]If vv. 18:1ff. followed v. 14:31c originally, as I
believe is the case, then the evangelist may be thinking in
very concrete terms as well: in v. 18:3 Judas--who, according
to v. 13:27, was controlled by Satan--and members of the chief
Priests and the Pharisees--who, according to v. 8:44, have the
devil as their father--come to arrest Jesus. One should
notice the use of ἔρχεται in v. 18:3 to refer to this group
(cf., v. 14:30b--ἔρχεται γὰρ ὁ τοῦ κόσμου ἄρχων). Thus, it is
through them that the encounter with "the ruler of the world"
takes place.

[116]Bultmann, p. 631, n. 2; Brown, p. 656; Schnackenburg, p. 100.

[117]A few manuscripts (B, L, et al.) read ἐντολὴν δέδωκεν rather than ἐνετείλατο (ℵ, A, D, Γ, Δ, Θ); however, textual
evidence alone supports the latter reading. In either case,
the meaning remains the same. The Gospel uses the verb elsewhere in v. 8:5 with reference to the Law of Moses.

[118]Although ἐντέλλομαι is not found elsewhere with
respect to a relationship between Jesus and the Father, the
noun ἐντολή is. First of all, in the brief, dislocated discourse of Jn 12:44-50, Jesus gives expression to the common
Johannine theme that it is the Father who sent him. Then, in
v. 12:49b he further declares that the Father has commanded
(ἐντολὴν δέδωκεν) what it is that he ought to say and speak.
Secondly, Jn 10:18 is closer than Jn 12:44-50 insofar as it

includes Jesus' death as part of that command--ταύτην τὴν
ἐντολὴν ἔλαβον παρὰ τοῦ πατρός μου.
      See also, vv. 4:34; 5:30; and 6:38, where the refer-
ence is to the will of the Father (τὸ θέλημα τοῦ πέμψαντός με).

[119]A sign which the world will not accept, as vv.
14:17, 19, and 22 confirm in the main body of the discourse.
However, from the point of view of the discourse, that event
is still outstanding.

[120]Indeed, it is more than an event; the ἐντολή of the
Father includes the whole of Jesus' life and mission (see
above, p. 159, n. 118). However, the conclusion of the discourse emphasizes Jesus' death above all (most probably
because of its original connection with vv. 18:1ff.).

[121]See above, pp. 155-56. I shall of course use these
verses at the conclusion of this specific examination for the
purpose of comparison.

[122]In this respect this group of verses is very similar to the originally independent discourse of vv. 12:44-50,
which is now found out of context at the end of ch. 12 (see
above, p. 148. One difference between the two discourses is
that, whereas vv. 12:44-50 are directly attributed to Jesus
('Ιησοῦς δὲ ἔκραξεν καὶ εἶπεν), vv. 3:31-36 do not identify
the speaker directly (i.e., from within).

[123]These last two sections, viz., vv. 22-24, 25-30,
represent a continuation of the apologetic tradition about
John the Baptist contained in ch. 1 (vv. 6-8, 15, 19-24,
25-34). For this reason some exegetes see the present position of these two sections as being highly controversial as
well. For example, Brown, I, pp. 153-55, argues that this
tradition originally belonged shortly after Jn 1:19-34 and
that it has been placed in its present position in order to
bring out the baptismal motif of the Nicodemus story.

[124]I take this list of objections from Wikenhauser,
p. 100, who concludes: "Die V 31-36 lassen sich schwerlich
als Worte des Täufers verstehen." Similarly, Brown, I, p.
159; Schulz, Das Evangelium, p. 66; Bultmann, p. 160; Schnackenburg, I, pp. 393-95.

[125]For specific similarities, see Brown, I, pp. 159-60.

[126]Bultmann, p. 160; Bernard, I, pp. xxiii, 123;
Wikenhauser, pp. 100-2. All three favor an original position
following vv. 3:1-21.

[127]Brown, I, p. 160; Schulz, Das Evangelium, p. 66;
Dodd, Interpretation, pp. 309-10. Dodd believes that the
evangelist placed these verses at this point in order to recapitulate the whole of vv. 3:1-30. Schulz raises the possibility that it may have been a redactor, not the evangelist, that
placed them here. Brown follows completely this latter line
of argumentation: it was a redactor, not the evangelist.
      Schnackenburg, I, pp. 374-77, also believes that these
verses formed part of an original discourse, but includes

within this independent discourse vv. 13-21 in the following
sequence: 3:31-36, 13-21.   This "kerygmatic" discourse--which
Schnackenburg further describes as a summary of the message of
Jesus designed as an addition to the Nicodemus scene--was then
added later to the Gospel by the "Jüngerredaktion."

[128]A dissenting voice is that of J. Becker ("J3,1-21
als Reflex johanneischer Schuldiskussion," in *Das Wort und die
Wörter. Festschrift G. Friedrich zum 65. Geburtstag*, ed. H.
Balz and S. Schulz [Stuttgart: Kohlhammer, 1973], pp. 85-95)
who sees vv. 3:31-36 as originally independent, but assigns
their composition and placement to the work of a redactor who
was a member of a "school." Becker does not distinguish the
theological standpoint of vv. 3:1-21 from that of vv. 3:31-36.

[129]This theme of "handing over," expressed by means of
the verb δίδωμι, is very frequent in the Gospel. The object
of the verb varies: judgment (vv. 5:22-27); life (v. 5:26);
his disciples (v. 6:37); the command concerning what to say
(v. 12:49); authority over all flesh (v. 17:2); followers
(v. 17:6); his name (vv. 17:11-12); his works (v. 17:8); glory
(v. 17:22).

[130]See above, p. 147. The threefold division has been
adopted from Martyn's work, *History and Theology*, pp. 49-50.

[131]See, e.g., v. 8:28, where the same description is
given as in ch. 5: καὶ ἀπ᾽ ἐμαυτοῦ ποιῶ οὐδέν. See also,
vv. 5:30; 6:38; 7:17-18, 28; 8:42; 12:49.

[132]See above, p. 159, n. 118.

[133]See above, pp. 134-35; p. 147, n. 62.

[134]See above, ch. III, pp. 125-29. At the beginning
of the discourse delineated above as 15:18-16:4a, "love" and
"hatred" are attitudes ascribed to the world with regard to
the disciples of Jesus. Thus, v. 15:18 has Jesus tell the
disciples that the world hates them just as it hated him
first. Then, in v. 15:19 the reason for the hatred is given:
the world hates the disciples because they are not--like Jesus--
"of the world." The world would love them only if they were
"of the world": εἰ ἐκ τοῦ κόσμου ἦτε, ὁ κόσμος ἂν τὸ ἴδιον
ἐφίλει. The specific channels of this hatred are described in
vv. 16:1-4a, the conclusion to this particular discourse.
    The relationship of love between "the world" and "its
own" does not occur elsewhere in the Gospel.

[135]See above, ch. I, pp. 21-22.

[136]Thyen, pp. 346ff.; Richter, "Die Fusswaschung,"
pp. 21-22.

[137]See Lattke, pp. 11-12; Bultmann, pp. 424-25, who
sees the evangelist as enlarging the saying of Mt 8:35 parr.
through the addition of the prepositional phrase, ἐν τῷ κόσμῳ
τούτῳ εἰς ζωὴν αἰώνιον. In the context it seems to refer
primarily to the approaching "hour" of Jesus, when he must lay
down his life and return to the Father.

[138]See above, p. 147.

[139]See above, pp. 146-51.

[140]See above, p. 151.

[141]See above, p. 161.

[142]See, e.g., J. Becker, "J3,1-21 als," p. 85.

[143]See Schnackenburg, I, p. 374, n. 2: Th. Calmes, J. E. Belser, F. Tillmann begin with v. 13; J. H. Bernard, M.-J. Lagrange, F.-M. Braun, R. H. Lightfoot begin with v. 16. Bernard, I, p. 117, lists the following reasons: (1) the dialogue framework is dropped; (2) past tenses are used; (3) the word μονογενής, while being thoroughly Johannine, is not placed on the lips of Jesus anywhere else in the discourse.

[144]The "original voice" may be taken as meaning the actual words of Jesus (e.g., Westcott, p. 54) or words of the evangelist that capture the essence of Jesus' own message (e.g., Lagrange, p. 72).

[145]Wikenhauser, p. 102, quotes a certain Gourbillon who would place vv. 3:14-21 between v. 12:31 and v. 12:32. Furthermore, Gourbillon would see vv. 3:31-36 as following upon vv. 3:11-13.

[146]Schnackenburg, I, pp. 374-77. See above, p. 161, n. 127. Schnackenburg argues that v. 12 provides a fitting conclusion to the Nicodemus dialogue: (1) it contains the last occurrence of the second person plural form of the verb; (2) the evangelist employs elsewhere a conclusion consisting of a question, e.g., v. 5:47.

[147]The only other ἀγάπη reference where "the world" is mentioned is that of v. 15:19. That example, however, is closer to the understanding of the κόσμος in vv. 14:15-26 than to that of v. 3:16, since the disciples are clearly differentiated from the world. The verse states that the world does not love the disciples because they are not "of the world." See above, p. 164, n. 134.

[148]Lagrange, p. 87.

[149]Spicq, III, p. 132. See also Schnackenburg, I, p. 423: "In einem Satz, der sich für alle Zeiten tief eingeprägt hat, fasst die kerygmatische Rede die ganze christliche Erlösungsbotschaft zusammen."

[150]Käsemann, p. 60; Lattke, pp. 64-85; Dibelius, pp. 214-15.

[151]Some exegetes prefer to take this οὕτως as an exclamation, i.e., "so much." Thus, Brown, I, p. 132. However, I would rather interpret it after the fashion of I Jn 4:9, 10. See Bultmann, p. 153, n. 1; Lattke, p. 64.

[152]This is the only instance of ὥστε in the Gospel and only the second instance of ὥστε with the indicative in the New Testament. See Blass-Debrunner-Funk, #391:2.

[153]See Lattke's sharp observation (p. 74): "Am Verständnis des διδόναι scheiden sich die Geister und oft genug tritt hier die jeweilige Gesamtauffassung vom Johannesevangelium zu Tage."

[154]Thus, the ἔδωκεν of the Gospel is to be seen in terms of the Pauline παρέδωκεν: Rom 4:25; 8:32; Gal 2:20. See Brown, I, p. 134; Lindars, The Gospel, p. 159; Wikenhauser, p. 90; Schnackenburg, I, p. 424; Lagrange, p. 87; Spicq, III, p. 130.

[155]Dibelius, p. 215; Lattke, pp. 74-77. Also, Bultmann, pp. 153-54.

[156]See Lattke, p. 64.

[157]Dibelius, p. 215.

[158]See above, p. 167, n. 150.

[159]Lattke, p. 69. Also, Dibelius, pp. 214-15. These authors also point to the Gnostic mythology that the evangelist of the Fourth Gospel has pretty much accepted.

[160]Thus, Bultmann, pp. 54-55; Brown, I, pp. 133, 147; Lindars, The Gospel, p. 159; Schnackenburg, I, p. 424.

[161]See above, ch. II, pp. 67-71, 78-79. As in the case of v. 3:16, the First Letter--despite a consistent and thoroughly hostile view of "the world"--also provides a couple of examples where "the world" seems to be more neutral in meaning. Furthermore, both of these examples are connected with the mission of Jesus to the world: (1) v. 2:2b states that Jesus came to take away the sins of "the world"--ἱλασμός ἐστιν περὶ τῶν ἁμαρτιῶν ἡμῶν, οὐ περὶ τῶν ἡμετέρων δὲ μόνον ἀλλὰ καὶ περὶ ὅλου τοῦ κόσμου; (2) v. 4:14 declares that Jesus is the "Savior of the world": ἀπέσταλκεν τὸν υἱὸν σωτῆρα τοῦ κόσμου. On this point, see above, ch. II, p. 64, n. 118.

[162]Lattke, p. 75. See above, ch. III, pp. 113-16.

[163]Both v. 12:43 and v. 3:19 attach the comparative μᾶλλον to the verb. Lattke, p. 12, does not consider either verse in his monograph: "Denn sie hat idiomatische Bedeutung: vorziehen, den Vorzug geben, bevorzugen, wobei μᾶλλον die Bedeutung von potius quam nicht von magis hat." However, these two verses parallel what is said elsewhere of the love of the disciples for Jesus.

[164]See above, pp. 143-45.

[165]Robert Kysar, The Fourth Evangelist and his Gospel. An Examination of Contemporary Scholarship (Minneapolis: Augsburg, 1975).

[166]The book consists of three main divisions: (1) The
Evangelist and his Tradition; (2) The Evangelist and his Situation; (3) The Evangelist and his Thought. The chapter in
question is #3 of Part 2: "The Situation and Purpose of the
Evangelist."

[167]T. C. Smith, *Jesus in the Gospel of John* (Nashville:
Broadman, 1959); W. C. van Unnik, "The Purpose of St. John's
Gospel," in *Studia Evangelica, I*, Texte und Untersuchungen,
no. 73, ed. K. Aland et al. (Berlin: Akademie Verlag, 1959),
pp. 382-411; J. A. T. Robinson, "The Destination and Purpose
of St. John's Gospel," *NTS* 6 (1959-60), pp. 117-31.

[168]Kysar, p. 149.

[169]Among others, Moody Smith, "Johannine Christianity,"
pp. 183-84; Culpepper, p. 268, n. 20; p. 275ff.; Schnackenburg,
"On the Origin of," pp. 228-30.

[170]Martyn, pp. 9-10, 77, 120-21. In pp. 127ff.
Martyn declares that this particular literary form of a two-
level drama was not John's own creation; rather, it was a form
commonly used in Jewish apocalypticism. John, however,
changes the form as follows: (1) both levels of the drama
take place on earth; (2) one level recalls the past, while
another describes the present time; (3) neither level is distinctly identified in the Gospel. On p. 128 Martyn concludes:
"Only the reflective scholar intent on *analyzing* the Gospel
will discover the seams which the Evangelist sowed together."
(Italics his.)

[171]Ibid., p. 9, n. 21.

[172]Ibid. Martyn suggests a translation of the *einmalig*
level as that which is "back there" as opposed to what is "here
and now."

[173]According to Martyn, p. 77, the evangelist is only
partly conscious of what he is doing: "His major concern in
this regard was to bear witness to the essential *integrity* of
the *einmalig* drama of Jesus' earthly life and the contemporary
drama in which the Risen Lord acts through his servants."
(Italics his.)

[174]This task of separation may often be a difficult
one, especially when the two levels overlie one another. Ibid.,
p. 10. In a work on the resurrection narratives that was post-
humously published, N. Perrin (*The Resurrection According to
Matthew, Mark, and Luke* [Philadelphia: Fortress, 1976]) also
distinguishes between the two levels in Mark and then states
precisely the same problem accompanying such differentiations
(p. 26): "These two levels at which the narrative of the gospel moves are extremely difficult to sort out, and there is
the obvious danger of assuming either that too much is symbolic or that too much is historical/physical/geographical."

[175]See above, p. 147, n. 68.

[176]The different stages are succinctly described in pp. 45-48 of the work. The theological nature of the dialogue is described in the last three chapters of the study, e.g., p. 79: "Precisely what do they talk about? We may begin to answer that question by recalling the contemporary dimensions of the two-level drama."

[177]As such, to use Martyn's terminology, these references would not concentrate on the *einmalig* level, but rather would describe the present stage of the community.

[178]This conclusion should not be altogether surprising. Contemporary exegesis has repeatedly shown that the discourses of Jesus--and, above all, the discourses that deal with the end, i.e., the apocalyptic discourses--provide a tremendous amount of information on the *Sitz im Leben* of the community in question. See above, ch. III, p. 81, n. 1.

[179]Martyn refers to Jn 13:31-14:31 only occasionally. In pp. 135ff. he points out the central role that the Paraclete plays in the two-level drama of the Gospel: it is the coming of the Paraclete to continue Jesus' work that allows the evangelist to jump from the *einmalig* level to the contemporary level at will. Jesus was present *back then* and is also present *here and now* through the Paraclete (pp. 141-42): "It is a dramatic union played out in the two-level drama in a way which creates an epistemological crisis. The world sees, of course, only one level of the drama . . . For John, on the other hand, the drama is real precisely because it is played simultaneously on the two levels."

[180]Although ch. 8 lies between the two series of events that duplicate each other in chapters 5-11, Martyn never addresses himself directly to the question of this seemingly pivotal position. It would seem, however, that he regards this debate as pointing beyond the *einmalig* level, since he includes several verses from the chapter in his delineation of the christological confession sought in John's church. Ibid., pp. 122-25.

[181]See above, p. 147.

[182]On the term οἱ ἄρχοντοι and its meaning in the two-level drama, see Martyn, pp. 74-77. In his opinion this verse points well beyond the *einmalig* level as well.

[183]See above, pp. 146-48.

CHAPTER V

[1]See above, ch. I, pp. 3-14.

[2]Meeks, "The Man," pp. 66-72.

[3]Moody Smith, "Johannine Christianity," pp. 222-25.

[4]Cullmann, *The Johannine Circle*, pp. 15, 40, 55, 58, 61, 86-88.

[5]Culpepper, pp. 258-59.

[6]Bogart, pp. 136-41.

[7]Meeks, "The Man," pp. 44-50, 66-72.

[8]Peter Berger, "The Sociological Study of Sectarianism," *Social Research* 21 (1954), pp. 467-85.

[9]I use the expression "to begin to provide" deliberately. See Berger's remark on p. 474: "The question under consideration is a very complex one, requiring a great deal of further discussion and clarification, but the following definitions are offered as a possible step toward such clarification."

[10]Ibid., pp. 468-73. Berger devotes most of his attention to Max Weber's distinction between the church as a political institution with a normative order, capable of enforcing that order over a continuing period of time; and the sect as a voluntary association, which uses no force and makes no effort to control all people within a certain sphere of power.

[11]By way of contrast, he defines the church as a "religious grouping based on the belief that *the spirit is remote*." Ibid., p. 474. (Italics his.)

[12]Ibid., p. 478. This idea of a "religious motif" Berger borrows from the Lund school of Swedish theology. Once the religious motif, the fundamental pattern, is understood, the totality of the religious experience is also understood.

[13]The study was originally published in the *American Sociological Review* 24 (1959), pp. 3-15. The version I use is a "slightly amended" reprint in *Patterns of Sectarianism: Ideology in Social and Religious Movements*, ed. Bryan Wilson (London: Heinemann, 1967), pp. 22-45.

[14]Unlike Berger, Wilson provides a long definition of the terms "sect" and "denomination." Ibid., pp. 23-25.

[15]Ibid., pp. 26; 29, n. 1. Wilson does say that each type finds support within the Christian scriptures, although he does not elaborate on this point.

[16]In Berger's typology this criterion may be found under the title, "attitude toward the world." See Wilson's remark on Berger (Ibid., p. 26, n. 25): "For an extremely suggestive classification of sects, which has come to my notice since this paper was written, but which shares certain similarities with the categorisation here proposed, see Peter L. Berger." The article that Wilson refers to is the one discussed in section #1 above, viz., "The Sociological Study of Sectarianism."

[17]Bryan R. Wilson, *Magic and the Millennium: A Socio-logical Study of Religious Movements of Protest among Tribal and Third-World Peoples* (New York: Harper & Row, 1973), pp. 9-30.

[18]See his "A Typology of Sects," in *Types, dimensions et mesure de la religiosité*, Actes de la Xe Conférence Inter-nationale de Sociologie Religieuse (Rome, 1969), pp. 29-56.

[19]Berger is exempted from this criticism. See Wilson, *Magic and the Millennium*, p. 12, n. 4: "For an important development in the differentiation of different types of sect, see Peter L. Berger, 'The Sociological Study of Sectarianism'."

[20]Wilson, *Magic and the Millennium*, p. 17.

[21]The shift from the earlier term "mission" to the present "response" is meant to represent the corresponding shift from an empirical basis to a logical one.

[22]Either the "reformist" response or the "utopian" response may be said to come close to Berger's second sub-division within the prophetic motif, viz., "a new order" sig-nified by the phrase "world to be conquered."

[23]I deliberately place quotation marks around the noun "the world" in order to emphasize all the possible different meanings that that term may have. See Wilson, *Magic and the Millennium*, p. 12: "It (the protest of the sect) may be against the state, against the secular institutions of society, or in opposition to or separation from particular institutions or groups within the society."

[24]See above, ch. I, pp. 3-5.

[25]Meeks, "The Man," p. 68.

[26]One need not interpret this separation solely from a geographical or physical point of view. B. Wilson speaks of either isolation or insulation in this regard. The former term stresses the physical aspect, while the latter means "behavioral rules calculated to protect sect values by reduc-ing the influence of the external world when contact neces-sarily occurs." Wilson, "An Analysis of Sect Development," pp. 36-37.

[27]Ibid., p. 28. See above, p. 207.

[28]There is simply not enough material to reconstruct what the position of the docetic-libertine group was vis-à-vis the world. It may very well be that they represent a movement away from sectarianism and toward a rapprochement with the world.

[29]The term "approximating" is a very important one. Wilson claims emphatically that, although the empirical corre-lates of a particular type may to a certain extent be deduced

logically, the actual historical phenomenon is far richer than
its type. The ideal type category does serve, however, to provide the main focus governing all the correlates. Wilson,
Magic and the Millennium, pp. 9-16.

[30]See above, ch. IV, p. 164.

[31]See above, ch. I, pp. 21-22.

[32]See above, ch. III, pp. 87-89.
For a complete and readable summary of Richter's views
on the Fourth Gospel, see the recent article by A. J. Mattill,
Jr., "Johannine Communities behind the Fourth Gospel: Georg
Richter's Analysis," *TS* 38 (1977), pp. 294-315.

[33]In "Die Fusswaschung," pp. 21-22 Richter presents
five basic arguments: (1) in vv. 6ff. the event is presented
as a sign; in vv. 12ff., it is an example of humble service.
(2) the two interpretations contradict each other somewhat:
(a) in vv. 6ff. the character of sign can only be understood
later, while in vv. 12ff. it is understood immediately after-
wards; (b) in vv. 6ff. the offering of Jesus is unique, while
in vv. 12ff. it is to be imitated by the disciples; (c) in
vv. 6ff. the centrality of salvation follows upon Jesus'
death; in vv. 12ff., it follows only when the action is
repeated. (3) one can read either vv. 6ff. or vv. 12ff. after
v. 5. (4) vv. 1-3 provide two different introductions. (5) the
conclusions to the two narratives show a parallel structure,
as if one (vv. 12ff.) had been modelled on the other (vv. 6ff.).

[34]Ibid., pp. 24-25.

[35]Ibid., p. 24: "Der V. 1 ist gleichsam das Vor-
zeichen, das dem Inhalt der zweiten Deutung neu bestimmt, das
einen neuen Akzent setzt."

[36]See Richter, "Die Deutung," pp. 21-27.

[37]Richter provides seven other literary and theological reasons why chs. 15-17 should be differentiated from the
Gospel. Ibid., pp. 30-34.

[38]Ibid., p. 29. Although ch. 17 contains both original
and redactional material, Richter does not give an explanation
of the literary structure of this chapter.

[39]Ibid., pp. 35-36.

[40]Ibid., p. 36.

[41]Thyen, pp. 344, n. 3; 345, n. 7; 350, n. 18.

[42]Ibid., p. 349.

[43]Ibid. See also, p. 347, n. 13, where Thyen states
that a sign can only be taken in its "semantischer Funktion,"
i.e., insofar as it points to the other world of Pneuma and

Glory. Therefore, a sign (and, by definition, the Washing of
the Feet) is "weltlos"--it takes out of the world if one sees
it correctly.

[44]Ibid., pp. 355-56. The redactor is also responsible
for the addition of ch. 21 and all the references to the
Beloved Disciple.

[45]Ibid., p. 350, n. 19. Thyen relies very heavily on
the theory propounded by E. Käsemann in his "Ketzer und Zeuge.
Zum johanneischem Verfasserproblem." See above, ch. I, p. 28,
n. 173.

[46]See above, ch. III, pp. 100-1.

SELECT BIBLIOGRAPHY

Reference Works

Aland, Kurt et al., eds. *The Greek New Testament*. 3rd ed.,
rev. New York: United Bible Societies, 1975.

Bauer, Walter. *A Greek-English Lexicon of the New Testament
and Other Early Christian Literature*. 4th ed., rev.
Edited by William F. Arndt and F. Wilbur Gingrich.
Chicago: The University Press, 1952.

Blass, F., and Debrunner, A. *A Greek Grammar of the New Testament and Other Early Christian Literature*. Edited
by R. W. Funk. Chicago: The University Press, 1961.

Koehler, Ludwig and Baumgartner, Walter. *Lexicon in Veteris
Testamenti Libros*. Leiden: Brill, 1958.

Metzger, Bruce M. *A Textual Commentary on the Greek New Testament*. New York: United Bible Societies, 1971.

Moulton, W. F., and Geden, A. S., eds. *A Concordance to the
Greek Testament*. 4th ed., rev. Edinburgh: T. &. T.
Clark, 1963.

Secondary Literature

Albertz, M. *Botschaft des Neuen Testaments*. 2 vols. Zürich:
Evangelischer Verlag, 1952.

Bacon, B. W. *The Fourth Gospel in Research and Debate*. New
Haven: Yale University Press, 1918.

Balz, H., and Schrage, W. *Die "katholischen" Briefe. Die
Briefe des Jakobus, Petrus, Johannes und Judas*. Das
Neue Testament Deutsch, no. 10. Göttingen: Vanden-
hoeck & Ruprecht, 1973.

Barrett, C. K. *The Gospel according to St. John*. London:
S.P.C.K., 1962.

Becker, H. *Die Reden des Johannesevangelium und der Stil der
gnostischen Offenbarungsrede*. Forschungen zur Religion und Literatur des Alten und Neuen Testaments, no.
68. Göttingen: Vandenhoeck & Ruprecht, 1956.

Becker, Jürgen. "Die Abschiedsreden Jesu im Johannesevan-
    gelium," *Zeitschrift für die neutestamentliche Wissen-
    schaft* 61 (1970), pp. 215-46.

_____. "Aufbau, Schichtung und theologiegeschichtliche
    Stellung des Gebets in Johannes 17," *Zeitschrift für
    die neutestamentliche Wissenschaft* 60 (1969), pp. 56-
    83.

_____. "J3, 1-21 als Reflex johanneischer Schuldiskussion."
    In *Das Wort und die Wörter. Festschrift G. Friedrich
    zum 65. Geburtstag*, pp. 85-95. Edited by H. Balz and
    S. Schulz. Stuttgart: Kohlhammer, 1973.

Berger, Peter. "The Sociological Study of Sectarianism,"
    Social Research 21 (1954), pp. 467-85.

Bernard, J. H. *The Gospel according to St. John.* 2 vols.
    The International Critical Commentary. New York:
    Charles Scribner's Sons, 1929.

Betz, Hans Dieter. "Spirit, Freedom, and Law," *Svensk Exege-
    tisk Arsbok* 39 (1974), pp. 145-60.

Bogart, John. *Orthodox and Heretical Perfectionism in the
    Johannine Community as Evident in the First Epistle
    of John.* SBL Dissertations, no. 33. Missoula, Mont.:
    Scholars Press, 1977.

Boismard, M.-É. "Le lavement des pieds," *Revue biblique* 71
    (1964), pp. 5-24.

Borgen, Peder. *Bread from Heaven.* Novum Testamentum Supple-
    ments, no. 10. Leiden: Brill, 1965.

Borig, Rainer. *Der wahre Weinstock, Untersuchungen zu Jo 15:
    1-10.* Studien zum Alten und Neuen Testament, no. 16.
    Munich: Kösel Verlag, 1967.

Bousset, W. *Jüdisch-Christlicher Schulbetrieb in Alexandria
    und Rom: Literarische Untersuchungen zu Philo und
    Clemens von Alexandria, Justin and Irenäus.* For-
    schungen zur Religion und Literatur des Alten und
    Neuen Testaments, n.F., no. 6. Göttingen: Vanden-
    hoeck & Ruprecht, 1915.

Bouyer, H. *Le quatrième Évangile.* Tournai: Castermann, 1955.

Braun, Herbert. "Literal-Analyse und theologische Schichtung
    im ersten Johannesbrief," *Zeitschrift für Theologie
    und Kirche* 48 (1951), pp. 262-92.

Brooke, A. E. *A Critical and Exegetical Commentary on the
    Johannine Epistles.* The International Critical Com-
    mentary. Edinburgh: T. & T. Clark, 1912.

Brown, Raymond. *The Gospel according to John.* 2 vols. The
    Anchor Bible, nos. 29, 29a. Garden City, N.J.:
    Doubleday, 1966-70.

_____. "Johannine Ecclesiology--The Community's Origins,"
Interpretation 31 (1977), pp. 379-93.

Bultmann, Rudolf. "Analyse des ersten Johannesbriefes." In
Festgabe für Adolf Jülicher, pp. 138-58. Tübingen:
Mohr-Siebeck, 1927.

_____. "Die Bedeutung des neuerschlossenen mandäischen und
manichäischen Quelle für das Verständnis des Johannesevangelium," *Zeitschrift für die neutestamentliche
Wissenschaft* 24 (1925), pp. 100-46.

_____. *The Gospel of John--A Commentary*. Translated by
G. R. Beasley-Murray et al. Philadelphia: Fortress,
1971.

_____. *The Johannine Epistles: A Commentary on the Johan-
nine Epistles*. Translated by R. Philip O'Hara et al.
Hermeneia. Philadelphia: Fortress, 1973.

_____. "Die kirchliche Redaktion des ersten Johannes-
briefes." In *In Memoriam Ernst Lohmeyer*, pp. 189-201.
Edited by Werner Schmauch. Stuttgart: Evangelisches
Verlagswerk, 1951.

Chmiel, Jerzy. *Lumière et charité d'après la première épître
de saint Jean*. Rome: Institut Pontifical des
Recherches Ecclesiastiques, 1971.

Clemen, C. *Die Entstehung des Johannesevangelium*. Halle:
M. Niemeyer, 1912.

Conzelmann, Hans. *An Outline of the Theology of the New Testament*. Translated by John Bowden. New York:
Harper & Row, 1968.

_____. "'Was von Anfang war.'" In *Neutestamentliche
Studien für Rudolf Bultmann zu seinem siebzigsten
Geburtstag am 20. August 1954*, 2nd ed., pp. 194-201.
Beihefte zur Zeitschrift für die neutestamentliche
Wissenschaft, no. 21. Berlin: Töpelmann, 1957.

Corssen, P. "Die Abschiedsreden Jesu in dem vierten Evangelium," *Zeitschrift für die neutestamentliche Wissenschaft* 8 (1907), pp. 125-42.

Cullmann, Oscar. *Early Christian Worship*. Translated by
A. Stewart Todd and James B. Torrance. Studies in
Biblical Theology, no. 10. London: SCM, 1953.

_____. *The Johannine Circle*. Translated by J. Bowman.
Philadelphia: Westminster, 1976.

_____. *Le problème litteraire du roman pseudo-Clementin*.
Études d'histoire et de philosophie religieuses.
no. 23. Paris: F. Alcan, 1930.

_____. "Samaria and the Origins of the Christian Mission."
        In *The Early Church*, pp. 185-92. Edited by A. J. B.
        Higgins, London: SCM, 1956.

Culpepper, R. Alan. *The Johannine School*. SBL Dissertations,
        no. 26. Missoula, Mont.: Scholars Press, 1975.

Dibelius, Martin. "Joh 15:13. Eine Studie zum Traditions-
        probleme des Johannesevangeliums." In *Festgabe für
        Adolf Deissmann zum 60. Geburtstag*, pp. 168-86.
        Tübingen: Mohr, 1927.

von Dobschütz, E. "Johanneische Studien. I," *Zeitschrift für
        die neutestamentliche Wissenschaft* 8 (1907), pp. 1-8.

Dodd, C. H. "The First Epistle of John and the Fourth Gospel,"
        Bulletin of the John Rylands Library 21 (1937), pp.
        129-56.

_____. *The Interpretation of the Fourth Gospel*. Cambridge:
        University Press, 1970.

_____. *The Johannine Epistles*. The Moffatt New Testament
        Commentary. London: Hodder & Stoughton, 1946.

Drummond, J. *An Inquiry into the Character and Authorship of
        the Fourth Gospel*. London: Williams & Norgate, 1903.

Feuillet, André. *Le mystère de l'amour divin dans la théologie
        johannique*. Études bibliques. Paris: J. Gabalda,
        1972.

Filson, Floyd. "First John: Message and Purpose," *Interpre-
        tation* 23 (1969), pp. 259-76.

Fortna, Robert T. *The Gospel of Signs: A Reconstruction of
        the Narrative Source Underlying the Fourth Gospel*.
        New Testament Studies Monograph Series, no. 11.
        Cambridge: University Press, 1970.

Furnish, Victor. *The Love Command in the New Testament*. New
        York: Abingdon Press, 1972.

George, A. "'L'heure' de Jean XVII," *Revue biblique* 61 (1954)
        pp. 392-97.

Gerhardsson, B. *Memory and Manuscript: Oral Tradition and
        Written Transmission in Rabbinical Judaism and Early
        Christianity*. Translated by E. J. Sharpe. Acta
        Seminarii Neotestamentici Upsaliensis, no. 22.
        Uppsala: C. W. K. Gleerup, 1961.

Haenchen, Ernst. "Neuere Literatur zu den Johannesbriefen,"
        Theologische Rundschau 26 (1960), pp. 1-43.

Häring, Theodor. "Gedankengang und Grundgedanke des ersten
        Johannesbriefes." In *Theologisches Abhandlungen. Carl*

von Weizsäcker zu seinem siebzigsten Geburtstage 11. Dezember 1892 gewidmet, pp. 171-200. Freiburg: Mohr-Siebeck, 1892.

Heise, J. *Bleiben. Menein in den Johanneischen Schriften.* Hermeneutische Untersuchungen zur Theologie, no. 8. Tübingen: J. C. B. Mohr, 1967.

Hirsch, Emanuel. *Studien zum vierten Evangelium.* Beiträge zur historischen Theologie, no. 11. Tübingen: J. C. B. Mohr, 1936.

Hoskyns, E. C. *The Fourth Gospel.* 2nd ed. Edited by F. N. Davey. London: Faber & Faber, 1947.

Houlden, J. L. *The Johannine Epistles.* Harper's New Testament Commentaries. New York: Harper & Row, 1973.

Howard, W. F. "The Common Authorship of the Johannine Gospel and Epistles," *Journal of Theological Studies* 48 (1947), pp. 12-25.

Käsemann, Ernst. "Ketzer und Zeuge. Zum johanneischen Verfasserproblem," *Zeitschrift für Theologie und Kirche* 48 (1951), pp. 292-311.

_____. *The Last Testament of Jesus.* Translated by Gerhard Krodel. Philadelphia: Fortress, 1968.

Klein, Günter. "'Das wahre Licht scheint schon!' Beobachtungen zur Zeit- und Geschichtserfahrung einer urchristliche Schule," *Zeitschrift für Theologie und Kirche* 68 (1971), pp. 261-326.

Kümmel, W. G. *Introduction to the New Testament.* 2nd ed. Translated by H. C. Kee. New York: Abingdon, 1975.

Kysar, Robert. *The Fourth Evangelist and his Gospel. An Examination of Contemporary Scholarship.* Minneapolis: Augsburg, 1975.

Lagrange, Marie-Joseph. *Évangile selon Saint Jean.* 4th ed. Études bibliques. Paris: J. Gabalda, 1927.

Lattke, Michael. *Einheit im Wort: Die spezifische Bedeutung von ἀγάπη/ἀγαπᾶν und φιλεῖν im Johannesevangelium.* Studien zum Alten und Neuen Testament, no. 41. Munich: Kösel Verlag, 1975.

Law, Robert. *The Tests of Life. A Study of the First Epistle of St. John.* Edinburgh: T. & T. Clark, 1912.

Lazure, Noël. *Les valeurs morales de la théologie johannique.* Études bibliques. Paris: J. Gabalda, 1965.

Lightfoot, R. H. *St. John's Gospel. A Commentary.* Edited by C. F. Evans. Oxford: University Press, 1956.

Lindars, Barnabas. *Behind the Fourth Gospel.* Studies in Creative Criticism, no. 3. London: S.P.C.K., 1971.

_____. *The Gospel of John.* New Century Bible. London: Oliphants, 1972.

Lohmeyer, Ernst. "Über Aufbau und Gliederung des ersten Johannesbriefes," *Zeitschrift für die neutestamentliche Wissenschaft* 27 (1928), pp. 225-63.

Loisy, A. *Le quatrième Évangile.* Paris: Alphonse Picard, 1903.

Martyn, J. L. *History and Theology in the Fourth Gospel.* New York: Harper & Row, 1968.

Marxsen, Willi. *Introduction to the New Testament.* Translated by G. Buswell. Philadelphia: Fortress, 1974.

Meeks, Wayne. "'Am I a Jew?' Johannine Christianity and Judaism." In *Christianity, Judaism and Other Graeco-Roman Cults: Studies for Morton Smith at Sixty,* I, pp. 163-86. 4 vols. Edited by Jacob Neusner. Studies in Judaism and Late Antiquity, no. 12. Leiden: Brill, 1975.

_____. "The Man from Heaven in Johannine Sectarianism," *Journal of Biblical Literature* 91 (1972), pp. 44-72.

Moffatt, J. *Love in the New Testament.* London: Hazell, Watson & Viney, 1930.

Nygrén, Anders. *Agape and Eros.* Translated by Philip S. Watson. Philadelphia: Westminster, 1953.

O'Neill, J. C. *The Puzzle of I John: A New Examination of Origins.* London: S.P.C.K., 1966.

Perrin, Norman. *The New Testament: An Introduction.* New York: Harcourt Brace Jovanovich, 1974.

Prunet, Olivier. *La morale chrétienne d'après les écrits johanniques.* Paris: Presses Universitaires de France, 1957.

Richter, Georg. "Die Deutung des Kreuzestodes Jesu in der Leidensgeschichte des Johannesevangeliums," *Bibel und Leben* 9 (1968), pp. 21-36.

_____. *Die Fusswaschung im Johannesevangelium: Geschichte ihrer Deutung.* Biblische Untersuchungen, no. 1. Regensburg: Friedrich Pustet, 1967.

_____. "Die Fusswaschung Joh 13:1-20," *Münchener Theologische Zeitschrift* 16 (1965), pp. 13-26.

_____. "Zur Formgeschichte und literarischen Einheit von Joh 6:31-58," *Zeitschrift für die neutestamentliche Wissenschaft* 60 (1969), pp. 21-55.

Robinson, J. A. T. "The Destination and Purpose of St. John's
     Gospel," *New Testament Studies* 6 (1959-60), pp. 117-31.

Roloff, J. "Der johanneische 'Lieblingsjünger' und der Lehrer
     der Gerechtigkeit," *New Testament Studies* 15 (1968),
     pp. 129-51.

Ruckstuhl, E. *Die literarische Einheit des Johannesevangeliums,
     der gegenwärtige Stand der einschlagigen Erforschung.*
     Studia Friburgensia, no. 3. Freiburg: Paulus-Verlag,
     1951.

Salom, A. P. "Some Aspects of the Grammatical Style of I
     John," *Journal of Biblical Literature* 74 (1955), pp.
     96-102.

Schlatter, Adolf. *Der Evangelist Johannes.* Stuttgart:
     Calwer, 1948.

Schnackenburg, Rudolf. "Das Anliegen der Abschiedsrede in
     Joh 14." In *Wort Gottes in der Zeit. Festschrift
     Karl Hermann Schelkle zum 65. Geburtstag,* pp. 95-110.
     Edited by H. Feld and J. Nolte. Düsseldorf: Patmos
     Verlag, 1973.

_____. *Die Johannesbriefe.* 2nd ed. Herders Theologischer
     Kommentar zum Neuen Testament, no. 12:3. Freiburg:
     Herder, 1963.

_____. *Das Johannesevangelium.* 3 vols. Herders Theo-
     logischer Kommentar zum Neuen Testament, no. 4.
     Freiburg: Herder, 1965-75.

_____. "On the Origin of the Fourth Gospel." In *Jesus
     and Man's Hope,* I, pp. 223-46. 2 vols. Edited by
     Donald G. Miller and Dikran Y. Hadidian. Pittsburgh:
     Pittsburgh Theological Seminary, 1971.

Schneider, J. "Die Abschiedsreden Jesu." In *Gott und die
     Götter. Festgabe für E. Fascher,* pp. 103-12. Berlin:
     Evangelische Verlaganstalt, 1958.

Schulz, Siegfried. *Das Evangelium nach Johannes.* Das Neue
     Testament Deutsch, no. 4. Göttingen: Vandenhoeck &
     Ruprecht, 1972.

_____. *Komposition und Herkunft der Johanneischen Reden.*
     Beiträge zur Wissenschaft vom Alten und Neuen Testa-
     ment, no. 81. Stuttgart: Kohlhammer, 1960.

_____. *Untersuchungen zur Menschensohn-Christologie im
     Johannesevangelium.* Göttingen: Vandenhoeck & Ruprecht,
     1957.

Schweizer, E. *Ego Eimi, die religionsgeschichtliche Herkunft
     und theologische Bedeutung der johanneischen Bildreden,
     zugleich ein Beitrag zur Quellenfrage des vierten*

Evangeliums. Forschungen zur Religion und Literatur
des Alten und Neuen Testaments, no. 38. Göttingen:
Vandenhoeck & Ruprecht, 1939.

_____. "Der Kirchenbegriff im Evangelium und den Briefen
des Johannes." In *Neotestamentica. Deutsche und
englische Aufsätze 1951 bis 1963,* pp. 254-71. Zürich:
Zwingli Verlag, 1963.

Scott, Ernest F. *The Fourth Gospel: Its Purpose and Theology.*
Edinburgh: T. & T. Clark, 1906.

Smith, D. Moody. *The Composition and Order of the Fourth
Gospel.* New Haven: Yale University Press, 1965.

_____. "Johannine Christianity: Some Reflections on its
Character and Delineation," *New Testament Studies* 21
(1974-75), pp. 222-48.

_____. "The Milieu of the Johannine Miracle Source: A
Proposal." In *Jews, Greeks, and Christians. Religious
Cultures in Late Antiquity. Essays in Honor of William
David Davies,* pp. 164-80. Edited by Robert Hamerton-
Kelly and Robin Scroggs. Studies in Judaism in Late
Antiquity, no. 21. Leiden: Brill, 1976.

Smith, T. C. *Jesus in the Gospel of John.* Nashville: Broadman, 1959.

Spicq, Ceslaus. *Agapè dans le Nouveau Testament.* 3 vols.
Études bibliques. Paris: J. Gabalda, 1959.

Spitta, F. *Das Johannesevangelium als Quelle der Geschichte
Jesu.* Göttingen: Vandenhoeck & Ruprecht, 1910.

Stendahl, Krister. *The School of St. Matthew: And its Use
of the Old Testament.* Philadelphia: Fortress, 1968.

Thyen, Hartwig. "Johannes 13 und die 'kirchliche Redaktion'
des vierten Evangeliums." In *Tradition und Glaube.
Festgabe für K. G. Kuhn,* pp. 343-56. Göttingen:
Vandenhoeck & Ruprecht, 1971.

van Unnik, W. C. "The Purpose of St. John's Gospel." In
Studia Evangelica, I, pp. 382-411. Edited by Kurt
Aland et al. Texte und Untersuchungen, no. 73.
Berlin: Akademie Verlag, 1959.

Vawter, Bruce. "The Johannine Epistles." In *The Jerome Bib-
lical Commentary,* Part II, pp. 404-13. Edited by
Raymond Brown et al. Englewood Cliffs, N.J.:
Prentice Hall, 1968.

Warnach, Victor. *Agape. Liebe als Grundmotiv der neutestamentlichen Theologie.* Düsseldorf: Patmos Verlag,
1951.

Wellhausen, Julius. *Erweiterungen und Änderungen im vierten
        Evangelium*. Berlin: Georg Reimer, 1907.

_____. *Das Evangelium Johannis*. Berlin: Georg Reimer,
        1908.

Wendt, H. H. *Das Johannesevangelium*. Göttingen: Vandenhoeck
        & Ruprecht, 1900.

Westcott, B. F. *The Epistles of St. John. The Greek Text
        with Notes And Essays*. 3rd ed. London: Macmillan,
        1892; reprint ed., Abingdon, Eng.: The Marcham Manor
        Press, 1966.

_____. *The Gospel according to St. John*. 2nd ed. London:
        John Murray, 1903.

Wikenhauser, Alfred. *Das Evangelium nach Johannes*. 2nd ed.
        Regensburger Neues Testament, no. 4. Regensburg:
        Friedrich Pustet, 1957.

Wilson, Bryan R. "An Analysis of Sect Development." In
        *Patterns of Sectarianism: Ideology in Social and
        Religious Movements*, pp. 22-45. Edited by Bryan R.
        Wilson. London: Heinemann, 1967.

_____. *Magic and the Millennium: A Sociological Study of
        Religious Movements of Protest among Tribal and Third-
        World Peoples*. New York: Harper & Row, 1973.

Wilson, W. G. "An Examination of the Linguistic Evidence
        Adduced Against the Unity of Authorship of the First
        Epistle of John and the Fourth Gospel," *Journal of
        Theological Studies* 49 (1948), pp. 147-56.

Windisch, H. *Die katholischen Briefe*. Handbuch zum Neuen
        Testament, no. 15. Tübingen: J. C. B. Mohr, 1930.

Wurm, Alois. *Die Irrlehrer im ersten Johannesbrief*. Bib-
        lische Studien, no. 8:1. Freiburg: Herder, 1903.

Zimmermann, H. "Struktur und Aussageabsicht der johanneischen
        Abschiedsreden (Jo 13-17)," *Bibel und Leben* 8 (1967),
        pp. 279-90.